STATS™ 1998 DIAMOND CHRONICLES

Don Zminda, Editor

Jim Callis, Ethan D. Cooperson, Kevin Fullam, Jim Henzler,

Chuck Miller, Tony Nistler and Mat Olkin, Assistant Editors

Published by STATS Publishing

A division of Sports Team Analysis & Tracking Systems, Inc.

Cover by Ron Freer

Cover photo by Ponzini Photography

STATS is a registered trademark of Sports Team Analysis and Tracking Systems, Inc.

First Edition: March, 1998

ISBN 1-884064-49-3

Acknowledgments

The STATS team is made up of a group of individuls who have myriad ideas and opinions. . . and who relish the opportunity to let those ideas and opinions be known. Thanks go out to the following people for making such entertaining and informative arguments.

John Dewan, STATS President and CEO, continues to position us as the No. 1 source for sports statistics. He's always up for a lively give-and-take and is STATS' biggest proponent of the free-flow of ideas you now have in your hand. STATS Chief Operating Officer Marty Gilbert also plays a key role in leading this company into the next millennium. They are assisted by Heather Schwarze, who somehow manages to keep up with the hectic pace they set.

The *content* of *Diamond Chronicles* is a bit different than any other book we publish, but as Vice President of Publications, Don Zminda ensures that the *quality* is the same. Don, as you will soon see, also shares his wealth of baseball knowledge through both the discussions and his "Zee-Man Reports" column, which also can be found on America Online.

Speaking of AOL, STATS has its army of experts enlightening you on the subject of baseball throughout the year in cyberspace, and here you'll find the best of what they had to say in 1997. Columnists Jim Henzler ("STATS Focus"), Steve Moyer ("Baseball Babble-On") and Mat Olkin ("Fantasy Baseball Advisor") give you widely varying perspectives of last season, and look for more of the same in '98!

Of course, one of the highlights of being on the STATS baseball e-mail list is seeing a thought from Bill James pop up on your computer sceeen. We share that excitement with you in the *Chronicles*, and his ideas on everything from the '97 NL MVP race to Harry Caray are not to be missed.

Special thanks go out to the members of the Publications department, who took a bunch of random parts and assembled a cohesive book. Kevin Fullam and Chuck Miller impressed us with their dexterity in using our publications software, while Jim Callis, Ethan D. Cooperson, Thom Henninger, Jim Henzler, Mat, Don and yours truly all spent time sharpening our editorial pencils.

The rest of the employees at STATS helped provide the most-important ingredients of this book: ideas and words. It all starts at the top, with a second-to-none team of managers: Art Ashley, Mike Canter, Sue Dewan (Systems); Doug Abel (Vice President of Operations); Steve Byrd (Vice President of Marketing); Jim Capuano (Vice President of Sales) and Bob Meyerhoff (Vice President of Finance and Administration). Stephanie Seburn (Human Resources) and Susan Zamechek (Administration) assist Bob Meyerhoff.

Then comes the hardest-working staff in sports: Kristen Beauregard, Andrew Bernstein, Grant Blair, Dave Carlson, Jeff Chernow, Brian Cousins, Steve Drago, Marc Elman, Drew Faust, Dan Ford, Ron Freer (who did another stellar job on the cover!), Angela Gabe, Mike Hammer, Mark Hong, Sherlinda Johnson, Antoinette Kelly, Jason Kinsey, Stefan Kretschmann, Tracy Lickton, Walter Lis, Betty Moy, Steve Moyer, Jim Musso, Jim Osborne, Brent Osland, Oscar Palacios, Dean Peterson, Dave Pinto, Pat Quinn, Corey Roberts, John Sasman, Jeff Schinski, Taasha Schroeder, Matt Senter, Leena Sheth, Lori Smith, Allan Spear, Kevin Thomas, Joseph Weindel, Mike Wenz and Peter Woelflein. Thanks one and all for sharing your thoughts.

—Tony Nistler

This book is dedicated to my mother and father,
who have always supported me throughout all my endeavors—
and pushed me to follow my dreams.

—Kevin Fullam

Table of Contents

Introduction

As you could perhaps tell from our name, we here at STATS, Inc. compile all sorts of statistics, from the common to the esoteric, for a variety of sports. But we're not just number-crunchers keeping track of how many homers Mark McGwire has hit. Most of us are passionate sports fans, and most of us are more passionate about baseball than any other sport. Rarely a day goes by when the national pastime doesn't provide us with news that we discuss, analyze, argue about and sometimes ridicule.

The second annual *STATS Diamond Chronicles* is a collection of those discussions, analyses, arguments and ridicules. A good portion of the book—the section entitled "Voices From the Network"—comes from our internal baseball e-mail list, which includes noted baseball expert Bill James. Bill and others provide their take on such subjects as the Braves-Indians blockbuster trade, Deion Sanders, the All-Star Game, amazing pitching debuts, Harry Caray, Josh Booty, the wild-card system, the postseason, the National League Most Valuable Player and Hot Stove League action.

And that's not all. We also include the best efforts from our regular America Online columnists. Don Zminda's "Zee-Man Reports" tackles topics such as peak age, how relievers are used and the 1952 World Series. Mat Olkin's "Fantasy Baseball Advisor" discusses the genius of Felipe Alou, the root of the Cubs' chronic ineptitude and the *real* reason today's pitchers no longer work 300 innings a year. Jim Henzler's "STATS Focus" explains concepts like the power-speed number, secondary average and offensive winning percentage. And Steve Moyer's "Baseball Babble-On" mixes baseball with kill-crazy goons. . . don't ask.

It won't take long for you to start reading and say, "Wait a minute. This guy doesn't know what he's talking about!" As you'll see, that's exactly how some of us reacted when one of our colleagues presented an opinion that we didn't agree with. With all the various voices, it should be quite obvious that the opinions expressed in this book aren't necessarily those of STATS, Inc. If they were, we wouldn't have had so many arguments.

—Jim Callis

Dramatis Personae

(in alphabetical order)

The following people contributed their opinions, insights, observations and analysis throughout this book:

Jamie Bataille	Dan Ford	Chuck Miller	John Sasman
Kristen Beauregard	Ron Freer	Mike Mittleman	Jeff Schinski
Andrew Bernstein	Kevin Fullam	Steve Moyer	Matt Senter
Jim Callis	Ken Gilbert	Dave Mundo	John Sickels
Mike Canter	Kevin Goldstein	Rob Neyer	Todd Skelton
Dave Carlson	Matt Greenberger	Mat Olkin	Allan Spear
Jeff Chernow	Ginny Hamill	Jim Osborne	Joseph Weindel
Ethan D. Cooperson	Thom Henninger	Brent Osland	Mike Wenz
Brian Cousins	Jim Henzler	Oscar Palacios	Peter Woelflein
John Dewan	Bill James	Dean Peterson	Craig Wright
Brian East	Jason Kinsey	Dave Pinto	Don Zminda
Marc Elman	Dave Klotz	Pat Quinn	
Drew Faust	Stefan Kretschmann	Kenn Ruby	

In addition, Jim Henzler, Steve Moyer, Mat Olkin and Don Zminda contributed numerous columns and essays, many of which can be found in the STATS Baseball area on America Online (keyword: STATS). Look for their fresh perspectives throughout the 1998 season on AOL.

Voices From the Network

March 3—The All-Things-You-Wear Team

OLKIN:

The all-things-you-wear team:

C	Lave Cross
1B	Harry "The Hat" Walker
2B	Ski Melillo
3B	Clete Boyer
SS	Monte Cross (thank God for those Cross boys)
LF	Socks Seybold
CF	Boots Day
RF	Cap Peterson
P	Orval Overall
P	Spec Shea
P	Jimmy Ring
P	(the other) Socks Seibold

March 5—Hall of Fame

ZMINDA: The Veterans Committee has elected Nellie Fox, Tommy Lasorda and Willie Wells to the Hall of Fame.

As many of you know, Fox was my favorite player when I was growing up. So naturally, I'm thrilled. I think I'll treat myself to a glass of bourbon and a big plug of chewing tobacco when I get home.

Well, *one* of those things.

SPEAR: With regard to Willie Wells making the Hall, isn't there a rule saying a guy can't make it if I've never heard of him?

PINTO: A bit of a did-you-know on Fox. He played more consecutive 150-game seasons than Gehrig did. For some reason the Yankees only played 149 games in 1935 and that stopped Gehrig's streak at nine.

ZMINDA: Wells was a Negro League shortstop in the 1930s and '40s. Definitely a worthy choice, according to people who know black baseball.

He currently goes for $101,000 in the Bill James Classic Game, so he *must* be good, right?

SCHINSKI: I had Wells once. He stunk.

WENZ: I'm not sure how to feel about Nellie Fox going into the Hall. On one hand, I'm happy that Don will get the opportunity to enjoy a nice big plug of chewing tobacco (I'm guessing that's the *one* of those things you're going to treat yourself to). But on the other hand, I can't fathom anybody getting so many chances to get in before finally making it on what I perceive as a sympathy vote. He had 15 times in front of the writers, then—I believe this is correct—eight times in front of the Veterans Committee. Sorry, but that's too many chances for my liking.

ZMINDA: Mike is right, that Fox got a second chance with the Veterans Committee, but what applies to Fox also applies to about half the members of the Hall of Fame, all of whom got their 15 chances with the writers. Fox got more support from the writers—he missed getting in by two votes in his last election, for God's sake—than *any* player elected by this process.

The writers make oversights, and I would say it's reasonable that any player who received a lot of support from the writers, but who just missed being elected, should get a chance with the Veterans Committee. The Veterans have made a lot of mistakes, too (to say the least), but Fox is in the same category as guys like Johnny Mize and Richie Ashburn—worthy players who belonged in the Hall, but who never got the 75 percent needed from the writers.

Look at Fox' playing record. We're not talking about Jesse Haines or Long George Kelly (two bogus members of the Hall of Fame). He belongs.

WENZ: I'm probably wrong, but didn't Nellie Fox get eight chances with the Veterans Committee? By the way, I'm not going to argue with his credentials, although I would in general like to see it become harder to get in if only because the NBA Hall of Fame has become a joke lately.

SPEAR: Since he got in, I think Manny Trillo should be a lock.

Did Fox ever win NLCS MVP? Enough said.

ZMINDA: Yes, Fox got a number of chances with the Veterans Committee as well. But that will happen when there are a number of good candidates, and the Committee is only allowed to elect one (Lasorda and Wells were chosen in a different category). Fox had the votes to get in last year, but only one former major leaguer was eligible, so Jim Bunning, who had received one more vote from the committee, went in instead.

In case you didn't know it, the writers took three years to elect *Joe DiMaggio* to the Hall of Fame! Should he have gotten one chance, and then forget it? And I guess we should tell Don Sutton to forget it, too.

I'll agree there are problems with the system. A lot of the writers who vote are simply unqualified, and the Veterans Committee has its own cliques and groups of fools. But with all the support Fox has received over the years, and particularly with his outstanding playing record, it seems weird to me that his election should be singled out as a sign of "a problem."

March 10—Free Agents & Ticket Sales

BEAUREGARD: There seems to be an interesting correlation here. For example, I know that Comiskey was mobbed this weekend (the first weekend tickets went on sale) and I have been told that this was the largest crowd since the new Comiskey opened. I imagine the reason is Albert Belle. But I wonder, is it happening in Florida, too, where another team that has been bogged down by lagging ticket sales went on a shopping spree this winter? St.

Louis did it last year. I'll bet their ticket sales before the season started all went up considerably.

And what about the other side? Take the Red Sox, for example. They lost Mike Greenwell, Jose Canseco and Roger Clemens, so are their ticket sales down?

WOELFLEIN:: I'm sure part of the White Sox' mob was due to Belle, but I'd bet a bigger part was due to the White Sox' plan to raise ticket prices come Opening Day.

BEAUREGARD: I don't buy into this. Tickets only went up $2 and there were people camped out at midnight outside of Comiskey. I don't think that they are that intent on getting tickets to save the $2 per game. I don't think that they would go to such measures, I mean.

March 10—Spring Training

PINTO: Is the Marlins' spring-training facility a hitters' park? Joe Robbie seems to be a great pitchers' park, and I wonder if coming out of Florida on such an offensive roll if they'll hit a wall at Joe Robbie and lose confidence in themselves?

SICKELS: Watch out! Darnell Coles is hitting .400 for the Rockies this spring.

If he makes the team, who will be the first sportswriter to talk about how Coors Field helped resurrect his career by "giving him more confidence"?

SPEAR: It appears that, since no one is wearing No. 9 for the Blue Jays this spring, Toronto has retired John Olerud's number.

March 14—Rickey Henderson

OLKIN: I'm hearing rumors on AOL that the Angels are going to deal Chuck McElroy for Rickey Henderson as soon as they're convinced that Troy Percival's back is sound.

"What are those idiots in the Padres' front office thinking? Chuck McElroy? I wouldn't give up an egg salad sandwich for that guy! The Angels just conned them out of one of the best leadoff men in baseball!"

Just thought I'd save you the trouble, Steve.

Seriously, do the Disney folks know that the rules put an absolute limit on the number of Angels in the outfield?

ZMINDA: If I were Garret Anderson, I'd be packing my bags.

OSLAND: I don't know if they are really looking to move anybody out of the outfield. On ESPN they were talking about Henderson playing DH and giving the regular outfielders days off. With Darin Erstad moving to first base it might be a possibility. I don't know what would happen with Eddie Murray if Henderson is the DH, but it might work out with everyone.

OLKIN: That's what I don't get—they just signed Garret Anderson to a multiyear deal (which was puzzling enough in the first place).

March 18—Homer Duos

PINTO:

Top homer duos

Year	Team	Players	HR
1961	Yankees	Roger Maris & Mickey Mantle	115
1927	Yankees	Babe Ruth & Lou Gehrig	107
1930	Cubs	Hack Wilson & Gabby Hartnett	93
1932	Athletics	Jimmy Foxx & Al Simmons	93
1996	Mariners	Ken Griffey Jr. & Jay Buhner	93
1931	Yankees	Lou Gehrig & Babe Ruth	92
1938	Tigers	Hank Greenberg & Rudy York	91
1965	Giants	Willie Mays & Willie McCovey	91
1930	Yankees	Babe Ruth & Lou Gehrig	90
1996	Orioles	Brady Anderson & Rafael Palmeiro	89
1996	Athletics	Mark McGwire & Geronimo Berroa	88
1947	Giants	Johnny Mize & Willard Marshall	87
1955	Reds	Ted Kluszewski & Wally Post	87
1996	Rockies	Andres Galarraga & Ellis Burks	87
1961	Giants	Orlando Cepeda & Willie Mays	86
1961	Tigers	Rocky Colavito & Norm Cash	86
1996	Indians	Albert Belle & Jim Thome	86
1959	Braves	Eddie Mathews & Hank Aaron	85
1996	Rangers	Juan Gonzalez & Dean Palmer	85

DEWAN: I predict a third-place all-time finish this year for Albert Belle/Frank Thomas!

PINTO: They only need 94 to set a record for a pair of righthanders.

ELMAN: I suspect that they will hit a bunch. What I find interesting is the lack of conversation re: Griffey and Buhner. The two of them combined for more taters than Belle & Thomas did last year. Is it the small- vs. large-market syndrome? Is it two big names vs. one big name? Why is everyone so sure Belle and Thomas will make a run at the big boys and not give Junior & Buhner their due?

OLKIN: My feelings exactly. Perhaps that's the reason Ben Oglivie and Gorman Thomas have never gotten their due. Besides, they were undoubtedly the best Panamanian-and-ugly-guy home-run duo of all time.

OSBORNE: I didn't know Ben Oglivie was Panamanian.

OLKIN: Are you kidding me? Oglivie *dug* the canal!

MILLER: I didn't know Ben Oglivie was Panamanian. I didn't know Gorman was ugly.

PINTO: There is a perception that somehow Thomas and Belle will make each other better. A number of people seem to think that Thomas will walk less with Belle behind him (as if this were a good thing). I simply point to Ruth and Gehrig. Ruth led the league in walks before Gehrig was batting behind him, and he continued to lead the league in walks after Gehrig was batting behind him. Yes, Ruth was walking in the 130s instead of the 140s, but I don't think the drop-off was significant. Gehrig was a devastating hitter, but he wasn't Babe Ruth. Likewise, as good as Belle is, he's not Frank Thomas.

Now people already know what Griffey and Buhner can do together, but Thomas and Belle are an unknown, so we will see. I look for 90-95 HR for the pair.

FULLAM: Why Griffey and Buhner aren't recognized probably has to do with the fact that:

1) Albert Belle has one of the biggest profiles in baseball.

2) Griffey and Buhner have already hit together for several years now; people are still under the delusion that the addition of Belle to the White Sox' lineup will make Frank Thomas a better hitter. They figure Frank will be able to bash about 70 longballs next season with the added "protection."

PINTO: As you all probably know, Gehrig holds the record for grand slam HR with 23. I don't think that would have been possible without pitchers walking Ruth to get to Gehrig. What would you do? Take your chances with Ruth and give up three runs, or take your chances with Gehrig and give up four? Seems like a no-win situation to me.

DEWAN: Griffey and Buhner deserve recognition, but the excitement is not there because it's not something you can *expect* them to do again. Fans generally know that the Griffey/Buhner duo is not as powerful as Thomas/Belle. Our projections support this: we project Griffey/Buhner for 87 homers this year (48 and 39, respectively). That's an impressive projection. Nevertheless, Belle and Thomas project to hit 92 (49 and 43). The differential is not huge, but it is there and fans intuitively know that.

COOPERSON: And Fred McGriff sure isn't Lou Gehrig, but he got sooooooo much credit for making Ron Gant and David Justice better after Atlanta acquired him in 1993. McGriff got some MVP consideration for "making the other guys better." To me that was a bunch of BS.

DEWAN: A *Scoreboard* article we did a couple of years ago showed that having a superstar bat behind another superstar *does* help the player earlier in the order. This only applied to superstars; no effect was shown for players of lesser ability.

March 25—Braves/Indians Trade

SENTER: It has been reported on ESPNnet that the Braves have shipped David Justice and Marquis Grissom to the Indians for Kenny Lofton and Alan Embree.

OSBORNE: Now it's official: Cleveland sports teams *hate* winning.

COOPERSON: There's something of a precedent for leadoff-man deals between these two teams—remember Brett Butler for Len Barker?

PINTO: So Atlanta has a real leadoff man again! I have never liked Marquis at the top of the order. Now if they can just get Mark Lemke and Jeff Blauser out of the No. 2 hole.

FULLAM: The latest in a series of ongoing debates between me and Mike Mittleman concerning the Braves-Indians trade:

MITTLEMAN: You were kidding, were you not?

Kevin:

The points you make with the statistical anomalies for range factors and zone ratings for tenths of a point don't impress me. I never said Grissom was as good or they were equal or that he was better, merely that you wildly overstated the facts based on sitting down at your desk and not scouting these guys properly. That means going to the park, watching their drills, work ethics, seeing them play live and on TV repeatedly to get a proper feel. Instead, you would rather base your opinions on imperfect ratings. Ridiculous! Grissom is recognized as one of the finer outfielders in the game, period!!!

As far as the offensive comparison, I see Lofton as having better command of the strike zone, which enables him to walk, which brings his OPB up. That's great. I also see Grissom with more home-run power, and the ability to drive in more runs and hit for similar average. Please don't quote me career stats. They are absolutely meaningless, as any GM will tell you when making comparisons on players. You can say Lofton's numbers were closer to his career averages and that may be true, but last season is the closest determinant we can find to make any comparison that is likely to occur for the future, not five years ago.

Look at the Indians, and you see what may be the most devastating lineup in the American League. Grissom isn't Lofton, but he is more of an AL leadoff hitter (he hit 22 homers) and runs a little less; defensively, Grissom plays a more shallow center field, but that's the only real difference, as they are arguably the two best defensive players at that position. Justice has looked terrific this spring, like the 40-homer hitter he was before his shoulder went. Grissom, Omar Vizquel, Jim Thome, Matt Williams, Justice, Julio Franco, Manny Ramirez, Kevin Mitchell and Sandy Alomar is the lineup, at least as long as Franco doesn't pull a hamstring. GM John Hart likes offense, and he says, "Second base is an offensive position." That remains to be seen, but Tony Fernandez can play the position and he is still an offensive player.

After Lofton turned down a $44 million offer, Hart was worried that he would end up in Phoenix or New York. The Indians also were hesitant to tie up $50 million for five years to someone who'll turn 30 next year and whose legs are his greatest tool.

FULLAM: Here are my long-awaited replies to yesterday's comments:

Grissom is an excellent outfielder—I'm not denying that. But the fact of the matter is that all of our recorded data leads us to believe that *Lofton* is an even *better* outfielder. Yes, I know, all of our methods are imperfect, but it sounds a bit arrogant when you claim that unless I watch the players in drills and know about their work ethics, I can't possibly know what I'm talking about. In any case, we have a difference of opinion—but leaving the entire fielding issue aside, how can you possibly say that "career stats are meaningless, as any GM will tell you on making comparisons between players?" What GMs? Where are they working? Please enlighten me. From that standpoint, we should expect Steve Finley and Terry Steinbach to hit 30 HR *every* year now, since the only stats that matter are their offensive numbers from '96.

There are a variety of factors that affect how players will perform in the future, such as age, injury history, ballpark change, and also career statistics. John Olerud hit .269 from the time he entered the league until '93, when, as you know, he exploded to a .363 average. Yet while he's hit .287 over the past three years—the main question about Olerud has been "What happened to him?" Maybe he *wasn't* a .360 hitter! Whenever a player produces a season that is out of whack with their usual level of production, nine times out of 10 that player will follow up the unusual season with a performance that more resembles his career numbers. Like Willie McGee after his '85 MVP year; or like Wade Boggs after the '87 year (when he exploded for 24 HR); or like Andres Galarraga after he hit .370 for the Rockies in '93. I can't believe that most baseball GMs think that career numbers are meaningless—if they do, my respect for baseball front offices is rapidly dwindling.

And finally, even if Lofton tests the free market, he couldn't possibly get more money than the Indians have locked up in the Grissom/Justice combo right now. The only reason I can fathom Cleveland making the trade would be Kenny telling the Indians' brass that *no matter what*, he wouldn't return next season. The Tribe could have replaced Justice with Brian Giles for a much cheaper price and hardly lost anything offensively.

March 26—Jose Cruz Jr.

MOYER: Jose Cruz Jr. was sent down by the Mariners. Maybe I was in another world, but from everything I'd read and heard, he pretty much had the everyday LF job locked up. Who plays left now? Lee Tinsley? Rich Amaral? Rickey Henderson?

PINTO: This could be one of those stupid arbitration moves. If they keep him down for a month now, they may get another year out of him before they have to deal with him in arbitration. These owners do think like that.

KRETSCHMANN: It's also Lou Piniella, who doesn't exactly give youngsters a chance. It took Alex Rodriguez two years to play, and he screwed with Bret Boone so much that the Mariners ended up trading him.

ZMINDA: Jose Cruz, 1997 Spring Training: .339 AVG, .645 SLG, 4 HR in 62 AB. Too bad he can't hit the curve.

MITTLEMAN: I had pointed out two days ago in the Daily that he would be going down after my man in Arizona saw him play and saw how badly he was struggling with curveballs. We looked good on that one.

Remember Carlos Delgado and his explosion onto the scene a couple of years ago in Toronto? I believe he hit nine homers in April and had gaudy stats until the curveball brought him to his knees.

Cruz' overall stats may look fine indeed, but he also went 2-for-18 during a stretch when Piniella was making his decision and it was the curveball that he looked weak against. Piniella probably figures it would do no harm for him to work on his adjustments before he brought him up.

ZMINDA: I see your point, but I only agree to an extent. Piniella's an excellent manager, but he has a definite impatience with young players that sometimes hurts his team, in my opinion. I would like this move better if the M's had a better alternative than Tinsley/Amaral. But I can understand his position: he's expected to win with this team, and it's hard to show much patience in developing a young player. I hope Cruz is back soon.

March 26—Spring-Training Comebacks

CANTER: HoJo just announced his retirement! *And* the Mets released Alvaro Espinoza!

PINTO: Have any of the players trying to make comebacks caught on with a team?

ZMINDA: I don't think any of them have made it yet, but Van Slyke was hitting over .500 for the Cardinals last time I looked, so I'd say he has a chance.

CARLSON: I am waiting for some players to follow Gordie Howe's lead. When is Joe DiMaggio going to get another tryout? I'll bet he could swing better than half the current Tigers.

March 27—Cubs

SICKELS: I can't understand why the Cubs are giving the LF platoon job to Brant Brown. He's not that great of a hitter, and his defense in LF is terrible. I suppose Brooks Kieschnick has too much power, Robin Jennings is too good a fielder and Pedro Valdes has too much potential. A bizarre decision.

OLKIN: Don't forget, they're going to use Doug Glanville against lefties. I guess they just got confused. After announcing that they wanted a power-hitting left fielder, they realized that they had four good candidates for the job (Kieschnick, Jennings, Timmons and Valdes). That was too much to deal with, so they decided they'd go for a singles hitter instead. That narrowed it down to two and they still couldn't make a decision, so they decided to platoon them.

MOYER: Hopefully, Brown still has his goatee, which made him a Babble-On separated at birth last year with Jeff Schinski. To paraphrase Jeff from *Diamond Chronicles 1997*, page 204, "No way man, Brown rulz!"

March 28—Vince Coleman

MOYER: From *USA Today* today:

"Veteran OF Vince Coleman survived the final cut. 'I think he's been a positive influence in the clubhouse,' GM Randy Smith said. 'And he legitimizes us a little.'"

ZMINDA: I'm sure Vince is a positive influence in the stadium parking lot, also.

PINTO: I guess there will be some fireworks in Detroit this year.

ELMAN: I understand Coleman's agent said he would take a $50,000 pay cut if he could be assured of a roster spot for Devil's Night.

April 1—Opening Day

DEWAN: It's Opening Day, the sun is shining, the birds are singing. Ah, all is well with the world.

It's a nice sunny day here in Chicago, not a bad day for a ballgame. But there won't be any on this day in this city. That's because of the a new MLB initiative to set up the schedule to start games in domed and warm-weather cities this year. Many agree that the major league baseball schedule is too long, and because of that, cold-weather baseball is inevitable. One solution, of course, is to shorten the schedule. But that's like asking baseball owners to cut a hole in their pockets so the money can dribble away. The next best thing is to avoid the cold weather whenever possible. Obviously it's not possible to avoid it in October. So they've decided to unleash the schedule makers and do the best they can early in the year (mainly this week, it appears) to handle this.

A good decision by MLB.

MOYER: We can't have too much of this positive stuff going on the @OFFICE:BBALL list. It is dangerous. Where's a GM I can pick on? (Actually, I'm as excited as John. I got giddy just putting the batteries in my SportsTrax this morning.)

PINTO: I noticed today that the entire Mets starting rotation is on the DL. So much for strong young arms.

You know you spend too much time in front of the computer when the highlight of your day is the correct ML schedule being on the beeper on Opening Day.

COOPERSON: It's OK, Steve, I'm sure Opening Day 1998 will include a game in Allentown.

CARLSON: I was just watching opening statements of the Jose Mesa trial on Court TV at lunch, waiting for the in-progress update on the AOL AL Scoreboard.

PINTO: Albert Belle now projects to 486 RBI on the season. And Frank Thomas hasn't drawn a walk, so Belle must be protecting him.

MUNDO: . . . and Norberto Martin projects to 162 HR.

OLKIN: Kevin Orie just allowed Edgar Renteria to bunt one past him for a double. The Cubs are alive and well.

OLKIN: Ryne Sandberg made two errors before being forced to leave the game. He fouled a ball off the plate and it came up and hit him in the face.

April 1—Jim Abbott

RUBY: Jim Abbott was released. Will he find another job? He was pitiful last year.

One of the things I find especially strange, considering the sports media's tendency to always remind us when someone is the first minority to do this or that, is that no one ever mentions Abbott's lack of a right hand. Does anyone think that there might be a relationship between his bad pitching and the fact that he has to have such a strange pitching motion just so he can find time on each pitch? Granted, he's turned his switching into an art form, but maybe it was really upsetting his mechanics.

He was a great story a few years ago: great college pitcher overcomes a handicap, goes straight to the majors, pitches a no-hitter, etc. Maybe the rush to get this novelty to the majors has ultimately damaged his career.

Happy Opening Day, everyone. The weather today rocks. Too bad the Cubs and Sox are out of town.

HENZLER: Peter Gammons has made the very point you suggested. He maintains that Abbott's lack of mass in his right arm has harmed his follow-through, and in the long run damaged the arm strength in his left.

Gammons also says that Abbott has actually thrown well on the side, but that once he gets in a game he just loses it. He suggests that Abbott might be helped by getting out of Anaheim. Montreal has shown interest, but that brings up an interesting point. How well would Abbott bat in the National League?

SPEAR: If memory serves me correctly, Abbott once went 4-for-4 in an intersquad game with California back in the early '90s.

HENZLER: And that triple was hit off of none other than Randy Johnson. That suggests he wouldn't necessarily be overpowered.

MOYER: Maybe Abbott is the new Babe Ruth (except Ruth was a good pitcher).

April 2—Mark Fuhrman

FREER: Yes, *that* Mark Fuhrman was spotted in the Yankees' dugout before Tuesday's opener. He was there because he's friends with David Wells' brother. He was *not* brought to Seattle to throw out the first *glove*.

OLKIN: I heard the grounds crew refused to let him on the field—they were afraid he'd plant something.

PINTO: He's probably a great admirer of Jackie Robinson and wanted one of the special commemorative balls.

MOYER: He was looking for an Indian pitcher named Chad.

MILLER: The rumor in southwest Ohio is that Marge Schott is looking into signing Mark Fuhrman as the Reds' closer!

April 2—Gary Sheffield

PINTO: Gary Sheffield signs for $61 million.

I love the way the owners try to get out of things. And salaries are all the players' fault.

ZMINDA: It's nuts, when you think about it. For all of Albert Belle's problems, he's been a consistently excellent power hitter—five straight seasons with 30+ HR and 100+ RBI. Sheffield's had two 30-100 seasons, four years apart, and those were the only seasons he's had 500 AB. In four of the eight seasons since 1989, he hasn't even played 100 games.

You give a guy with a record of durability like that a $61 million guaranteed contract?

COOPERSON: And the team from the largest market with only one team won't give Curt Schilling $16 million.

WENZ: Just a hunch. . . I wonder if his other good year was a contract year. It is pretty tough to question his ability, though.

April 3—Wade Boggs

ELMAN: It was with great pleasure and *much* surprise that I saw Wade Boggs play on Opening Night. In a time when it seems ballplayers will sit themselves down for a strain, ingrown toenail, or just not feeling right, Boggs played with a bandage covering 45+ stitches above his nose and eye that he received just one or two days earlier. Truly unusual in this day when too many players appear to be more concerned with their future (read: financial) instead of concerned for what happens between the foul lines. Great job, Wade!!!

April 3—Bill Buckner

FREER: Recently hired New York Jets coach Bill Parcells, on how he has been treated by the Boston media since leaving the New England Patriots:

"The way things are going up there, before too long, they'll be blaming me for the ball going through Buckner's legs."

April 8—Joe Crawford

OLKIN: Mets pitcher Joe Crawford made his major league debut last night—as a pinch hitter. He went on to pitch and took the loss in extra innings. It's not as crazy as it sounds. In his minor league career, Crawford batted .455 (15-for-33) with eight RBI and a .697 slugging percentage.

ZMINDA: I'm sure this does make sense as Mat says, but I'm also sure that we'll see at least one article about how Bobby Valentine was used to managing in the DH league for so many years and didn't leave himself enough pinch hitters. In the world of baseball, managing without the DH is the equivalent of splitting the atom (at least according to a big chunk of the sportswriting fraternity).

April 9—Streaks

RUBY: The Phoenix Suns now have a 10-game winning streak and are headed to the playoffs despite starting the season 0-13.

Does anyone know of an occurrence in either hoops or baseball in which a team had at least a 10-game winning streak *and* a 10-game losing streak in the same season? This seems pretty unprecedented to me.

KLOTZ: Didn't the Brewers do something like this a couple years ago?

OLKIN: The '87 Milwaukee Brewers began the season 13-0, but embarked upon a 12-game losing streak soon thereafter. They finished the season in third place in the AL East with a record of 91-71.

OLKIN: Didn't the '81 Oakland A's have a long winning streak and a long losing streak? I know they made the playoffs that year.

GILBERT: The Cubs seem to be on there way to a 10-game losing streak, but the odds of a 10-game winning streak do not look good.

KRETSCHMANN: The '82 Braves won their first 13 games and then lost 11 in a row when they got stuck on 62 wins. They lost to the Cardinals in the playoffs.

HENZLER: Similarly, the Texas Rangers won 14 straight games in 1991 before immediately losing 11 of 12. Only eight of those losses came consecutively, however.

COOPERSON: During the Braves' 11-game slide, Bob Watson said it was like "watching someone steal your furniture while you stood and watched."

In the NHL, the 1983-84 Washington Capitols started the year with seven straight losses, then later had a 14-game unbeaten streak (13-0-1) that included 10 straight wins. The Caps finished with the fifth-best record in the league that year.

What's really amazing is that the Braves actually endured a 2-19 slide yet still won the division!

FULLAM: The 1991 Phils won 13 in a row directly after a seven-game losing streak. I think Mitch Williams picked up five wins during the run.

COOPERSON: It appears that every win in that streak guaranteed Lee Thomas another year as Phils GM, no matter how bad the subsequent results.

ZMINDA: The 1951 New York Giants in baseball had an 11-game losing streak early in the year, and a 16-game winning streak (if memory serves) late in the year as they came from way back to force a playoff with the Dodgers. Don't recall any other sports teams with both losing and winning streaks of 10+ games in the same year.

HENZLER: Twelve MLB teams have had winning and losing streaks of 10 or more games since 1950.

10-Game Winning and Losing Streaks in Same Season (since 1950)

Year	Team	W Streak	L Streak
1951	New York Giants	16	11
1955	Philadelphia Phillies	11	13
1957	Cincinnati Reds	12	10
1959	Kansas City Athletics	11	13
1970	Chicago Cubs	11	12
1976	Chicago White Sox	10	10
1979	Cleveland Indians	10	10
1982	Atlanta Braves	13	11
1985	Minnesota Twins	10	10
1987	Baltimore Orioles	11	10
1987	Milwaukee Brewers	13	12
1991	New York Mets	10	11

PINTO: I know the Cubs can tie an NL record for losses to start a season, but has anyone seen the top five or six ML list? I know two AL teams lost 13, but I wonder if any other AL teams lost 11 or 12 or 10 to start a season.

DEWAN: I recall the White Sox losing 10 to start the 1968 season.

RUBY: How soon we forget. . . Baltimore started 0-21 in 1988, I believe.

CANTER: Yes. The O's started 0-21. I went to the game at Comiskey when they finally won. They *crushed* the White Sox 9-0. Billy Ripken got beaned in the head and was carried off on a stretcher, too. So they couldn't even really feel good about finally winning one.

April 9—Young Infielders

NEYER: While researching a piece on Edgar Renteria and Luis Castillo, I ran across this:

From 1901 through 1968, only six of 136 pennant-winning teams featured a regular middle infielder age 21 or younger.

All six were managed by a Hall of Famer.

Year	Team	Infielder	Manager
1905	Athletics	Jack Knight	Connie Mack
1924	Giants	Travis Jackson	John McGraw
1931	Athletics	Dib Williams	Connie Mack
1932	Yankees	Frank Crosetti	Joe McCarthy
1957	Yankees	Bobby Richardson	Casey Stengel
1958	Yankees	Tony Kubek	Casey Stengel

Maybe I'm reading too much into this list, but it might say something about those guys, even taking into consideration the large number of pennants they accounted for.

April 9—White Sox Attendance

PINTO: Official attendance, 1,677. Less than 1,000 were actually in the stands. I wonder if Albert Belle is worried that his paycheck is going to bounce?

OSBORNE: New official attendance number is 746!

OLKIN: And falling!

CARLSON: Maybe they should start playing indoor lacrosse or something where the attendance is higher.

I can just see, Jerry Reinsdorf is calling dome builders as we speak.

FULLAM: How can that be? Isn't official attendance based on tickets sold? Season-ticket sales have to be higher than *that*.

April 16—Cubs

HAMILL: Why was the Cubs' web page kicked off the Internet?

Because they couldn't string together 3 W's in a row!

CHERNOW: Averages

The Cubs, top to bottom: .146, .154, .128, .179, .250, .167, .226, .000, .000

The Rockies: .308, .357, .522, .357, .000, .356, .333, .250, .400

Which team is 9-3?

ZMINDA: After getting shut out by the immortal Roger Bailey today, the Cubs are hitting .177. They have yet to reach double figures in hits in any game; they've had nine hits twice, no more than seven hits in any of their other games.

Bailey's shutout was the first ever by a Rockies pitcher on the road, and only the third complete-game shutout in team history. The others were by David Nied (1994) and Mark Thompson (1996), both in Colorado.

Leave it to the Cubbies to keep making history!

HENZLER: Bailey also failed to record a single strikeout while recording a complete-game shutout. In addition, he walked only one batter.

The last pitcher to go the distance and register a shutout while while allowing one or fewer walks and striking out no one was Mike Morgan on 4/19/91, when he blanked the Padres for the Dodgers.

If you're interested in the last complete-game shutout without any strikeouts, regardless of walks issued, that would have been Zane Smith's performance for the Pirates against the Expos on 8/11/94.

We all know what happened the next day. I'm guessing the Cubs may be wishing for a strike right about now themselves.

April 16—Deion Sanders

MUNDO: One advantage of being home sick is that you get to watch some baseball!

In today's Reds/Braves game, Terrell Wade threw to second to try and pick off Deion Sanders. The ball sailed into the outfield, allowing Sanders to round third and head home.

The official scorer gave Deion a caught stealing on the play. Skip Caray said he checked with the scorer and he showed Skip something in the rule book that made the ruling "make sense."

What's the rule? Can the official scorer haphazardly give out a CS in cases like this?

By the way, that was Deion's first CS of the season. Let's hope the official scorer reverses his decision.

OSBORNE: Rule 10.08(g)

When in the scorer's judgment a runner attempting to steal is safe because of a muffed throw, do not credit a stolen base. Credit an assist to the fielder who made the throw; charge an error to the fielder who muffed the throw, and charge the runner with "caught stealing."

Is it possible that Sanders first broke for third, and would, in the scorer's judgment, have been out, if not for the a muffed catch at second base, and therefore awarded the "caught stealing"?

He also is considered "caught stealing" if he is picked off a base and tries to advance. Any move toward the next base is considered an attempt to advance. 10.08(h2)

NEYER: I was watching the game, too (one advantage of having a TV six feet from your desk), and Dave—probably suffering from delirium brought on by his illness—doesn't have his facts quite right.

Wade did *not* attempt a pickoff throw. Sanders was on second base, and broke for third before Wade went into his motion. Somebody yelled, Wade looked, and saw Sanders halfway. He turned and threw to third base, trying to lead Mike Mordecai. But Mordecai wasn't moving to the bag, and the throw sailed into foul territory. Sanders, who had slammed on the brakes when Wade first threw, now jogged home.

Essentially, this is a variation on a scoring decision you'll see from time to time, when a catcher's throw to second appears to beat the runner, but the infielder drops the ball. They'll often give the runner a CS and the infielder an error, though I suppose it's strange to assume the umpire would definitely have made the right call.

On the other hand, they *never* give the runner a CS on an errant throw; it's always a SB and an error (assuming the runner moves to third). And one might argue that today's situation is analogous.

One last point. Even if Wade's throw had been perfect, there would have been a rundown, and it's not inconceivable that Sanders would have escaped.

All in all, a questionable scoring decision, but one with which I agree. Sanders did something dumb and doesn't deserve a stolen base, and Wade did something stupid and does deserve an error. Bet you didn't think anyone would write this much, did you, Dave?

April 21—All-Geezer Team

CARLSON:

The all-geezer team (oldest active player at each position):

C	Tony Pena	6/4/57
1B	Eddie Murray	2/24/56
2B	Ryne Sandberg	9/18/59
3B	Wade Boggs	6/15/58
SS	Rafael Belliard	10/24/61
LF	Tim Raines	9/16/59
CF	Brett Butler	6/15/57
RF	Willie McGee	11/2/58
P	Rick Honeycutt	6/29/54

April 23—Homer Duos

CARLSON: Just came across on a wire story. . . what two teammates have homered in the same game the most times in history?

OLKIN: Aaron & Mathews? (Not Tommie & Nellie.)

CARLSON: The answer, and top 15 list:

Hank Aaron & Eddie Mathews	75
Babe Ruth & Lou Gehrig	73
Willie Mays & Willie McCovey	68
Duke Snider & Gil Hodges	67
Ron Santo & Billy Williams	64
Bob Allison & Harmon Killebrew	61
Joe Adcock & Eddie Mathews	56
Jim Rice & Dwight Evans	56
Mickey Mantle & Yogi Berra	55
Willie Mays & Orlando Cepeda	50
Bob Meusel & Babe Ruth	47
Ernie Banks & Ron Santo	43
MARK McGWIRE & JOSE CANSECO	43
Mickey Mantle & Roger Maris	42
Ernie Banks & Billy Williams	42
Harmon Killebrew & Tony Oliva	42

Considering they all make the list with their other two teammates, I wonder if Banks, Santo and Williams would lead the list of trios that hit HR in the same game?

April 24—Terry Steinbach

KRETSCHMANN: I was just flipping through the box scores and noticed Steinbach hit a homer against his ex-mates and was wondering how catchers hit against guys they had caught (both before they started catching them and after).

All Catchers	AB	Avg	OBP	Slg
Before	16,235	.244	.308	.375
After	10,563	.258	.333	.409
Steinbach	**AB**	**Avg**	**OBP**	**Slg**
Before	276	.239	.289	.373
After	385	.351	.369	.478

If he had played on a few more teams, he could have been a Hall of Famer.

Attached is a list of other guys with 200+ ABs hitting against ex-batterymates.

Disclaimers: Our data on who caught who only goes back to 1987, so that affects some of the older guys drastically (like Gary Carter). I didn't bother to check exact days they caught, I just assumed once he caught the guy, anything he did against that pitcher that year was afterwards.

Pat Borders	AB	Avg	OBP	Slg
Before	544	.270	.304	.414
After	287	.230	.301	.331
Gary Carter	AB	Avg	OBP	Slg
Before	499	.291	.336	.459
After	238	.202	.296	.361
Darren Daulton	AB	Avg	OBP	Slg
Before	291	.186	.337	.330
After	251	.239	.337	.363
Joe Girardi	AB	Avg	OBP	Slg
Before	208	.284	.333	.399
After	221	.276	.344	.330
Matt Nokes	AB	Avg	OBP	Slg
Before	400	.220	.285	.378
After	296	.280	.318	.524
Tom Pagnozzi	AB	Avg	OBP	Slg
Before	217	.189	.252	.263
After	271	.284	.313	.428
Benito Santiago	AB	Avg	OBP	Slg
Before	555	.234	.268	.346
After	335	.257	.318	.442
Don Slaught	AB	Avg	OBP	Slg
Before	465	.249	.313	.381
After	226	.314	.389	.456
Mike Stanley	AB	Avg	OBP	Slg
Before	345	.281	.386	.443
After	344	.302	.412	.555
Mickey Tettleton	AB	Avg	OBP	Slg
Before	439	.271	.381	.465
After	506	.271	.411	.472
Dave Valle	AB	Avg	OBP	Slg
Before	377	.244	.319	.358
After	330	.288	.358	.433
Rick Wilkins	AB	Avg	OBP	Slg
Before	285	.242	.324	.421
After	227	.238	.377	.383

April 25—Carlos Baerga

FAUST: What happened to Carlos Baerga?

He's now hitting .182 in his career as a Met—25-for-137 in 41 games.

ZMINDA: He's had some injuries, but the biggest problem is that he's really slowed down. His bat speed just isn't what it used to be, and he's too out of shape to be of any use in the field. I'd pontificate that being out of shape has hurt his hitting, but it never seems to hurt Tony Gwynn. So who knows? Also, Carlos loves to party.

Remember how the other Indians were whining when they dumped Baerga last year? It looks like they got rid of him right in the nick of time.

MOYER: Funny you ask. There's an article in today's *New York Post* focusing on the decline of five bright stars: Jim Abbott, Baerga, Jack McDowell, Brian McRae, and Ruben Sierra. The general blame for all four (and any other youngster who peters out suddenly) is: 1) multiyear contracts, 2) weightlifting, 3) increased media attention. Specific Baerga blame can be summed up by this quote in the article: "You can't run around 24 hours a day for a number of years and not impact your body. He lost the range of motion in his swing. Now all you have to do is pound him inside and he'll get himself out."

Personally (as I'm sure you'd guess), I think most of those reasons are hooey, the usual "things were better in the good old days" nonsense. There is a side issue to the weightlifting thing that I could believe a bit: "I think you have guys who take the steroids, put up the numbers, get the long-term contract and once they have the money start worrying about their health and get off the steroids and lose some of their strength."

I don't think McDowell and especially Abbott were ever really that good in the first place. McRae and especially Baerga and Sierra have always been undisciplined and, as we good sabermetricians know, when things dry up for a non-walker, they dry up a lot drier than for a walker. McRae had a real good year last year and April 25th is way too early to write off his season. Sierra is now hitting .290. Baerga is as big a mystery to me as anybody. I thought after he quit the heavy partying this winter he'd be good again. Maybe, like Bill once said about Lonnie Smith and Darrell Porter, the shocking change of lifestyle did more harm than good.

ZMINDA: He may have quit, but all those years of living in the fast lane must have an awfully wearing effect on his body. Baseball history is full of guys who partied hard and flamed out early.

April 25—Steve Howe

FREER: Nine Lives

Steve Howe is making a minor league comeback with an independent team. How long before some MLB team is able to forget his eight suspensions, deem him cured, and start his ninth major league life?

I bet Dwight Gooden and Darryl Strawberry court him on behalf of the Yanks.

ZMINDA: Actually, Howe seems to have gotten his act together. Whatever you think about him getting all those chances, he seems to have straightened himself out (famous last words). Drug problems didn't drive him out of the big leagues this time, the hitters did.

ELMAN: He must be trying to work his arm into shape for expansion next year. Could he be one of the top 22 arms that is not pitching in the bigs this year???

May 1—Jose Canseco

RUBY: Did anyone see how Jose Canseco made a smart defensive play last night to preserve an A's victory?

With the bases loaded and the score tied in the bottom of the ninth or 10th, a long foul ball was hit that he could clearly catch, but he was smart enough to let it drop so there would be no sacrifice fly. The batter was eventually retired and the A's went on to win. I don't think I've ever seen that happen.

May 3—New Haven Ravens

SABRMAN (AOL name): At last night's New Haven Ravens' game, I witnessed the following amazing occurrence:

The New Britain Rock Cats' game at New Haven on Thursday, May 1, 1997, had been suspended with one out in the top of the fifth, due to rain. On Friday, May 2, 1997, the game was completed and the regularly scheduled game was shortened to seven innings and played after the completion of the suspended game.

In the top of the seventh of the regularly scheduled (second) game, New Britain had a 10-7 lead, two out and runners on first and third. Ryan Lane, the Rock Cats' second baseman and No. 7 hitter was due up. The PA announcer announced Lane as the batter. Amazingly, instead of Lane, up stepped Keith Legree, the right fielder and No. 8 hitter. No one except the umpire appeared to notice. (The umpire, incidentally, did exactly as the Rule 6.07 specifies in such circumstances, and did not point this fact out to anyone, although he did stare curiously at the New Haven dugout for a moment, seeming to wonder whether Ravens manager Bill Hayes had any objection).

As the count went to 3-0 to Legree, Ravens catcher Blake Barthol called for an intentional ball. Since the last ball was intentional, this play is scored as an intentional walk. Then the No. 7 hitter Lane came to bat, and struck out swinging to end the inning. The Ravens mounted a rally in the bottom of the seventh but ultimately fell short and lost 10-9.

This series of events is fascinating on many levels. First, batting out of order is a phenomenon that I have never witnessed in a professional baseball game. Additionally, this faux pas seems to have escaped the attention of virtually everyone except the home-plate umpire and the PA announcer, including Hayes and the 4,013 fans in attendance. A neighboring Rock Cats pitcher who was charting pitches on his day off confirmed that his team had, in fact, just batted out of order without getting caught.

But the true beauty of this achievement lies in the fact that, for quite possibly the first and only time in the history of baseball, a batter was, in effect, intentionally walked in order to reach the hitter in front of him!

May 4—Deion Sanders

MOYER: From today's *New York Post* "Behind The Seams" column:

"Anyone who believes (Deion) Sanders is bad for baseball is a racist. Period." Geez, has this touchy-touchy business come so far now that if one doesn't like a minority player for any reason, it's racism?

RUBY: Oh man, does this stuff get me going.

When are people going to say stuff like "Tiger Woods dominated the Masters" before (or better yet instead of) saying "Tiger Woods is the first black to win the Masters"?

I'm so tired of people feeling like they have to bring race into every issue involving a person of color. I don't like Deion because he's a jerk. I hate all jerks. If they're black, white or whatever. If that makes me a jerkist, then I guess I'm a jerkist. Someday people will describe Deion as a baseball player, football player, basketball player, or whatever else he tries to play rather than as a "black baseball player," etc.

I personally think the comments in the *Post* contribute far more to racism than the author thinks a Deion-basher does. If that author could avoid bringing race into it, maybe others would and eventually we'd all realize that Deion is either a nice guy or a jerk, but who cares about his race. OK, maybe this wasn't too coherent of an argument, but I'm just sick of hearing about it.

P.S. I don't think Deion is bad for baseball (what a relief, I'm not a racist), but I do think he's overrated. What does that make me?

SCHINSKI: I agree with Kenn. Too often race is mentioned in the media. I don't look at someone's race to judge their ability.

MOYER: From today's *USA Today*, Felipe Alou is annoyed that Dusty Baker thinks the Expos are stealing signals: "I would like to spread the word: I'd like to express my concern about a minority manager accusing another minority manager about stealing signs."

I guess these days we don't go by names anymore, just races. That's progress.

PINTO: Didn't the Giants under Roger Craig make sign stealing an art form?

MOYER: Don't you mean "white man manager"?

PINTO: The real funny thing is that there's an ESPN ad with the baseball detectives where Baker calls them up and asks them to steal the Dodgers' signs.

May 6—Roger Clemens

OLKIN: In his last four starts against the Tigers, Roger Clemens has gone 4-0 with an 0.79 ERA, striking out 53 batters while walking only two. Project that out to 34 starts and you get 451 strikeouts and 17 walks.

MITTLEMAN: He's also 11-2 with a 1.58 ERA since last August, striking out approximately 128 batters in 120 innings.

His rebound was evident to everyone during the latter half of last season, which is another reason why his seemingly mediocre season record was so deceiving. Shame on the Red Sox for this serious miscalculation.

May 8—Bases-Loaded Walks

HENZLER: As per a recent inquiry, there have been more walks than usual with the bases loaded this season. We've seen a bases-loaded walk roughly every fifth game in 1997. That's a far higher rate than any previous year going back to 1987. And it does continue a developing trend since 1988.

Bases-Loaded Walks Per Game

Year	BB	G	Per Game
1987	240	2,105	.114
1988	198	2,100	.094
1989	208	2,106	.099
1990	211	2,105	.100
1991	207	2,104	.098
1992	235	2,106	.112
1993	272	2,269	.120
1994	190	1,600	.119
1995	270	2,017	.134
1996	332	2,267	.146
1997	81	436	.186

FULLAM: This brings up an interesting question. Would the Phillies intentionally walk Barry Bonds with the bases loaded? They've walked him nine times in 22 plate appearances this season.

SCHINSKI: Didn't that happen to Ernie Banks?

ZMINDA: No. The last occurrence of this (IBB with the bases loaded) that's been documented occurred in the 1940s with Bill Nicholson of the Cubs.

May 8—Bob Hamelin

MOYER: What's the first noteworthy thing Bob Hamelin does for the Tigers?

He walks and steals a base.

The Royals were confused, thinking this Bob Hamelin was the same big, fat, slow Bob Hamelin that used be one of them.

ZMINDA: I saw Hamelin steal a base when I was in Kansas City last year. If I were Jerry Coleman, I would say something like, "He's surprisingly fast for a slow guy."

May 9—Moose Stubing

ZMINDA: Moose Stubing was in the Comiskey Park press box scouting for somebody a couple of weeks ago. Hawk Harrelson walks up to him and says to everybody, "Here's the only guy in history who played in the majors and didn't get a hit, and managed in the majors and didn't win a game!"

I looked it up and don't know if there are any other cases like this, but the Hawkeroo was absolutely right about Stubing. Moose went 0-for-5 with four strikeouts as a player with the '67 Angels, and he was 0-8 finishing out the 1988 season as the Angels' manager.

That's some record.

MOYER: That should go as an addendum to Bill's book.

May 9—Barry Bonds

RUBY: The season is 20 percent over and Bobby Bonilla has yet to hit a homer and Barry Bonds doesn't have any doubles. Pretty strange.

HENZLER: Bonds now has 30 walks to go along with the zero doubles that Kenn mentioned. In the history of major league baseball, only one other player had a higher "ratio" of walks to doubles, although both ratios are technically infinite.

In 1890, Herman Pitz, a catcher with Brooklyn and Syracuse in the American Association, walked *58* times with no doubles in 284 at-bats. He had no triples or homers, either. Perhaps unsurprisingly, that was his only season in the majors.

Something tells me Bonds won't be shut out in doubles much longer, however.

FYI, the legendary Rafael Belliard had 26 walks and no doubles for the 1988 Pirates. Maybe he should have stopped at second base on one of his four triples.

Mickey Lolich had a year in which he walked 20 times with no doubles. Of course Mickey, with his girth, was better at walking than running.

Another girthful walker? Babe Ruth in 1935. He walked 20 times with no doubles. He also retired after 72 at-bats.

May 13—Doug Jones

MOYER: Today, with ace closer Doug Jones unavailable since he pitched last night, Milwaukee had to settle for stinky Mike Fetters, who promptly blew the 1-0 lead Jose Mercedes had protected all game long. Where's Jeff Reardon when you need him?

PINTO: How could a player who throws 60 MPH get tired?

DEWAN: Based on his strikeout/innings ratio you would think he throws at 90. I'm sure he must be up to at least 61 by now, however.

May 15—Terry Bevington

NEYER: You guys see the game today?

Top of the ninth, first and second, 2-0 count on Albert Belle, Sox down one run.

Double-steal attempt? Yep, and Ray Durham is thrown out at third. That takes the bat out of Belle's hands, as he is intentionally walked.

Why steal here?

Of course, it worked out when Chris Snopek hit one off the wall. But this could have been the last straw.

MUNDO: According to the *Trib*, Durham stole it on his own. Terry Bevington's quote on Durham: "Most times he makes good decisions. I don't think he'll try the next time."

Either that, or Bev and Durham made an agreement to tell the press it was Ray's idea so Bevington doesn't get the ax.

May 17—Todd Dunwoody

SPEAR: Something kind of cool. . .

Todd Dunwoody's first four major league hits have been a single, double, triple and home run. A cycle in just 10 at bats!

PINTO: Way cool!

May 19—Tony Phillips

ZMINDA: The White Sox didn't get much for Tony Phillips, if you ask me, but I'm glad to see him gone. He's a great leadoff man, but the constant chip on his shoulder got really tiresome. The final straw for me was when he said Gene Budig, a very decent man, was a racist because he upheld Phillips' suspension (which Phillips deserved).

Let someone else deal with his idiotic behavior.

WENZ: Between Albert Belle, Frank Thomas, Jaime Navarro, Phillips and even Terry Bevington, they must have one of the most tense clubhouses in baseball. Not the kind you want when the going gets tough. I don't usually put too much weight on people's "clubhouse presence." Either they can play or they can't, but when you're underachieving it's pretty tough to turn things around when you keep getting more and more tight. So getting rid of Phillips was certainly a good start.

COOPERSON: If Phillips was Dennis Rodman, all he would need was Michael Jordan and Scottie Pippen to keep him in line. Apparently Thomas & Belle didn't fit the bill.

May 19—Offense

HENZLER: I was rather surprised to see the Expos are creating so many runs per 27 outs. They're even outproducing the Rockies, and are only slightly behind the major league-leading Indians.

Not surprisingly, nine of the bottom 10 teams are from the National League. The only AL club in the bottom 10 is Toronto.

Oh boy, the Phillies are in town.

Runs Created Per 27 Outs by Team—1997

Team	RC	RC/27
1. Indians	257.75	5.40
2. Expos	241.81	5.35
3. Rockies	251.40	5.32
4. Mariners	250.58	5.12
5. Yankees	268.46	5.09
6. Red Sox	232.34	4.97
7. Orioles	230.05	4.80
8. Braves	223.35	4.66
9. White Sox	220.00	4.54
10. Rangers	192.20	4.26
11. Brewers	190.33	4.25
12. Angels	195.19	4.21
13. Tigers	204.45	4.19
14. Twins	208.32	4.13
15. Athletics	209.13	3.94
16. Marlins	195.46	3.89
17. Royals	184.80	3.89
18. Pirates	179.48	3.67
19. Astros	182.17	3.64
20. Cubs	170.99	3.58

PINTO: If the Blue Jays knew anything about runs created, they never would have gotten rid of Olerud.

I'm surprised the Expos are ahead of the Yankees in runs created. The Yankees lead the AL in hits and walks, and have hit a decent number of HR. The Expos never walk (they've drawn the fewest in the NL). At some point the opposition is going to realize this and stop throwing these players strikes, and I think their offense will go down (unless, of course, this is a team of eight Kirby Pucketts).

At least in real life, the Yankees are scoring more runs per game than the Expos.

May 19—Secondary Average

HENZLER: The Indians have compiled a team secondary average of .361 this season. I know it's early, but that's historically high. No other club since 1900 has compiled a secondary average within 37 points of the Indians' current rate.

Here again, we see how the offense of the 1990s is unusually high.

Team Secondary Average—Since 1900

Year	Team	AB	2B	3B	HR	BB	SB	CS	Sec Avg
1997	Indians	1399	76	5	71	192	25	11	.361
1994	Tigers	3955	216	25	161	520	46	33	.324
1996	Mariners	5668	343	19	245	670	90	39	.324
1938	Yankees	5410	283	63	174	749	91	28	.322
1996	Indians	5681	335	23	218	671	160	50	.320
1953	Dodgers	5373	274	59	208	655	90	47	.319
1996	Orioles	5689	299	29	257	645	76	40	.318
1936	Yankees	5587	315	83	182	700	77	40	.316
1997	Rockies	1409	72	7	57	159	44	16	.315
1995	Indians	5028	279	23	207	542	132	53	.312

May 22—Jack Hamilton

OLKIN: Guess the significance:

Pitcher Jack Hamilton threw 119.1 innings in the AL in 1967 and hit only one batter.

HENZLER: He hit Tony Conigliaro. It was the fifth time Tony had been hit that year.

May 26—Birthdays

PINTO: Did you know that Frank Thomas and Jeff Bagwell have the same birthday? They will both be 29 tomorrow. I wonder:

How many players have been born on the exact same day? What's the best group born on the exact same day?

The leaders for HR being born on the same day are Bill (Bull) Johnson and Ted Williams, 582. Bagwell and Thomas are currently eighth with 392. Third is Fred McGriff and Matt Nokes (with Mike Smith contributing 0 HR on the same date). Two pairs, Ernie Banks and Hank Aguirre and Murray Wall and Duke Snider had all their HR come from only one of the pair. I think the most interesting pair other than Bagwell and Thomas is Cecil Cooper and Oscar Gamble, who are fifth with 441.

DEWAN: That means that Babe Ruth and Hank Aaron and a few others have unique birthdays. That's a bit surprising on its own.

CARLSON: Not really. Dave, I think, was doing pairs born on the exact same day (in the same year), not just pairs who were born on the same date.

ZMINDA: Milt Wilcox and I were born on the exact same day—April 20, 1950—and we've hit exactly the same number of home runs: zero!

Actually, I was born in 1948, but I still think this is amazing.

MOYER: When I was at ESPN, I just happened to look up Harold Reynolds' *Bill James Encyclopedia* listing since I was working with him. To my surprise, I found out we were born less than two months apart (I'm a little older). I told Harold and he was mildly amused. He called me onto the set during "Baseball Tonight" and we sang "Happy Birthday" to each other. Only the previous sentence is a lie.

SPEAR: Braulio Castillo and I have combined for two homers. Three if you include Skokie Park District Softball as a major league.

MOYER: Joe Boever and I share the same birthday and body shape.

GREENBERGER: I share a birthday/year with Spike Lee, and between us we've written six major motion pictures and 114 BJFB newsletters.

May 31—Inside-The-Park Homers

SPEAR: With the recent outburst of inside-the-park homers, I started thinking and have come up with a great new rule for baseball!

What if when a player hits an ITP homer, the game is automatically over and that player's team wins? It would be like a pin in wrestling. . . no matter what inning it is or how many runs down you are, if you get an ITP homer, you win!!

Of course, this would apply to four-base errors as well. Basically, anytime a batter scores on his own hit that doesn't leave the park, you win!

Sure, all the "purists" out there will probably would be against this, but I'm telling you, what a way to get those kids back to the ballpark. Anybody can win at any time! Very MTV!

When I become All Sport Commissioner, I'm going to decree this to be law on my first day on the job, right after mandating all first basemen must wear helmets in the field.

June 7—Switch-Hitting Homers

OSLAND: With a home run from each side of the plate today, Chili Davis is now tied with Mickey Mantle with 10 games with a home run from each side of the plate. Eddie Murray is first with 11 such games.

There are two active players among the next three players on the list. Can you guess who they are?

OSLAND: With F.P. Santangelo hitting a HR from both sides of the plate this is only the third time ever that that has ever been done by two players on the same day.

The other times:

June 8th, 1989—Steve Jeltz for Philly and Ruben Sierra for Texas

August 21, 1996—Chili Davis for California and Ken Caminiti for San Diego

The answer to my quiz is:

Eddie Murray, 11; Chili Davis, 10; Mickey Mantle, 10; Ken Caminiti, 8; Bobby Bonilla, 6; Reggie Smith, 6.

June 12—Mariners Hall of Fame

ZMINDA: "Just a couple more good years, Junior, and you too might. . ."

Alvin Davis will be the first player inducted into the Seattle Mariners Hall of Fame.

Next year's inductees: Bill Stein and Diego Segui.

I'm joking about the last two, but it's possible. . .

PINTO: What about Ken Phelps, first and greatest member of the Ken Phelps All-Stars?

ZMINDA: The M's Veterans Committee considers Phelps a strong candidate, but let's face it: he was no Julio Cruz.

MILLER: What about Harold Reynolds or Bruce Bochte?

PINTO: Don't forget Julio's brother, Ernest.

MILLER: Mario Mendoza didn't reach the Mendoza Line in 1979 when he hit .198 for the M's. However, his career as a Mariner ended above the line at .218.

PETERSON: My vote is for Wimpy (Tom Paciorek).

OLKIN: Some sort of honorable mention should go to pitcher Mike Parrott, who suffered through perhaps the worst season of all time in 1980: 1-16 with a 7.28 ERA.

MUNDO: Mike Parrott!!

OLKIN: Don't parrot me.

June 16—Streaks

SPEAR: Ryan McGuire has now started off his career with an 11-game hit streak, which is the longest streak to begin a career since 1987 (when our data begins). Mike Lansing and Johnny Damon began with eight-game streaks, and Jerome Walton and Russ Johnson began with seven-gamers.

June 17—300-Game Winners

JAMES: Of the 12 pitchers identified in this year's *Scoreboard* as having at least a five-percent chance to win 300 games, it appears that all of them except Dennis Martinez and Chuck Finley will improve their standing with the 1997 season. Among the group (Greg Maddux, Roger Clemens, John Smoltz, Tom Glavine, Mike Mussina, Alex Fernandez, Kevin Appier, Pat Hentgen, Kevin Brown, Andy Benes, Martinez and Finley) we would have predicted 1.75 300-game winners before the season started. Next year that number will probably be over 2.00.

June 18—Glenallen Hill

OLKIN: Giants right fielder Glenallen Hill, on his recent benchings: "I'm not going to go quietly into the night."

Major League Leaders, Most Times Quoting Keats, 1997

Glenallen Hill	1
Several Tied With	0

GREENBERGER: Actually, that was Dylan Thomas. What a sad state of affairs when our own writers don't know their poetry.

OLKIN: Thanks for the correction. You know, when I dropped my English major, no one tried to talk me out of it. In hindsight, should I have just gritted my teeth and stuck with it? Another five semesters and I might have known the difference between Keats and Dylan Thomas. Oh well, like John Paciorek said, "Nobody's perfect."

WENZ: Damn. I'd have gotten it wrong too. I thought it was Rodney Dangerfield from "Back to School" or Michelle Pfieffer in "Dangerous Minds" or the guy who played the president in "Independence Day." One of them.

CANTER: I think I heard Lyle Mouton say, "Shakespeare for everyone!" on "SportsCenter" last week. Or maybe that was me.

GREENBERGER: That's just too much to bear. Read it and weep.

"Do Not Go Gentle into That Good Night"

Do not go gentle into that good night, Old age should burn and rave at close of day; Rage, rage against the dying of the light.

Though wise men at their end know dark is right, Because their words had forked no lightning they Do not go gentle into that good night.

Good men, the last wave by, crying how bright Their frail deeds might have danced in a green bay, Rage, rage against the dying of the light.

Wild men who caught and sang the sun in flight, And learn, too late, they grieved it on its way, Do not go gentle into that good night.

Grave men, near death, who see with blinding sight Blind eyes could blaze like meteors and be gay, Rage, rage against the dying of the light.

And you, my father, there on the sad height, Curse, bless, me now with your fierce tears, I pray. Do not go gentle into that good night. Rage, rage against the dying of the light.

After all, we are sports fans, not beasts.

COOPERSON: Did Dylan Thomas know something when he mentioned ''Green Bay'' in this?

June 26—Pat Hentgen

WENZ: Did anyone notice that Pat Hentgen gave up 11 runs on 13 hits, including homers in five different innings, and still lasted through the eighth inning?

Why?

ELMAN: Cito Gaston and Terry Bevington grew up together? Watching how he handles Jaime Navarro, this is my best guess.

CHERNOW: The funny thing is that if Paul Quantrill hadn't given up two runs in the ninth, Hentgen could have won that game—maybe Gaston was doing him a favor.

JAMES: I watched a little bit of that game on TV, the Pat Hentgen game. Predictably, the announcer intoned that this really illustrates the effects of the DH rule on the American League pitchers. If this was a National League game, he explained, Hentgen would have been long gone. . .

So I checked the league profiles, to see how many innings have been pitched in each league by the starting pitchers and the bullpen. It's essentially identical between the two leagues. The average American League team had gotten, I think, 443 innings out of their starting pitchers; the average National League team 446 innings. But most of the National League had played one extra game, so the percentage was a tiny, tiny fraction lower in the National League.

July 1—Greg Maddux

RUBY: Greg Maddux has walked zero guys in his last four starts.

What is the record for the most consecutive starts without walking anyone? I'm not saying that he's even close to such a record (it's probably not even his personal-best streak), but it seems to me to go four straight starts without a single walk is pretty hard to do.

MILLER: I think Andre Dawson, Shawon Dunston and Ozzie Guillen would be near the top of the list of consecutive games without a walk!!!

FULLAM: Don't forget Mariano Duncan. . .

CARLSON:

Longest Personal Pitcher/Batter Games-Started Streak w/o a Walk (Active Players)

Pitchers

Jimmy Key	7
Orel Hershiser	6
Bob Tewksbury	6
Greg Maddux	6
Bret Saberhagen	5
Eric Hillman	5

Batters

Mariano Duncan	70
Luis Sojo	51
Ozzie Guillen	48
Kim Batiste	46
Orlando Miller	44

ZMINDA: These guys are pikers. One year Rob Picciolo didn't get his first walk of the season until early September!

CARLSON: Among active players:

Longest Streaks Without a Walk—Pitchers

Pitcher	GS	Date Ended
Jimmy Key	7	5/6/90
Orel Hershiser	6	9/21/91
Bob Tewksbury	6	7/22/93
Greg Maddux	6	7/13/95
Bret Saberhagen	5	6/13/94
Eric Hillman	5	8/5/93

GOLDSTEIN: . . . and Alfredo Griffin once had less than one BB per 100 AB in 140+ games in '84.

CARLSON:

Longest Streaks Without a Walk—Hitters

Hitter	G	Date Ended
Mariano Duncan	70	8/29/95
Luis Sojo	51	8/19/92
Ozzie Guillen	48	10/3/93
Kim Batiste	46	7/31/94
Orlando Miller	44	6/16/97
Jeff Kent	42	7/11/93

RUBY: Maddux pitched a three-hit shutout. . .

That's five straight starts without a walk!

July 2—All-Star Game

QUINN: Here's the result of 24 STATS baseball experts picking the 1997 All-Stars. We voted from June 26 thru July 2.

NATIONAL LEAGUE		AMERICAN LEAGUE	
CATCHER			
Mike Piazza	20	Ivan Rodriguez	15
Todd Hundley	4	Sandy Alomar Jr.	7
		Dan Wilson	1
		George Williams	1
FIRST BASE			
Jeff Bagwell	18	Frank Thomas	14
Andres Galarraga	4	Tino Martinez	7
John Olerud	2	Mark McGwire	2
		Rafael Palmeiro	1
SECOND BASE			
Craig Biggio	21	Chuck Knoblauch	13
Jeff Kent	1	Joey Cora	6
Quilvio Veras	1	Roberto Alomar	3
Wilton Guerrero	1	Damion Easley	1
		Jose Offerman	1
THIRD BASE			
Chipper Jones	17	Cal Ripken	12
Vinny Castilla	4	Travis Fryman	6
Ken Caminiti	1	Jeff Cirillo	3
Bobby Bonilla	1	Matt Williams	1
Scott Rolen	1	Dean Palmer	1
		Russ Davis	1
SHORTSTOP			
Jeff Blauser	17	Alex Rodriguez	18
Barry Larkin	6	Nomar Garciaparra	5
Mark Grudzielanek	1	Jay Bell	1
OUTFIELD			
Larry Walker	22	Ken Griffey Jr.	23
Tony Gwynn	16	Dave Justice	14

Barry Bonds	14	Rusty Greer	10
Ray Lankford	10	Albert Belle	7
Kenny Lofton	5	Bernie Williams	6
Gary Sheffield	1	Manny Ramirez	5
Sammy Sosa	1	Brady Anderson	2
Moises Alou	1	B.J. Surhoff	1
Steve Finley	1	Wil Cordero	1
Ryan Klesko	1	Darren Bragg	1
Ricky Henderson	1	Jim Edmonds	1

DESIGNATED HITTER

Edgar Martinez	16
Frank Thomas	2
Geronimo Berroa	2
Mark McGwire	1
Albert Belle	1
Paul Molitor	1
Chili Davis	1

PALACIOS: I don't know if this has been discussed, but I believe that the real victim of interleague play will not be the World Series. The real victim will be the All-Star Game.

It's true the Randy Johnson-Larry Walker matchup will be memorable, but history shows that attendance declined between 1959 and 1962, when they had two All-Star Games and the novelty of the game itself declined.

The Nielsen ratings for the All-Star Game were low and they'll continue to diminish because the matchups like Tony Gwynn vs. Johnson will no longer capture the imagination.

PINTO: I think players like Albert Belle refusing to play, or not showing up becuase they'd rather have the time off, is hurting the All-Star Game more than interleague play. Also, the ability to see players from out of your area more often also takes the luster off of it.

Think about it. In the 1970s, someone in New England would only get to see Ken Griffey Jr. maybe a dozen times a year. Now, with highlight shows, superstations, ESPN and Fox, you can probably catch Griffey 30 times a year. It's probably making a difference.

RUBY: Every year I get up for the All-Star Game and every year I'm disappointed that it's so boring. This year was probably one of the better All-Star Games of recent years, but that's not saying much.

Usually the most interesting parts of the All-Star game are: 1) The commercials, especially the classic first "Bo Knows" commercial. 2) Introducing the players beforehand. I always enjoy the special cheer the fans give their own players. (The first game I ever remember seeing, the 1979 All-Star Game at Seattle, the biggest ovation went to Bruce Bochte!)

But the game itself is usually pretty dull. I don't mind pitchers' duels, but it is no fun if the pitcher is changing every inning.

Just out of curiosity, does anyone know if more people watch the NBA all-star game than MLB's now?

HENZLER: The ratings for the MLB All-Star Game were still higher than for any other sport's all-star game this year.

Remember, too, the All-Star Game was on Fox, which probably didn't help the ratings. That was used as an excuse for last season's World Series ratings.

FREER: Using that approach, you are correct in that the All-Star Game would suffer. We might have already seen Gwynn vs. Johnson in the regular season, and an All-Star matchup would not be as historic.

But, at the same time, in the regular-season games, we might see Gwynn vs. Johnson! Or a repeat of last year's Series (Yanks vs. Braves). The regular season has become more exciting, as interleague attendance has proven.

There is never a guarantee for any matchup. At any moment The Big Unit can up and injure himself into retirement, or Gwynn could pull a Darryl Strawberry or Vince Coleman and get suspended. The point is, moments like those should be cherished whenever or wherever they occur. Gwynn vs. Johnson is as exciting in the All-Star Game as in the World Series or an interleague game.

That's just one warm-weather fan's opinion.

COOPERSON: I would feel not a tinge of remorse if interleague play made the game better as a whole while detracting from the All-Star Game. All-Star Games are meaningless.

FULLAM: Over the last decade, I've probably seen about five times as much NBA all-star game action as I have the MLB. . . It's just a lot more entertaining to watch.

RUBY: By the way, I don't think interleague play has very much to do with the All-Star Game. Do people really tune in to see the epic matchup of Johnson and Gwynn? The game is (supposedly) fun because so many of our favorite players and/or the best players are all in one place playing together. I enjoy the camaraderie of all-star teammates a lot more than I do the matchups. I agree—who wins and who loses is pretty meaningless. (I love it when announcers talk about All-Star Game streaks.)

FREER: Is any all-star game, in any sport, except maybe for college football (North-South, Blue-Gray, etc.) really exciting?

COOPERSON: Other than the Don Zminda/Mat Olkin/Dave Pinto types, who here can even remember what happened in the '95 All-Star Game?

PINTO: Was there an All-Star Game in 1995?

The only one I really remember is 1986. Roger Clemens pitched three perfect innings, Cal Ripken made a fantastic play at short that the announcers didn't even acknowledge and Frank White and Lou Whitaker accounted for all the scoring with HRs in the Astrodome.

COOPERSON: Just my point. All-star games are forgotten the day after they're played. Who cares if they are detracted from? Could anyone imagine the NBA making schedule decisions so as to protect the integrity of the All-Star Game? Please. By the way, did the Bulls/Jazz games in November and January detract from this past year's Finals?

ELMAN: Sorry, but I think you are out in left field (pun intended). Most all-star games are a complete hoax because they don't look anything like a regular game. Most of it stems from a lack of defense (West 160-East 155 comes to mind with hoops). You can still see some great matchups and defense in the MLB game. Granted that with interleague play it may be a matchup that has already taken place in the regular season, but it still is pitcher/batter/fielder, all of them trying their best not to be outdone. I will take a competitive effort over offensive highlights any day. As far as I am concerned, the most fun surrounding the NBA game is the three-point contest. Individuals giving their very best effort, something that does not happen in the game itself.

HENZLER: Frankly, I'm surprised.

I think there's little doubt that MLB has had, and continues to have, the *best* All-Star Game of any sport. The Pro Bowl occurs at the end of football's season, and players are more concerned about avoiding injury than putting out their best effort. Basketball's all-star game completely forgets about defense. Can anyone remember anything significant in any NBA all-star game, other than Magic Johnson's comeback?

But in baseball, there are plenty of memorable moments. Pete Rose running into catcher Ray Fosse. . . Ted Williams' homer off the "eephus" pitch. . . Carl Hubbell's strikeouts. . . Bo Jackson's homer. . . heck, even Sandy Alomar's home run this season has a chance to be remembered years from now.

FREER: I remember Jordan's dunks in the dunk contest in 1988 most. Oh yeah, and Steve Kerr in the three-point shootout this year.

Spoken like a true Bulls fan.

No all-star contest in any sport is a memorable event. Each will have moments to take home, depending on your individual preferences.

GREENBERGER: In the BJFB newsletter I talked about interleague play diluting the already-weak draw of the All-Star Game. As hard as I tried to work myself into a lather about it, it just came out as geezerism. I think all those games should turn into trash sport events like the three-point contest, home-run contest, fastest around the bases, throwing footballs through a tire, etc. It's more fun to watch that stuff anyway.

HENZLER: By the way, did you notice that the All-Star Home Run Derby was an absolute ratings hit for ESPN? Its rating was 5.7, which means it was ESPN's most-watched program of 1997. More than any college basketball game, more than any college football bowl, more than any NHL playoff game. Even more than any WNBA basketball game, for gosh sakes.

CARLSON: I agree, the three-point contest is the best of the "novelty" events that surrounds an all-star game.

My order of the "novelty events:" (1) Three-point shootout, (2) Hockey's shooting accuracy competition, (3) Home-run derby (would be better if they showed it live).

I think the biggest decline is in the slam dunk competition. It used to be pretty exciting, then they changed the rules because it seemed to be losing its luster, and the new rules ruined it even more.

July 9—Bob Boone/Tony Muser

QUINN: The Royals announced today the firing of manager Bob Boone with Tony Muser being his replacement.

OLKIN: Upon leaving, Boone tried to steal his desk but was thrown out (of the stadium).

EAST: I guess this puts an end to the Cincinnati Reds' "Boone" County, KY Night they hoped to have when the Royals came to Cincinnati. Although two (Bret, Aaron) out of three ain't bad.

July 21—Mickey Tettleton

HENZLER: From the *1991 Bill James Baseball Book*, regarding Mickey Tettleton:

"He's Gene Tenace all over again. . . My guess is that, like (Tenace), he will be extremely consistent at a level between 1989 and 1990—somewhere around .240 with 18 homers, 55 RBI."

Well, now that Tettleton has retired. . .

Most Similar Players to Mickey Tettleton

Player	Pos	AB	R	H	2B	3B	HR	RBI	BB	K	SB	Avg	Slg	Score
M. Tettleton	C	4698	711	1132	210	16	245	732	949	1307	23	.241	.449	1000
G. Tenace	C	4390	653	1060	179	20	201	674	984	998	36	.241	.429	927
D. Porter	C	5539	765	1369	237	48	188	826	905	1025	39	.247	.409	859
R. Campanella	C	4205	627	1161	178	18	242	856	533	501	25	.276	.500	847
D. Crandall	C	5026	585	1276	179	18	179	657	424	477	26	.254	.404	843
B. Freehan	C	6073	706	1591	241	35	200	758	626	753	24	.262	.412	832
W. Cooper	C	4702	573	1341	240	40	173	812	309	357	18	.285	.464	829
A. Seminick	C	3921	495	953	139	26	164	556	582	780	23	.243	.417	827
B. Santiago	C	4623	521	1200	203	25	154	613	283	861	78	.260	.414	826
E. Howard	C	5363	619	1471	218	50	167	762	373	786	9	.274	.427	825
R. Petrocelli	SS	5390	653	1352	237	22	210	773	661	926	10	.251	.420	820

Tettleton actually did a little better than Bill expected, averaging 28 homers and 82 RBI between 1991 and 1996. His batting average since 1991 was close, though, at .244. But I'd say Tenace was a pretty good match, wouldn't you?

Just one Hall of Famer appears among the top 10 comps. Campanella, of course, had his career shortened by the exclusion of African-Americans, as well as his tragic car accident. I'm sure the Hall of Fame voters took that under consideration when electing Campy, and it's unlikely Tettleton will ever be inducted.

Benito Santiago is the eighth-best comp to Tettleton? Here again, Bill was perspicacious. From the *1990 Baseball Book*:

"The most-comparable major league player: Benito Santiago. I didn't say he was comparable, mind you; I said he was the closest. . . ."

July 21—Luis Castillo

OLKIN: Florida second baseman Luis Castillo is about a dozen plate appearances short of qualifying for the major league lead in groundball-to-flyball ratio, but we should just give it to him anyway. According to STATS reporters, Castillo has hit 160 groundballs this season and only 14 flyballs, for an earth-loving ratio of 11.43. The current major league leader is Julio Franco, with a G/F ratio of 3.84.

Castillo's hit only 14 flyballs. . . maybe that's why he's slugging .271. Thank God somebody taught him to hit the ball on the ground and take advantage of his speed.

July 21—Billy McMillon

ZMINDA: The Philllies have traded Darren Daulton to the Marlins for Billy McMillon. Presumably McMillon will finally get a chance to play now.

FULLAM: Can he play? He's almost 26 years old now and hasn't done anything with his career.

BATAILLE: Not yet. Tony Barron has been called up by Philadelphia to take Daulton's roster spot.

OLKIN: He hasn't because the Marlins haven't let him. I think he could hit .300 if the Phillies let him play.

ZMINDA: Steve Moyer Memorial Quote of the Day

From Peter Gammons on the Daulton-McMillon trade: "This really helps Florida. Daulton will add the veteran leadership to help them in the stretch drive."

Can't beat that "veteran leadership," eh, Steve?

OLKIN: Yeah, without Daulton's leadership, the Phils might have been *really* bad.

FULLAM: Irrespective of leadership, Daulton can still flat-out hit; his OBP is hovering around .380, and he's slugging almost .500. I checked out his fielding stats and, surprisingly, they're not bad. He definitely won't *hurt* Florida's chances.

OLKIN: Plus, he's got the intangibles. Don't ask me what they are; they're intangible.

GOLDSTEIN: McMillon was expendable as the Marlins had both Todd Dunwoody and Mark Kotsay ahead of him as far as their outfield plans go. I think McMillon is capable of .280/.360/.450 type of numbers, which are serviceable, but less than what one would ask for from a corner OF.

OLKIN: The Marlins shelled out big bucks to get those kind of numbers out of Moises Alou.

HENZLER: Daulton's production has been better than the typical right fielder's this season.

Sammy Sosa, by the way, doesn't even rank in the top 15. Is he really worth $10 million per season?

Right Field—Runs Created

Player, Team(s)	Runs Created	Per 27 Outs
1 Larry Walker, Col	130	15.22
2 Tony Gwynn, SD	94	10.11
3 Paul O'Neill, NYA	73	8.27
4 Manny Ramirez, Cle	66	8.04
5 Tim Salmon, Ana	73	7.61
6 Jeromy Burnitz, Mil	61	7.58
7 Gary Sheffield, Fla	54	7.40
8 Darren Daulton, Phi	55	7.14
9 F.P. Santangelo, Mon	48	7.11
10 Jay Buhner, Sea	71	7.09
11 Stan Javier, SF	47	6.92
12 Tony Phillips, Ana/ChA	65	6.52
13 Raul Mondesi, LA	65	6.22
14 Geronimo Berroa, Oak/Bal	59	6.21
15 Troy O'Leary, Bos	47	5.89
Avg at Position with 240 PA		**6.68**

(minimum 240 PA)

SPEAR: In Darren "10 Knee Operations" Daulton's last game as a Phillie, he had a triple and a stolen base.

CANTER: That gives Darren a career-high six triples. He's got the third-highest triple/AB rate in the league—edging out slowpoke Deion Sanders.

COOPERSON: Even after Daulton's first major knee operation in '86, he was considered a "plus runner" for a catcher.

FULLAM: He may have suffered a bunch of injuries, but the fact that he caught very few games when he was young probably helped him retain his speed. Can you name all of the catchers the Phils used between '86 and '91?

HENZLER: Daulton the speed demon. . .

Highest Stolen Base Percentage—Since 1990

Player	SB	CS	Pct
Tony Womack	41	3	93.18
Darren Daulton	39	4	90.70
Mike Benjamin	24	3	88.89
Oddibe McDowell	27	4	87.10
Chipper Jones	38	6	86.36
Eric Owens	19	3	86.36
Lou Frazier	54	9	85.71
Barry Larkin	208	35	85.60
Henry Cotto	76	13	85.39
Chico Walker	35	6	85.37
Eric Davis	122	22	84.72
Ced Landrum	27	5	84.38
Alex Rodriguez	42	8	84.00
Andy Van Slyke	61	12	83.56
Paul Molitor	146	29	83.43

(minimum 20 attempts)

July 22—Melvin Nieves

FAUST: Well, Melvin continues his march towards 200 Ks. He's struck out 20 times in his last eight games to bring his total to 121 through 86 games. In his career, he's struck out 405 times in 345 games, a ratio of 1.17 Ks per game. Dan Ford and I were looking last night to see if we could find someone who topped that ratio. Bo Jackson was the only one we found—841 Ks in 694 games for a ratio of 1.21 K/G.

Anyone else in their league?

FULLAM: Rob Deer: 1,409 Ks, 1,155 games—a ratio of 1.22 K/G

PINTO: They should do a movie about Rob Deer. They can call it "Deer Strikes Out."

HENZLER: Here's where Deer fits in all-time:

Highest Career Strikeout Per Game Rate

Player	K	G	Rate
Rob Deer	1,409	1,155	1.220
Bo Jackson	841	694	1.212
Melvin Nieves	405	345	1.174
Tony Clark	245	222	1.104
Dave Nicholson	573	538	1.065
Jose Canseco	1,455	1,433	1.015

(non-pitcher, minimum 150 games)

July 22—Greg Maddux

OLKIN: Greg Maddux just went nine innings against the Cubs, using only 78 pitches and likely wrapping up the 1997 STATS Red Barrett Trophy. Last year, Bob Wolcott took the prize with his complete-game, 79-pitch effort. No other pitcher completed a game last year throwing less than 90 pitches. Maddux has now done it twice this year.

PINTO: It's the second-lowest total this decade for a nine-inning complete game.

SPEAR: Lowest since Tewksbury 8/29/90, with 76.

OLKIN: I wonder if they'll let him start the second game of the doubleheader? He's probably just getting warm.

ELMAN: When I was driving in this morning the Score (WSCR) mentioned that of Maddux' 78 pitches yesterday, only 10 were called balls. That blew me away. Is that some sort of record? If it's not, it has to be real close. One ball an inning is just mind-boggling to me, especially considering purpose pitches.

July 23—AL vs. NL

HENNINGER: This may be a mild case of sour grapes from a player who was traded out of the National League by the Pirates, but in the *Baseball Weekly* out today (page 6), Orlando Merced maintains the AL has better pitching and that AL clubs run 10-11 deep in "real good" players, while NL teams have roughly five players of similar stature.

Merced cites the O's, Yanks, Boston, Seattle and Toronto as teams with four solid starters, while he implies the Braves are alone in this category. (What about those Cards?) He doesn't get into specifics of AL team depth vs. NL team depth, but notes the movement of Matt Williams, Eddie Murray and Will Clark to the AL as proof. While it seems over the past few years the free-agent movement has brought more front-line players to the AL, does he have a defensible position regarding the talent pool in both leagues?

I've waged a discussion with a few friends in recent months, one of whom believes the AL has become a superior league, but I've never seen a player make such a claim. What do you think? Does either league have a substantial edge in any facet of the game? Pitching? Hitting? Running game?

By the way, Merced claims NL teams have stronger benches, which seems to contradict his point that the AL has the advantage in talent.

FAUST: It seems to me that he probably has this perception because NL teams use their benches more (no DH).

It's a small sample, but what was the AL vs. NL record in interleague play? It might be even better to look at runs scored.

MILLER: As Drew pointed out, the NL uses its bench more often, but Merced's claim is about "real good" players. I think a "real good" player would be in the starting lineup regardless of which league he was in, so to say that one league's bench is stronger than the other shouldn't at all say anything about how "good" the players are in general.

HENNINGER: The small-market thing brings up an issue, though. Do the concentration of big-market or big-dollar teams (O's, Yanks, Boston, Cleveland) create an illusion of a talent surplus in the AL? The NL has the Phillies, but the AL has the Brewers, Twins, K.C. and others.)

I also wonder who Merced would include among Pittsburgh's "elite five." Maybe the Pirates would have a better contingent now than a year ago.

HENZLER: It appears there may be something to Merced's comments. 1996 AL players who switched to the NL in 1997 have improved their batting average by an average of two points, and their on-base percentage by five points. Their slugging percentage has experienced a four-point drop, however. . .

Players With New Teams in 1997

Player Team(s)	1996			1997		
	Avg	OBP	SLG	Avg	OBP	SLG
AL to NL Player Totals	.269	.334	.422	.270	.339	.418
(minimum 100 AB with both teams)						

Meanwhile, 1996 NL players that have switched to the AL in 1997 have experienced a far larger relative drop in production. . .

Players With New Teams in 1997

Player Team(s)	1996			1997		
	Avg	OBP	SLG	Avg	OBP	SLG
NL to AL Player Totals	.269	.335	.424	.255	.328	.401
(minimum 100 AB with both teams)						

WENZ: Is 4-5 points really negligible? I wouldn't think so. That's a pretty big sample, about 40 or so players.

CARLSON: And it was actually bigger. AL players to the NL gained .004 on their average, but NL to AL lost .013, and that is huge, for example, players going from .290 to .277.

FULLAM: In a one-year sample, I really don't believe that it's that significant. For one thing, I'd want to isolate the players on a number of characteristics:

1.) Did the players who jumped ship differ greatly in age? If more of the older players went from the NL to the AL, the age-based decline would affect the data.

2.) Again, the park differences are significant. I'd want to find out exactly which parks the players traveled to and from before making any judgments. A 4-5 (or even a 12) point difference is nothing compared to the impact of different ballparks on statistics.

PINTO: Atlanta, L.A., Chicago, St. Louis and the Mets appear to be large-market teams to me. The Rockies are for all intents and purposes a large-market club. I don't see any advantage there.

This century, the NL has seldom outscored the AL in a season, even before the DH. I believe this is due to a little-ball mentality that has always dominated the league (they just love to bunt and steal over there: "Oh look, someone took an extra base!") while the AL has been a power league. It's easy to put up sub-2.00 ERAs when wimpy teams are giving away outs on bunts and caught stealings. It's a lot harder when everyone is trying to hit the cover off the ball.

This is why no NL team has ever been able to dominate the World Series. There have only been three times an NL team has won back-to-back World Series: the '07-'08 Cubs, the '21-'22 Giants and the '75-'76 Reds. The AL has had three teams win three or more in a row. You can keep the NL.

COOPERSON: Isn't it funny that postage stamp-sized St. Louis is considered large market, while Philadelphia is considered small market. Unfortunately, if you look at revenue, it's probably true. Funny—just looking at demographics, Philly is the largest market with only one team.

JAMES: There are two tests here:

1) Whether the data would convince a reasonable skeptic, and

2) Would the data cause an uninvolved third party to draw a conclusion.

I think it is clear that this data would not meet the first test—it would not convince a skeptic. I think it's questionable whether it would meet the second. It *might* cause a curious bystander to draw the conclusion that the American League was tougher, but I wouldn't want to rest too heavily on it. . . Just my thought.

HENZLER: I'm sending this list for informational purposes only. You're more than welcome to draw your own conclusions.

But in every single instance (with the exception of 1991-92) batters switching from the AL to the NL posted better relative batting average and on-base percentage differences than those moving from the NL to the AL. And in every single instance (with the exception of 1995-96) the hitters generated better relative slugging percentage differences when switching to the NL.

Obviously, there are other factors we would need to consider before deciding the AL is really the stronger league. Sounds like it could be a *Scoreboard* essay. . .

Players Changing Leagues

Years	Event	Avg	Year 1 OBP	SLG	Avg	Year 2 OBP	SLG
1990-91	AL to NL	.257	.319	.383	.270	.335	.402
1990-91	NL to AL	.255	.339	.402	.256	.336	.399
1991-92	AL to NL	.254	.321	.350	.253	.317	.377
1991-92	NL to AL	.251	.309	.372	.254	.308	.368
1992-93	AL to NL	.261	.325	.372	.280	.340	.435
1992-93	NL to AL	.258	.320	.363	.258	.315	.366
1993-94	AL to NL	.262	.323	.381	.279	.347	.422
1993-94	NL to AL	.265	.326	.402	.271	.342	.416
1994-95	AL to NL	.258	.322	.399	.253	.328	.373
1994-95	NL to AL	.285	.362	.432	.264	.337	.374
1995-96	AL to NL	.265	.333	.407	.268	.345	.405
1995-96	NL to AL	.268	.332	.401	.270	.337	.415
1996-97	AL to NL	.273	.340	.422	.277	.346	.427
1996-97	NL to AL	.271	.337	.429	.258	.332	.407
Totals:	AL to NL	.262	.327	.389	.270	.338	.411
Totals:	NL to AL	.264	.330	.399	.262	.329	.393

(minimum 100 AB with both leagues)

FAUST: Wait a second. Does this imply that the talent continually moves from the AL to the NL, yet the AL remains stronger? We must be missing something.

Shouldn't we look at pitchers switching leagues?

July 24—Ron Mahay

SASMAN: You can have Bo Jackson, or Deion Sanders or Dan O'Brien. I'll take Ron Mahay as the most versatile athlete around. Mahay has pitched three games for the Red Sox this year. OK, so he has a 7.71 ERA in only 2⅓ innings, but he's a converted outfielder. In fact, he started five games in center field for the Red Sox in 1995. With two more outings on the mound, he'll become the first player since Vance Law to total at least five career appearances in the field and on the mound. Here are the eight players since 1960 who pitched in at least five games and played another position in at least five:

Player	Last Yr	Games As P	Games Other
Vance Law	1991	7	1,273
Skip Lockwood	1980	420	7
Mel Queen	1972	140	53
Dick Hall	1971	495	132
Wonderful Smith	1971	29	432
Danny Murphy	1970	68	30
Granny Hamner	1962	7	1,533
Jack Harshman	1960	217	14

July 28—Steve Woodard

FORD: Who is this guy?

Facing back-to-back doubleheaders against Toronto today and tomorrow, the Brewers brought up Steve Woodward from AAA Tucson to pitch against Roger Clemens today. He outdueled Clemens 1-0, giving up one hit and one walk in eight innings, striking out 12.

His Tucson stats, according to our on-line:

15-3, 3.01 ERA, 143 IP, 139 H, 26 BB, 103 K

He isn't listed in our *Minor League Scouting Notebook*. Who is he? How old is he? Is he for real?

OLKIN: Woodard's a 22-year-old righthander and a classic control pitcher-slash-over-achiever. Lacking an above-average fastball, he gets by with a decent curve and change and superb command. He was leading the minor leagues with 15 wins when he was called up yesterday, although 14 of them came at Double-A El Paso.

His previous high in pro ball was 10 strikeouts in a game, so I don't think we have another Hideo Nomo here. From what I saw on the highlights, his style looks a lot more like Bobby Jones than Nolan Ryan. And for what it's worth, radio commentator Bob Uecker was making frequent mention of home plate ump Dale Scott's generous strike zone last night before the fifth inning was even in the books. Yes, Woodard was fantastic, but the two teams combined for five hits, two walks and 23 strikeouts.

Don August had a big run his first time around the league in '88. I see a lot of similarities.

PINTO: The other thing about his minor league numbers that I noticed yesterday was a 4-to-1 K-to-BB ratio. Secondly, he's striking out 7.3 batters per nine innings in the minors. Now, correct me if I'm wrong, but 7.3 K per nine is pretty good. We have some great power pitchers around these days, so 7.3 may not seem that high, but for his career, Clemens is 8.4. Now, if I remember my *Baseball Abstracts* correctly, pitchers who strike out a lot of batters and don't walk many tend to be very good pitchers. I don't have Don August's minor league numbers, but in the majors he walked close to the number he K'd.

MITTLEMAN: I covered Woodard's game from the opening pitch and what people don't realize is that he threw against the weakest-hitting team in baseball at 5 pm EST. In other words, the twilight shadows were definitely in his favor.

He throws his curve from anywhere in the count and from a three-quarter arm slot as well as semi-sidearm. He has great control, but his fastball never gets over 88 mph. He will likely face Seattle this weekend for a much sterner test.

PINTO: You're absolutely right. But I do like to see clubs give a new kid a start against a patsy to get the butterflies out (although it didn't seem to work for Hideki Irabu). How long before Cito Gaston gets fired? Or is it the GM getting the ax for failing to build a winner?

MITTLEMAN: Blue Jays GM Gord Ash just learned that his contract was being extended yesterday, so he's on board. As for Cito, his guardian was Paul Beeston, who as you know is now gone to Major League Baseball's New York offices. I think this will be Cito's last hurrah as he and Ash have separated themselves this year.

OLKIN: David, I agree that 7.3 K/9 is an excellent ratio, and that power pitchers do tend to last longer. But one thing I have noticed is that there isn't a simple and predictable relationship between a pitcher's minor league strikeout rates and his major league strikeout rates. In fact, it's been my impression (and I may be completely wrong about this, but I've been watching it happen for years) that control artists aren't able to maintain their high K rates upon promotion nearly as well as the true flamethrowers do.

If you pressed me (and I suspect that you're about to), I could rattle off a list of control pitchers who had K rates well over six in the minors but had trouble breaking five K/9 in the majors. Off the top of my head, you've got Chris Haney (6.83 K/9 in the minors, 4.87 in the majors), Rick Reed (5.98, 4.93), Chris Holt (6.96, 4.13), Jason Dickson (6.28, 5.03), Bobby Jones (7.85, 5.42) and Mark Clark (6.62, 4.83).

I'm sure you could cite examples of pitchers who had good control and lots of Ks in the minors and kept fanning people in the bigs. But let me ask you this: if you set up a study where you matched up minor league pitchers who were similar in every respect except for their walk rate, and you looked at how many K/9 they notched in the majors, which group would end up with higher K rates in the majors—the low-walk guys or the high-walk guys? I would bet on the high-walk guys, just from experience. Can't really explain it.

GOLDSTEIN: 7.3 in nice, but that's for a career, much of it in Class-A or Rookie ball. His Double-A numbers are 6.4 K/9. 7.3 is good in the majors, above average for Double-A and average-to-below average in A ball and below. The lower you go, the higher the K rates get. 1996 numbers:

Class	League		K/9
MLB	AL		6.24
	NL		6.77
AAA	International		6.62
	Pacific Coast		6.49
	American Assc.		6.52
AA	Eastern		6.89
	Southern		7.09
	Texas	Woodard's AA league–the lowest rate—	6.00
A+	California		7.71
	Carolina		6.92
	Florida		6.58
A	Midwest		7.22
	Sally		7.91
A-	Northwest		8.28
	NYP		7.96
R+	Appalachian		8.54
	Pioneer		7.86
R	Arizona		8.34
	Gulf Coast		7.59

Just a hunch, but I'd guess the increased rates are due to a combination of strikeout-prone players who don't advance and bad lighting.

PINTO: Nice job. It is interesting to note that his league did have a low K/9 vs. the rest of the minors, which makes Woodard's numbers a little more impressive.

HENZLER: There are some great names on this list of pitchers who had strong debuts since 1987. To qualify, the pitcher had to either strike out at least nine batters or pitch at least seven innings and allow four or fewer hits plus walks.

The likes of Jeff Pico, Brian Barnes, Kevin Morton and Mo Sanford never really amounted to much. I believe Sam Militello soon fell victim to "Steve Blass disease." And yes, that's the same Rick Reed who's pitched so well for the Mets in 1997. And it's the same Roberto Hernandez who soon became the White Sox' closer.

Is it too soon to ask whatever became of Hideki Irabu?

Best Pitching Debuts Since 1987

Player	IP	H	R	ER	BB	K	W/L	Date	Team vs Opp
Jack McDowell	7.0	4	0	0	0	3	W	9/15/1987	ChA vs Min
Jeff Pico	9.0	4	0	0	0	6	W	5/31/1988	ChN vs Cin
Rick Reed	8.0	3	0	0	1	4	W	8/8/1988	Pit vs NYN
Brian Barnes	7.0	4	2	2	3	9	N	9/14/1990	Mon vs Pit
Roberto Hernandez	7.0	1	1	1	2	4	W	9/2/1991	ChA vs KC
Kevin Morton	9.0	5	1	1	1	9	W	7/5/1991	Bos vs Det
Mo Sanford	7.0	2	1	0	1	8	W	8/9/1991	Cin vs SD
Ricky Bones	7.0	2	0	0	2	6	W	8/11/1991	SD vs Cin
Pedro Astacio	9.0	3	0	0	4	10	W	7/3/1992	LA vs Phi
Tim Wakefield	9.0	6	2	0	5	10	W	7/31/1992	Pit vs StL
Sam Militello	7.0	1	0	0	3	5	W	8/9/1992	NYA vs Bos
Jason Isringhausen	7.0	2	2	2	2	6	N	7/17/1995	NYN vs ChN
Hideki Irabu	6.2	5	2	2	4	9	W	7/10/1997	NYA vs Det
Steve Woodard	8.0	1	0	0	1	12	W	7/28/1997	Mil vs Tor

(minimum 9 K or (7+ IP and 4 or fewer H+BB))

JAMES: How hard would it be to run this by game scores? I'd be interested to know whether this was the best game score for a first game since we have data.

HENNINGER: He certainly slipped through the cracks on me. I've been working on a database of minor league pitchers, and I missed him. One thing of note: I saw his name as Woodward early in the evening on ESPN, but it was Woodard without the second "W" on the second edition of "Baseball Tonight," which is correct.

OLKIN: I spell it W-E-G-M-A-N.

MILLER: Didn't this kid's dad break the news on that Watergate thing several years ago?

MUNDO: I think he kinda looks like Joe Cowley.

HENZLER: Yes, using game scores as the definition, Woodard's performance last night was the best pitching debut since 1987.

By my estimation, we need to get down to the 19th-best game score, 72, to find the first arguable "star" in Jack McDowell. John Smoltz, at 71, may be the only other star in the top 27:

Best Pitching Debuts Since 1987

Player	IP	H	R	ER	BB	K	Pt	W/L	Date	Team vs Opp
Steve Woodard	8.0	1	0	0	1	12	91	W	7/28/1997	Mil vs Tor
Pedro Astacio	9.0	3	0	0	4	10	87	W	7/3/1992	LA vs Phi
Jeff Pico	9.0	4	0	0	0	6	85	W	5/31/1988	ChN vs Cin
Mike Remlinger	9.0	3	0	0	3	4	82	W	6/15/1991	SF vs Pit
Kirk Rueter	8.1	2	0	0	3	5	81	W	7/7/1993	Mon vs SF
Kevin Morton	9.0	5	1	1	1	9	81	W	7/5/1991	Bos vs Det
Bob Milacki	8.0	1	0	0	4	4	80	W	9/18/1988	Bal vs Det
Rick Reed	8.0	3	0	0	1	4	79	W	8/8/1988	Pit vs NYN
Mo Sanford	7.0	2	1	0	1	8	78	W	8/9/1991	Cin vs SD
Shawn Boskie	9.0	5	1	1	1	6	78	W	5/20/1990	ChN vs Hou

(based on game scores)

PINTO: I don't know, Pedro Astacio is a pretty good pitcher.

ZMINDA: Bob Feller struck out 15 batters in his first major league start.

On the other hand, so did Karl Spooner.

HENZLER: Pedro Astacio is now a 47-45 pitcher over the course of his career. Since 1994, Astacio is actually two games *under* .500 while pitching for a Dodger team which is 40 games *over* .500 during the same span.

His ERA's over that period:

1994	4.29
1995	4.24
1996	3.44
1997	3.90

Considering the park in which he pitches, those marks are certainly nothing special.

While Astacio may be a serviceable starter, I was commenting on those pitchers who could reasonably be considered stars. With all due respect to Pedro, I don't think he qualifies.

WOELFLEIN: Where's Irabu on this list? Oh that's right, in the minors.

COOPERSON: Hmmm. . . the recent fate of Irabu brings to mind the EDC philosophy on things that are over-hyped.

PINTO: Astacio is certainly starring today.

HENZLER: One could make the argument that Irabu did likewise in his first start on July 10.

ELMAN: He is spending his time in the minors writing a column for his local Japanese paper praising the American Capitalistic Society and how we often overpay for our commodities.

July 31—Brien Taylor

OLKIN: Brien Taylor has now made 25 starts over the last three years since the fight:

W	L	G	GS	IP	H	R	ER	BB	SO	ERA
3	13	25	25	75.1	71	107	88	130	60	10.51

Perhaps Hideki Irabu can take solace in the fact that he isn't the biggest mistake George Steinbrenner's ever made.

GOLDSTEIN: He reminds one of former Yank phenom Sam Militello, who just never returned from his first injury and then couldn't find the plate at all. His last 11 minor league starts, covering three seasons.

W	L	G	GS	IP	H	R	ER	BB	SO	ERA
0	6	11	11	20.1	12	33	28	54	25	12.39

This includes 19 walks in 3.2 IP (four starts) in '94. If I remember right his complete loss of control was somewhat of a mystery, and I think he was hired as a Marlins pitching coach for their GCL team this year.

MILLER: But Militello was nearly unhittable!!! 12 hits in 20.1 innings isn't bad.

July 31—Brad Radke

OSLAND: I smell an ESPN "Baseball Tonight" full-screen.

I know I'm biased because he's a Twins pitcher, but I would say that Brad Radke's win streak is pretty darn amazing. He is currently tied with last year's NL Cy Young winner with the longest streak for wins in consecutive starts since 1987. Even more amazing is the fact that he probably won't get any consideration for a Cy Young this year. I'm not saying he should, considering the incredible years Roger Clemens and Randy Johnson are having, but it speaks volumes about the level of pitching we're seeing this season. Sure there are plenty of Rich Robertsons and Steve Karsays out there, and it will only get more diluted next year with expansion, but there have just been some downright excellent and entertaining individual pitching efforts this year.

Longest Streaks for Wins in Consecutive Starts Since 1987

Player	Wins	Start Date	End Date
John Smoltz	11	4/9/96	5/29/96
Brad Radke*	11	6/7/97	7/30/97
Cal Eldred	10	8/8/92	9/29/92
Tim Wakefield	10	6/29/95	8/13/95
Bob Welch	9	5/21/90	6/30/90
Frank Viola	9	9/23/89	5/12/90

*Current Streak

July 31—Trades

ZMINDA: First trade of the day: the Reds trade John Smiley and Jeff Branson to the Tribe for Danny Graves, Jim Crowell, Scott Winchester and Damian Jackson. Cleveland gave up a *lot* of young talent in this deal.

OLKIN: But they got a starter without losing Brian Giles, Bartolo Colon, Jaret Wright or Enrique Wilson. I like it.

HENNINGER: Methinks the Tribe was more willing to give up Graves and Jackson than Colon and Giles. And I suspect Cleveland wasn't inclined to give up Graves until the trade possibilities had thinned out—with Curt Schilling off the market and Ken Hill off to Anaheim.

PINTO: Wilson Alvarez, Roberto Hernandez and Danny Darwin to Giants for six minor leaguers. You Sox fans should revolt. I guess the management thinks that there's no way they can catch Cleveland now that they have John Smiley.

MOYER: Wow. What do Roberto Hernandez and Rod Beck do on the same team?

Answer A: Roberto goes back to that super starting form Jim Henzler showed us the other day.

Answer B: Go out to eat a lot together.

August 4—Ryne Sandberg

HENZLER: Did you see Bernie Lincicome's column in today's *Chicago Tribune*? In it he says:

> "If (Ryne) Sandberg had played any other position but second base, he would be considered much less remarkable."

Well, sure, that makes sense. I guess if Rickey Henderson couldn't steal bases, he'd be considered much less remarkable, too. Likewise, Mark McGwire should feel fortunate that he can hit home runs. Otherwise McGwire might be considered much less "remarkable."

PINTO: If McGwire's name weren't Mark, he wouldn't be as remarkable.

FULLAM: If Greg Maddux had played any other position but pitcher, he would have been cut from his high school team.

COOPERSON: If Michael Jordan hadn't played basketball, he'd be considered less "remarkable."

RUBY: If Sandberg played third base, first base or one of the other more "remarkable" positions and finished his career with. . .

1,300 runs scored; 280 homers; 340 stolen bases; 2,400 hits; 400 doubles; 75 triples; nine Gold Gloves; one MVP

. . . wouldn't we find those numbers pretty remarkable? I know he stunk his last few years, but he's a first-ballot Hall of Famer, no matter the position.

August 4—Hitters Supporting Pitchers

OSLAND: Tidbit No. 1: Through yesterday's games, since 1987 there have been exactly 39,999 home runs hit in the majors. Tidbit No. 2: Following are the lists of home runs hit by a player for the pitcher of record for 1997 and since 1987.

HR Hit For Pitcher—1997

Batter	Pitcher	HR
Barry Bonds	Kirk Rueter	9
Ken Griffey Jr	Jeff Fassero	9
Mark McGwire	Steve Karsay	8
Tino Martinez	David Cone	8
Tino Martinez	Andy Pettitte	8
Jeff Bagwell	Shane Reynolds	8
Barry Bonds	Shawn Estes	7
Larry Walker	Roger Bailey	7
Sammy Sosa	Kevin Foster	7
Jim Thome	Chad Ogea	7
Jeff Kent	Mark Gardner	7
Dave Nilsson	Scott Karl	7
Jeromy Burnitz	Scott Karl	7
Carlos Delgado	Roger Clemens	7

HR Hit For Pitcher—1987-1997

Batter	Pitcher	HR
Ken Griffey Jr	Randy Johnson	46
Mark McGwire	Dave Stewart	37
Albert Belle	Charles Nagy	35
Jose Canseco	Dave Stewart	33
Frank Thomas	Jack McDowell	33
Frank Thomas	Wilson Alvarez	33
Mark McGwire	Bob Welch	32
David Justice	Tom Glavine	32
Andre Dawson	Greg Maddux	30
Fred McGriff	Greg Maddux	30

August 8—Trades

ZMINDA: The Cubs have traded Turk Wendell, Mel Rojas and Brian McRae to the Mets for Lance Johnson and two players to be named.

The Cubs also sold Terry Mulholland to the Giants on waivers.

COOPERSON: This will be Mulholland's third stint with the Giants, and it marks the sixth time he's changed teams since the end of the 1993 season. Maybe he'll sign with the Phillies in the offseason, for his third stint there, then get dealt to the Giants next August for his *fourth* stint in San Francisco.

Note that on page 202 of the 1997 *Diamond Chronicles*, someone named COOPERSON made the following offer, on the day Mulholland signed with the Cubs:

"I'll bet anyone 2.3 million dollars that if Mulholland has any kind of a decent season, he'll be dealt to a contender late in the year."

OLKIN: Thom Henninger says the Score is reporting that Mark Clark and Manny Alexander are the two players to be named.

ZMINDA: WGN says the same thing: Clark and Alexander.

PINTO: How can they be named later? They already have names!

OLKIN: Hey, Candlestick Park and Riverfront Stadium used to have names, too.

August 13—Matt Beech

RUBY: Matt Beech went into tonight's game at Colorado with these career stats: one win, 11 losses, 6.20 ERA in 123⅓ IP, a homer given up every 5⅓ IP, 14.3 baserunners/9.

Yet he went into the greatest hitters' park ever and shut out the Rockies on four hits and zero walks over seven innings.

(By the way, he struck out six, giving him 117 Ks in 130.1 IP in his career—not bad!)

MOYER: For what it's worth (nothing), I've been keeping an eye on Beech since the beginning of the season. I think he's one of the most promising young pitchers in baseball. I was scared his run of bad luck might make the Phillies give up on him and stunt his growth. Hopefully things are looking up now. He's particularly interesting if you're in a fantasy league that counts strikeouts.

August 13—Rickey Henderson

GOLDSTEIN: From Padres GM Kevin Towers on the impending trade of Rickey Henderson to Cleveland, Anaheim or Seattle (why did they trade Jose Cruz Jr.?!?):

"If we're able to bring prospects back from these teams, we'd certainly do it. . . Something could happen by the end of the week. It's not easy because he's been the lifeblood of the club. If we do trade him, by no means are we conceding the season."

MOYER: What I want to know is why is it always such a priority to trade Rickey? Why can barrels of cash be thrown at every Schmoe in the league, but Rickey's always not worth it? Line up Lofton's stats this year (partially due to injury) against Henderson's (partial due to stupidity) and tell me who's the most productive top-of-the-order guy. It's a tie at best for Lofton.

There's a great *Sporting News* feature on Henderson from a couple weeks ago where he says he might play until he's 50. He wants Ty Cobb's runs record and Babe Ruth's walk record. He's about five seasons away from both. I swear, if some team will be smart enough to let him play (ahead of a Tom Goodwin or Tony Womack, which certainly is doubtful), I think he can do it.

PINTO: I've said it before, and I'll say it again, I want a player who wants to break the run record, because there's nothing selfish about that record. You have to get on base to break that record, and that helps the team.

DEWAN: I can't agree more! Good comments, Steve.

August 13—Protection

MOYER: Did you know?

That *James Mouton* batted cleanup for the division-leading Astros yesterday? And he went 2-for-4 with three RBI in Houston's 13-2 romp over Al Leiter and the Marlins. After years of failure as an inning-starter, has he finally found his niche as an RBI man?

If you want some proof of all the hooey that "protection" crap is that everyone in baseball is always talking about, check out the protection Jeff Bagwell's gotten from the Astros' No. 4 and No. 5 hitters this season.

ZMINDA: Of course, we'll be hearing now that:

1) Mark McGwire can't hit for the Cardinals because there's nobody in the lineup to protect him.

2) Albert Belle's slumping because he doesn't have Harold Baines protecting him any more.

3) Give good old Sammy Sosa some proection in the Cub lineup and he wouldn't strike out so much.

and blah blah blah.

I'm afraid it's a losing fight, Steve.

DEWAN: Reminder: we researched this topic a few years ago and found that "protection" only works between major superstars. Thus, Belle protecting Thomas should work (to a limited extent) while Mouton protecting Bagwell (or anyone else in the Houston lineup protecting Bagwell) is in fact "hooey." We should redo the study this year and analyze Belle/Thomas.

ZMINDA: I definitely want to look at the issue again in the *Scoreboard*. But no matter how much evidence we present, people will keep writing the same old crapola.

FAUST: Here's Thomas' 1997 numbers compared with 1996 through 102 games:

AVG	G	AB	R	H	2B	3B	HR	RBI	TBB	IBB	SO
.347	102	372	77	129	26	0	26	94	77	7	52
.354	102	379	78	134	20	0	25	95	90	23	53

So. . . which one has Belle behind him?

August 18—Turk Wendell

SCHINSKI: Turk Wendell on hunting: "Whenever I bag a species for the first time I cut the animal open and I reach in and take the heart and I take a bite out of it. It's a ritual to preserve the spirit of the animal."

This is the kind of player I would want on my team!

PINTO: I'd like to see him fight Mike Tyson.

SCHINSKI: It would be a promoter's dream. The fighters would eat each other until there's nothing left and the promoters would get to keep all the money.

RUBY: Stop. . . you're making me hungry. . .

August 18—Billy Wagner

SASMAN: OK, so Billy Wagner's K/9 IP rate is currently 14.32. If he can maintain this rate, he will post the best single-season mark for anyone with at least 50 innings pitched. But what happens if we lower our qualifications? Well, Wagner's rate is still the best among anyone who has pitched at least eight innings in a season!

Wagner's performance, however, isn't even close to the best of all-time. In fact, there have been 15 players who have posted single-season K/9 rates of 27.00. The last players to post a perfect 27 Ks per 9 innings were Ken Dayley (2 Ks, 0.2 inning) and Kevin Seitzer (he struck out the only batter he faced). Both accomplished this in 1993. The record for the most innings pitched with a 27.00 k/9 rate belongs to the immortal Ray Krawczyk. In 1989 he pitched two innings and struck out six batters! Of course, he allowed three runs in those two innings, making his ERA 13.50.

Sure, Wagner's a fine pitcher, but if I've heard it once, I've heard it a thousand times: "Billy Wagner, he ain't no Ray Krawczyk."

August 19—Trades

ZMINDA: The Dodgers have traded Pedro Astacio to the Rockies for Eric Young.

HENZLER: Astacio since 1995 at Colorado:

15⅔ IP, 10.91 ERA, .351 Avg Allowed, .676 Slug Allowed, 3.45 HR / 9 IP

ZMINDA: Get me a glove and a seat in left field!

DEWAN: Jim, that's incredible. I suspect the Rockies have no idea.

Only redeeming value of this info for the Rockies: it's not a large sample size—only 15 innings.

HENZLER: As Chuck Miller inquired. . .

Eric Young Since 1993

	Home	Road
Games	306	307
AB	1,071	1,049
Avg	.345	.245
Slug	.489	.334
HR	23	7
RBI	158	69
Runs	245	133
SB	109	71
Triples	20	8

However, he's hit .277 at Dodger Stadium over the course of his career, including a .296 mark there since 1993.

FYI, Astacio's 15.2 innings at Coors since '95 is over five games (three starts).

RUBY: So both teams traded for guys they didn't need who would perform poorly at their new venues? Can anyone explain this one to me?

I know Wilton Guerrero isn't *that* good, but are the Dodgers only trading for Young so that none of their competitors will get him?

As for Astacio—a mediocre pitcher going from the best pitching park in the NL to the worst, it'll be a rude awakening.

MOYER: What can be better in baseball than pitcher/hitter trades involving the Rockies?

PINTO: I disagree a little here. Young has a pretty good OBP, something that the Dodgers need. An Otis Nixon/Brett Butler/Young combination at the top of the order is going to give Mike Piazza more opportunities to drive in runs.

ZMINDA: The Dodgers were desperate to replace Guerrero, whom they feel is a big defensive liability. They've been trying to get a second baseman for weeks, and this was apparently the best they could do.

SASMAN: Last year Young had an OBP on the road of .298. This year it's .309. That's not someone I'd want at the top of the order. Heck, wasn't Delino DeShields run out of L.A. for a similar performance?

ZMINDA: Home parks and all that aside, how come when a deal like this is made, nobody among the "baseball insiders" in and out of the game ever says something like, "The Rockies got robbed. They traded an everyday player for *a guy who only works once every five days*!" Nah, they just analyze the deal like they would any other trade.

But this is the same stupid argument those people make when someone like Greg Maddux or Roger Clemens is offered as an MVP candidate. I know I wrote about this in the *Scoreboard* two years ago, but it still drives me up the wall.

CANTER: Pitchers will never get a fair shake at the MVP until there is a Cy Young-like award for batters! We need the right batter to name it after, too.

MILLER: It should be the Mickey Mantle Award:

He could hit for average, power, draw walks, steal bases and strike out. There's still hope for Melvin Nieves!

ZMINDA: I can almost buy the argument that a pitcher should usually not get the MVP award, since they already have the Cy Young. What I hate is the idiotic argument that a starting pitcher doesn't deserve the MVP because he doesn't play every day.

DEWAN: I concur, Don.

FULLAM: I totally agree with the fact that starting pitchers deserve the MVP as much as anyone else, but what about relievers? It seems hard to believe that any reliever—even Dennis Eckersley in his prime—could possibly face enough hitters to have an MVP-type impact on his team's performance. . . but Eck did win in '92 (and Willie Hernandez won in '84).

DEWAN: These relievers face batters in much more critical situations, and hence, are "worth" more. The awards for Eckersley and Hernandez were well deserved.

FULLAM: I'm not so sure. . . but I think it'd be a great topic for a *Scoreboard* article next year; I'd definitely be interested in researching it.

SICKELS: For what it is worth, Wilton Guerrero has only made four errors this year.

On the other hand, his range factor is well below average.

August 20—Wade Boggs

ZMINDA: Todd Greene is. . .

The answer to a the new trivia question: "What batter struck out against Wade Boggs in Boggs' first major league pitching appearance?"

In case you haven't heard, Boggs pitched a scoreless eighth in the Angels' 12-2 blowout last night. He walked Luis Alicea on a full count, retired Tim Salmon and Garret Anderson on groundouts, then struck out Greene. Not a ball left the infield!

I'd always heard Boggsie had a wicked knuckleball. Who knows, he may have added another 10 years to his career last night!

COOPERSON: Most guys who can swing the bat and are old go to the AL so they can DH and prolong their careers. Maybe Boggs needs to go to the NL where he can *pitch* and still get to hit, to prolong his career!

FULLAM: I'm kind of surprised that managers are continuing to let their position players occasionally take the mound, considering the Jose Canseco fiasco a few seasons ago.

COOPERSON: Put him on the mound, pray he gets hurt, put him on the DL and you never have to hear from him again. Thus you eliminate a potentially controversial roster decision.

OLKIN: Boggs didn't appear to be throwing hard enough to hurt himself. Canseco claimed that he was throwing knucklers too, but he was so wild that it didn't really matter if his ball had any movement or not. The interesting thing about Boggs' performance was that he was making such an effort to throw strikes. He wasn't even trying to get it up into the '70s—he just wanted to get it through that imaginary tire. It makes a lot of sense, given his approach at the plate (control of the strike zone is paramount).

COOPERSON: Perhaps this explains the pitching woes of free-swinging Larry Biittner, who allowed three HRs in the one inning he pitched in his career. But, hey, Biittner only walked one guy.

OLKIN: It certainly would explain Manny Alexander's inability to put his "great arm" to use on the mound. He issued four walks in his only appearance; as a hitter, he's drawn 32 walks in his career (471 at-bats).

GOLDSTEIN: We would be foolish not to mention the brilliant career of Doug Dascenzo, who has put up a career line of 5 IP, 3 H, 0 R, 0 ER, 2 BB, 2 K in four appearances. He's still in the Padres' system, so Orel Hershisher's scoreless inning streak isn't safe yet.

WENZ: They showed a highlight of a pitch Boggs threw to Luis Alicea that had to drop a foot and a half. It didn't look like a knuckleball from the spin, but it sure moved like one.

ZMINDA: I understand Boggs spent an hour reviewing videotapes of Dascenzo on the mound before his appearance last night.

Well not really, but you could easily imagine this. . .

COOPERSON: If he eats chicken before every other game, what does he eat before he pitches?

OLKIN: Eggs.

DEWAN: The pitch dropped that much simply because it was going so slow!

CANTER: A friend of mine has a Larry Biittner custom-made, game-used bat. But the fine folks in Louisville spelled his name with but one "i." I bet that wouldn't happen to Ken Grifey.

ZMINDA: Eat your heart out, Phil Niekro.

CRAIG: In watching the highlight of Boggs whiffing Todd Greene, no one mentioned that the pitch was. . . a knuckleball. Boggs actually has a pretty good one. Back when he was still with Boston, when they were getting ready to face Charlie Hough, Boggs would sometimes throw batting practice so his teammates could hit against the knuckler. I watched him do it from behind the cage one night in Texas and they had a harder time hitting him than they did Charlie.

Just a little note to enrich your season pleasure.

SASMAN: Clearly the only reason Boggs pitched last night was because he wants to get into the Hall of Fame. Check out the list of Hall of Famers who took their turn on the mound: C, Roger Bresnahan; 1B, Jimmie Foxx; SS, Honus Wagner; LF, Ted Williams; CF, Ty Cobb; and RF, Babe Ruth. Then you have Stan Musial, Tris Speaker, Cap Anson, George Sisler, Buck Ewing, et al on the bench. Boggs fills the need at third. Now, if Ryne Sandberg would only squeeze in an appearance before *he* retires.

ZMINDA: Actually, you could fill out the team with Ewing, who played 51 games at second base in his career.

August 29—Harry Caray

GOLDSTEIN: A friend's account of Harry Caray's reaction to Six-Finger Antonio Alfonseca yesterday: Harry was flipping out when he was told that. It took almost the whole inning to get him to believe that Stoney wasn't pissing up his leg (a phrase he almost used on air!). Then when they showed a good close-up, he went "AAH! What the heck is that? The Marlins have some kind of freak up on the mound. Is that legal, Arne?" I about died.

JAMES: I watched the game. In fact, I'm watchin' the Cubs every day. I may be a minority of one, but I firmly believe that Harry Caray is one of the three or four best announcers working right now.

It's true that Harry's voice is awful, and he does slip a name to a similar name from 30 years ago several times a game. But on the other side, you have:

1) Genuine enthusiasm.

2) Genuine love of the game.

3) Outstanding knowledge about how the game is played.

4) Outstanding knowledge of the history of the game.

5) A level of integrity unmatched by any other active announcer, in terms of a willingness to face frankly the fact that his team stinks and to say why.

6) A lack of fear about what he says, which makes it possible for him to have fun on the air. The six-fingered guy is an excellent example. A modern announcer would be like, "Don't mention that twice in any game; don't make any big deal about it. We don't want people to think he's some kind of a freak." Harry is more like, "Hey, man, this is *wonderful*. We've got some kind of a friggin' freak on the mound."

Most announcers, you watch them two innings and you're tired of them. Harry is a guy you can spend a hundred hours with and never get tired of. He mixes up a name now and then. So what? I love the guy.

OLKIN: Wait 'til Harry finds out about Jim Abbott.

COOPERSON: But Bill, any cynic could easily point out how easy it would be for any baseball fan to be "enthusiastic" if they were getting paid that much to talk about the game. I wonder how Harry saying that the batter and the pitcher he's currently facing "were once teammates, I think" can be misconstrued as "outstanding knowledge of the history of the game." Please.

WENZ: I love Harry too, but beyond slipping on a few names, he's about as poorly prepared for games as they come. He may know the history of the game, but he doesn't know a big chunk of the players playing now. It is nice to have an announcer who can rip the home team, though.

I try to think of Harry as a team mascot. It helps me to forgive his frequent errors and still laugh my tail off.

GOLDSTEIN: I have to disagree. I hate the Cubs, but I really like Harry, and I think the occasional embarrassing slips make too many people think he doesn't know the game. I think he has a solid knowledge of the players today. He totally surprised me earlier this year with an excellent summary of Karim Garcia, of all people.

On another Harry note, earlier this week Harry said, "You know, Steve, this kid shortstop for the Red Sox got another hit today, and that ties the AL hitting streak record." I immediately was glued to my television, knowing that he was going to say the name. . . "Yup, this Nomar Garciaparra is something special." And he *nailed* it, said it perfect. It was great.

Later, Harry quipped, "You know, they named him Nomar, because it's Ramon backwards, so I'm not the only one doing that, heh heh."

JAMES: If it is so easy to be enthusiastic about the game if you're getting paid for it, why do 99.7 percent of announcers under the age of 40 sound as if they were taking a test? And Harry knows 400 times more about the history of baseball than any of us.

OLKIN: Don't say that, Bill—we don't want Harry to start writing books too. Chapter One: Illegal Freaks!

JAMES: There are different ways to know history. You may study *Who's Who in Baseball* and the *Handbook* three hours a day. . . I do, anyway. But if the group of us were walking down the street and we met Wally Post, Roy McMillan and Marty Barrett on their way into a restaurant, not a damn one of us would know it. Harry would immediately bellow out, "Roy, Wally, Sam. . . um, um. . . Mr. Barnes. How the hell are you? Wally, what ever happened to that redhead you used to know in Philadelphia? I was thinking about her just the other night."

OLKIN: Chapter Two: I Wonder What Happened to that Redhead Wally Post Used to Know.

COOPERSON: What the heck is that worth? I know of some drunks who probably haven't left their South Philly barstool since the day the Phillies moved out of Shibe Park who could do the same thing with recognizing baseball people. Does that mean we'd want them on the air?

Besides, the redheads they'd be thinking about probably have no teeth.

PINTO: One of the great things about the Internet is that you can now listen to a radio broadcast of almost any game. I happened to be home yesterday working and was listening to the White Sox game. I don't remember the names of the announcers, but I enjoyed the broadcast.

I grew up listening to Phil Rizzuto and Bill White call games for the Yankees on both radio and TV, and that was a great duo. I enjoy listening to Harry and making fun of his voice, and even Ken Harrelson you love to hate. But baseball TV and radio in Boston is the pits.

(Actually, there is one good thing, Jerry Remy, who I think is a much better broadcaster than he was a player.)

DEWAN: I haven't heard Harry that much this year, but I have to say what little I did hear made me feel sorry for him. When I've been listening (radio), he's relegated to a role where he can occasionally get in a very weak comment which is usually way off the topic that the other announcers are discussing.

Bill, you watch him every day so I'm sure you know better, but I find that when I hear him on the radio I have to turn the station because I actually get embarrassed for him!

David, I concur with you on Hawk Harrelson. He adds a tremendous amount of color to announcing. I haven't seen it recently, but the White Sox came out with a Hawk Harrelson dictionary a couple of years ago. It had definitions for all his pet phrases (like duck-snort). It was great.

He is also the last of the great nicknamers. Big Hurt, The Deacon, Little Hurt, One Dog.

He is the ultimate home announcer ("You can put it on the board. . . Yes!"), but I find that a big plus and adds to my enjoyment of the game.

FAUST: I like both good and bad announcers. I like good ones, well, for the obvious reasons, but I can have just as much fun with bad announcers. It's mind-boggling how many myths they perpetuate, or how much they miss in their off-the-cuff analysis. Last night I watched a good part of the Braves-Astros game. With Neagle and Kile pitching, the announcers got into a discussion of the four NL Cy Young candidates (Denny Neagle, Darryl Kile, Greg Maddux and Pedro Martinez).

One of the points made for Kile was something like this: "He's the unquestioned ace of his staff. When teams go to face Houston, all the batters know that they have to get geared up for Kile. When they face Atlanta, no one pitcher stands out like that." Huh?

". . . and Pedro Martinez just doesn't have as many wins." Um, guys, his team isn't as good. You could mention that.

And, I have to admit, I don't know whether the Braves' new park is a hitters' park, pitchers' park or neutral park, but not once did they mention that both Kile and Martinez get to pitch in pitchers' havens.

Next time you get a bad announcer or two, grab a notepad. By the end of the game, you'll have half a dozen *Scoreboard* questions. I'm sure we'll analyze the NL Cy Young candidates and the voting results in next year's book.

COOPERSON: A couple of things should be pointed out:

1. Look at the AL Cy Young voting in 1990. Right or wrong, Bob Welch won the award because he had so many wins. Rightly or wrongly this year, Martinez will be slighted because of fewer victories. As Neyer points out, this has been true throughout the history of Cy Young voting. The voters will certainly consider victory totals when they make their decision. Remember, the announcers have to consider that when they talk about who will win Cy Young.

2. Keep this in mind: Not everyone who watches a baseball game wants to analyze the game to the extent that the "figure filberts at STATS, Inc." do. Not that the announcers shouldn't try to educate the less-knowing, but sometimes they have more appeal if they forget about numbers and keep things basic. Why do you think you'll never hear about runs created per 27 outs on a game broadcast? Because you'll lose 90 percent of your audience. Some stats belong on TV, some belong in STATS books.

DEWAN: Ethan, well said!

FAUST: Good points, but it's hardly a leap to mention that Houston and Montreal play in pitcher-friendly parks.

I forgot my favorite point, though—they thought it was a bit odd that Houston had to bat Craig Biggio at leadoff. They thought it was an absolute shame that Houston didn't have Brian Hunter any more (with all his speed).

Then they rattled off the "prototype" leadoff hitters in the game today—Kenny Lofton, Hunter, Marquis Grissom, etc. . . I'd have laughed out loud, but I was too busy rolling my eyes. Not only did they fail to mention Chuck Knoblauch, I doubt they even thought of him.

WENZ: There's something to be said for announcers keeping their statistics simple in their broadcasts. However, they ought to know the complex ones themselves and to speak with this knowledge. If a simple statistic—say batting average—makes one guy look better than someone else, even though he's worse in just about every other category (Shawon Dunston, if you're looking for an example) they as announcers should not try to sell Shawon Dunston as a better hitter than someone else because his simple statistics might seem to indicate it.

JAMES: Which brings us back to Harry. Just yesterday, Harry was explaining why batting average, while it is certainly important, is often not *as* important as, for example, power. Harry knows, and says, that the Cubs are losing because:

a) they have a closer who gives up a .300 batting average, and b) they are short of power at several power positions.

Harry knows, and says, that Dunston does some things well but still can't resist chasing a 3-1 pitch in the dirt. He does a better job than almost any other announcer of passing along *accurate* judgments about the players without boring you with lists of stats.

I mean, stats really don't *work* in a broadcast. You can't focus on them, you can't relate to them. Out of all the stats used in a typical broadcast, what percentage are actually pertinent and informative? Use your own number, but I don't think anybody would try to tell you it is 30 percent. But whether you say that Dunston's on-base percentage stinks or that he really helped the pitcher out that time, it amounts to about the same thing. Harry's understanding of the game is just exceptionally good, and his knowledge of how to relate this to the fan in a form the fan can assimilate in a broadcast is just extraordinary.

GREENBERGER: Maybe some things do belong in the STATS books, but stuff like Sammy Sosa coming in nearly last in runs created among right fielders should be on the air. I guess I can't hear Harry or Stoney saying that about Sosa since the *Tribune* signs all the checks, but hell, the opposing announcer can do it. That kind of information improves my enjoyment of baseball, and knucklehead announcers who praise a player whose stats show to be a bum make me mad. Or at least irritate me.

BEAUREGARD: In the middle of these discussions about Harry, I received a voice-mail message from him. Although I wanted to think that he called just because his ears were burning, he was actually responding to a letter I had written to him just yesterday asking him to offer a testimonial quote for one of our upcoming fall publications.

When I got the message I at first thought it was one of you guys calling and imitating him to joke around. Rather quickly, though, his highly recognizable voice came through. I just called him back and got him directly. He is not familiar with the three books so he said that he didn't feel comfortable vouching for the books if he didn't use them, but he asked that I send them to him and he will review them and possibly offer a quote for next year's editions. However, he did indicate that he had read almost every one of your own books, Bill, and said, and I quote, "I would vouch for anything that Bill James has ever written."

I went on to say that I understand that he may not use our books in the booth and that we were actually just having a discussion about this topic while he had called me initially. He said that he "barely has enough time to get everyone's name straight, never mind look up their career stats." Truly, that is what he said. I guess he doesn't buy into the "game is slowing down" theory.

In any case, we talked for about five minutes and he sounded like a very intelligent, honest and entertaining guy.

PALACIOS: Cooperson, you are the cynic and enjoy being a cynic.

John, Harry is like an old grandfather with a wealth of information. Would you stop listening to your grandfather or father because you're embarrassed about the way they sound? I just had a conversation with my ancient grandmother. We spoke about how my family has been in the Americas for 11 generations. I wouldn't stop listening to her because I'm embarrassed of her.

Harry is the grandfather of baseball. He should be listened as such. Get the wealth, ignore the mistakes. We're all going to be old, too, some day.

I love baseball because of the stories, the folklore, the humanity that comes across through the ages thanks to baseball. I love baseball because it teaches me about American culture as it changes through the ages. Studying historical baseball is like studying Art History. Baseball records are like pottery shards or fossils. We're lucky to have baseball as a medium with which to understand the past of our country. History is too concerned about understanding powerful and wealthy people's lives and ideas, and often ignoring the life of the everyday person. Baseball gives voices to the common folk. Some day people will wonder about America's race relation history. The voices of Ty Cobb, Hank Aaron and Jackie Robinson will be more valuable than the voices of Henry Ford, J.F.K. or Richard Nixon.

Harry, in this context, should be heard as the old poet, ready to tell valuable information about our past. If you can't put up with a mispronounced name, get a life.

COOPERSON: What about all the announcers who prepare, and learn the game and learn the pronunciations—how should they feel about a guy who gets away with not doing that? Another question: if baseball tells the story of our country and race relations, how come no one knows that the color barrier was broken in football before Jackie Robinson?

PALACIOS: The reason why Robinson is so well known is a tribute to Robinson, himself. He's well known because of his activism and the power baseball gave to his activism.

Besides, Robinson was not the first player of black descent to play in the majors in the 20th century. Armando Marsans, who played in the early teens, was half black. Roberto Estalella was the first black player in the 20th century. He played in 1935.

However, we're not having Bobby Estalella Day. Estalella makes us ask many questions, such as "What is black?" Roy Campanella was of mixed heritage. So is Tiger Woods, so was Smokey Joe Williams.

JAMES: Joe Morgan doesn't make any effort to learn how to pronounce anybody's name, either, but a lot of people seem to enjoy his announcing. He's been on the air six years and he still calls Mike Macfarlane Mike McFarling and Mark Thompson Mark Thomas, etc., etc. There is no doubt that if you studied the issue, you would find that Morgan misses more names than Harry does, but he gets a free ride because he's younger and was a player and hasn't had a stroke.

On the larger issue, who gives a rat's ass *what* any announcer thinks about the way that any other announcer does his job? Announcers don't work for other announcers; they work for us, the people who watch. And my point about Harry was not that he deserves compassion because he is old; my point is that Harry is very, very good at the job. Not *was* good at it; *is* good at it, right now.

An announcer's job, as I see it, is to make the game fun to watch. I mean, you can evaluate announcers by the high-school English-teacher test if you want to; Cooperson apparently thinks that is the only relevant test, and I'm sure he'd make a hell of a good high school English teacher. I evaluate an announcer by whether he makes the game fun and interesting, or whether he makes the game tedious and boring. Harry makes the game fun and interesting. How much he prepares and *how* he prepares, to me, doesn't have squat to do with it.

[Editor's note: Just as this book went to press, Harry Caray was hospitalized and listed in critical condition after collapsing at a Valentine's Day dinner. All of us at STATS have the highest respect for Harry and his contributions to baseball broadcasting. Our prayers are with his family.]

September 6—Tom Kelly

SICKELS: I have lost what respect I had left for Tom Kelly. The Twins are buried, 20 games out. There are three weeks left in the season. And Todd Walker is rotting on the bench.

Is it possible that Tom Kelly and Cito Gaston have switched minds as a result of some sort of experiment gone awry?

ZMINDA: Kelly has apparently decided that Walker can't play, based on the evidence he's seen. I'm sure this decision is based on Kelly's experience with other "can't-miss" prospects like Dave McCarty, Willie Banks and LaTroy Hawkins.

Maybe Kelly's right about this, maybe he's wrong. What's annoying about this situation is that he's got the perfect opportunity this month to find out more definitively. But I wouldn't be shocked if he were absolutely right in his assessment.

JAMES: Well, I would be absolutely shocked if it turned out Walker couldn't play. If Kelly is generalizing his experience with Willie Banks and LaTroy Hawkins to Todd Walker, then we can definitely conclude that the man is a moron, since only a moron would think that the problems with young hitters are comparable to those with young pitchers. This would be equivalent to learning appropriate behavior at a rock concert from studying family reunions, and reasoning that they're all public gatherings.

I remember a couple of years ago, when Rich Becker was going through this, John Sickels wondered whether there might be something odd about the Minnesota park which makes minors-to-majors projections unreliable in that park. We looked at it, and concluded that, with the exceptions of Dave McCarty and (at that time) Becker, the minors-to-majors projections for Minnesota players were uncannily accurate—even more so than for most other parks. Everybody who had gotten a chance to play in that park, except McCarty, had done what he should have been expected to do, as Becker has this year.

But I remember that we used to think he was never going to let Becker play, either. It may be that his thinking is more subtle than we're giving him credit for. It may be, for example, that Walker is in a frustration cycle, has made some inappropriate adjustments to his initial struggles, and really wouldn't hit anything the way he is going right now. It may be that Kelly simply doesn't want him piling up 150 unnecessary at-bats while his head is all screwed up, finishing the year at .165 in 200 at-bats, and going home all winter stewing about it. Maybe he wants him to get some things straightened out first.

Or it could be, perhaps, that Kelly *knows* that Walker is going to hit everything you can throw him in a year or two. As such, he might be reasoning that, "When I turn this kid loose, he's going to hit .320, and I'm going to lose all control over him. The only leverage I have, to make him do the things that I want him to do—to work on his defense, to establish the habit of going home and getting a good night's sleep after a ballgame—is right now, when he's not playing. Therefore, I'm not cutting him loose and allowing him to make big money on his hitting stats until he clearly understands a few things."

SICKELS: Well, I can't see making a decision like that based on less than 200 at-bats.

September 7—Ken Griffey Jr.

PINTO: Some information on Junior from David Vincent of SABR.

Griffey on September 7 is 27.290.

Youngest Players to Hit 300 Home Runs

Player	Years.Days
Jimmie Foxx	27.328
Mel Ott	28.171
Eddie Mathews	28.186
Mickey Mantle	28.257
Hank Aaron	29.073
Frank Robinson	29.283
Harmon Killebrew	29.326
Willie Mays	30.059
Ralph Kiner	30.210
Babe Ruth	30.214

Earliest Date for HR No. 50

Roger Maris	8/22/1961
Babe Ruth	9/3/1921
Jimmie Foxx	9/3/1932
Mickey Mantle	9/3/1961
Ken Griffey	9/7/1997
Babe Ruth	9/11/1927
Hank Greenberg	9/12/1938
Mark McGwire	9/14/1996
Babe Ruth	9/15/1928
Hack Wilson	9/15/1930

September 8—Eddie Cicotte

JAMES: Did any of you ever notice how profoundly unusual Eddie Cicotte's career ratio of batters faced to innings is? I realize that, as obscure references go, this one takes the Ding Dong, but then that's why I asked you guys.

Anyway, if you take Cicotte's career record of batters facing pitcher, subtract out the baserunners, and figure the outs per inning, it comes out to about 24.8 "explained outs" per nine innings. This figure is like off-the-charts unusual. A normal figure is about 26.1 outs per nine innings, and the next-lowest pitcher that I am aware of is Red Ames, who is at about 25.5.

When I saw Cicotte at 24.8, I assumed of course that there was some sort of an error. But working through it, apparently there isn't. Anyway, the data on-line matches the data from old guides, and his averages are around 24.5 to 25.0 every season.

This could be explained by:

a) a genuinely exceptional pickoff move—but it would have to be genuinely exceptional.

b) a marginally unbelievable groundball rate.

c) some combination of the above, combined with exceptional outfield arms and infield defense on the teams he played for.

Any of you know anything?

September 10—Third Basemen

JAMES: Hey, what do you guys honestly think of Dean Palmer? How would you rate the American League third basemen, for example. Obviously as a group they're pretty pathetic, but would you regard Palmer as about the best of the group, or over-rated?

OLKIN: He's in the middle of the pack, I guess. Robin Ventura, Travis Fryman and John Valentin are at the top, and I'd rather have Cal Ripken or Jeff Cirillo. Matt Williams has to rate an edge over Palmer; they're similar in style but not quality. Then you get to the mid-level guys like Ed Sprague, Dave Hollins, Russ Davis and Palmer.

What player is this?

Year	Team	G	AB	R	H	2B	3B	HR	RBI	BB	SO	AVG	OBP	SLG
1996	KC	118	429	61	111	15	1	22	67	23	101	.259	.296	.452
1997	2TM	128	481	63	123	27	0	19	77	36	120	.256	.309	.430

Why, it's the Royals' third baseman. Remarkably consistent, isn't he? The only thing is that he's two different players. That's Craig Paquette, 1996, and Dean Palmer, 1997.

Bill, you've seen more of Palmer than any of us. Is he closer to Paquette or Matt Williams?

PINTO: I have to agree with Mat here. Cirillo has a higher OBP and his slugging is about the same. I don't know how Cirillo is as a fielder. I still like Wade Boggs at third, and I wish the Yankees would play him every day. I know he was injured this year, but Robin Ventura is still good.

JAMES: I just said the same thing to Neyer in another message, but I don't understand why you would rate Fryman ahead of Palmer. They're the same age, about the same on-base percentage most years, but Palmer has far more power.

I checked their on-base plus slugging in road games over a three-year period, and I didn't write down the exact figures, but it was something like Fryman, .750, Palmer, .860.

Also, why is Williams far ahead of Palmer? Power? Palmer has hit 38 and 33 homers or something in recent years. What am I missing here?

As for the Royals' third basemen, that was a career year for Craig Paquette, and it's an off year for Palmer.

Is Palmer closer to Paquette or Matt Williams? That's what I'm trying to sort out in my own mind. He's far better defensively than Paquette. He will make Brooks Robinson plays, but he'll also make mistakes.

WENZ: I hope you're not using those numbers to argue that Paquette is as good as Palmer. Seemingly everybody put up big offensive numbers last year.

OLKIN: I mean nothing of the kind. I wouldn't even argue that Paquette is better than beating your head against a telephone pole. I just thought it was an odd coincidence since no one would consider Palmer and Paquette of comparable quality.

JAMES: I checked the on-line again and made some notes. Compared by this season's batting, on-base and slugging, Fryman has a slim edge:

	Avg	OBP	SLG
Palmer	.256	.309	.430
Fryman	.273	.328	.437
Williams	.260	.302	.489
Paquette	.230	.263	.393

In career totals, it's a wash:

	Avg	OBP	SLG
Palmer	.248	.321	.469
Fryman	.274	.335	.444
Williams	.263	.311	.497
Paquette	.232	.263	.405

But in the three-year road data, which I think is a fair test, Palmer has a big edge—in fact, bigger than I said:

	Avg	OBP	SLG
Palmer	.284	.354	.524
Fryman	.263	.319	.428
Williams	.297	.344	.586
Paquette	.228	.267	.385

OLKIN: I guess it depends on how much you factor in defense. Fryman and Williams are two of the best defensive third basemen in the league, and from what I've seen of Palmer and his numbers, he isn't nearly as good, and may even be below average. Again, you've probably got a better handle on Palmer here than we do. But it seems clear to me that even if you consider Williams and Palmer to be offensive equals—which is a bit generous to Palmer, I think—Williams' defense has to give his the edge overall. Fryman has less power, and I didn't realize the gap was quite as large as it is, but I'd still take him over Palmer for his defense and durability.

JAMES: Appreciate your thoughts. Fryman's defensive numbers are vastly better than Palmer's in his career. Playing about the same number of games at third base (761-750) in the same league in the same years, Fryman has 36 more double plays (133-97), 46 fewer errors (73-119), a much better fielding percentage (.965-.938) and range factor (2.71-2.35).

MOYER: I don't have much of an idea about his defense (who cares anyway, right?), but I wish by some miracle the Jays would dump Sprague and give Tom Evans a shot next season. Lots of swishes, lots of walks, lots of homers. My kinda guy.

OLKIN: Not Cito Gaston's kind of guy. Evans isn't even 30 yet. If he's lucky, he'll work his way into a platoon with Juan Samuel in a couple of years.

September 10—Mark McGwire

PINTO: Just some tidbits.

This is just the fifth year when two players have reached the 50-HR mark. We've never had three reach it.

McGwire is now fifth all-time with HR in consecutive seasons (102). Ruth is first with 114 in 1927 and 1928.

Ruth is the only other player to have back-to-back 50-HR seasons. He did it twice, in 1920-21 and 1927-28.

McGwire has broken Greg Vaughn's record of HR playing for more than one team in a season. Vaughn had 41 for the Brewers and Padres last year.

It's possible that McGwire will have the most HR in majors this year without winning a HR title. It's similar to 1990 when Eddie Murray had the best batting average in the majors, but didn't win the NL batting title because Willie McGee was traded to the AL.

September 15—Scott Spiezio

OLKIN: Genetics

Year	Team	Lg	G	AB	R	H	2B	3B	HR	RBI	BB	SO	AVG	OBP	SLG
1969	SD	NL	121	355	29	83	9	0	13	43	38	64	.234	.313	.369
1997	Oak	AL	135	496	52	120	26	4	13	62	36	71	.242	.292	.389

Ed Spiezio in his first season as a regular, and his son, Scott, in his first full season. Score one for nature against nurture.

DEWAN: Nature 1, Nurture 0? Don't be so quick. It's quite likely nurture was similar, too! (Dad teaches son the way he was taught, etc.)

September 16—Terry Bevington

ZMINDA: Nobody commented on this yesterday, so maybe not everybody knows about it. In Sunday's White Sox-Indians game, Cleveland went into the eighth losing 2-0, but started to rally. Terry Bevington began bringing in pitchers, one after another. Finally it got to the point where he wanted to bring Matt Karchner in, only Karchner wasn't warming up. In fact *nobody* was warming up.

So in order to stall while Karchner got in some warmup pitchers, Bevington brought in Keith Foulke, who wasn't up, either, right off the bullpen bench and had him give Matt Williams an intentional walk. There were runners on first and third with one out at the time, so an IBB was definitely bizarre strategy. Anyway, after the walk he brought in Karchner, who still wasn't ready. He got pounded and the Indians wound up scoring seven runs. Bevington also tied a major league record by using nine pitchers. This is one of the craziest things I've ever seen in a baseball game.

COOPERSON: Instead of trading all their pitching in July, they could have changed managers in May, and they'd probably be right in the middle of the race.

JAMES: I'd hate to judge a manager on one bad game, but man, that is inept. That almost tops those Maury Wills stories when Wills was mismanaging Seattle for a couple of months. I can't recall that I've *ever* heard of a manager screwing up a game any worse than that, and I just wrote a book on the subject.

COOPERSON: I agree, don't judge a manager on one game. But, let's just say Karchner isn't ready to pitch, he has to pitch, hurts him arm and his career is ruined. . . then what? If I were Mr. Karchner, I'd have torn into Bevington—in the media, in front of the team, whatever. No excuse for that.

DEWAN: Why should Karchner tear into Bevington? Because he didn't plan it properly, he intentionally walked a batter *in order to* give Karchner time to warm up. You might suggest he still wasn't ready, hence his performance. But I wouldn't necessarily agree with that. I think one batter is enough time to warm up (plus the warmups on the mound).

Only Karchner can tell you if he was ready or not. I'll bet he was.

The blunder, of course, was having no one warming up when he signaled to the pen. Then, he tried to recover somewhat with an intentional walk. The walk was necessary damage control at that point.

COOPERSON: Most pitchers need a lot more than four pitches in the pen to get loose. OK, the intentional BB may give him time for about seven or eight throws—but remember, Karchner wasn't even up yet. His first four or five "pitches" in the pen probably would've been lobs, not even real pitches. For most relievers, that's not enough of a warmup.

Again, the issue goes beyond performance. How much is a young closer's arm worth? Potentially as much $50 million over the course of a long career (granted, that might be a best-case figure, but salaries certainly aren't declining). To have the manager put a pitcher's arm at risk through sheer stupidity is absolutely inexcusable. Yes, the IBB was the best he could have done at that point, but Bevington can't be let off the hook for this one.

DEWAN: I'll bet Karchner had at least 20 warmup pitches. Probably 25 or 30. I think that's enough to warm up.

Again, only Karchner knows for sure. With the intentional walk, I believe Bevington gave Karchner enough time.

By the way, I'm not saying Bevington should be off the hook. He made a huge blunder, but did all he could to recover from it with the IBB.

So, the scorecard reads (in my book):

Not warming up pitchers and signaling for a new pitcher: -100

Call for IBB to make up for it: +10

Net: Huge Blunder!

MUNDO: Don, I saw that stroke of brilliance on Bevington's part the other day and was astounded, too.

Bevington is incredibly inept. Darn it, Bill, if you could've held off on your book for another year you could have dedicated a whole chapter to him. He's terrible at handling pitchers. Last year the bullpen was pretty shaky, but I think was a little better towards the end of the season. Regardless, Boom-Boom would let Kevin Tapani (without his best pitch *and* pitching injured) throw at least 120 pitches per start, often pulling him way too late.

This year, same kind of thing. The Sox bullpen has had stretches where it has looked great. Never mind, though, as Bev lets Navarro throw 120+ pitches and put up lines like 7-12-7-7-3-2. And when prompted with questions about it, Bev sounds practically illiterate and blurts out, "I give Navarro a lot of credit for coming back after those bad outings." Like, he's impressed Navarro's ready to go five days after one of his shellings? Isn't that his job? I never remember Canter saying, "Gee, Dave, I'm really impressed that you showed up for work today!"

That Foulke/Karchner thing really takes the cake, though.

Why else don't I like him? He keeps playing Ozzie Guillen. And he has Norberto Martin pinch-hit a lot. And he keeps bringing in Tony Castillo to blow leads.

COUSINS: Either way, it was still another case of bad management by Bevington. He has always had trouble utilizing his bullpen correctly.

FORD: This wasn't the first time Bevington's been caught napping this year. Earlier, he made a visit to the mound after three balls were issued for an intentional walk. After reaching the mound, he was informed that the batter had one more ball coming. He hung around there for a while, just to make it look good, I suppose (if there's any way to look good in that situation). I just wonder what the conversation was.

September 18—Jaime Navarro

FREER: Itchy Trigger

You can't say *that* about Terry Bevington. The Chisox lead baseball in starter shellings. 1997 MLB leaders in number of games where the starting pitcher surrendered nine or more runs:

Team	Shellings
Chicago White Sox	11
Kansas City Royals	3
Toronto Blue Jays	3
Baltimore Orioles	2
Colorado Rockies	2
New York Yankees	2

Can anyone figure out why the Sox are a runaway in this category?

CALLIS: How many of those 11 are Jaime Navarro starts?

OSLAND: Six of those 11 are Navarro.

MUNDO: The Sox are a runaway because of Navarro, and Bevington's attitude towards him: "We paid him the big bucks and he's gonna start, dammit, no matter how bad he is."

OSLAND: Navarro's six "shellings" lead the league by a wide margin:

1997 Leaders in Shellings

Pitcher	Shellings
Jaime Navarro	6
Doug Drabek	2
Tim Belcher	2

Nobody else has more than one.

DEWAN: Now that's a good stat! That's an incredible usage pattern that Bevington has established with Navarro. I'd be curious to know if there's a pattern in Navarro's career that shows him getting stronger as a game goes on. I've been imagining all year that this must be the reason Bevington sticks so long with Navarro.

BERNSTEIN: Oddly enough, Navarro's ERA is a bit high in these games: 29 IP, 47 ER for a 14.59 ERA.

In his other starts he's only giving up 4.26 runs per game. So those six starts raise his season ERA by over 1.5!

September 19—Josh Booty

ZMINDA: Who else but our boy Rod Beaton:

". . . the critics of Florida third-base prospect Josh Booty (.210-20-60 at Class AA) have no sense of history. Booty, once the nation's top college quarterback recruit, is a great fielder with power. Buddy Bell, Steve Buechele and Graig Nettles had long careers with Bootyesque skills."

I almost don't know where to begin with this one. But I'm sure gonna have fun with that phrase, "Bootyesque skills." Every time I see a guy with a .203 lifetime minor league average and a 6-to-1 strikeout-to-walk ratio, I'm going to think, "Bootyesque skills! This must be the next Buddy Bell!"

I can't wait to see those MLEs for Josh.

FULLAM: A .210 average in AA ball? What do you think his MLEs would come out to??

ZMINDA: An exciting thought just occurred to me: Michael Jordan had Bootyesque skills!

FULLAM: How good of a college quarterback do you think Jordan would have been? (At least he wouldn't have any problems seeing over his linemen.)

GOLDSTEIN: Booty set a Midwest League record with 195 K last year at Kane County (.206-21-87), and I became quite excited to learn that this year he was closing in on the Eastern league mark of 165. Two whiffs on the last day brought Josh up to 166 and I was a happy, happy man. As I started scrambling for the International League record (Charlotte, here we come!), knowing that three strikeout records in three seasons at three different levels would most likely be an unprecedented feat, Jim Callis shattered my hopes by informing me that Mets "prospect" Matt Raleigh struck out 169 times for Binghamton this year.

Comparing the two great seasons:

Year	Team	G	AB	R	H	2B	3B	HR	RBI	BB	SO	SB	AVG	OBP	SLG
1997	Portl, AA	122	448	42	94	19	2	20	69	27	166	2	.210	.254	.395
1997	Bingh, AA	122	398	71	78	15	0	37	74	79	169	0	.196	.330	.513

The top season is Booty. Looking at Raleigh's season, an .843 OPS with a .196 average must be some sort of record.

SPEAR: Steve, this Matt Raleigh guy looks like a future "Moyer Favorite"!

FULLAM: What's more impressive: the fact that Raleigh had more walks than hits (79 to 78), or the fact that he hit more homers than singles (37 to 26)?!

JAMES: The interesting question here, not to be too vulgar, is whose ass Beaton is trying to kiss. The only apparent reason that Beaton would write something like this is that Booty's agent or the front-office moron who drafted and signed him must be a valued source for

Beaton and has been under pressure because Booty can't play. If you charted Beaton's column for a couple of weeks, you could figure out who Beaton was trying to pacify or protect.

BERNSTEIN: Didn't McGwire have more HR than singles in '95—39 homers, 13 doubles, 87 total hits, giving him 35 singles?

But I'm not sure anybody else did. I'd be more impressed with the more HR than singles. After all, didn't Gene Tenace pretty much make a living walking as much as he hit?

PINTO: Wasn't there a John Big Booty in the Buckaroo Banzai movie?

Didn't Mike Schmidt have a rookie year like Raleigh's? He could be another Rob Deer!

MOYER: I was just sitting up here in Bristol eating lunch at a Boston Market when I read that. I figured, "Good, I won't even have to think of anything for my Babble-On next week." However, Rob Neyer already informed me that he's ripped Beaton a new rectum orifice. I fear that by the time I write again, Rod may have about 1,000 new ones on the sports net. I do think that probably tops anything else he's said before.

I also wanted to mention that during my lonely Bristol Radisson morning, my mind wandered onto the thought that Craig Paquette is probably the closest thing to a real "Bootyesque" ballplayer. That's probably an insult to Craig Paquette, however.

September 20—Mark McGwire

MOYER: I just happened to notice that Mark McGwire only has 82 runs scored this season. Is that not exceptionally low for a guy with a .392 OBP and 54 HR? If you subtract his homer at-bats and add his walk plate appearances to his at-bat total, it means in most of his non-homer plate appearances, 549, he's only scored 28 runs. Why? I'm saying it's nothing more than an unlucky fluke.

PINTO: Yes, it is strange. If you look at the top run scorers of all time, they are dominated by power hitters with high OBPs. I think what happened is that he's played for teams with lousy offenses this year, and nobody was behind him to drive him in. I don't know this for sure, but I bet the A's and Cards' 5-9 have low slugging percentages.

PALACIOS: Maybe you shouldn't have punished McGwire for his HR. If a guy had 54 triples and no homers and 82 runs scored, he'd get praised for his runs scored.

It's like when our dearly departed Kenn Ruby showed up Dave Wannstedt. Coach Wannie said once, "If you took away the biggest four rushes against our team, our rushing defense would be one of the best in the league." So when Ruby, in his finite wisdom took the best four rushes from every team, the Bears were still one of the worst.

It's similar here. If you take away all the runs McGwire scored after his extra-base hits, then you'd have to do the same thing for all RBI men. He'd still stink, but that's because, as has already been mentioned, he has poor sluggers behind him, and. . . he doesn't steal bases, Ha!

I love the stat, but what does it mean?!? It's killing me. This isn't like math class, when you flip the book and find the right answer.

Bill, help!

JAMES: It's an odd one, for sure. In all seriousness, there is no doubt that his extreme lack of speed does play a role in this. The number is odd enough that it's hard to find parallels for it. Gus Triandos in 1958 hit 30 homers but scored only 29 runs otherwise, but

a) Gus Triandos was famous for his unusual slowness afoot, and b) That's really not a match.

Willie Stargell in his odd MVP year (1979) scored only 28 runs other than his 32 on home runs. Dave Kingman in 1975 scored only 29 runs other than the 36 he scored on home runs. A lot of people are somewhere around 30. Probably the best match is Harmon Killebrew in 1962, when he hit .243 with 48 homers, 126 RBI, also 106 walks, but scored only 37 runs other than the 48 on homers (85 total).

The performance of Oakland and St. Louis 5-6-7 hitters doesn't look to be notably bad. Oakland No. 5 hitters have hit over 30 home runs, as I recall, with a respectable average.

I would be interested to know how many times McGwire has been pinch-ran for and how many runs the pinch runners have scored.

September 20—Royals

JAMES: There can't be anyone in the majors who has done more to save his career after the All-Star break than two aging Royals, Jeff Montgomery and Mike Macfarlane. In his first 23 appearances this season (through July 10), Montgomery had an ERA of 7.09. As of right now he hasn't given up an earned run since July 16, a stretch of 23 appearances in which he has pitched 26 and a third innings, giving up only 10 hits and four walks, one run, which was unearned. His ERA is now 3.49—less than one-half of what it was at the All-Star break.

Macfarlane hit .106 in April and .172 in May. He rallied for a .226 mark in June, but hit .188 in July until the last day, through July 30. At that point he was 30-for-170 on the season, having never topped out above .200, and it seemed enormously unlikely that he ever would.

Since July 31 he has hit .400 (30-for-75), with 60 percent of his hits for extra bases. Improbably enough, he has a shot to finish the season over .250. He has also not committed an error during his hot streak (I don't know when his last one was), and has 56 total bases in 75 at-bats. He has grounded into only three double plays all year.

At the All-Star break, anyone would have assumed that both of these players would be released during the winter.

September 22—Graig Nettles

SASMAN: Who am I?

I led three different teams in HR a total of 10 times from 1970-1984.

I went to the postseason with three different teams.

I won more than one Gold Glove.

I am not in the Hall of Fame.

SASMAN: And the winner is. . .

David Pinto, who correctly guessed Graig Nettles. He led the Indians three times in homers, the Padres once and the Yankees six times. If Reggie was the straw, Nettles was, at least, the swizzle stick.

PINTO: I really think if you do a complete comparison of Nettles and Brooks Robinson, Nettles beats him everywhere but batting average.

JAMES: For the new *Historical Abstract,* I have Nettles (for now) ranked as the sixth-best third baseman in baseball history. And I have him *behind* Brooks Robinson.

COOPERSON: Nettles allegedly was born with a chip on his shoulder, maybe because his parents named him Graig instead of Craig.

JAMES: I have it Mike Schmidt, George Brett, Eddie Mathews, Robinson, Ron Santo and Nettles. Dean Palmer, in all seriousness, will probably rank about 50th, although it is too early to rate him. I have Bill Melton 52nd among third basemen; Palmer is probably going to edge past Melton, at a guess.

As to why Robinson over Nettles. . . well, Robinson played 200 more games than Nettles, and drove in a few more runs. His batting average is 20 points higher, and Robinson's career centers in the 1960s, when runs were very scarce, whereas Nettles' centers in the 1970s, when run-scoring levels were more normal.

The key question is defense. Intuitively, I don't believe that Nettles was an even match for Robinson, although in all honesty I haven't studied it exhaustively. Nettles certainly was very, very good defensively; Robinson was probably the best ever.

September 23—Playoff Races

ZMINDA: Along with the Dodgers falling apart, how about the Orioles? After beating the Yankees on September 5, they had a 9½-game lead. . . 10 in the loss column. Now it's down to three.

Of course nobody cares because both teams have clinched playoff spots. But as Bob Costas pointed out in *The Sporting News* a few weeks ago, that's precisely what's wrong with the whole wild-card thing. When they brought this thing in, the owners said the idea was to "give us September back," that is, create some excitement over battles for playoff spots. But in both 1996 and 1997, the wild-card has rendered meaningless what might have been two very dramatic races: Dodgers-Padres in 1996, O's-Yanks this year. And the Mariners-Angels race in 1995 was dramatic only because the loser wound up being eliminated from the playoffs. In baseball, nothing can compare with two quality teams battling for first place down to the wire. The wild-card has basically ensured that this won't happen.

MOYER: Even though I think Bob Costas is too big for his britches, I read that *TSN* article, thoroughly enjoyed it, and wholeheartedly agree.

PINTO: I agree 100 percent. Does anyone really care about the Astros-Pirates race? These are two lousy teams battling for a playoff spot.

The great things about 1978 and 1993 was the fact that there was tragedy. The Red Sox were a great team, but not good enough. The Giants were a great team, but not good enough.

The only meaningful races we can have now are among second-rate teams. That may be fine for the other major sports, but I'd like some real drama in my regular season once in a while.

COOPERSON: As Moyer correctly pointed out months ago, when everyone was talking about the Pirates winning despite the small payroll, no one will care about the Pirates later in the year. David just confirmed that.

SCHINSKI: I care about the Astros-Pirates race. The winner gets in, the loser doesn't. Besides I don't want the 'Stros to clinch against the Cubs!

1993 was horrible. Any Giants fan out there has to be crying about that one. How can you win 90+ games and not get into the postseason? It's a travesty.

To me, the races aren't as exciting as Griffey's and McGwire's chase for 61 dingers. That's the real fun!

PINTO: That's the whole point, the fans *were* crying. It's the real world. Losing is as important as winning, because if you never lose, you can't appreciate the win.

COOPERSON: 1993 was a travesty? Lest we all forget, that 104-win team that beat out the 103-team lost the LCS to a 97-win team. Should we sit here and cry that the Phillies beating the Braves was a travesty too?

CARLSON: And if 1993 was a "travesty," what about all of the teams that won't make the playoffs that will have records better than the worst division leader, and won't make it just because they are caught in the wrong division (despite the fact that they are playing a balanced schedule, so "division leader" means squat)?

QUINN: I agree with your point, David, but you picked a bad example. In 1993, the NL played a balanced schedule. Since everyone played virtually the same schedule, the division championship is meaningless. San Francisco missed the playoffs despite 103 wins and the second-best record in baseball. Jeff correctly describes this as a travesty.

ZMINDA: I'm going to *really* appreciate it when the White Sox finally win a title (and I don't mean just the AL Central, either). Or maybe I should say *if*.

CARLSON: I don't dispute that, but I am saying, we will have a travesty this year also. You can't have divisions and a balanced schedule. It doesn't make any logical sense to allow teams into a playoff based upon being in a "division" when you are not playing your division's teams more than the others.

COOPERSON: Exactly. The Phillies won 97 games, went 3-6 over their last nine games that meant essentially nothing. Of course you "travesty"-whining people didn't consider that, did you? You would be better served working with Kenn Ruby on some conspiracy theory about the 1993 NL.

PINTO: Imagine how happy White Sox fans will be when they get an owner who actually likes baseball and wants to win.

FULLAM: It's kind of off the topic, but do you think the Phils might have won more games in '93 if they had been pushed by a division rival? They started the season 51-21 and basically had the race locked up by the end of July. Complacency definitely had to be a factor for most of the final two months of the year.

JAMES: I, for example, am really appreciative when the Royals win a ballgame. For me, as a Royals fan, winning a ballgame is essentially equivalent, for anyone else, to winning a series. Winning a series, to me, is equivalent to a month-long hot streak for fans of a competitive team.

If the Royals actually play well for a month, this, to me, is equivalent to your team winning a pennant. For example, the Royals played exceptionally well in late July/early August, 1994. I still remember this event as if it was yesterday. Making the playoffs, for us, would be like winning the World Series for you. It's all the science of *relative* appreciation. The Royals are masters of it.

GOLDSTEIN: I'm offended by the word "travesty" here. The word infers that it was unfair and that there was a wrong that deserves to be righted. To get into the playoffs in 1993, you had to win your division. To win your division you had to have the best record. The Giants knew this going into the season. They didn't do it. I'd understand someone saying, "Gee, that kinda sucks for them," but it's not a travesty.

FULLAM: What's gonna happen to Bill when the Royals actually win a *World Series*? I'd stay clear of Lawrence, Kansas, that's for sure.

CARLSON: I am not saying that the Giants did not know this coming in, I am just saying the setup is goofy to begin with. If there are 14 teams in a "league," and you all play each other the same number of "x" times, then the top two teams should make the playoffs, not the best one from the left side of the page and the best one from the right side, when there were four teams as good as that one from the right side on the left side. So, I guess I'm just saying, "Gee, that kinda sucks for them that baseball doesn't know how to set up the schedule correctly."

OLKIN: If we're talking about the aspects of the current setup that kinda suck, I'll put my two cents in. I think it's more than a little unfair that the Giants only have to outplay three other teams to make the postseason while the Brewers have to top four other clubs.

As to your point, Bill, you're right—it is all relative. My Brewers haven't won a World Series, *ever*, so quit whining. And I'm not even going to mention how many Cubs fans work in this office. Get on the wrong side of those fellas, and they can make those Classic Game meetings last longer than a tripleheader at Coors.

ELMAN: The party line here (Chicago, not STATS) is that Jerry Reinsdorf's true love is baseball and not hoops. This can be traced to his Brooklyn days. He has always said if he can win one or the other, he would want to win the World Series, not the NBA championship. That has always been his dream. David, are you questioning the validity of what Mr. Reinsdorf says?

PINTO: I guess that's why Bill devoted half of his *1986 Abstract* to the Royals winning the World Series.

QUINN: Yes, "travesty" meaning unfair and a wrong that deserves to be righted fits. If baseball wants divisions, they need an unbalanced schedule. If baseball wants a balanced schedule, there should be no divisions.

Maybe the Phillies could win seven more games if they needed, maybe they could have won all 162 if they wanted. This is not the point. The point is the system is not fair.

COOPERSON: Maybe the system is not perfect, but no practical system (no divisions? you're dreaming) is going to be perfect. Why doesn't the NFL put every team in a single division (i.e. do away with divisions)? Because it's not practical and would be more confusing than it's worth. A balanced vs. unbalanced schedule is only *one* issue of the schedule. Maybe, somewhere during the course of a season, a team has to endure a ridiculous stretch of travel—what if one team plays more Sunday nights than the other, making for more short nights on the road prior to a Monday game? The schedule can not be perfectly equal for any two teams. Any system is imperfect. The 1993 NL was imperfect and fair.

Why doesn't someone, in their spare time, go through records for all four major sports and find every case where a team making the postseason had a worse record than a team that missed out? Let's try to correct all of those travesties too.

QUINN: No change needed in the NFL, they play an unbalanced schedule. The NFL has a legitimate division champion.

Yes, many issues are problematic. The balanced vs. unbalanced can be easily fixed.

NFL does it right. NBA does it right. And sometimes baseball does it right (divisions are a recent addition and some seasons used an unbalanced schedule). The only two times it went wrong that I can think of: MLB NL 1993 and the 1981 strike.

I'm not trying to correct the past, only point out a problem with a simple solution.

By the way, an unbalanced schedule not only makes the division winner legitimate, it increases the likelihood the contenders play each other in the last week of the season. Which gets back to David's point of making the races more exciting.

PINTO: I disagree with you, Pat. It doesn't matter if the schedule is balanced or unbalanced, it just matters that you play the same competition the same amount. If there were an unbalanced schedule in 1993, the Giants and Braves might have won a few less games, and the Phillies might have won a few more, but it should not have mattered that much in the final outcome.

The Braves and Giants would have played five more games that year under the old schedule, but the Giants lost 6-7, and it's not likely that those five games wouldn't have been split either. The real difference that year was that the Braves swept the Rockies, while the Giants lost three to Colorado.

Any system is fair as long as you play the same competition. What's not fair is what the NFL does, giving poor teams easier schedules to make them look better.

CARLSON: I would disagree. If you are setting it up that teams will make the playoffs solely based on finishing at the top of a certain column of teams (i.e. divisions), then you should have to play each of the teams in that column more than you play the other teams. If you play the same competition the same amount throughout all of the teams, then you shouldn't put teams in "columns" (divisions), it should just be from 1-14 (in the case of baseball). You're saying, "Any system is fair as long as you play the same competition," rolls right into this. How is it fair, if you are playing a balanced schedule, that just because someone finishes atop an arbitrary column, that they should make the playoffs ahead of you even though you had a better record?

COOPERSON: Fine, gripe about the setup. But don't just gripe in hindsight. Don't tell me who would have gotten in the playoffs, etc., etc. Think of all the strategies that would've been different had the teams all been competing with each other. You can't sit there and say that every team would've won exactly the same number of games that they did.

JAMES: Whining? *Whining?* I thought I was explaining how much I *enjoyed* this system, how the Royals' performance teaches you to savor each victory as one might savor a fresh coconut in the middle of the desert.

CARLSON: I am not griping in hindsight at all. The Phillies won the 1993 National League pennant, I have no problem with that. I just say, fix the future.

SKELTON: Correct me if I'm wrong, but only one team gets a wild-card berth from each league. Thus, there are still two divisions in which it's winner take all (the way it was from '69-93). Mind you, the races are not very exciting this year, but that's not a flaw in the system. That's a result of insufficient competition from inferior teams. If we were still in a two-league, four-division format the division leaders would be Atlanta, Baltimore, Seattle, and a race between S.F. and L.A. How's that different from this year?

Now I'm not trying to be argumentative or defend the wild-card system as a whole (I still like my job), but the plus side of this is a little surge by the young Pirates, a first-time trip to the postseason for Florida, and we've brought October back once more to the Bronx. These things are good.

I agree at least 100 percent with Ethan regarding the imperfections of the system. Why is it so bad that a lower-caliber team wins a division, or LCS or WS? I thought everyone loves an underdog in America! Unless of course you're a STATS person who believes underdogs simply can't win because the numbers say so. Weren't the WS Champion Royals of 1985 outscored by their opponents in the regular season?!?!?

JAMES: 1) As to the 1985 Royals being outscored by their opponents in the regular season, no, they weren't. That was the 1987 Twins.

2) If you get real ambitious, why don't you build a computer model of the various alignments. Properly constructed, a model could give you objective answers to questions such as:

a) How often does each format select the best team in baseball as the world champion?

b) How often does each format select an essentially average team as the world champion?

c) How many meaningful September games per season do you get with each format?

I did all of this once, but it's all been rendered obsolete by the restructuring.

PINTO: The division-champion 1984 Royals were outscored. The World Series-champion 1987 Twins were outscored. Those are the only two teams to make the playoffs (in a full season) while being outscored. The Giants will be the third this year.

PALACIOS: The whole purpose of the postseason is to make money, and it must be argued within that premise.

Why should the team with the hottest month win the whole thing? The arguments should be:

A) Pool all the teams in one huge division, and whoever has the best record at the end of the season wins. Period.

B) Let's make more money and have a playoff system.

Once you have agreed to Plan B, you have agreed to some sort of "unfairness."

SKELTON: Before you all freak out . . .

Dave Pinto already reminded me that the Braves were in the West and that the Marlins would win the East. MLB was still functioning under the same logic that keeps the Atlanta Falcons in the NFC West.

Gee, Mat, maybe Bud Selig has something with this Geographic Realignment Overhaul.

Had you all a little scared, didn't I?

OLKIN: Bill, I'm not sure if it's fair to fault me for "choosing" the Brewers as my team. I think that in many ways, our teams choose *us*. Whatever follows, you're stuck with, whether it's Selig, Herk Robinson or Bob Boone.

MOYER: If you want an argument for how crappy the wild card is, take a look at the lineup the Yankees put on the field last night, as they entered the game only three games from the division lead. Do you think that same lineup would've been out there if they were three games from being out of the playoffs altogether? Do you think they have any desire whatsoever to play the Mariners as the division winner? This is what I call the new September drama.

SCHINSKI: That is what's wrong with the current playoff system. The wild card should play the division winner with the best record. Home-field advantage should be based on record, not this stupid alternating division system!

And while I am at it, a five-game playoff series should be in the format 2-2-1, and the seven-game playoff series should be in the format 2-2-1-1-1. The 2-3-2 format should be reserved for the World Series. Take the travel days, dammit!

COOPERSON: Sorry, baseball purists—home-field for the LCS and WS has been on a rotating system for years!

OSBORNE: And for years, there was no wild card. When the wild card was instituted, the home-field advantage system should have been altered. It is absurd that a wild-card team should have an easier first-round matchup than the team that beat it out for the division title. Yet, that is exactly what will happen this year based on won-loss records. Jeff, I'm with you on this.

HENNINGER: Now that the wild card comes into the discussion, it's my turn to rag on baseball owners and schedule makers. Not only is it idiotic to go to a balanced schedule under a divisional arrangement, which *does* make the divisional winners the champions of *random* categories or divisions, it's equally idiotic to add interleague play under a wild-card system. So, while wild-card contestants in the NL Central (which, of course, there are none this year) get to feast on the Twinks, Royals, Brewers and Chisox, the wild-card candidates in the NL East have to battle the O's and Yanks. This year the Cubs fared well against the AL Central, which sends a warning about a wild-card race potentially being overly influenced by interleague play, but the fact is the Cubs seem light years away from wild-card contention anyway. Still, interleague play runs the risk of determining a wild-card winner at some point in time.

September 23—Albert Belle

OLKIN: Who Am I?

Year	Team	Lg	G	AB	R	H	2B	3B	HR	RBI	BB	SO	AVG	OBP	SLG
1996	ChA	AL	132	472	58	120	23	3	27	101	64	128	.254	.340	.487
1997	ChA	AL	155	609	86	165	43	1	29	110	53	103	.271	.331	.488

Answer: Danny Tartabull, 1996; and Albert Belle, 1997.

SCHINSKI: Gee, that was worth the $50 million.

MUNDO: A while back there was a mini-discussion involving Frank Thomas' '96 and '97 seasons and how similar they were. A couple of people commented on how it was more evidence that the "protection" theory is bunk.

Now I'm not saying the theory *isn't* garbage, but what if Belle had a Belle year in '97? Would Thomas' numbers be even more incredible this year?

JAMES: Maybe we're looking at this backwards. Maybe, rather than a good hitter making Frank Thomas better, Frank Thomas makes the hitter coming up behind him *worse*. The logic, I think, works just as well one way as the other, and there is much better empirical evidence for the "anti-protection" theory than there is for the protection racket theory. After all, remember how George Bell went down the tubes after the Sox signed *him* to hit behind Frank? I bet you could put his line up above, and he'd look just like Tartabull and Belle.

September 29—Barry Bonds

JAMES: Barry Bonds wound up the season with 40 homers, 37 stolen bases, 145 walks, and led a down-and-out team to a division championship.

Anybody else in baseball does that, you gotta figure people will notice.

PINTO: Two weeks ago Dan Patrick and I were arguing the NL MVP. At that point the argument was Piazza and Walker. I pointed out that if Bonds picked it up and carried the Giants to the title, he might get it. He did, and I'm hoping he does. In his last 13 games, he hit .342 with 10 XBH, 7 HR and 13 RBI.

JAMES: On the NL MVP. . . just based on what I know, I'd vote for Larry Walker. But Bonds is. . . what, one of the top three? And this has got to be about the eighth straight year that he was one of the top three players in the league. That's *really* amazing. Even Willie Mays didn't do that.

OLKIN: I'd still vote for Piazza ahead of Walker. Gee, Bill, I thought you'd be with me on this one.

JAMES: It could be you're right. Piazza plays dreadful defense for a team that folded down the stretch. Walker has the best raw numbers, so he starts out ahead. Maybe Piazza would pull ahead on a careful analysis.

PINTO: You are right about Walker, of course, but I think Bonds should have four MVPs already, so I'd like to see them make it up to him.

COOPERSON: Or if a nice guy does it. . .

PINTO: Part of my argument with Patrick was trying to debunk the dreadful defense argument. The fact is that the Dodgers always have a lower ERA with Piazza catching. So if his defense is so dreadful, it doesn't seem to hurt his staff.

JAMES: My God. . . Cooperson is now reminding us of the value of being a nice guy.

COOPERSON: Right. Pendleton is a joke.

Not so fast, Willie. I didn't say this was the way it *should* be; this might be the way it is. Fewer people want to see Bonds do well than they do Griffey; thus they are less willing to acknowledge Bonds' great performance.

JAMES: Nice Guys win MVP Awards

I understand this, Ethan. I have understood this since long before you began to instruct me on it. What I was astonished by is the fact that *you* pretended to understand the value of being politic.

COUSINS: Barry definitely deserves some respect for his excellent year but even more so for his incredible month. He was the definition of a *clutch* player in the month of September—coming through when his team needed him most. Does anyone know what his numbers were in the month of September or even from August 15 'til the end? It was definitely impressive and exciting to watch.

PINTO: Remember, clutch is in the eye of the beholder!

JAMES: I did a little analysis here. Bonds created an estimated 147 runs while using 403 outs. An average NL left fielder created .1867 runs per out this season.

The Giants, however, scored 377 runs and allowed 387 runs in I-forget-who-we-sold-this-name-to Park, whereas they scored 407 and allowed 406 on the road, which creates a raw park factor of .93972, and an adjusted park factor of .9440. Applying that to one-half of his games, an average NL left fielder could be expected to create .18152 runs per out in (Candlestick), which means 73 runs with 403 outs. Bonds was 74 runs better than average—147 over 73, almost exactly twice as productive as an average NL left fielder.

Same analysis for Walker. . . Walker created an estimated 178 runs (!!!) while using 387 outs. An average NL right fielder created .200 runs per out this season. The Rockies scored 545 runs and allowed 501 at home, with figures of 378 and 407 on the road (fortunately, all three teams played 81 games home and road, so we can ignore that.) This creates a raw park factor of 1.33248, adjusted 1.3087, which creates an expectation for a Colorado right fielder of .23087 runs/out. This would be 89.3 runs for a man using up Walker's outs, which means that Walker was 88.3 runs better than average.

This figure, however, would need to be adjusted again for *game* impact, since it takes more runs to win a game in Colorado than it does in (Candlestick). Making that adjustment, there is essentially no difference between the value of Bonds' numbers and the value of Walker's. Bonds was 2.01 times as effective as an average left fielder. Walker was 1.99 times as effective.

Piazza, however, blows them both away. That may be an overstatement, but it's clear who wins. Piazza created 149 runs (probably a record for a catcher, I don't know) while using 379 outs, and did so in a park where runs were scarce; the Dodgers scored 346 runs and allowing 280 runs at home, 396 and 365 on the road. That's a park factor of .8226, an adjusted park factor of .8352.

National League catchers this year actually hit better than left fielders did, and created .1883 runs per out. Adjusting this for Dodger Stadium, we have .17280 runs/out for a Dodger catcher, which is 65.5 runs for 379 outs. Piazza beat that by 83.6 runs. He was 2.28 times as productive as a typical National League catcher, making him a clear winner in this analysis.

Part of the problem of doing this type of analysis is that the standard of what constitutes a truly sophisticated analysis expand relentlessly, since we are now able to do things which were simply impossible 15 years ago. We should consider, for example:

a) Defense.

b) Situational Hitting Stats.

c) Big Game Impact.

d) Whether it is really appropriate to apply the left-field average to Bonds and the (higher) right-field average to Walker, since after all, left fielders are just right fielders who can't throw. It may not be entirely logical to say that because Bonds can't throw well enough to play right field, we won't hold him to the same expectations that we hold Walker.

I think you can, in good conscience, vote for any of the three.

Or David Segui.

Anyway, just for the halibut, I decided to add Jeff Bagwell and Craig Biggio to the study above. This led me to the discovery that I had made a significant (although non-fatal) error to the study as reported before. The statement that NL left fielders created more runs/out than catchers was incorrect. . . the actual averages are .1943 for left fielders and .1868 for catchers (.2178 for right fielders). The conclusion remains the same in outline although different in details:

1. Piazza was +84 runs, and 2.295 times as productive as a typical NL catcher.

2. Bonds was +71 runs, and 1.93 times as productive as a typical left fielder.

3. Walker was +80 runs, and 1.83 times as productive as a typical right fielder.

4. Craig Biggio comes in at +56 runs, and 1.75 times as productive as a typical second baseman.

5. Jeff Bagwell comes in at +49 runs, and 1.51 times as productive as a typical first baseman.

The selection of Biggio over Bagwell as the MVA (Most Valuable Astro) is surprising, but seems to hold up. The technical versions of the runs created version are largely consistent with the cruder versions *except* when a player has odd data in terms of HBP and GIDP. Biggio has the oddest and most remarkable data in terms of HBP and GIDP this season of any player in the history of baseball. He was hit by pitchers 34 times (which is. . .what, the third- or fourth-highest total of the century?) and grounded into no double plays. Ordinarily, a player *loses* on Times on Base when you consider GIDP and HBP; Biggio goes *up* by 34. Thus, Biggio is actually much better than you think he is when you just glance at his line.

Biggio still didn't create as many runs as Bagwell (145 to 131) and still used more outs (445 to 432), but when you consider that Biggio is a second baseman, he turns out (in this analysis, at least) to be slightly more valuable.

While we are on the subject of MVPs, the Cubs' MVP may be Sammy Sosa. Somebody made a comment here a month ago about Sammy being actually a below-average right fielder, which I found surprising and somewhat offensive, since I've always liked the guy. But I ran Sammy through the MVP work also, and actually it's correct—in fact, he was far worse than an average NL right fielder, adjusting for Wrigley Field. Thirty-four runs worse, 85 versus an expectation of 119.

You realize the Cubs this year scored just 284 runs in road games? They scored 403 at home, and still had one of the worst offenses in the league, even without adjusting. Ugh.

COUSINS: Regarding Sammy, he was definitely the MVP for the Cubs this year. Although he had a down year in the average department and a horrific year in the strikeout department; he drove in 119 runs for a team that was not putting very many people on base. Without his power the Cubs would have been lucky to win 50 games. For a team so bad, Sosa had pretty impressive home run and RBI numbers.

FAUST: Without Sammy they'd have been lucky to win 50? Does that assume they replace him with a zero? I think we've reasonably concluded he was below average as a right fielder this year, meaning that if they were without him (and got an average right fielder), they'd have won more games. Of course, maybe he's the best right fielder you can get for $8 or $10 million per year.

And how did he have impressive home-run numbers for a team so bad? How does that relate? Oh, must be impressive considering the lack of protection in the lineup.

COUSINS: You have to admit, it doesn't take much to be the MVP for a team such as the Cubs this year. Who else would you give it to? Grace—who hit .320 but doesn't drive in enough runs and can't even hit 15 homers playing in Wrigley as a home park.

JAMES: Good point. The Cubs may not have an MVP. Dave Clark, maybe? Only guy on the team I was actually happy to see come up in a key situation.

COUSINS: I agree, Clark was very impressive after coming over to the Cubs. Tapani was impressive, especially coming off hand surgery and losing his "best" pitch.

JAMES: I have Grace as four runs better than an average NL first baseman, which may make him the Cubs' best everyday player. Tapani was great. So we have a choice of a third of a season of "great," a full season of "hardly ever played but was pretty good," a full season of "average" and a full season of "frankly terrible but at least he does *something*." I suppose I may have to vote for Tapani.

FREER: Hands down: Mark Clark. He was the catalyst in dumping highly overrated and overpaid Mel Rojas and McRae.

SCHINSKI: Don't knock Grace. His RBI are a function of the guys in front of him getting on base. He didn't have that. He's a contact hitter, not a home-run hitter. I would take a single over a whiff (which Sosa excels at) anytime. He's also one of the few Cubs to take walks. A real rarity. Besides, he's a Gold Glove first baseman.

COUSINS: With the kind of season the Cubs had, you try to look for any bright spots as a fan and I would say that one of the most overlooked bright spots for the Cubs would have to be Dave Clark and his contributions in pinch hitting. I don't know exactly how many pinch-hit RBI he had, but I know it was impressive and he also hit .301 for the season. Maybe I'm looking too hard, but I would have to give Dave Clark a thumbs-up on the season.

October 4—Hit Batters

JAMES: The Houston Astros this year had an even 100 batters hit by pitches. This is the highest total in the major leagues at least since 1989, and I suspect that it may be the highest total since the dawn of the lively ball era in 1920. Anybody know?

SKELTON: The funny thing is, 73 of those 100 Astros HBP hit Jeff Bagwell in the hand.

KRETSCHMANN: It is the most since 1899, when two teams got plunked 100+ times. Since 1920, the highest total prior to Astros was the 1996 Blue Jays getting hit 92 times.

October 7—Indians vs. Yankees

COUSINS: I just thought I would make a few comments about the Division Series between between the Yankees and the Indians. Although I would consider myself a "National League fan," I thought that this series featured some of the most exciting baseball I have seen all year. Between last night's game and Game 4 you could not ask for more excitement and better baseball. What a series!! Although he did not pitch flawlessly in his two starts, I think Jaret Wright showed that he has what it takes to be a successful pitcher in the league. As a 21-year-old rookie, he handled the pressure at Yankee Stadium pretty well, especially after falling behind 3-0 in the first inning in Game 2. And then he comes back in Game 5 and pitches an excellent game that was finished nicely by the bullpen. One last thought: I found it kind of interesting that Joe Torre benched Wade Boggs in the series to go with Charlie Hayes for "his defense," and Hayes thanked him by making three errors in the series. However, he did hit .333 and made an excellent play at second last night, diving to the middle to take away a hit.

OLKIN: Ask Jaret Wright about "experience."

Moyer's out sick, so I'm covering for him.

PINTO: I think there was a matter here of dislike of a player interfering in a manager's judgment. I'm told Torre does not like Boggs. Now that's fine. But that doesn't take away from the fact that Boggs is a much better hitter than Hayes, and his defense isn't bad enough to counter that. I was not only surprised that Boggs did not start Game 4, I was surprised that he was never used as a pinch hitter in that game. I think this bit of mismanaging could have cost the Yankees the series. Hayes did hit .333, but his OBP was .313, and he had no extra-base hits, so I think his offensive contribution was minimal.

JAMES: Boggs hit .362 this year after the All-Star break.

OLKIN: And didn't allow a single earned run.

COUSINS: Boggs had struggled in the middle of the season and been replaced by Hayes, but toward the end of the season Boggs "won" his job back by doing what he does best and that is putting the bat on the ball. His average started to come back up to a respectable number and then he is rewarded by being benched in the Division Series. I agree with Pinto in that this is a case of poor managing due to a manager's dislike for a particular player.

PINTO: Yes, and Hayes' average faded toward the end of the year. If you want Charlie for defense, wait until you have a lead in the seventh. Don't hamstring your offense when you have a better player on the bench.

COOPERSON: Funny that Hayes apparently made some enemies in both his stints in Philly—Jim Fregosi said that Hayes was one of his biggest disappointments there—twice. Yet, he plays in the postseason because his manager doesn't like the other guy.

MITTLEMAN: Please keep in mind that after Boggs theoretically won his job back, he came up injured again during the final week of the season with an Achilles tendon problem. It's also possible that Torre felt his aches and pains would limit his range at third. That's not an excuse for not going to him earlier as a pinch hitter, but it does reflect on the defensive decision.

October 7—NL Championship Series

COUSINS: Does the Braves' postseason experience override the fact that the Marlins have had the Braves' number this year? The Marlins won eight out of their 12 meetings in the regular season.

PINTO: Four of those eight losses came in games started by the Braves' fifth starters. The main starters pitched very well against Florida, and three of the games started by the top four were lost by the bullpen.

ZMINDA: I agree that Florida's regular-season success against the Braves doesn't mean much at all. Wait'll we get to Game 4, when the Braves trot out the league's only 20-game winner and the Marlins have to start Charlie Hough.

I'm exaggerating, but you get my drift. Braves in six.

COUSINS: What a feeling knowing that come Game 4, one of the top four pitchers in the whole league will be starting for your team. If that doesn't give your team some confidence, not much will. Boasting the best pitching rotation in a long time combined with the past six years of postseason experience, the Braves are going to be hard to stop. I agree with Don, Braves in six (maybe five)!!

MOYER: I know in my mind I shouldn't be writing this. I am sick today, but "the past six years of postseason experience" as a reason for picking the Braves in a STATS mail message just might kill me. So why didn't the past five years of postseason experience beat the Yankees last year? Why didn't the past two years beat the Phillies in 1993? Why didn't the past year beat the Blue Jays in 1992? The Braves have won one World Series in four tries since 1991. I've already been told that examples don't count, but then, please, show me examples of postseason experience counting. I think the Braves have as good a chance to win as anyone this year, but it's because the players they've assembled (especially the pitchers) have as good a chance of catching fire for a couple of short series as any other team. I just can't believe for a second that it has anything to do with postseason experience. I feel totally confident any objective study (I've been begging for one for years) would prove this out. I have to go lay on the couch now.

PINTO: The other thing here is, who on the Braves actually has six years postseason experience? The team has radically changed since 1991. Only Blauser, Glavine, Smoltz and Belliard are left from that team (Lemke is injured for the playoffs).

JAMES: I think Moyer is probably wrong. I think if you studied teams in postseason play with essentially the same won-lost record, you would find that the one which has more recent postseason experience would probably win 55 percent of the time.

I'll run it myself if nobody else gets to it.

SKELTON: Is winning 55 percent of the time because you have more players with greater postseason experience a significant indicator?

You could probably find stuff like:

Teams with more players who still wear low-top cleats win 77 percent of the time in the postseason.

or

Teams with a higher percentage of players who chew gum rather than tobacco are likely to win 73 percent of their postseason games.

The postseason experience factor seems too arbitrary. Is Jeff Blauser more valuable to the Braves than Chipper Jones? Or Belliard over Andruw Jones coming off the bench? Certainly not.

Were the Indians at a disadvantage last year with 34-year-old Julio Franco as their 1B/DH because he had never been to the postseason? What good was Mitch Williams' postseason experience in 1993? He still made a bad pitch.

Good players should be good players in the postseason, regardless of their experience. Guys like Barry Bonds do poorly because they don't match up well against the opponent's pitchers or he picked the wrong time of the year to slump. Gritty "winners" like Jack McDowell and Randy Johnson have failed because they had to face teams (Toronto and Baltimore) who had always beaten them up. One had experience, the other didn't. I think it's safe to say experience had little to do with it.

How is it the Braves have been to five of the last six World Series, but lost four of them? There *have* to be *more* important factors that determine World Series winners or postseason success than experience. Factors that would virtually nullify the effects of previous experience.

That's just my opinion. I could be wrong.

PINTO: A little "Baseball Tonight" preview: Maddux allowed one unearned run all season, five unearned runs tonight. In his career with the Braves, in 157 regular-season starts, he had allowed 27 unearned runs. In the postseason with the Braves, he has now allowed 15 unearned runs in 14 starts.

And the walk was intentional.

My point with the Maddux unearned runs is that his defense has let him down in the postseason. Maddux has a bad rap in the postseason, but he's had some poor defense behind him.

JAMES: Not to argue with you, David, a better explanation of the odd data on Maddux' UER can be found in a common bumper sticker. S--- Happens.

PINTO: Sure. I just find it interesting that the feces seem to be concentrated in the postseason.

MOYER: Maybe I'm up a tree again, but did anyone else wonder if maybe Maddux on the mound had anything to do with the official scorer's decision to give Lofton the three-base error. It's my notion that I see easier messed-up plays than that one get scored hits all the time. My usual rule of thumb is, if it's hit hard, it's a hit. I think a ball hit to the center-field wall qualifies. I don't mean to open a discussion of what *should* and *shouldn't* be an error, in general. I'm just saying it seems to me that Gary Sheffield's ball is usually scored a hit.

ZMINDA: I agree with Steve that the call on the Lofton error was ridiculous. The official scorer's guideline on what's an error is a play that could be made "with ordinary effort." There's no way a catch where a player's about to crash into the wall is ordinary.

Unearned runs or not, Maddux pitched badly last night. His defense could have helped him, sure, but he didn't do a lot to help himself. There were a *lot* of hard-hit balls off him.

The "postseason experience factor" is a natural for the *Scoreboard*. Until we see some real data, we're just talking off the tops of our heads here. We'll do it (but first we have to enter the missing postseason data into our system!).

COOPERSON: Also, Lofton's defensive ability is considered. Lofton's good, he should catch that, call it an E. If Pete Incaviglia fails to catch the exact same ball, the scorer might call it a hit because, hey, we can't really expect Inky to make that play.

ZMINDA: That's out-and-out wrong. Carrying this to its logical extreme, good fielders could wind up getting charged with more errors than bad fielders due to miscues on plays like the one last night. Makes no sense, and that's why the scorer's guidelines are the way they are.

COOPERSON: You're right—it's wrong that it should happen that way, but I believe it does sometimes. Scorer's guidelines are nice, but we're talking about a world where scorers go into the clubhouse after the game and let players try to convince them to change their decisions. Plenty of politics and illogical ideas figure into their decisions.

PINTO: I tend to agree with you. However, it did look like Lofton was under it, and should have caught it. If the game had been a no-hitter at the time, it definitely would have been an error.

MUNDO: . . . similar to Ryan Klesko's goofy catch last night. Yet another easy fly ball that Klesko turned into an adventure.

I don't know if he was kidding, but Joe Morgan said something like, "That was a routine play that Klesko turned into a *great* play!"

NEYER: I suspect Bill is right, but not necessarily for the reason most people might think.

If a team is in the postseason two years in a row, that suggests a high level of quality, right?

If a team is in the postseason this year but wasn't last year, they're more likely a fluke, right?

You probably see what I'm getting at. Reaching the postseason six straight times suggests an amazing organizational strength, and *that* is what wins ballgames, more than experience per se.

Or so my theory goes.

My best friend once came up with the idea that if the best player ever at the position would have made the play and you don't, it's an error. Using this criteria, Chipper Jones' play in the first should have been an error.

October 10—AL Championship Series

ZMINDA: I really thought Davey Johnson blew last night's game (Game 2 of the ALCS) by not bringing in Jesse Orosco to pitch to Jim Thome. There are all kinds of reasons why this move should have been made:

1. Lefthanded batters hit .107 against Orosco this year.

2. Thome was 1-for-13 lifetime against Orosco.

3. While Thome hit better against lefties this year than in the past, he had 36 HR vs. RHP, four vs. LHP.

4. Despite the fact that he'd had a fine year in '97, Armando Benitez has been shaky in the postseason in both '96 and '97. He gave up three HR in the '96 playoffs, and another in this year's Division Series.

5. Benitez was throwing pitches that were moving all over the place with an umpire who had a tight strike zone (Jim Joyce) behind the plate.

As soon as I realized that Johnson was going to let Benitez pitch to Thome, I thought, "He's either going to hit a home run or get a walk." Benitez got the lesser of the two evils, at which point I went to hide in the kitchen (I'm pulling for the Birds, as you might have guessed). I wasn't the least bit surprised when Grissom crushed the game-winning homer.

I think Johnson is a terrific manager, but I still don't understand this strategy at all. The key at-bat was Thome. . . why didn't Johnson bring in the guy who could get him out? I just don't get it.

COOPERSON: Should we renew the Davey Johnson debate?

NEYER: Well said. If I'd had my wits about me last night, I would have written something similar for today's column.

I'm going to check the Baltimore papers today and see if Davey supplied any rationale for the non-move. Quite curious.

OLKIN: I'm not sure if I would have gone to Orosco or not, but I could see why Johnson decided to leave Benitez in. As to points 1, 2 & 3, they're all valid; the numbers indicated pretty strongly that Orosco was the man for the situation. But just watching Benitez with the naked eye, he looked especially unhittable on this particular night. He was throwing 95-99 MPH consistently, with great movement, and no one was making solid contact off him. As to point No. 4, it's true that he hasn't pitched well in the postseason, but I'd put more weight on his tremendous performance this season. There's little doubt that he's a quality pitcher, and a handful of failures doesn't do much to dissuade me of that.

I was aware of what the numbers said, but my eyes told me Benitez could get Thome out. I think what happened is that he got mad and lost his focus when the ump called ball four instead of strike three on Thome. Thome did go around, and Benitez did get hot about it. Maybe Johnson should have gotten him out of there right then; I don't know. But I do know that the Indians hadn't been hitting him at all, and then he got distracted and threw a fat one to Grissom. But I don't think the home run would have happened if he'd just given Thome a crystal-clear, no-doubt-about-it base on balls.

HENNINGER: I agree, especially considering how important command was, in light of the home-plate ump's strike zone. For instance, he squeezed Charles Nagy on his 2-1 pitch to Mike Bordick, setting up the hitter-friendly count on which Bordick delivered his two-run double that appeared to be the game-winner. Nagy's chances were better if he faced a 2-2 count with Bordick. As for Benitez, his command hasn't been overly impressive when I've seen him pitch on TV. I certainly was more fearful of what Thome was going to do than Marquis Grissom, but I like an Orosco-Grissom matchup better than Benitez-Thome, anyway. (I'm assuming only Benitez and Orosco were candidates to pitch in the inning; I don't know if Myers was warming up at the time.)

MOYER: I can say something like:

"Davey Johnson can manage like Chuck Tanner for the rest of the postseason for all I care," if you'd like, Don. Then he'll get hit by a truck.

PINTO: I believe Johnson was thinking that he wanted Benitez to pitch to Grissom, so he would allow a walk to Thome. Obviously it backfired.

October 13—MVP

OLKIN: Who am I?

Year	Team	Lg	G	AB	R	H	2B	3B	HR	RBI	BB	SO	AVG	OBP	SLG
1996	Col	NL	156	613	142	211	45	8	40	128	61	114	.344	.408	.639
1997	Col	NL	153	568	143	208	46	4	49	130	78	90	.366	.452	.720

That's Ellis Burks, 1996, and Larry Walker, 1997. Burks finished third in the NL MVP voting behind Piazza and Caminiti.

October 15—NL Championship Series

HENZLER: It will be interesting to see how Kevin Brown recovers from his 140-pitch effort last night (in Game 6 of the NLCS), especially considering the possible lingering effects from his recent illness. The Marlins have done an admirable job of limiting Brown's pitch counts since he joined them in 1996. In 65 regular-season starts for the Marlins, Brown topped the 122-pitch mark only once, and that was a 127-pitch effort this September.

With the unavailability of Alex Fernandez, the Marlins probably can't afford to have Brown be ineffective during the World Series. If last night's effort has an adverse effect on him, Jim Leyland might be second-guessed for not bringing in a reliever late in the game. Of course, I can understand Leyland's logic. You need to get to the World Series before you can worry about winning it, and I'm sure he didn't want a Stan Belinda repeat.

OLKIN: And if Livan Hernandez' 141-pitch outing takes its toll, they're really screwed.

COOPERSON: Didn't it stand to reason that the longer the Series went, the better for Atlanta, with Florida facing the prospect of running out of pitching? Leyland needed lots of innings from his starters.

ZMINDA: He's really going to extremes not to use his bullpen, isn't he? It's almost like there's this voice in his head going "1992, 1992, 1992. . ."

The situations aren't really comparable, though. He has a much better pen with the Marlins than he did in Pittsburgh. It was awfully risky having Brown pitch to Chipper Jones last night when logic dictated that he bring in Dennis Cook. Joe Morgan's comment—"He doesn't want to bring in Cook because Cook's role isn't to close games"—makes no sense at all, of course.

OLKIN: Wasn't he criticized (in hindsight, of course) for staying with Doug Drabek "too long" in Game 7 of the '92 NLCS?

MOYER: A friend of mine years ago always used to say that someday it's going to be discovered that all sports are just fixed entertainment events, like pro wrestling. A game like last night really makes one wonder. I would have to guess that the heavy betting action was on the Braves and the under. So Tom Glavine gives up seven walks (probably hasn't done that since 1988, if ever), the Marlins win, and the two teams combine for a whopping 11 runs. I like to believe thoughts like this are total nonsense, but I still wonder sometimes.

CALLIS: I had a friend who said the same thing, though just about the NFL. Agreed, this does seem impossible, but all those "botched" field goals this year? Hmmmm.

OLKIN: At least he was consistent about the use of his pitchers. He didn't make a move this time based on the criticism he received for failing to make a similar move in the past. Gene Mauch tried it both ways. . . he refused to bring in the lefthander (Hassler) to pitch to Cecil Cooper in the fifth game of the '82 ALCS, and he lost. Then, in the fifth game of the '86 ALCS, he *did* bring in the lefthander (Lucas) to pitch to Gedman, replacing Witt, who was throwing a hell of a game. And he lost with that one too. It makes you wonder, somewhere in the back of his mind, when he called for Lucas, was he really calling for Hassler?

COOPERSON: Whose fault was '64?

PINTO: Actually, I think Leyland wanted to take him out, but Brown talked him out of it.

ZMINDA: I love good conspiracy theories, but if the games were really fixed, wouldn't MLB and NBC have arranged things for the Braves to win last night to give them bigger ratings for Game 7?

This isn't totally twisted, though. I often feel that in the NBA playoffs, the league helps one team or another during a series by assigning certain referees. Whenever they want the Bulls to lose so NBC will get another game or two to broadcast, Hue Hollins always shows up.

So maybe we should be asking ourselves: Did someone from another network poison Frank Pulli?

CALLIS: I thought Brown said in the postgame interview that he was surprised they left him in. After all, Nen just blew away Atlanta this year.

ZMINDA: And Leyland would have taken Brown out in the ninth, but he couldn't because he was under the stands smoking another cigarette.

PINTO: Peter Gammons told me a great story about Mauch and the '82 LCS. Mauch used to play out the game in his mind before hand. He basically told Peter that Game 5 would come down to Cooper with men on base and he'd have to decide if he should bring in Hassler. He thought there would be no way Hassler could get Cooper out, and figured he'd get Cooper to line to third. Well, he didn't bring in Hassler, Cooper lined the ball into left and the Angels lost.

SCHINSKI: Brown wanted to stay in the game for the seventh and eighth. He was surprised they left him in in the ninth especially since a few guys got on base.

WEINDEL: On the way in today I heard a man on the radio wonder if the NBA doesn't fix the NBA lottery so premier players go to big markets. I think he cited Ewing to New York and Shaq to the Magic as examples.

ELMAN: Have you quietly added Oliver Stone to the STATS roster?

MUNDO: I've always thought Albert Belle kinda looks like Junkyard Dog.

OLKIN: Notice how the pitch that tipped off Lenny Webster's glove went back and to the left, back and to the left, back and. . .

COOPERSON: Take note tonight. Look for some activity in the sixth-floor window of the B&O Warehouse outside Camden Yards. Special delivery to O's clubhouse was a bunch of bats? I don't think so. I'm sure if the Orioles lose tonight, the autopsy will be badly botched.

With those 14 Fox microphones, many sounds will confuse the viewers, who will have no idea what direction some of the sounds came from. It's all a plot, I tell you.

OLKIN: And who's this kid named "Jamey" who pitches for Colorado? A "second" Wright?

HENNINGER: Look for the second Wright on the grassy knoll.

JAMES: Isn't the Congressional Representative from Miami named Clay Shaw? By the way, I think I saw Keith Hernandez in the bullpen, hiding behind Kramer's hair. . .

MOYER: I heard a Hideo Nomo interview earlier this season. The Dodgers were playing the Astros and there were suspicions that the Astros' backup catcher had partied a little too hard the evening before. Nomo referred to a "glassy Knorr." See, I told you.

PINTO: Call Mulder and Scully!

October 16—World Series Managers

FREER: This will be Cleveland skipper Mike Hargrove's second World Series (he also managed the Indians in the 1995 Series), while his managerial foe, Jim Leyland, has never been to the Series before. Does Hargrove's experience give him "the edge"? Not necessarily. Since WWII, the 46 managers in their first World Series have been more successful than the 21 managers who've made it to a second.

Experience	W-L	Pct
1st Series	23-23	.500
2nd Series	9-12	.429

Any guesses why this is?

HENZLER: Those winning percentages sure look like random chance to me. Twenty-one events is a relatively small sample size, and 9-12 is not an outrageous percentage. The larger the sample size gets, the more likely that winning percentage should gravitate toward the .500 mark, which would indicate that the experience of World Series managers actually has a negligible effect.

OLKIN: I agree with you Jim, to a point. It's true that the sample sizes are too small to lead to any definitive conclusions, but in a way, that's the point. We both know that one of the first things we're going to hear is how Hargrove has an edge because he's been there before. The point is that the evidence does not support this assertion, and suggests that the opposite may be true. That's all.

MOYER: Not that it's worth anything, but here's my stupid theory:

Anything can happen in a short series. To take the NFL adage one step further, anything can happen on any given seven days. The only thing I think that really matters at all in a short series is pure player ability—a great rookie will be great more times than not, a stinky veteran will still stink more times than not. But don't bet on that stuff, either. Anybody who has enough talent to be on the postseason roster in the first place has enough talent to be lucky for a few games. I think luck is, by far, the most overlooked aspect in all of baseball. Sometimes the grounder goes through the hole, sometimes it goes right to the shortstop. Sometimes the errant pitch gets lined right to the center fielder, sometimes it goes over the wall or into the gap. In a short series, the luck factor is magnified X times over. In a seven- or five-game series, flip a coin, you'll be correct as many times as anyone else.

MILLER: Al Weis, in response to Steve Moyer's e-mail.

DEWAN: Amazing! I actually agree with Mr. Moyer on this one!!

ZMINDA: I agree with Steve that luck is a much bigger factor than most people realize. Rob Neyer wrote his SportsZone column the other day on the Braves in postseason; by the Pythagorean Theorem, they should have won two-thirds of their games, but instead they were 27-29 (if memory serves). And they *didn't* lose because of a shaky bullpen, either. . . Rob's figures showed the Braves' pen has been excellent overall in the postseason.

There's also this. Reggie Jackson will be known forever as a great clutch hitter because he batted .357 with 10 HR in 27 World Series games. But in the LCS—where the players always say the pressure is greater—Jackson hit .227 with six HR and only 20 RBI in 45 games. Had his A's and Yankees lost most of those LCS instead of winning them—and they would have, if his teams had performed like he did—Jackson would probably have a postseason reputation about equal to Barry Bonds. Luck's a huge factor in a short series.

OLKIN: Obviously, as Steve says, luck is a huge factor in a short series. Anyone who disagrees can go review a game or two from the Cleveland-Baltimore series. But I would still argue that if you ignore luck and just focus on the relative importance of managing versus talent, a manager can have more impact on the outcome of a World Series than on a typical stretch of seven regular-season games.

In the World Series, a million different circumstances create unique situations that the managers must deal with. They make their choices, and they succeed or fail, but many of the decisions would have been unnecessary in the regular season.

In the World Series, one of the most important things a manager must do is set up his starting rotation. He can use his ace in Games 1, 4 and 7, or he can use his No. 4 starter. He can bring back a guy on short rest if he needs to. During the regular season, the rotation pretty much runs itself, and most managers don't need to tinker with it, outside of injuries, doubleheaders or demotions to the bullpen.

There are also a million options that are perfectly viable for a seven-game series that don't exist during the regular season, for practical purposes. Some of the most creative and daring managerial maneuvers have taken place in the World Series. Connie Mack put Lefty Grove in the bullpen. Mayo Smith put his center fielder at shortstop. Bob Lemon pinch-hit for Tommy John, who was pitching well, in the fifth inning. The Phillies gave a start to their relief ace, Jim Konstanty. Two years later, the Dodgers used their closer, Joe Black, to start Games 1, 4 and 7.

We've already seen Hargrove and Leyland do some odd things. Hargrove wouldn't platoon Jim Thome during the season, and Leyland wouldn't let Kevin Brown or Livan Hernandez throw 140 pitches.

It seems to me that managers have more of an opportunity to make an impact—positive or negative—in the postseason. With the players, in the aggregate, nothing changes. They just play.

MOYER: But so much of what are historically considered genius or stupid short-series manager moves come down to luck too. If Mickey Stanley boots a ball to lose a game (which certainly can happen to the best of shortstops), Mayo Smith looks like a dunce. If Salomon Torres happens to have a great day against the Dodgers in 1993 for Dusty Baker, he's not questioned for all time, but looks like Connie Mack with Howard Ehmke. I was amazed that Leyland was prepared to start Tony Saunders in Game 7 (or had him in the rotation at all, for that matter). In a short series, the worst of players can be the hero (ask Buddy Biancalana) and the best of players can be the goat (ask Tom Glavine). The "right" managerial choice all comes down to results and the results are as much luck as anything else in a game or two.

JAMES: 1) Mathematically, a one-game edge in won-lost record translates to approximately a .007 edge in expected wins head-to-head, generally speaking. When a 100-win team plays a 90-win team in regular season, the 10 wins become .070, and the 100-win team will win about 57 percent of the games.

2) This edge almost precisely doubles in a seven-game series, within normal ranges of comparison. If a team would win 51 percent of games against a given opponent, they will win a seven-game series 52 percent of the time. If they would win 55 percent of the games, they will win 60 percent of the series. You can work out the math if you don't believe me.

3) If you study historical World Series and playoffs, it is amazing how well this holds up after the fact. If you put a 100-win team against a 90-win team in the World Series, the 100-win team is going to win about 64 percent of the time.

4) Thus, the idea that in a seven-game match you can flip a coin and do as well as anybody else is not exactly correct. If team A is actually better than team B, team A can be expected to win 60 percent of the time or a little more.

Of course there are many, many upsets (like Cleveland vs. Baltimore and Florida vs. Atlanta), but if you study it, you'll find that there are quite significantly more non-upsets than upsets. The better team does win a clear majority of the time.

5) Whether there are patterns in upsets, such as veteran teams upsetting experienced teams, good bullpens being extra important, top starting pitchers being extra important, power teams doing better than singles-hitting teams. . . all of those are harder to prove. I am inclined to think that some of these distinctions are meaningful. But I doubt that any of them is more

telling than the quality of the team. If you bet on the better team, you'll win more often than you lose.

MUNDO: Bill, are you implying you're a betting man? For shame!

Speaking of which, according to today's *Tribune* the opening line for the Series favors Florida at -140 (which means in order to win $100 you'd have to bet $140 that Florida would win it all). A line of -140 is the same as saying the Marlins have a 58 percent chance of winning the Series.

GREENBERGER: A manager makes a decision—a player just plays. You think the manager is somehow more responsible for the outcome in a given situation because he has options; pinch-hit, new pitcher, change the rotation. But Robbie Alomar doesn't decide to fly out to end the series. He just fails, or is unlucky, depending on how you look at it. Comparing players and managers is apples and oranges.

October 16—Braves/Indians Trade

FULLAM: The arguments in favor of Marquis Grissom lead me to believe that a number of Associated Press reporters need some serious therapy. "Hey, Grissom is such a swell guy, he didn't complain about being moved to the bottom of the Indians' lineup even though his OBP is a phenomenal .317! What a team player!" Come on, the guy scored 74 runs despite spending part of the season at the top of one of the best lineups in baseball. . . but hey, is that important when he gets hugs and handshakes from opposing players?

Justice had a career year at the plate—no doubt about it. Anyone who thinks Grissom helped Cleveland take home the pennant is kidding themselves.

MOYER: I look at it this way: Grissom is a crappy leadoff hitter, but he's a mighty fine No. 9 hitter. At least the Indians had the sense to bat him where he looks good, which the Braves never had.

FULLAM: Grissom is an above-average No. 9 hitter—I don't think I'd go so far as to say he's "mighty fine." But in any case, all the talk in the preseason concerning the Braves-Indians trade was about how Cleveland "got two All-Stars in exchange for one." Grissom is hardly an All-Star, and I still contend that Lofton has far more value now than either of the two players he was traded for (assuming the Braves can keep him).

MOYER: You're right, Kevin. The AL average No. 9 hitter is better than I thought. (The NL ain't so hot.) However, I'm not so sure I'd take Lofton anymore over a healthy (wishful thinking) Justice and Grissom, no matter how overrated he is. Lofton isn't going to hit .350 or whatever every year, which was his whole value this season. In my mind, Kenny Lofton is the biggest individual player mystery going into 1998.

MITTLEMAN: The point has always been that the Braves traded Justice and Grissom for Lofton and Alan Embree. You continually want to point to OBP and Grissom just as a leadoff hitter and that's never been the way to evaluate this trade, which I told you back in the spring when it originally happened.

There were so many intangibles that these two players brought to the Indians' clubhouse that you could readily see when you walked in there as compared to last year. Belle and Lofton were major problems in Cleveland, something you don't see in the stats.

Did Kenny Lofton have a better statistical year than Marquis Grissom? Yes, no one is arguing that, but neither player lived up to expectations. Were the Indians a better team after trading Lofton for these two players? Yes, and that is the point. Will the Indians be more secure in the future as a result of the deal? Yes, and that's point No. 2. Did Marquis Grissom outperform Lofton during the crucial postseason? Yes, Grissom hit only .250 in the ninth spot, but Lofton had a stellar .175 batting leadoff.

The point has always been whether the Braves gave up too much in this blockbuster deal. There's no argument anymore, they did and they will be the first to admit it. Of course, the primary factor for the imbalance was Justice's comeback, but here's the real salt in the wound—Lofton is gone now and the Braves have Alan Embree and no World Series appearance to show for it. Lofton not only hurt the Braves with his lackluster playoff, he hurt his pocketbook as well because of his inability to play big, and his incredible falloff in stolen-base percentage this year is going to drive his market price downward. It's not just about OBP and who is a better leadoff man. It's about team results, chemistry, playing big at the right time and signability for the future.

DEWAN: "Mighty fine" and "above-average"—seem about the same to me!

ZMINDA: I have to say I agree with Mike M. on this one. My main objection to the trade at the time it was made was that it would prevent Giles from getting playing time. As it turned out, he played about as much as anyone could have reasonably expected (and very well, also). It also turned out that Justice was far from finished. . . and a lot more signable than Lofton was. Justice wound up having a lot better year than Lofton did. Whatever the Tribe got from Grissom was a bonus.

All in all, this turned out to be a great trade for Cleveland.

MOYER: "It's about team results, chemistry, playing big at the right time and signability for the future."

Hoo, baby. Where do I start?

ELMAN: Not having the baseball knowledge of everyone receiving this message, and representing the general fan, can't one conclude that for this year, Cleveland got the better of the trade because the Indians are in the Series and the Braves are not. I realize that may sound simplistic and does not take into account all factors involved, but isn't that the idea of any trade (make your team better and get to the Series)?

FULLAM: First of all, how could you say Lofton didn't live up to expectations? He had a stellar defensive year in center field and had an OBP of .409! What more were they expecting out of him? I know you want to discount these numbers and talk more about "team results" and "chemistry," but the fact of the matter is that Grissom was at best an average center fielder and Lofton turned in an All-Star performance. Based on Justice's injury history, age, and salary, he was (and still is) a risky investment; the Indians cashed in big on his stellar season this year, but I think everyone would agree that Lofton has a lot more "left in the tank" career-wise than Justice does. You say that the Indians had better chemistry than the Braves did this year, but Atlanta had a far better regular season. True, they didn't make it to the Series, but I wouldn't say that Lofton's struggles were the chief reason why. . . nor would I say that Grissom was anywhere near the MVP of the ALCS.

OLKIN: But Mike—the Indians didn't improve with Justice and Grissom this year. They declined by 12½ games. Cleveland's good fortune in the postseason (and Atlanta's ill fortune) have little to do with determining who got the better end of the deal. One last point: Atlanta isn't going to "lose" Lofton for nothing. They used the money they freed up to sign their starters. Anyone can come up with outfielders. The Indians have hitters like Bruce Aven, Richie Sexson and Sean Casey coming up, but they have no place to put them, because they've locked up all their outfielders. They sure could use some starters, though.

MITTLEMAN: They expected him to be more of a basestealing threat as well, the type of player who could change the outcome of ballgames all by himself as he did in Cleveland. Lofton's caught stealings were 20 and fully negated the dividends they expected on the basepaths. On this, he fell way short. Your comment that Grissom is at best an average center fielder (I assume you are talking about his defense only here and not the combination of offense and defense), is way out of bounds. Lofton made more errors, had a few less assists, consequently less of a range factor, and their zone ratings (a stat which I hesitate to even quote) were about equal. Lofton batted .244 during September and had a poor postseason. Grissom came on strong when it counted the most hitting .290 in September and furnished key hits in the playoffs.

Again, and for the last time, you keep wanting to make this a Lofton vs. Grissom deal. If that were the case, I would be singing your song right alongside you. But it wasn't. You also never want to address the future insofar as where each team stands after this. Grissom is not the offensive force that Lofton is, but he is equal defensively and he's a decent hitter that can do some things better than Lofton like hit for more power. Who knows? Next year, without having to deal with the injury and the trade shock, he may return to his '96 performance. They stole roughly the same amount of bases and I am not going to go into the intangibles anymore because you scoff at them even though every major league team strives to get them.

Cleveland ended up going further, got more overall talent split between two players, and got more future out of the deal assuming everyone stays healthy. This whole argument was about which club ended up with the better deal, not who is better between Lofton and Grissom and not just about one season, although that's precisely the shelf life of Lofton's existence in

Atlanta. Cleveland was the winner from day one, they are now and they will be in the longer term. Case closed.

OLKIN: On the most basic level, yes, but. . . if you trade your Yugo for a Mercedes so you can drive to California, and on the way you get struck and killed by a meteorite, have you made a bad deal?

SCHINSKI: I agree with Elman on this. What matters is you got to the Series. It doesn't matter that Cleveland was 12½ games worse in the standings. If you call getting Justice and going the Series "getting hit by a meteorite," then I hope all the Cubs get hit by meteorites.

COOPERSON: This doesn't directly relate to Lofton/Grissom, but:

Atlanta is perhaps the one team in baseball that has tried to build around pitching; look at their results in this decade. Now, compare that to the other clubs, all of them less successful, who tried to build around offensive stars: San Fran (Barry Bonds), Chisox (Frank Thomas), Cleveland (Albert Belle/Lofton), Oakland (Mark McGwire). From Ron Gant to Justice to Fred McGriff to Ryan Klesko to Lofton to Grissom to Chipper Jones, the Braves seem to have no trouble finding—then discarding—big bats. But the pitching has stayed pretty much intact (except Steve Avery, when he bombed).

Maybe the point of this all is (as Mat said), Atlanta will lose Lofton and his salary, which is OK because that will have helped them keep Tom Glavine and Greg Maddux.

MITTLEMAN: The 12½-game falloff was mostly to do with pitching, not offense. The Indians retained their position as one of the most powerful teams in the AL, second only to the Mariners in most statistical categories. There's no way you could make an argument that the trade cost them 12½ games, that's ludicrous. Their offense was nearly as potent as it was in '96, save for a few percentage points in hitting and scoring about .5 runs less per game. But, then again, I seem to remember that they lost some other guy who had nothing to do with this trade. Damn. . . his name escapes me right now but I know it rhymes with "Hell." Also, their club ERA went up by more than .5 runs per game which is where the falloff occurred.

My God, if they didn't have those two guys (Justice and Grissom) they wouldn't have even been close.

The money being freed up by trading away those guys to sign one of their aces (take your pick which one, because they gained roughly $8 million per year) is a good point and that's where Atlanta at least saves some face insofar as their future is concerned. But, player for player and overall, they lost.

MOYER: So, from here forth, any trades made by teams that make it to the World Series the following season are good ones. Trade evaluation has become so much easier for me now.

CALLIS: This was a great trade—for the Braves, no question. Their top priority was getting the money for Glavine and Maddux. They did that. They also got the best player in the deal, Lofton. If Lofton leaves, they'll probably get two high draft picks as compensation. And while the trade helped Cleveland this year, they will regret giving long-term deals to Grissom and Justice.

FULLAM: We can take it one step further, and say that any players who contribute to championship-winning teams are obviously championship-quality players as well, right?

It's even easier now, Steve!

MITTLEMAN: See what I mean? You have a way of simplifying the simplest of equations. And the contrary could be true as well. Any player that goes to a team that has made it to the World Series four out of the last five times and then doesn't get in, is a cancer on the body politic. Right, Kevin.

COOPERSON: You're all missing the point.

The two teams that had Darren Daulton defeated the Braves in the NLCS. Thus the Marlins' acquisition of Daulton counts as a great trade!

HENNINGER: Both teams achieved their goals with this trade. And it's possible the Braves will re-sign Lofton, and win two or three World Series with Lofton and Tucker at the top of the order. After all, Lofton may never come cheaper than his price right now. This deal may still benefit the Braves the most in the long run.

ELMAN: Oh ye of microscopic vision! Isn't that the point of the game? So what if it's luck, the experience factor, the ability of Joe Morgan to analyze a game, or an overt act of God (feel free to fill in your favorite recent discussion topic). The team is in the Series. If the Cubs traded their entire roster for Jose Offerman and they somehow made the Series, after all this time I'd think it would be considered a good trade by the baseball gods, No?

HENNINGER: The Cubs might be the only team to which Offerman could go, and actually provide a boost to the team's on-base average. Sounds like a good deal to me.

October 19—Vin Scully

SPEAR: I'm not a big Vin Scully fan, but listening to the first 1½ games of the Series on radio, I have been quite impressed by Mr. Scully. He's about 10,000 percent better on radio than on TV.

He also just said something pretty funny. Talking to Joe DiMaggio in the booth, he said. . . "Joe, you hit 361 home runs in your career and only struck out 369 times. That's incredible! These days, guys are striking out during the anthem."

PALACIOS: I agree. Scully should be doing TV, but I can also think of plenty of good announcers that are not on TV, but aren't because they don't have a TV face.

COOPERSON: Vin Scully? It's a shame there's a game going on—it occasionally interrupts Scully.

FULLAM: C'mon, Ethan. . . Scully and Joe Garagiola were outstanding when they had the "Game of the Week" on NBC 10 years ago.

COOPERSON: During Saturday's game, Scully enlightened me with a 3-5 minute discussion of the ethnic composition of his hometown neighborhood, then and now. If I wanted to hear that kind of stuff, that's what grandparents are for. Sorry, Vin, it's a World Series broadcast, not a fireside chat with relatives.

MOYER: I know it's silly, but I'd love to, someday, see one of us get an announcer or analyst position of national prominence. Then, the rest of us could rip him or her to shreds.

JAMES: I like Vin Scully on the radio a great deal. I thought he was terrible on television. This is kind of a seat-of-the-pants analysis, but I think that on the radio he is able to control the mood, and he creates a "feel" that seems very appropriate to the game. On TV, the pictures drive everything, and he reacts or distracts from what is going on.

There is every reason that somebody like us should be on TV in the next generation. It's just a matter of setting that goal and working toward it.

ZMINDA: Gee, I thought he was fine on television. He understood the medium and talked a lot less than he does on radio. I would venture that Scully and whoever he was paired with talked much less than the guys who are around today.

I have a tape of Game 6 of the 1986 World Series, the Bill Buckner game, with Scully and Joe Garagiola. After Scully's "Here comes Knight and the Mets win it!" he said absolutely nothing for the next three minutes (I actually timed this once) and let the pictures tell the story. He understood that nothing he could say could add to the scene. Absolutely the right decision. I wonder how many current announcers would have that much restraint.

COOPERSON: He might be guilty of the same thing Jeff Torborg is—over-compensating when on radio as opposed to TV. Maybe he's thinking, "I'm on radio, I have no pictures, I need to talk more." And I'm not kidding, he did discuss the ethnic background of his home neighborhood.

DEWAN: I remember the silence of Scully's call from 1986—it was superb, as is Mr. Scully overall. There are very few announcers I'd rather listen to.

October 31—Pedro Martinez

ZMINDA: Rumor has it that the Dodgers are offering the Expos a ton of players to get Pedro Martinez back.

MOYER: Wow, Adrian Beltre, Dennis Reyes, Wilton Guerrero and one or two minor leaguers. Holy smokes, I'd take that deal in a second if I were the Expos. I can't imagine they'll get a better offer elsewhere. Guerrero, Mark Grudzielanek, and Beltre would make a mighty fine three-fourths of an infield. All they'd need is a real first baseman. Go, 'Spos.

CALLIS: Brad Fullmer could be that first baseman for Montreal, but I'm underwhelmed by the DP combo. Guerrero might hit .300—with a .301 OBP and a .302 SLG. Grudz is a decent player, but could he be more overrated? His OBP was .304 (Ordonez drew more walks) and he slugged just .384 despite hitting 54 doubles. The three guys mentioned in that trade are, respectively, a budding superstar, an overweight lefty who gives up a lot of hits and an overrated second baseman whose sole value is his batting average. Well, at least Vladimir would be happy. But I'd want to make sure those other minor league prospects were pretty decent, like maybe a Mike Judd and Ted Lilly, before I'd jump at that deal. Of course, I also wouldn't keep the team in Montreal. Montreal doesn't deserve a baseball team and neither does Claude Brochu. Move to D.C. and get it over with.

MOYER: I agree 100 percent that Grudz is overrated. He wouldn't be so bad, however, if they'd bat him at the bottom of the lineup, where he belongs, and not at the top. I'd take a shot at Reyes any day, and who else is going to give them a "budding superstar" at all? Russ Branyan? Cripes, bring Rob Deer out of retirement. You'll get the same thing. Mariano Rivera (whom the Yankees don't even want to give up)? Let me tell you how to make a closer. Find a guy in your organization with good control. Only give him the ball when you're in a save situation in the ninth inning. There. You've got your closer.

CALLIS: Points well taken, especially about the closer. They're not going to get a better player than Beltre, but I wanted to hammer on your other points. Wilton Guerrero is all Dodger hype. If he came up with the Phillies, we'd never hear about him. Jack Perconte was probably better. And in a nod to Kevin Goldstein, I'd probably rather have Arquimedez Pozo as my second baseman over Wilton.

COOPERSON: If Wilton came up with the Phillies, instead of Rolen, he's still be their best prospect in 10 years, and we'd hear all about how Lee Thomas was turning the farm system around.

November 5—Davey Johnson

GOLDSTEIN: WBAL-TV in Baltimore is reporting that Davey Johnson has resigned because he "was growing tired of waiting" for Peter Angelos.

MOYER: Bye bye, birdies. I can't wait to see Scott Erickson's ERA next year. And Randy Myers'. And Jeffrey Hammonds leading off.

JAMES: Hank Bauer, who managed Davey in his rookie season in the majors, quit as Kansas City manager in the winter of 1962-63, under almost precisely the same circumstances. Charles Finley wouldn't fire him; he just wanted him to hang around a couple of months so he could decide whether he wanted to fire him.

Does this count as cutting off your head to get rid of a headache?

PINTO: Bill, since you are now an expert on the subject of managers, has there ever been as successful a manager as Johnson who had this much trouble hanging on to a job?

OLKIN: Billy Martin?

JAMES: Bill McKechnie. McKechnie won the pennant with the Pirates in 1925, was fired after 1926, won the pennant with the Cardinals in 1928, was fired that winter. And McKechnie was a likable guy.

November 10—Mike Morgan

JAMES: Is Mike Morgan some sort of historical one-of-a-kind? I get the feeling he must be, but I can't quite put my finger on it. Morgan has now been in the majors 17 seasons, and has had 13 losing records, two winning records (1992-93 with the Cubs) and two even records (1-1 and 7-7). He has posted ERAs over 4.50 10 times.

CARLSON: Bill is once again correct on his prediction, although Mike does have some close company:

Most Seasons with a Losing W-L Record

Pitcher	Years
Mike Morgan	11
Bob Friend	10
Tom Zachary	10
11 tied with	9
(minimum 10 GS in a season)	

CARLSON: Going back and looking at the list I made of players who have played on the most major league teams, Mike Morgan is the only person to be on the "leader board" of both that list and most seasons with a losing record (nine different MLB teams played on, 11 losing seasons as a starter).

ELMAN: I find the most amazing part of this story is that his only two winning seasons were spent with the Cubs (perennial losers). I'd guess that most pitchers' career numbers go in the opposite direction after a stint with the Cubs rather than their numbers improving. Could pitching for the Cubs afford the opportunity to go out with very little expectations, allowing you to perform up to or beyond your normal capabilities?

JAMES: Bob Friend had 10 losing seasons, including four quick ones with Pittsburgh teams that couldn't beat the Hooters girls, but he also had seasons of 14-9 (leading the league in ERA), 17-17, 22-14, 18-12, 18-14 and 17-16. In 1957, one of his "losing" years (14-18) he led the NL in innings pitched and posted a 3.38 ERA. He won 197 games in his career.

Zachary is similar; he had 10 losing seasons in a 19-year career (actually 12 losing seasons including a 1-5 mark and 0-3), but he also won 18 games in 1921, went 15-9 in 1924 and, of course, went 12-0 in 1929, I believe the only 12-0 season in major league history. (Howie Krist or somebody may have about the same record.) He won 186 games in his career.

Morgan, on the other hand, is just legitimately bad, all of his career. He's more like Milt Gaston or Sid Hudson or somebody, Matt Young, except that he's done it for so long. That, I think, is what makes him historically unique: he has extended a dreadful career on the illusion of untapped potential longer than anybody else in major league history.

I think you have to give Jim Lefebvre a lot of credit for his 1992-93 seasons.

HENZLER: Howie Krist went 10-0 in 1941. Dennis Lamp went 11-0 as primarily a reliever in 1985. They and Zachary are the only pitchers to win at least 10 games without a loss in any season in baseball history.

November 10—Men on Base

JAMES: Obviously Manny Ramirez is a better hitter than Jeff King, but King drove in 112 runs this year, Ramirez 88, and the difference is *not* a function of opportunities. It's a difference in production in RBI situations. Ramirez had 295 at-bats with the bases empty this year, 266 with men on base. King had about the same data, 280 and 263. But Ramirez had 41 extra-base hits with the bases empty, only 33 with men on base. King had 23 with the bases empty, but 36 with men on base.

Also, Ramirez had 152 at-bats with men in scoring position, King 148. But Ramirez hit .237 in those at-bats and drove in 62 runs; King hit .277 in those at-bats and drove in 76 runs.

PINTO: I have a program that I use quite often to show the difference in RBI opportunities between two batters (a good example was Ken Griffey Jr. and Tino Martinez this year). King and Ramirez were separated by one baserunner. I'm sending the top of the list. The players with similar baserunners to King and Ramirez is quite interesting.

Player	Run On	RBI	RBI/RO
Tino Martinez	550	97	.176
Albert Belle	542	86	.159
Jeff Kent	532	92	.173
Jay Buhner	499	69	.138
Tim Salmon	499	96	.192
Andres Galarraga	498	99	.199
Garrett Anderson	497	84	.169
Jeff Bagwell	493	92	.187
Sammy Sosa	491	83	.169
Bobby Bonilla	484	79	.163

The first stat column is the total number of players on base, regardless of base. The second is the number of those runners that were driven in (as opposed to scored) by the batter. The third column is the percentage.

November 10—Randy Johnson

JAMES: Randy Johnson over the last three seasons is now 43-6. Is this the highest winning percentage ever over a three-season span? Did somebody already cover this?

HENZLER:

Winning Percentage Over Three-Year Span

Player	Years	W	L	Pct
Howie Krist	1940-42	23	3	.885
Freddie Fitzsimmons	1940-42	22	3	.880
Randy Johnson	1995-97	43	6	.878
Terry Leach	1986-88	18	3	.857
Preacher Roe	1951-53	44	8	.846
Lefty Grove	1929-31	79	15	.840
Jim Coates	1958-60	19	4	.826
Ron Davis	1978-80	23	5	.821
Sal Maglie	1948-50	18	4	.818
Randy Johnson	1994-96	36	8	.818

(minimum 20 decisions)

SPEAR: What is Terry Leach doing on this list?!?

HENZLER: If you'd prefer a higher minimum of decisions. . .

Winning Percentage Over Three-Year Span

Player	Years	W	L	Pct
Randy Johnson	1995-97	43	6	.878
Preacher Roe	1951-53	44	8	.846
Lefty Grove	1929-31	79	15	.840
Randy Johnson	1994-96	36	8	.818
Lefty Grove	1930-32	84	19	.816
Howie Krist	1941-43	34	8	.810
Joe Wood	1912-14	54	13	.806
Sal Maglie	1949-51	41	10	.804
Ron Guidry	1976-78	41	10	.804
Spud Chandler	1942-44	36	9	.800
Ed Reulbach	1906-08	60	15	.800

(minimum 40 decisions)

November 11—Trades

GOLDSTEIN: The Yankees have traded third baseman Charlie Hayes to the San Francisco Giants for minor leaguers Chris Singleton and lefthander Alberto Castillo.

The Marlins have traded Moises Alou to the Astros for minor league closer Oscar Henriquez, RHP Manuel Barrios and a player to be named later.

HENZLER: I'm a little surprised the Astros took on Alou's salary. Some might see this as the beginning of a payroll purge for Florida, but I think Henriquez and Barrios are decent prospects. And Alou's talents are not unique.

PINTO: I wonder if the Astros are trying to fix their cleanup spot. When Florida tried to fix it with Alou, he did not hit either.

PINTO: I understand that Bagwell and Biggio are willing to restructure their contracts so the Astros can keep Kile.

CALLIS: I've seen that too, but Alou costs a lot of money.

HENNINGER: Will the 'Stros buck up for Kile after taking on Alou's contract?

MOYER: The Astros already have the poor man's lefty Moises Alou in Luis Gonzalez. I prefer the Yankee trade—take Charlie Hayes. . . please.

PINTO: I was hoping the Yankees would lose Charlie Hayes twice in expansion.

COOPERSON: Amazingly, the Giants will become the third team for which Hayes has served two different stints. Comparable to Terry Mulholland, who's served three different stints with the Giants.

November 12—Hideki Irabu

PINTO: Why would the Yankees protect Hideki Irabu in the expansion draft? First of all, no one is going to take him with his huge contract and bigger ERA. You would think there would be someone in the organization who would be more important to protect.

CALLIS: Two words: George Steinbrenner. I also think Irabu's big contract contained a huge bonus, so the salary obligation to him might not be really high. He had an awful year, but does have a good arm and several teams wanted him. If they didn't protect him and he got picked, Steinbrenner probably would fire the entire staff. I'm actually surprised they remembered to protect Mike Lowell. I think that Donzell McDonald will be one of the first 10 picks, and Steinbrenner will fire someone over this in the next two to three years.

November 17—Pedro Martinez

ZMINDA: The Red Sox finally completed their big deal for Pedro Martinez.

MOYER: I'll bet Dan Duquette's thinking of a place Roger Clemens can stick his Cy Young Award about now.

PINTO: He probably could have kept Clemens for less, but it'll be fun watching Pedro pitch in Fenway. AL batters should get used to being hit.

November 21— McGriff vs. Galarraga

ZMINDA: The Braves just signed Andres Galarraga. I don't get it.

PINTO: I don't understand this signing at all. We know for two years the Braves have wanted to dump Fred McGriff's salary and move Ryan Klesko to first. Something here has changed very suddenly, or someone has lost his mind.

Here's McGriff and Galarraga on the road the last three years:

	Avg	G	AB	R	H	2B	3B	HR	RBI	SB	CS	BB	SO	GDP	OBP	SLG
McGriff	.290	224	842	114	244	45	1	37	136	8	5	107	168	28	.372	.477
Galarraga	.268	229	889	130	238	44	5	48	149	23	7	55	241	18	.324	.490

McGriff has been declining the last three years, but Galarraga did not have much of a career outside 1) Colorado and 2) Baylor's influence. I have a feeling we are looking at the end of the Braves dynasty. This is the first time in a while I can think of them making a move that didn't make any sense.

SCHINSKI: I agree the "swap" was a bad move. You think they did this in order to allow them to ship Klesko off somewhere?

PINTO: Yes, shipping off Klesko is one of the few things that might make sense, but if you are going to do that, why not keep McGriff? Something has had to happen in the last few days to totally change the direction this franchise is going. The other thing I can think of (and I hate to think this was the case) was that the Braves were sitting there thinking, "Our strength is our pitching, we should do what Baltimore did and get great glove men in there." So they sign Walt Weiss, then decide Klesko would botch all the throws, so they sign the "Glove Man" Galarragga and get his offense as a bonus.

MOYER: If they're shipping Klesko, I hope it's for Ken Griffey Jr. or something, to make up for the drop-off they're going to see in Galarraga. Why wouldn't you want to give Klesko a chance at first and see what he can do against lefties? Instead, they'll keep him bumbling around in left where he has no business. Throw everything else out of the equation and you've gotta remember that Galarraga turns 37 in June. He could conk out any year just on the age factor alone.

COOPERSON: "Change the direction of the franchise?" Wrong, wrong, wrong. The franchise didn't change anything—they've retained the pitching that defines the team. They have a history over the last nine years of bringing in, then discarding, big-name position players. I don't see this as a dramatic change by any means.

PINTO: No, I disagree. Atlanta has been very good at letting players go at the right time, the one exception being Dave Justice, but I understood that move. And they usually bring in someone better, either a kid they developed in their farm system (Andruw Jones, Javy Lopez, Ryan Klesko) or a star quality player (Kenny Lofton, McGriff, Greg Maddux, Denny Neagle). This is the first big move they've made where I can't see the improvement or hope of improvement. I can understand wanting to save money. I can understand wanting to move Klesko to first. I can't understand, having made the moves to make that possible, giving more money to Galarraga, an old righthanded first baseman, than keeping McGriff, an old lefthanded first baseman with a better OBP and similar power. Someone's brain wasn't working here.

MOYER: It's like the one guy in my rotisserie league still says (I thought he may have learned something in the years I was away, but no): "If a guy can hit at one park, he can hit anywhere." (He acquired Dante Bichette shortly before the end of last season, too.)

HENNINGER: The signing may or may not represent a directional change for the organization, but it leaves a few questions:

1) If trading Klesko is part of this equation, what about the team's dearth of lefthanded pop? Signing the Big Cat is countered by trading the two lefthanded power bats on the team.

2) Who bats leadoff on this team in '98? Walt Weiss? To Weiss' credit, his OBP has been .381 and .377 the past two seasons, but he's not the man for the job. It's hard to comprehend giving a 36-year-old first baseman a three-year deal for that kind of money when a leadoff man with a .400+ on-base average is what this team needs. Brady Anderson was the best bet to fill Atlanta's needs. (John Schuerholz has come out and said they're out of the running for Anderson. Is there anybody of Anderson's caliber who could be acquired for a few Braves prospects?)

PINTO: I just read a report that the Braves have given up on Anderson and Lofton, and that they won't sign anymore big-money free agents. They may sign Otis Nixon to play center field.

There is a rumor of a three-way deal where the Braves get Bernie Williams, the Mariners get John Smoltz, and the Yankees get Herr Grosse Unit. But unless that happens, I'm picking the Mets to beat the Braves this year if:

They keep John Olerud and get Gary Sheffield. The Mets' seven-year purgatory is over. It's their year.

SPEAR: I don't get it. . . why would the Mariners essentially trade Randy Johnson for Smoltz? The $$ difference can't be *that* big, can it?

If I were Seattle, I'd be signing RJ to a three-year or more deal ASAP.

HENNINGER: That's an interesting rumor. Still, who would bat leadoff for the Braves if Williams comes aboard?

MOYER: Who is Herr Grosse Unit? The Braves get Williams, the M's Smoltz and the Yankees get Tommy Herr and Wayne Gross?

PINTO: I'm a believer in unconventional leadoff men. I'd probably do something like:

Williams, Weiss, Chipper Jones, Klesko, Galarraga, Lopez, Andruw Jones, Other Outfielder, Lemke, Pitcher

PINTO: Herr Grosse Unit is German for Mr. Big Unit.

COUSINS: The Mariners must be uncertain about RJ's health and ability to dominate in the future like he has in the past. Otherwise, I don't think they would entertain the offer to give him up and get another high-paid player like Smoltz.

COUSINS: Maybe the Braves are going to look to one of their younger guys to step up into that leadoff spot. Tony Graffanino? Or maybe they are planning on putting Michael Tucker in that spot. However, the thought of bringing Otis Nixon back to Atlanta doesn't sound too bad to me.

HENNINGER: Graffanino's the guy I would like to see given a chance to play every day. As much as I like him, there's not much in his minor league numbers to suggest he could be a leadoff man. I would love to see him prove me wrong.

MITTLEMAN: I don't know why you think they are out of the running for Brady Anderson, They have a four-year, $28-million offer on the table to him right now.

MUNDO: A German-speaking friend of mine just told me that ''The Big Unit'' is more properly translated as: Der Grosse Teil.

December 1—Hall of Fame

PINTO: I was reading the AP story in my local paper about this year's Hall of Fame ballot. The story list the top three new players as Gary Carter, Jack Clark and Bert Blyleven. It then listed (in this order) others on for the first time:

Rick Dempsey

Brian Downing

Mike Flanagan

Pedro Guerrero

Carney Lansford

Willie Randolph

Now, I don't know how any of you feel, but Randolph is one of my favorites. He was a good fielder and an excellent leadoff man. His main drawback as a Hall of Famer is that he didn't hit for power. I don't think he belongs in the Hall, but I certainly would put him on the level of Jack Clark or Brian Downing, if for nothing else than for his fielding. But if Bobby Grich didn't make the Hall, I guess there's no hope for Willie.

MOYER: I don't want to infer that your mind is at the same rudimentary level as mine in any way, but your mail message out-and-out scared me. I read that same article and had the same thought process—exactly.

PINTO: Thanks for confirming my thoughts. Sometimes, I think I let my love for those '70s Yankees teams cloud my thinking.

If you think about it, there were five teams that dominated the '70s; the Reds, A's, Yankees, Royals and Orioles. But if you think about it, they were not dominated by Hall of Famers. You have Bench and Morgan, Jackson and Hunter (Yankees and A's), the Robinsons and Palmer, and I can't think of anyone from the Royals except Brett, who will go in next year. (Of course you can add Rose to the Reds list if you'd like to.) I'm sure Bill can come up with a list of Royals who should get more consideration than they have, but if I had to pick three Yankees who got overlooked, I'd have to say Ron Guidry, Graig Nettles and Randolph (as much as I loved Thurman Munson, I can't put him in the Hall).

Any thoughts, anyone?

WENZ: Frank White pops into my head as a decent person to compare to Willie Randolph. I don't think White's a Hall of Famer, but he won eight Gold Gloves and had a very similar career to Randolph (same league, same era, almost all with the same team). So here it is:

	G	AB	R	H	2B	3B	HR	RBI	BB	SO	AVG	OBP	SLG
White	2,324	7,859	912	2,006	407	58	160	886	412	1,035	.255	.293	.383
Randolph	2,202	8,018	1,239	2,210	316	65	54	687	1,243	675	.276	.373	.351

A little more pop from White, a lot more on-base from Randolph, and outstanding gloves from both.

JAMES: I'm repeating something I'm sure I've written, but one of the most popular Hall of Fame candidates is Bill Mazeroski. White and Mazeroski are closely comparable, and White appears to have an edge, probably.

	G	AB	R	H	2B	3B	HR	RBI	BB	SO	AVG	OBP	SLG
White	2,324	7,859	912	2,006	407	58	160	886	412	1,035	.255	.293	.383
Mazeroski	2,163	7,755	769	2,016	294	62	138	853	447	706	.260	.302	.367

I believe that both players won the same number of Gold Gloves, which is like twice as many as anybody else won.

WENZ: For the record. . .

Sandberg won nine Gold Gloves, White and Mazeroski won eight each.

December 1—Fathers & Sons

OLKIN: You could make up two pretty decent teams of second-generation major leaguers:

		First Team	Second Team
C		Todd Hundley	Sandy Alomar
			Jason Kendall
1B		David Segui	Eduardo Perez
2B		Roberto Alomar	Bret Boone
3B		Ed Sprague	Aaron Boone
SS		David Howard	David Bell

LF	Barry Bonds	Jose Cruz Jr.
CF	Ken Griffey Jr.	Brian McRae
RF	Ben Grieve	Moises Alou
SP	Todd Stottlemyre	Jaime Navarro
	Jaret Wright	Chris Haney
	Darren Oliver	Omar Olivares
RP	Robb Nen	T.J. Mathews

The first one looks like a sure division winner, and the second looks more like an expansion team. Still, that ain't bad. I doubt you could find a stronger team of "sons" at any other time in major league history. To all the responsible fathers: nice procreating, guys.

JAMES: The 1994 Royals had, as I recall, six players on their roster whose fathers had played in the majors. I'm not sure if I can remember them all. . . David Howard, Mel Stottlemyre Jr., Brian McRae, Chris Haney, Kurt Stillwell. . . I think there was one more. What are the odds?

PINTO: Wasn't Chris Haney's father on Green Acres?

MOYER: The lists look good except for shortstops David Howard and David Bell. Those guys are at least similarly as bad as each other though. How about that trivia question: Name two active second-generation major league (using the term loosely) infielders who are as bad as each other.

JAMES: It wouldn't be too much of a reach to count Cal Ripken Jr. as a second-generation baseball player. In fact, this is about the second or third generation for Cal Jr., even if you don't count his father.

MOYER: Sorry, I meant to put "named David" in that question too. And, on second thought, I think we might be able to ask the same question substituting the phrase "named Boone" about a year from now.

OLKIN: Seems like a pattern: almost all of the second-generation shortstops are lousy hitters:

Mike Brumley

Gary Green

Keith Kessinger

Jeff Kunkel

Jeff McKnight

Dick Schofield

Kurt Stillwell

Roy Smalley Jr. is the only one who could really hit. Dale Berra got by with a little help from his friends.

December 1—Bo Jackson

FAUST: Yesterday was Bo Jackson's birthday, so I sent Bill this list of players most similar to Bo:

Player	Score	Pos	G	Avg	H	2B	3B	HR	RBI	SB	BB	K
Bo Jackson	1000	OF	694	.250	598	86	14	141	415	82	200	841
Ron Kittle	945	OF	843	.239	648	100	3	176	460	16	236	744
Glenallen Hill	936	OF	821	.263	711	144	17	118	415	90	201	609
Dan Pasqua	920	OF	905	.244	638	129	15	117	390	7	335	642
Jimmie Hall	917	OF	963	.254	724	100	24	121	391	38	287	529
Bob Cerv	913	OF	829	.276	624	96	26	105	374	12	212	392

JAMES: You might think, from Drew's list, that the Bo story was all hype. It wasn't. I saw Bo do far more spectacular things on a baseball field than any other player ever, probably more spectacular things than all other players I ever saw. I saw him break bats over his head. I saw him nail Carlton Fisk off first base when Fisk tried to play a fly ball halfway. I saw him hit baseballs 500 feet. He was the most spectacular athlete ever to play in the majors.

But he wasn't a good player.

PINTO: I have to agree with Bill here about Bo. At his peak, I remember saying to someone that even though I didn't think he was that good, he was the player I'd be most willing to pay to see play.

DEWAN: I'll never forget how he "ran off the wall" after making a spectacular catch once. Running full speed toward the wall, he made the catch and then ran up the wall and back down instead of simply running into it like every outfielder in the history of baseball has done after a similar catch!

December 8—Braves/Indians Trade

ZMINDA: Kenny Lofton is apparently about to re-sign with the Indians as a free agent. Great. . . now we can talk about that trade some more.

PINTO: It's a great move on Cleveland's part possibly getting Kenny Lofton back. It will be like getting Dave Justice and a good pitcher for a one-year lease of Lofton.

CALLIS: It's a great move on Atlanta's part. They found the money to sign Greg Maddux and Tom Glavine, and rented Lofton to buy a year of development time for Andruw Jones. Cleveland now will have Marquis Grissom, Justice and Lofton tied up to long-term contracts that could hamstring them in the future. That said, I will not defend the signings of Andres Galarraga and Walt Weiss. Atlanta should have gotten Brady Anderson and moved Ryan Klesko to first base.

117

PINTO: I really doubt that long-term contracts hamstring clubs. One reason Cleveland was able to trade Lofton to Atlanta was that they had signed him to a long-term contract, which meant that last year Lofton was cheap compared to his abilities. Take Ken Griffey Jr. as an example. The Mariners by signing him to a long-term contract at about $8 million a year may easily save $30 million over the life of the contract, vs. signing him to a number of short-term deals. And if they ever decided to trade him, price isn't going to be a problem, because he'll be cheaper than signing a superstar free agent.

CALLIS: Long-term contracts do hamstring clubs. Lofton was in the last year of his contract, and was traded because he was thought to want $10 million a year, long-term.

Griffey is a poor example. Especially because of his marketing appeal to go with his talent, he's Michael Jordanesque. No matter what you pay him, you are going to get value. If you can sign a guy below market value, obviously that's good.

Of course, if you do that, the guy will bitch and moan like Tony Gwynn did. He may hold out or demand a trade. So it doesn't always help you in the long run.

If you want an example from the other end of the spectrum, look at Sammy Sosa. The Cubs aren't going to contend, and they're going to pay him a boatload of money. Can they trade him for prospects in the stretch drive? No.

PINTO: Well, if the Cubs had a better idea of what Sammy Sosa's value was, they

a) would not have signed him to a long-term contract

b) would not have paid him so much money.

You miss my point on Lofton. Yes, he was traded for the reason you give, but Atlanta was willing to take that risk for a year, because he had been signed to a long-term contract in 1992. I don't know offhand how much he made last year, but it certainly was a lot less than what he was worth. If Cleveland had done what Pittsburgh did with Barry Bonds every year, that is, take him to arbitration and not give him a long-term contract, Lofton would have been playing for someone else, and the Indians would have gotten nothing.

These contracts only hamstring clubs when the value is not there, as in the case of Sosa.

COOPERSON: The Cubs signed Sosa for one and only reason: to deflect all inevitable criticism about the *Tribune* not being willing to spend the money and not being interested in building a winner. The Cubs can shoot back with, "We're paying Sosa $10 million/year." The reality is that they'll use Sosa as an excuse to have a team of 24 cheap no-names and Sosa, and claim they're really trying to win. They'll have a smaller payroll that way than if they really did try to build a winner.

PINTO: No, I'm saying that you use them wisely. At the end of the 1990 season, I bet the Pirates could have signed Bonds to a 10-year contract worth $20 million. They could have made Bonds the highest-paid player in baseball, and it still would have been worth it.

If you have someone who isn't that special, it's silly to sign them to a long-term contract (i.e., Sammy Sosa). But if you have someone special, like Bonds or Griffey, or even someone young and good, like Lofton, Carlos Baerga, Sandy Alomar and Albert Belle were in 1992, it's crazy not to.

Look what it did for Cleveland:

They did not have arbitration battles.

They were able to make trades based on talent not price.

They gave themselves room to bring in free agents to fill in holes, and economic stability for a decade.

The Cubs just threw money at a bad player because he hits a few HR.

CALLIS: I seriously doubt Bonds would still be honoring a 10-year, $20 million contract if he had signed it.

Yes, Cleveland had a great strategy. Why isn't everyone else doing it? Simple—the players won't take these deals. Chipper Jones and Javy Lopez did with Atlanta, but Klesko refused. Players generally won't give away their arbitration and free-agent rights, so the only long-term deals are going to go to free agents, not young guys who are cheaper.

You won't see another situation like Cleveland again where all the young guys signed those deals. The only reason the Indians may get Lofton back is he had a year that caused him to greatly lower his salary expectations.

COOPERSON: Sign Bonds to $20 mil over 10 years? How long would it have taken him to cry about renegotiating??

The Lakers signed Magic Johnson to a 20-year deal in 1980, worth $1 million a year. How long do you think it took for them to tear that deal up?

PINTO: Why wouldn't Bonds honor the contract? I don't know of many players who have held out holding a long-term contract (Actually, I can't think of any). What they do is negotiate an extension, or if a club is smart, they pay him some kind of bonus. Either, way it's still cheaper for the club in the long run.

CALLIS: I guess I watch a different sport. Rickey Henderson comes to mind. Players get unhappy and they disrupt the team.

MUNDO: So the moral of the story is: smart contracts help you, dumb contracts hurt you.

PINTO: Rickey also plays his behind off every game, but that's another argument.

Sure it can come back to bite you later, but I think the long term odds are in your favor when you sign a player to a long-term contract.

KINSEY: This story has been all over Cleveland news since about this time last week. The only broadcast that would go out on a limb said that the Tribe would send Grissom to L.A. for Ismael Valdes and possibly another player.

JAMES: Anybody who thinks you are going to get Ismael Valdes-plus for Marquis Grissom is obviously:

a) Nuts, or

b) A local sportscaster.

I wouldn't trade Ismael Valdes for three Marquis Grissoms if you gave me the money to sign the Marquis players.

OLKIN: Anyone who thinks you should give up Ben McDonald-plus for Marquis Grissom is either:

a) Nuts, or

b) Sal Bando, or

c) both.

OSBORNE: Good trade/bad trade, long-term/short-term, I don't know what is right or wrong. But, if the Indians do sign Lofton, it would be a great PR move. Remember the ovation he received at the All-Star game? I really hope that they do sign him. Win or lose, I'll enjoy Tribe games much more with him on the field. (Of course, more so in wins than losses.)

ZMINDA: I can see this deal (Valdes for Grissom, even Valdes plus for Grissom) being made. There's a substantial element in baseball circles that believes:

a) the real problem with the Dodgers is not their bad on-base percentage or bad infield defense or bad closer, but their "bad clubhouse chemistry."

b) Valdes, who got into it with Bill Russell last year, was supposedly part of that bad chemistry.

So. . .

c) So what the Dodgers really need is a guy like good old Marquis, who's supposed to be "great in the clubhouse."

This sort of thing has happened before, of course. In the early 1980s, the Montreal Expos supposedly had "great talent," just like the Dodgers are supposed to have now, but they could never make it to the World Series. Eventually they decided their problems were in the clubhouse ("bad chemistry"), so they went out and signed that proven winner and team player, Pete Rose. Of course, that didn't work, either; pretty soon the Expos started trading away all their best players because they were "losers," and went down the drain completely.

So I could see this deal happening.

GREENBERGER: What you want is to get a good player in the last year(s) of a long-term contract, when he's a bargain, like Lofton.

OLKIN: It's a done deal. The Indians signed Lofton and traded Grissom and Jeff Juden to Milwaukee for Ben McDonald, Mike Fetters and Ron Villone. Then Cleveland turned around and traded Fetters to Oakland for Steve Karsay.

Grissom, age 31, batted .262 with 12 homers and 74 runs scored last year. He replaces Gerald Williams, age 31, who batted .253 with 10 homers and 73 runs scored last year. The Brewers must figure they can break even on the deal if they can trade Williams for a new staff ace.

PINTO: Yeah, maybe they can get Dave Mlicki for Williams.

December 10—Jeff Blauser

ZMINDA: The Cubs have signed Jeff Blauser. Blauser's career numbers at Wrigley: .311-11-28 with a .636 slugging percentage in 39 games.

ELMAN: I figure I might as well be the first. . . yes, but he doesn't get to face Cub pitching.

MILLER: My guess for Blauser's stats as a Cub in Wrigley this year: .275-7-33.

DEWAN: My guess: .253-12-57.

COOPERSON: Wrong. Pulled groin in March. Hamstring problems through much of June. Only .219-2-19 for the Cubs, traded to a contender in August.

SCHINSKI: OK. Being a loyal Cub fan and all: .277-7-52.

PINTO: Why not just keep Dunston?

SCHINSKI: I woulda kept him.

CALLIS: Excuse me. I thought I was at STATS. People are espousing the virtues of Shawon Dunston now? I'm not a huge Jeff Blauser fan and he did overachieve last year, but his 70 walks in 1997 are more than Dunston has in the last six seasons.

PINTO: What virtues? I agree Blauser walks more, and that's something the Cubs need. But overall at shortstop, is he really that much better than Dunston? I haven't taken the time to look yet, but my gut feeling is that overall they are probably pretty close. Blauser's never been known as a great defensive shortstop, but Dunston's always had the reputation of having a great arm.

CALLIS: Great arm? Yes. Significantly better defensively? I don't think so. I would give Dunston a slight edge, but both have slowed down. Blauser is three years younger, and they have virtually the same career AVG and SLG. OBP? Blauser's is a mere 57 points higher over their careers. Blauser also is coming off a much better year than Dunston. At worst, he'll have the same year as Dunston with at least 50-60 more walks. I know the Cubs don't like players who walk, but this was a much better move than signing Dunston. Much better.

PINTO: OK, it was a good move.

CARLSON: Three-Year Profiles

	Avg	G	AB	R	H	2B	3B	HR	RBI	SB	BB	SO	OBP	SLG
Dunston	.298	341	1,254	156	374	64	13	33	151	50	31	190	.318	.449
Blauser	.260	349	1,215	198	316	61	7	39	136	19	167	262	.364	.418

Comparable number of games, Dunston beats him hands down in average and slugging but Blauser does get on base quite a bit more, which is what the Cubs really need anyway (although another good power hitter with Sammy Sosa wouldn't hurt either). Also, Dunston, although not taking walks, isn't getting struck out as much either anymore.

PINTO: But Blauser looks 10 years older than Dunston.

CALLIS: I'm not necessarily saying it was a good move to sign a 32 year old whose range at shortstop is declining. It's just a much better move than getting 35-year-old Dunston. That's my only point.

HENZLER: Just to be clear, while Dave Carlson pointed out that Dunston's slugging percentage is 31 points higher than Blauser's over the past three years, that does not necessarily indicate that Dunston has more power. In this case, it's entirely a function of Dunston's batting average advantage over Blauser. In fact, Blauser's isolated power over the past three years was slightly higher than Dunston's.

Also, no shortstop had a better offensive season than Blauser in 1997, at least according to runs created per 27 outs. Even Nomar Garciaparra, who obviously enjoyed a terrific season, was comfortably behind Blauser. And wunderkind Alex Rodriguez was over a full run lower.

Shortstop

Player, Team	RC	RC/27
1. Jeff Blauser, Atl	107	7.45
2. Nomar Garciaparra, Bos	124	6.65
3. Alex Rodriguez, Sea	101	6.28
4. Jay Bell, KC	99	6.15
5. Walt Weiss, Col	61	5.46
6. Derek Jeter, NYA	101	5.44
7. Neifi Perez, Col	47	5.33
8. Shawon Dunston, ChN/Pit	68	4.95
9. Omar Vizquel, Cle	75	4.47
10. Pat Meares, Min	57	4.47
Average at position with 300 PA: (minimum 300 PA)		4.17

QUINN: Jim's chart makes the Jay Bell signing by Arizona look better, especially considering he moves from a pitchers' park to the second-best hitters' park in baseball (according to my prediction).

December 10—Runs Created

JAMES: I have just been working on a project to re-rate all the great offensive seasons in history, based on the new runs created estimates in the *All-Time Handbook* and a new super-structure tying runs created to team wins. Anyway, my conclusion is that the best offensive season of the 1980s (by a fairly wide margin) was turned in by a player who *didn't* win the MVP Award, although his team won its division. A teammate won the award. Any guesses?

FAUST: Rickey Henderson (when Don Mattingly won in 1985)?

JAMES: No, it isn't Rickey. Rickey's 1985 season is better than Mattingly's, but rates below Brett the same year and also below Tim Raines the same year. . . it's like the seventh-best season of the 1980s or something.

COOPERSON: Yanks didn't win the division in 1985 anyway.

ZMINDA: Eddie Murray in '83?

JAMES: Good guess, but no cigar. Murray in '83 was quite a bit ahead of Cal Ripken Jr. (strictly as a hitter), but not one of the top 25 seasons of the 1980s.

FAUST: Will Clark in 1989?

JAMES: We have a winner! Will Clark in '89.

Clark's season looks good, at a glance, but not sensational. He hit .333 with 38 doubles, 23 homers, 74 walks. Clark is almost dead even with Kevin Mitchell in runs created, old style, and Mitchell won the MVP award because the writers were surprised by his big season, whereas they *expected* Clark to have a great year.

Clark is bumped ahead of Mitchell, and ahead of everybody else, by two things. First, the National League in 1989 is one of the lowest run environments of the 1980s, with teams scoring less than 4.00 runs per game on average. Clark had his 1989 season in a low-run league in a pitcher's park, which makes it more valuable than it appears to be at a glance.

Second, in figuring the new runs created estimates, we used situational stats, since we have them and they increase the accuracy of the estimates. Mitchell had OK situational stats, hitting .286 with men in scoring position (.291 overall) and hitting 25 of his 47 homers with the bases empty, although 53 percent of his at-bats were with men on base.

But Clark had sensational situational stats, hitting .389 with runners in scoring position, and hitting 13 of his 23 homers with men on base, although 61 percent of his at-bats were with the bases empty. This bumps him up by about 10 runs created, which makes it a genuinely superb season, a high-impact season in context.

This is kind of a loaded contest, because we only have situational stats for the last couple of years of the 1980s, and for all I know, Gorman Thomas in '82 may have hit .340 with runners in scoring position, too. But I thought it was interesting, anyway, in that we don't think of that as a historically great season, but in my current analysis, it ranks No. 1 in the period 1962-1990.

December 12—MVPs

JAMES: It is too late to have any impact on the discussion, but do you remember the discussion we were having in early October about the best hitter in the National League this year, the Larry Walker/Barry Bonds/Mike Piazza discussion? I have now come to the conclusion that by far the most valuable offensive player in the National League this year wasn't Walker or Bonds or Piazza, but Tony Gwynn. The rank goes Gwynn, Piazza, Jeff Bagwell, Bonds, Walker.

As to why this is true and why we missed it, there are a couple of keys. Studying the history of MVP Awards, one is struck by the prevalence of the Willie Mays syndrome. There are about eight years between 1954 and 1965 when Willie Mays probably could have or should have won the MVP award, but didn't (in six of them) because. . . well, you can't give the award to Willie every year. This is a general truth, that the more often a player plays at a given level, the more we take it for granted, and stop giving any real consideration to it. Mike Schmidt, Bonds, Joe Morgan, Mickey Mantle, Rickey Henderson and others have lost countless MVP awards to this phenomenon, and I think it got *us* as it does the MVP voters. Because Gwynn *always* has a great year, we didn't stop to think about exactly how good it was.

Second, the Padres data this year is very odd. They jiggled a couple of fences there two years ago, you'll remember, and this year the Padres were second in the National League in runs scored (795, behind Colorado), but also second in runs allowed (891, also behind Coorsorado). So I tended to assume, without thinking about it, that this was now a hitters' park, and the runs created there needed to be downgraded a little.

But actually, it remains one of the best pitchers' parks in the National League; it's just an odd team. The Padres scored and allowed far more runs on the road than they did in San Diego.

Third, the situational stats. Gwynn hit 11 of his 17 home runs with men on base—no big deal, but it helps a little. Piazza and Larry Walker both hit very well with men in scoring position. Piazza hit .361, Walker .365. Tony Gwynn outhit them (with men in scoring position) by almost a hundred points! The man hit .459 with runners in scoring position, in 150+ at bats.

When you take that quite phenomenal stat into account, Gwynn created 138 runs—six more than Bonds and one more than Piazza, but still four fewer than Bagwell and 20 fewer than Walker.

As to why this makes Gwynn more valuable than Bagwell and Piazza, who also played in pitchers' parks, it has to do with the won-lost record of their teams. This also is counter intuitive, since the Dodgers and Astros both had better records than the Padres.

But the Dodgers and Astros, while they had better records than the Padres, both under performed in terms of wins relative to runs scored. The Astros scored 777 runs, allowed 660, which means that we would expect them to finish 94-68. They finished 84-78. The Dodgers were also four games under expectation, while the Padres, although a poorer team, were four games over their expected wins.

I don't figure expected wins in calculating the win value of the runs, but the fact is that while the Padres were a weaker team, they still won more games, *run for run*, than the other two teams did. That means that Gwynn's runs are more valuable, one for one, than those of the other guys—consequently, Gwynn ranks as easily the top performing hitter in the league.

Surprising, I know, but think about it this way. If anybody else hit .372 with 49 doubles and 17 homers in a pitcher's park, we'd probably notice him right away. Even if we didn't know he had hit .459 with runners in scoring position.

December 12—Clutch Hitting

JAMES: Dick Cramer has argued for years that there probably is no such thing as an ability to hit in the clutch. I have been timid in supporting him on this, out of deference to baseball dogma, but I'm not going to argue that he is wrong.

Recently I was reading an old issue of *Sport* magazine, from the mid-fifties, which was titled something like "Baseball's best clutch hitters—*Sport* asks the managers." The author of this article, to his credit, had done exactly what he claimed to have done: he went to each and every major league manager, and asked him who he regarded as the best clutch hitters in baseball.

Bobby Bragan, an icon to analytic types anyway, told the reporter frankly that there wasn't any such thing as clutch ability. He said that Stan Musial and Willie Mays and Duke Snider were the best clutch hitters in the National League, because they were *always* the best hitters in the league, regardless of what the situation was. The writer reported this with astonishment and disbelief, but, again to his credit, he did report it.

PALACIOS: I'll take the extreme in this position. I don't quite feel that strongly about it, but heck, it's probably true, anyway. There's no clutch hitting in baseball because there's no thinking in hitting.

Yeah, as a hitter, thanks to watching miles of film, you may have an idea what a pitcher may throw you with a 1-1 count, but what makes you a great hitter is probably your ability to guess wrong and still get a hit. Reflexes are everything. There's no hitting equivalent for a knuckleball pitcher. Because of this, I find it tiresome when people argue who the best clutch hitters are. I'd much rather discuss who are the best clutch pitchers. I'll agree that the conventional wisdom is "clutch" hitters may intimidate some pitchers into not pitching right based on the hitters' reputation. I agree with Bill. A good hitter is a good hitter. Looking at good hitters' stats as results and not causes is wise, too.

PINTO: Every so often, I look at the best hitters with runners in scoring position over a long time period. What I see is what Bobby Bragan knew; the best hitters are also the best hitters with runners in scoring position. Paul Molitor goes way up in these studies, but you don't ever see a .250 hitter hitting .320 with RISP. You see Tony Gwynn, Wade Boggs, Molitor and Barry Bonds at the top of the list, just as you would expect.

Best batting average, 1990s

Batter	AB	H	HR	RBI	Avg
Tony Gwynn	4,109	1,426	62	557	.347
Mike Piazza	2,558	854	168	533	.334
Frank Thomas	3,821	1,261	257	854	.330
Edgar Martinez	3,572	1,144	143	562	.320
Paul Molitor	4,505	1,427	111	657	.317
Kenny Lofton	3,314	1,047	44	309	.316
Rusty Greer	1,837	573	67	294	.312
Mark Grace	4,462	1,387	84	606	.311
Roberto Alomar	4,292	1,330	97	556	.310
Hal Morris	3,217	987	72	439	.307
Wade Boggs	3,919	1,203	45	410	.307
Ken Griffey Jr.	4,138	1,269	278	811	.307
Barry Bonds	3,987	1,218	290	871	.305
Willie McGee	3,025	924	27	319	.305

(minimum 2000 PA)

With RISP, 1990s

Batter	AB	H	HR	RBI	Avg
Tony Gwynn	929	340	18	467	.366
Mike Piazza	687	238	46	358	.346
Paul Molitor	1,177	402	21	514	.342
Frank Thomas	1,046	352	56	570	.337
Barry Bonds	978	322	63	543	.329
Mo Vaughn	870	277	56	452	.318
Bernard Gilkey	763	242	24	337	.317
Moises Alou	804	255	33	381	.317
B.J. Surhoff	928	293	20	450	.316
Mark Grace	1,083	342	9	478	.316
Chuck Knoblauch	836	263	3	324	.315
Julio Franco	842	264	23	367	.314
Barry Larkin	917	287	22	372	.313
Wally Joyner	955	297	23	442	.311
Tim Raines	759	236	12	327	.311

(minimum 800 PA)

As you can see, the only difference in the top five is Bonds for Edgar Martinez. (Martinez hit .297 with RISP in this period). Molitor's jump is impressive. The two biggest surprises on the list to me are Gilkey and Surhoff, who have hit .283 and .282 respectively over this time period. But sample sizes are small.

DEWAN: I don't believe that RISP is the best measurement of hitting in the clutch. You need a situation where a hitter feels the pressure. RISP happens too often to feel the pressure. Our own clutch stats would be better to look at (hitting in the late innings of close games). But even in many of those situations, the hitter might not feel the pressure.

Therefore, one of the problems in measuring true clutch hitting (or pitching, or whatever) is that by definition, the sample size is small. And, if the sample size is small, it's hard to get meaningful results that can be attributed to true clutch hitting, as opposed to simple random variations due to sample-size problems.

Personally, I do believe that clutch ability exists in a very limited way. Let me relate my own personal experiences. As folks here in the office can attest, my level of competitiveness in athletic endeavors is quite a bit higher than average. They can also attest, however, that my athletic abilities are pretty average. Despite this, there are times that I believe that I can rise to the occasion. It doesn't happen very often, but it happens. It happens whenever a temporarily very high confidence level happens to coincide with a "clutch" situation.

But more importantly, there are times when my confidence level is very low, and I just *know* I'm going to blow it! I really play below my abilities at those times.

I believe that this same thing happens in all sports, regardless of the level. At the professional level, choking in the clutch occurs less often, but it does occur. I'm sure of it. The batter steps to the plate knowing he just has to get a hit (or he just has to make the game-tying free throws). I believe that *some* players can rise to the occasion. There are more players, however, that will choke.

My purely speculative guesses are that there are about 10-15 players in all of professional baseball who can *regularly* rise above there own level of performance in true clutch situations. However, I would expect that there might be as much as 10-15 *percent* of all players (that's over 100 players) who generally would fall below their regular level of performance in true clutch situations. The rest, I would expect, would generally be average.

In summary:

1. It's not a clutch situation unless you feel the pressure.

2. True clutch ability is almost impossible to measure.

3. Clutch ability is rare. Choke ability is less rare.

JAMES: The simplest interpretation of the data is that clutch ability is enormously difficult to measure because it doesn't exist.

DEWAN: I agree that this is the simplest interpretation, but I also believe it is the wrong one.

SKELTON: All this talk about clutch hitting has me wondering. . .

Last season, for the *10th* time in his career, Joe Carter drove in over 100 runs. He managed to do it with a .234 batting average, too.

Although Joe's not likely to be among the worst, what are the lowest single season batting averages for players who still managed to drive in at least 100 runs?

HENZLER:

Lowest Average in 100-RBI Season

Player	Year	H	AB	RBI	Avg
Tony Armas	1983	125	574	107	.218
Roy Sievers	1954	119	514	102	.232
Joe Carter	1990	147	634	115	.232
Ruben Sierra	1993	147	630	101	.233
Joe Carter	1997	143	612	102	.234
Mark McGwire	1990	123	523	108	.235
Carlton Fisk	1985	129	543	107	.238
Jeff King	1997	129	543	112	.238
Gorman Thomas	1980	150	628	105	.239
Jose Canseco	1986	144	600	117	.240
Phil Plantier	1993	111	462	100	.240
Ron Cey	1977	136	564	110	.241
Harmon Killebrew	1959	132	546	105	.242

PINTO: Yes, I think it was pretty amazing. For a number of years, I thought Carter drove in 100 runs because he was surrounded by great players; in San Diego he had Jerald Clark, Tony Gwynn and Roberto Alomar; in Toronto he had Alomar, Molitor and John Olerud. So the guy is always coming up with men on base. Plus, I think that pitchers feel (rightly so) that they can get Carter out. Carter has only been IBB'd 82 times in his career, and 30 of those came in 1990 and 1991, the only time he's been in double digits. (He's been IBB'd 27 times from 1992-1997.) So pitchers pitch to Carter with men on base, and he has enough power and gets enough hits in these situations to drive in 100 runs.

Players like Bonds and Fred McGriff don't get these opportunities, because they are tough outs who can hurt you with power. And because they are tough outs, they don't chase bad pitches that usually result in outs, but sometimes turn into hits that drive in runs.

I think one of the advances we have made through the work of people like Bill James is to realize that RBI are not a be-all and end-all. There are still a lot of fans who think Joe Carter is a great player due to the fact that he drives in 100 runs a year. Joe is also one of the nice guys in the game (reporters love him) so no one is going to criticize him due to a personal grudge. It's really hard to convince people that Joe has serious offensive flaws.

1990 was a really strange season for Carter. 115 RBI in 1990 was huge. He had 59 at the All-Star break, and Carter's praises were being sung far and wide. Carter hit .266 with runners in scoring position that year, better than his overall average but not outstanding. What was outstanding was that he had more men on base than any other batter in the majors that year. And with men on, he batted 50 points higher and slugged 100 points higher. To Carter's credit, when reporters asked him about his great RBI year, he said that with the men on base in front of him he should have driven in 150 runs.

December 23—Cubs

ZMINDA: The Cubs have traded Doug Glanville for Mickey Morandini.

PALACIOS:

Year	Player	G	AB	R	H	2B	3B	HR	RBI	BB	SO	AVG	OBP	SLG
1997	Morandini	150	553	83	163	40	2	1	39	62	91	.295	.371	.380
1997	Sandberg	135	447	54	118	26	0	12	64	28	94	.264	.308	.403

All of a sudden, the Cubs are making a little noise. Coincidentally, getting another Phillie to play second base for them. The Cubs are no longer six players away from contending. They are probably down to three, and three "ifs" are better than six.

The three "ifs" remaining are:

1. signing Rod Beck,

2. Kerry Wood develops by June 1,

3. getting a better catcher, 1B or 3B

Question: Is Cooperson now a Cubs fan?

WENZ: Damn them, I may actually spend the next few months believing they have a chance. They actually did something positive yesterday. I understand it's just Mickey Morandini, but they actually got *something* for one of their Triple-A outfielders, Doug Glanville.

COUSINS: What happened to the John Valentin rumors? Was it true that they were asking for Jeremi Gonzalez and Glanville? If so, then it was smart not to make the trade. I guess it will be nice to have a legitimate No. 2 hitter with a good OBP, but I hate to see the youth and talent of Glanville gone.

JAMES: I've always liked Mickey Morandini, but signing a 32-year-old player coming off a career year is just *not* a smart strategy. Look up Tommy Herr, Cookie Rojas, Julian Javier, Bobby Richardson, Sandy Alomar Sr., Tommy Helms, Johnny Temple, Eddie Miksis, etc. I'll bet that players of this type typically lose 70 percent of their value or more between the ages of 32 and 34.

January 5—Untouchable Pitchers

HENZLER: In the history of baseball, there have been only six pitching seasons in which hurlers have posted strikeout to hit-plus-walk ratios of 1.19 or better (minimum 125 IP). Three of those pitching seasons occurred in 1997.

Does anyone else find that ironic? I mean, we're in the middle of a hitter's era, right? Is there an explanation?

Best K/(H+BB) Ratios

Year	Player	K	H+BB	Ratio
1997	Pedro Martinez	305	225	1.356
1965	Sandy Koufax	382	287	1.331
1995	Randy Johnson	294	224	1.313
1997	Randy Johnson	291	224	1.299
1986	Mike Scott	306	254	1.205
1997	Curt Schilling	319	266	1.199
1977	Goose Gossage	151	127	1.189
1984	Dwight Gooden	276	234	1.179
1968	Luis Tiant	264	225	1.173
1995	Hideo Nomo	236	202	1.168

(minimum 125 IP)

FAUST: Yes, it's a hitter's era, but wouldn't you say that hitters are striking out at historically high levels these days? That would make it easier to get a high numerator. . .

Could we look at Ks per plate appearance year-to-year for batters?

PINTO: I believe the explanation is that there is a wider variance in pitching ability than in hitting ability. The best pitchers are incredible, and the worst pitchers are really awful. Since you have more bad pitchers at the lower end, it appears to be a hitters' era. I think this should be properly categorized as a bad pitching era.

HENZLER: As Dave Carlson suggested, last year's MLB strikeout to hit-plus-walk ratio was the largest since the historic "year of the pitcher" in 1968. It also continued the general trend since the late '70s.

Just think what would happen if the Lords of Baseball decide to tinker with the rules to help depress a perceived overabundance of offense (i.e., change the strike zone, lower the mound, reduce the liveliness of the baseball, etc).

CARLSON: I think it may be ironic in what you are saying, but that doesn't mean it needs an explanation. Even when the league tendencies might be going in a certain direction, certain individuals can buck the trend (having outstanding power totals in a dead-ball era, or in this case, a spectacular pitching ratio during a hitters' era). All that means is what the player did is even more significant considering when it was done.

January 11—Cuban Defectors

PALACIOS: I lived in a Communist country for a good number of years, and I found out that the keys to success in a Communist regime were:

1. Following directions

2. Discipline

3. Respect for your superiors

4. Belief in your superiors

5. Hard work

I don't endorse totalitarian governments; however, the qualities to be successful in communist countries are extremely similar to the qualities necessary to succeed in team sports.

Sadly, defections are the only way we can see great Cuban-born talent in the U.S. Sadly, because the apples that arrive here are those players who leave something to be desired when it comes to discipline, following directions and respecting superiors. This is why most defectors who come to the U.S. will leave something to be desired when it comes to their major league careers. I would not be shelling much dough after these guys.

This doesn't mean that there aren't potentially awesome baseball players in Cuba, but we'll never see those players because they won't defect. Omar Linares is an awesome talent, though now declining. In the late '80s, he was probably the best third baseman in the world. But his personality was like Stan Musial's. Stan didn't leave for Mexico when he was offered an outrageous salary (by the standards in his day), and if Linares ever gets to play in the U.S., he'll be too old to make any sort of impact.

Obviously, not all defectors are alike, but usually it means abandoning their extended family, wives and young children. (Yes, Osvaldo Fernandez did bring his whole family from Cuba after he settled in the U.S., but he's exceptional in that regard.)

We already have plenty of people who disrespect their family (Wil Cordero) and who are dumb (Cordero, again, if you will) in the majors. We don't need any more. And let's get something straight, you have to be pretty dumb to get on a raft and cross the Caribbean on shark-infested waters—not to mention having no shelter from the sun and being at mercy of the capricious winds and storms of the area.

If getting on a raft was the smart thing to do, we'd have more 30- and 40-year-old people doing the same thing. Instead we have youngsters doing it, some of whom can play baseball.

It's just like the Russian kids who died defending the White House in Moscow: They were all under 18. The kids who carried the arms in Somalia, the ones who dragged the American corpses, they were around 13. When I was in a Communist country, I saw those who died trying to be heroic: they were all kids. Living in a Communist country was no fun, but seldom did I see a mature person trying to wage war.

Once again, same thing with the baseball player defectors. The mature, the sane, the intelligent, the leaders, the winners—they will never defect. It will be the immature kids, ready to join any madmen's revolutions, the ones who have nothing to lose, who will risk nothing to make in the majors. And the majors will shell out money—a lot of money—to them.

Too bad we're staging no revolutions in the U.S. right now. Too bad for Latrell Sprewell, Vernon Maxwell, Isaiah Rider, Brian Cox. They'd be the leaders of the revolutions. They'd be our heroes. Too bad they were born in such great times when we need no heroes. (Since I'm already digressing, I'll wander away some more: Low voter turnout means great times. Don't believe me, then check South Korea's voter turnout now that their economy is in trouble.)

Anyway, don't place much stock on Cuban defectors. They don't have what it takes to endure. They may have done something heroic in defecting (though I question that heroism), but the second they step on U.S. soil, they'll no longer need to be heroic. They'll need patience, the ability to follow directions, the ability to endure. Unfortunately for them, the lack of these qualities is exactly what got them to the U.S. They will fail.

P.S. I really wish Linares had played in the majors. I really wish Julio Moya had pitched against Nolan Ryan (Moya was from Nicaragua, but he too missed his chance). In a weird way I imagine them to be happy people. Almost like Buck O'Neil.

PINTO: You make an interesting point. A sports writer I know has been very high on almost every Cuban defector, but except for Livan Hernandez, they have been very disappointing.

I would disagree with you on one point, however. The reason the 40 year olds don't lead revolutions is that the revolutionaries in Communist countries never live to be 40.

Secondly, as Bill James has pointed out to me, baseball is a conservative sport, full of conservative people. So you are more likely to find people in baseball who are unwilling to buck the system. (It's an interesting irony that the most successful union in the world is full of members who would likely be on the union-busting side in any other endeavor.) So baseball players, by their very nature, are unlikely to leave.

Finally, I bet baseball players in Cuba have it pretty good compared to their countrymen. But word will start filtering back, that the United States isn't such a bad place and you can really make a lot of money there. And some really good Cuban player is going to look at the current lot of defectors, say "I'm better than they are," and start thinking about defecting. And there are safer ways to defect than a raft in the Caribbean, especially for someone who's playing games internationally.

JAMES: It's a small point relative to the discussion, but unions are now *conservative* institutions, institutions with privileged, well-off members whose basic function is to protect their privileges. The failure to recognize this is among the critical dysfunctions which is tying our political system in knots.

It is true that baseball players are, as a group, exceptionally conservative in most respects. Their union is an excellent symbol of the union movement in America today. It deliberately excludes all of the genuinely exploited workers who work for peanuts (the minor leaguers, the service workers, etc.), and exploits every device in labor law to protect the privileges of its obscenely wealthy members.

Top 100 (Well, Almost) Players
of All Time

January 2, 1998—The Greatest Players of All Time

FAUST: One of our customers, Bruce Grossberg, asked knowledgeable baseball fans to submit Top 40 lists to him via e-mail, which he used to compile a list of the top players of all time (by consensus). A player listed at No. 40 got one point; a player listed No. 1 got 40 points. Additionally, players got bonus points for being listed in the top 10. Without further ado, here's the countdown he posted on America Online on New Year's Day. Enjoy.

Happy New Year, folks: The baseball survey is officially closed. The results have been tabulated. There were 124 different players who got at least one mention among the total of 47 top 40 lists that were tabulated. Only those players that got at least two mentions will be listed in the final rankings. There are 97 players who got at least two mentions. Players are listed in order of total points accumulated with ties broken first by total number of mentions and then by the highest individual listing the player got. There is one incident of an exact tie at No. 85. Two players each got the exact same mentions at the exact same positions. Despite the low point totals on the players near the bottom of the survey there are only one or two questionable players listed, in my opinion. Most of the 27 players who only got one mention would have been questionable choices to make the top 100 in my opinion, so in that regard I think you will all be pretty comfortable with the results. Let's start with the No. 97 player:

No. 97—WADE BOGGS—5 points—2 mentions—Finally got a second mention yesterday to squeak into the rankings. Would have done better a few years ago before these last few so-so Yankee seasons. Even those are better than you think. OBP with Yanks is still about .400.

No. 96—ROLLIE FINGERS—10 points—2 mentions—One of three relief pitchers to crack the list.

No. 95—BROOKS ROBINSON—10 points—3 mentions—Stats don't seem to add up to it, but people's opinions sure do. Second of six third basemen on the list.

No. 94—WHITEY FORD—12 points—3 mentions—The first of 22 starting pitchers to make the list. First of only six lefthanded pitchers to make the top 97.

No. 93—EDDIE MURRAY—13 points—2 mentions—Like Boggs he got a late second mention to propel him into the final rankings. Like the Hall of Fame, 500 homers was enough to get you on to this list. All-time great clutch hitter. The first of 13 first basemen on the list.

No. 92—DUKE SNIDER—14 points—4 mentions—The first of eight center fielders on the list. The next one will not show up for a while.

No. 91—ROBIN YOUNT—15 points—2 mentions—Also got a late second mention to put him into the final rankings. Unlike the 500-homer plateau, 3,000 hits did not guarantee a spot on this final list, as you will see as we count them down.

No. 90—PAUL WANER—16 points—3 mentions—"Big Poison" definitely belongs on this list. He's the first of 10 right fielders to show up. A Classic Game favorite for great offense, excellent defense and great durability for a reasonable price that just went up 9K (123K last year, now 132K).

No. 89—BILL DAHLEN—17 points—2 mentions—I'm very glad that he made the list as our voters recognized his greatness. Interesting that he's the only guy who made the top 97 whose Classic Game salary is under 100K.

No. 88—ED WALSH—20 points—2 mentions—Had an *unbelievable* seven-season stretch and baseball's all-time lowest career ERA (1.82).

No. 87—HARMON KILLEBREW—20 points—6 mentions—That's a lot of mentions to only total 20 points. Obviously he just got on to the bottom of several top-40 lists. One of the most feared sluggers in the history of baseball.

No. 85 (tie)—ARKY VAUGHAN—21 points—2 mentions—One of baseball's greatest shortstops.

No. 85 (tie)—KING KELLY—21 points—2 mentions—Glad to see him make it. Baseball's biggest star for a while in the mid-1880s.

No. 84—THREE FINGER BROWN—25 points—3 mentions—Probably should be higher. His five-year stretch from 1906-1910 (127-44, ERA under 1.50) was at least as good as Koufax' five-year stretch, plus Brown's other years were not exactly bad.

No. 83—RALPH KINER—27 points—2 mentions—All-time great slugger with a short career. May or may not deserve to be on this list, but made it as one voter had him in the top 20.

No. 82—MICKEY COCHRANE—27 points—4 mentions—Somewhat short career discouraged voters from putting him on their lists, I believe.

No. 81—MARTIN DIHIGO—28 points—3 mentions—Apparently he was the second-greatest pitcher in the history of the Negro Leagues although, I admit that I don't know that much about him.

No. 80—HOYT WILHELM—31 points—4 mentions—Opposing hitters hit just .216 against him in over 2,250 innings pitched. Even led his league in ERA once without starting a game!!!

No. 79—REGGIE JACKSON—32 points—3 mentions—Mr. October checks in with the all-time greats, which is where he always thought he belonged.

No. 78—JUAN MARICHAL—33 points—3 mentions—A somewhat surprising choice here, not that he doesn't deserve it but he is usually underrated. I guess a couple of the voters realized that he may have been even better than Sandy Koufax in '65-'66.

No. 77—TONY GWYNN—34 points—4 mentions—Should probably be even higher. Still in his prime.

No. 76—LOU BOUDREAU—35 points—2 mentions—He's better than a couple of higher-salaried Classic Game shortstops according to our voters.

No. 75—PIE TRAYNOR—38 points—2 mentions—This one seems questionable but like I've said before, he must have been better than his stats seem to indicate. Still him being at No. 75 is a bit of a fluke because one list had him at No. 15.

No. 74—OZZIE SMITH—39 points—7 mentions—Deserves to be here for obvious reasons.

No. 73—WILLIE McCOVEY—40 points—4 mentions—Devastating slugger.

No. 72—DENNIS ECKERSLEY—42 points—8 mentions—Should be the highest-salaried swing man in the Classic Game when he gets in. It'll be hard to code him correctly, as his career has had so many different stages.

No. 71—TIM RAINES—43 points—3 mentions—The numbers say that he's an all-time great, but many of us don't want to accept it, as indicated by his only being on three different lists. All three of his mentions were in the top 30.

No. 70—AL SIMMONS—43 points—7 mentions—Five of his seven mentions came right at the bottom of different lists (from Nos. 36-40) which explains the low point total for seven mentions. Only player ever to drive in 100 or more runs in each of his first 10 seasons. He topped it off by doing it in his 11th season, too.

No. 69—CAP ANSON—44 points—4 mentions—Throw in his first five seasons in the National Association and he hit .300 for 20 consecutive seasons. One list had him in the top 20.

No. 68—MARK McGWIRE—46 points—3 mentions—Hard to say yet where he really belongs.

No. 67—KID NICHOLS—46 points—4 mentions—I'm glad to see him make it. Only pitcher ever to win 20 or more games in each of his first 10 seasons.

No. 66—BUCK EWING—55 points—6 mentions. Thought of as perhaps the greatest player of all time before Wagner and Cobb showed up.

No. 65—GEORGE SISLER—56 points—4 mentions—Two lists had him in the top 20. Perhaps the quintessential transitional player (from dead ball into live ball).

No. 64—JOHNNY MIZE—60 points—5 mentions—Another all-time great slugger with a somewhat short career. He missed three mid-prime seasons during the war that you can't hold against him.

No. 63—AL KALINE—71 points—7 mentions—Super solid star even made the top 20 on one list. Numbers say that he's as good or better than Clemente.

No. 62—CHARLIE GEHRINGER—73 points—10 mentions—Eight out of his 10 mentions were near the bottom of lists. He did make the top 20 on one list.

No. 61—DAN BROUTHERS—74 points—6 mentions—Perhaps the greatest slugger of the 19th century. One list had him at No. 13.

No. 60—NOLAN RYAN—77 points—10 mentions. Was he the 60th-best player of all time? Probably not, but he was such an unbelievable phenomenon that he may belong here anyway.

No. 59—ROY CAMPANELLA—80 points—7 mentions—The first of three catchers in a row in the rankings. These three came in as a notch below the top three catchers who come up later.

No. 58—BILL DICKEY—84 points—4 mentions—Made the top 20 on two different lists.

No. 57—MIKE PIAZZA—86 points—7 mentions—The shortest career of anyone on the list (six seasons). The voters are obviously trying to estimate how his career will turn out. He also made the top 20 on two lists.

No. 56—ED DELAHANTY—86 points—9 mentions—Tremendous superstar was still going strong right up until his mysterious death. Would have been No. 41 on my list. Nobody listed him in their top 20.

No. 55—GEORGE DAVIS—98 points—10 mentions—I guess he'll never make the Hall of Fame, but the real people know the real deal. Made the top 20 on one list.

No. 54—CARL HUBBELL—108 points—12 mentions—In the top 20 on two lists but also down near the bottom of nine different top 40 lists.

No. 53—BUCK LEONARD—112 points—10 mentions—All-time great Negro League slugger was in the top 20 on two lists.

No. 52—POP LLOYD—117 points—6 mentions—One list ranked him in the top 10. His coding in the Classic Game should be better if he was really this good.

No. 51—CARL YASTRZEMSKI—120 points—14 mentions—Only four mentions in the top 30 of any lists, but had 10 mentions between 31 and 40.

No. 50—CAL RIPKEN—128 points—14 mentions—The top shortstop in the history of the AL. Cal should be a unanimous Hall of Fame selection. I wonder how many of those moron sportswriters will leave him off their ballots ? Only two lists had him in the top 25.

No. 49—JOE JACKSON—139 points—12 mentions. How high would he rank if he hadn't been banned? Two lists had him in the top 20.

No. 48—HANK GREENBERG—144 points—14 mentions—Had one mention at No. 12 and he may have been up in that area if he hadn't missed those war years. Anybody who slugs over .600 lifetime is mind-boggling.

No. 47—BOB FELLER—144 points—16 mentions—I always though that he was slightly overrated, but then again he also missed almost four super prime seasons during the war.

No. 46—PETE ROSE—148 points—10 mentions—I guess he's the Nolan Ryan of position players. I'm sure there were a lot more than 45 guys who were better players, but not many who wanted it more than he did. Voted by old-time players in a book as "the player who did the most to inspire his teammates." Certain things can't be coded unfortunately. "Charlie Hustle" had two votes in the top 15, including one in the top 10.

No. 45—ROBERTO CLEMENTE—164 points—17 mentions—All 17 mentions were between No. 21 and No. 40 as many voters felt that he had to be on their top 40 list somewhere. Stats say he was great, but he was even better than that.

No. 44—ROGER CLEMENS—177 points—19 mentions—Probably should be even higher, but I think some voters did not fully comprehend the context of his numbers (Fenway Park in the AL with the DH). Only one mention in the top 20, with 14 of his 19 mentions coming between No. 31 and No. 40.

No. 43—BOB GIBSON—185 points—16 mentions—Some things stick in your mind forever. I was only 11 years old but I remember the buildup to the Gibson/Denny McLain matchup to open up the 1968 series. I also remember the results of that first game as Gibson mowed down the Tigers. I'll bet that the bookies made a fortune when Gibson lost the seventh game of that Series. Bob had three of his mentions in the top 20 of various lists.

No. 42—JACKIE ROBINSON—188 points—16 mentions—He had one mention in the top 15 and all the rest were between No. 21 and No. 40.

No. 41—OSCAR CHARLESTON—232 points—13 mentions—Ironic choice to follow Jackie Robinson with. Oscar was supposed to have been the Ty Cobb of the Negro Leagues, although analysis of historical accounts seem to indicate a closer likeness to Speaker. He received five mentions in the top 20 on different lists including two in the top 10. One voter placed him at No. 3.

No. 40—SANDY KOUFAX—238 points—20 mentions—Sandy had four mentions in the top 20 including one in the top 10, but most lists that included him had him in the 30s. If players and/or writers did this survey, he'd be higher.

No. 39—ERNIE BANKS—269 points—23 mentions—Ernie had three mentions in the top 15, but most of his listings came from 21-40. Hard for me personally to rank with the immediate switch from shortstop to 1B after a few games in the OF.

No. 38—KEN GRIFFEY JR.—271 points—15 mentions—Had four mentions in the top 10 including one at No. 5, which is where he may finally end up.

No. 37—STEVE CARLTON—318 points—27 mentions—Lefty was mentioned on 57 percent of the lists, although not on mine as I feel he's a little overrated. People tend to think of the four Cy Youngs rather than the six or seven just so-so years he had in between. Had two mentions in the top 15 and another two between 16 and 20.

No. 36—FRANK THOMAS—322 points—20 mentions—Frank's nickname came from a song ("The Big Hurt" by Miss Toni Fisher) and was bestowed upon him by Ken "Hawk" Harrelson. Casey Kasem might have played that song on a countdown if his show had been around in those days (1959-1960). Had six mentions in the top 15, including two in the top 10. His fielding scares me though. I'd want him as a DH in a future Classic Game league.

No. 35—MEL OTT—348 points—29 mentions—Named on 62 percent of the ballots, this guy must have been amazing to do what he did at 5'9" and 170 pounds. Only one mention in the top 20, but on 28 ballots between No. 21 and No. 40.

No. 34—GEORGE BRETT—356 points—24 mentions—As a Yankee fan this was the guy I feared most as an opposition player coming to bat in a big spot. A real stud. Had seven mentions in the top 20, with most of his rankings coming in the 20s. One of these guys who could hit any pitcher at any time, unlike some of the bigger swinging sluggers of the day.

No. 33—RICKEY HENDERSON—367 points—26 mentions—He was my favorite player for many years, but even I ranked him a little lower than I would like to have because of his attitude. I never saw any non-pitcher dominate a game like Rickey did, especially in 1985. Had three mentions in the top 20 including one in the top 10.

No. 32—YOGI BERRA—415 points—29 mentions—Had three mentions in the top 20 including one in the top 10. My choice for the top catcher, but he's only No. 3 according to these rankings. Montclair State University, which is in the next town over from me here in New Jersey, just named their new baseball stadium after him. Yogi is a longtime resident of Montclair and the school has won a couple of NCAA Division III championships in the last 10-15 years.

No. 31—EDDIE MATHEWS—425 points—37 mentions. Only one mention in the top 20, as most voters had him between 21 and 30. He was named on 79 percent of the lists as most voters decided that a decent fielding third baseman who hits like him has to be on the list.

No. 30—GREG MADDUX—450 points—31 mentions—On about two-thirds of the lists, Maddux was top 10 on one list and top 20 on a total of nine lists. I don't see how he's a notch above Clemens, but the majority rules here.

No. 29—TOM SEAVER—500 points—29 mentions—Only one mention in the top 15 but nine more between 16 and 20. Did not win the Cy Young in his best season (1971).

No. 28—JOHNNY BENCH—548 points—39 ballots—Mentioned on 83 percent of the lists, this all-time great places right next to one of his old batterymates (Tom Terrific). One mention in the top 10 and six more between 11 and 20 for Bench. Most lists had him in the 20s or 30s.

No. 27—WARREN SPAHN—577 points—39 mentions—Only one mention in the top 15, but 13 more between 16 and 20. Got hurt by WWII at the start of his career and did not win his first ML game until he was 25.

No. 26—SATCHEL PAIGE—629 points—27 mentions—Five mentions in the top 10 for Satch, including one in the top five, which is where he might really belong. A total of 16 mentions in the top 20. Major league hitters hit .241 against him in a hitter's era when he was already an old man.

No. 25—NAP LAJOIE—657 points—29 mentions—Nap's momentum was slowed some after Bill James posted his list and left him off of his top 40. Lajoie was headed for the top 20 at the time but his listings slowed down after Bill somewhat denounced him. Maybe No. 25 is a good compromise for a guy whose teams never contended much and who dominated a new "major" league early on. It's always impressive to me when you open the page of your encyclopedia and see a ton of bolded (league leading) numbers for a player. *Total Baseball* ranks him as the best player in the AL for nine different seasons. He was in the top 10 on seven different lists, between 11-20 on 10 others.

No. 24—JOSH GIBSON—671 points—32 mentions—At No. 24 Josh is the lowest-ranked player to be the best ever at his position according to our voters. Bench was named on more total ballots but Josh was top five on two lists, top 10 on another and between 11-20 on 14 more. Over one-third of the voters had him in their top 20.

No. 23—JOE MORGAN—677 points—40 mentions—85 percent of the lists included Joe in their top 40. Only seven voters left him off their lists. Would have been higher, but only had one top 10 mention and only 11 others between 11-20. Most of his mentions (21) came between 21-30, which is where he ended up.

No. 22—GROVER CLEVELAND ALEXANDER—697 points—36 mentions—You think anyone will break his record of 16 shutouts in a season? The 1993 Braves were the last *team* to have 16 shutouts in a season. This guy was a "Maddux" type who could go over 300 innings in a season. In 1923 he walked 30 batters all year in over 300 IP. Only had two mentions in the top 10, but 13 more between 11-20.

No. 21—FRANK ROBINSON—703 points—42 mentions—Only five lists did not contain Mr. Robinson's name. When Maury Allen's book came out years ago, it was a joke when he had Frank down at No. 63. Don't forget this was many years ago, before the Griffeys, Madduxes, Ripkens, etc. were around. Frank had 12 mentions between 11 and 20. Most voters had him in the 20s, and that's where he ended up.

No. 20—CY YOUNG—769 points—37 mentions—Cy was between 6-10 on six ballots and between 11-20 on 17 others. He accumulated 66 more points than the No. 21 player, which is enough of a difference to give the top 20 a little separation from the next few players down. Had 749 complete games in his career. I think that record is safe.

No. 19—BARRY BONDS—790 points—29 mentions—After Barry everyone in the top 18 has at least 40 mentions apiece. For him to garner 790 points tells you that he got a lot of votes very high up. He had 13 mentions in the top 10 and nine more between 11-20. Considering that some voters did not even consider current players in mid-career, this is astounding. May be the best ever at his position (left field) before he's through.

No. 18—EDDIE COLLINS—801 points—41 mentions—Only one mention in the top 10 and two others between 11 and 15. He did, however, have 14 mentions between 16 and 20, which is exactly where he ended up. Only six lists did not contain his name. Not quite the best ever at his position, though, according to the voting.

No. 17—JOE DiMAGGIO—831 points—42 mentions—Only five lists did not contain "The Yankee Clipper's" name. Had eight mentions in the top 10 and another 11 mentions between 11 and 20. I think there's some others coming up who are still alive, so Joe will have to relinquish his title as "The Greatest Living Player."

No. 16—JIMMIE FOXX—955 points—45 mentions—Over 95 percent of the lists contained his name, with only two voters leaving it off. Only one voter placed him in his top 10, but he had 26 mentions between 11 and 20. He had 125 more points than Joltin' Joe, which places him at the start of the "Best of the Best" so to speak. Most every player from here on down was listed on virtually every ballot.

No. 15—CHRISTY MATHEWSON—990 points—45 mentions—As with Double X, only two lists did not contain Matty's name. He was only in the top 10 on two lists but was between 11 and 20 on 26 lists. Starting with the next player, everyone who is still left was listed in the top 10 on at least 10 ballots.

No. 14—ROGERS HORNSBY—1,058 points—40 mentions. Everybody loves defense at second base and somehow seven lists did not contain Hornsby's name, but he still finished as the top second baseman due to 14 top-10 mentions and another 16 mentions between 11 and 20. Eddie Collins had 41 mentions, but Eddie did not have near the top-10 mentions that Rogers accumulated. Hornsby had four different lists include him in their top five, with two of those listing him as the third-greatest player ever. Even Bill James' slight of Hornsby could not derail the Rajah Train.

No. 13—TRIS SPEAKER—1,183 points—46 mentions. One voter somehow left Tris off his list. I hope it was just an oversight on his part. I can understand taking him over Cobb, especially for Classic Game purposes. Cobb may be slightly better offensively, but Speaker gives you the tremendous defense while Cobb in center is probably slightly above average. Cobb played more career games, but Speaker played more than enough games where his durability will be the same as Cobb's as far as the Classic Game is concerned. *Total Baseball* rates Speaker as better than Cobb on a per game basis (see page 2278 of the current edition—total player rating per 150 games). Barry Bonds is No. 2 on that list, which does not include pitchers. As for intangibles, it's not even close between Tris and Ty. *The Pitch That Killed,* which is a book about Carl Mays and Ben Chapman gives you the impression that Speaker's teammates would have killed for him. Ty's teammates wanted to kill Ty. The voters have spoken though and Ty is still to appear on the survey. Tris had 14 mentions in the top 10 but only three in the top five.

No. 12—MIKE SCHMIDT—1,201 points—44 mentions—Mike flirted with finishing in the top 10 but came up a little short. Like Speaker, Mike also had 14 mentions in the top 10 with only three of those being in the top five. He did however have 15 mentions between 11 and 15 which is where he ended up. Schmidt was easily the highest-ranking third basemen.

No. 11—MICKEY MANTLE—1,357 points—47 mentions—"The Commerce Comet" is the first player to show up who was mentioned on all 47 lists. The Mick was in the top 10 for most of the time the survey was being tabulated, but a late surge by another player who finished at No. 9 knocked Mickey down to No. 11. As it was, he only missed the top 10 by 21 points. Mick had four mentions in the top five and another 12 mentions between six and 10. He also had 16 mentions between 11 and 15, which is where he ended up. Not only was he on every list, but he was in the top 30 on every list. Only 23 points separated No. 9 through No. 11.

Coming up at No. 10 we have another player who is *not* the best ever at his position according to our voters.

At this point I would like to thank all of you who took the time to participate in this survey. Anyone can draw up their own list of the greatest players ever, but most of us have certain pet players that we like to push and others that we like to knock. Using this democratic method hopefully we have removed at least some of those prejudices from the process and have come up with a representative list. So far we had Josh Gibson as the top catcher, Schmidt as the top third basemen, Hornsby as the top second baseman and Eckersley as the top relief pitcher. The top players at the other positions are still to come. Here we go with the Top 10:

No. 10—STAN MUSIAL—1,378 points—46 mentions—Some klutz left him off their list, I hope by accident. When I was growing up and reading baseball record books, Stan's name was all over the place for extra-base hits, most bases on long hits, total bases, etc. How'd you like to get a Classic Game year from him like the one he had in 1948? Only two mentions in the top five, but 14 others between six and 10, and 23 mentions between 11 and 15. This means 83 percent of the lists had Stan in their top 15. Next at No. 9 with only two more points than Musial is. . .

No. 9—LEFTY GROVE—1,380 points—45 mentions—We should have the heads examined of the two voters who did not include Lefty in their top 40. Grove had 11 mentions in the top five and another 13 mentions between six and 10. This means that more than half the voters feel that he belongs in the top 10 and he made it. Three different voters listed Lefty as one of the three greatest players of all time. The Classic Game computer manager needs to be modified so guys like Lefty can pitch more in relief in between starts. Grove had 55 saves in his career and averaged six or seven a year for a five- to six-year period. I know he had a lot of relief wins too. Lefthanded pitcher is not really a position, but Grove is easily the top southpaw of all time on the survey, unless you count hitters who used to be pitchers at one time. Coming up at No. 8 is another all-time great who cannot be considered the best ever at his position. . .

No. 8—HANK AARON—1,640 points—46 mentions—Some knucklehead left Henry off his top 40 (I know who it was, I'm assuming it was an oversight) but it didn't matter as he was well entrenched in the top 10 some 260 points ahead of Grove. Hank was in the top five on 14 lists and between six and 10 on another 17 lists. This means that about two-thirds of the voters thought that he belonged in the top 10. In fact, 45 of the 47 lists had Hank in the top 15. It's kind of a matter-of-fact pick. You know he's gotta be way up there somewhere and you find a nice slot for him. Nobody had him at No. 1 or No. 2, but from No. 3 on down he got plenty of mentions. Coming up next at No. 7 is a player who has to be considered as the *best ever* at his position.

No. 7—LOU GEHRIG—1,683 points—47 mentions—All 47 lists included Lou somewhere in the top 40. He even got one first-place vote. Thirteen lists had Lou in the top five and another 18 lists had him between six and 10. He was in the top 20 on *every* ballot with only four voters not placing him in their top 15. I thought that he belonged just outside the top 10 with either Speaker or Schmidt replacing him, but the public has spoken. Next at No. 6 is still another player who finished as the *best ever* at his position.

No. 6—WALTER JOHNSON—1,704 points—47 mentions—Thirteen mentions in the top five and another 23 mentions between six and 10 means that over three-quarters of the voters think that "Barney" belongs in the top 10. He averaged one shutout for every six starts in his career, and I think he lost a lot of 1-0 games in his career too, including a couple to another player who is still coming up on the survey. Walter was in the top 15 on 46 out of 47 lists. Somehow one voter had him at No. 32. I'll send his copy of the results to Bellevue.

No. 5—TY COBB—1,771 points—46 mentions—It's fitting that one voter left Ty off his list, citing Cobb's racial stance among other reasons for not ranking him. This guy was universally thought of as the greatest player in baseball and at the same time was the most hated player in the game. I left him out of my top 10 thinking him to be a terrible guy to have in the clubhouse. He would also make headstrong moves, like attempting to steal home with no outs and a guy like Sam Crawford at the plate. Fourteen different lists had Ty in the top three with one first-place vote. Altogether 21 voters placed Ty in their top five, and here he is.

No. 4—TED WILLIAMS"—1,906 points—47 mentions—Forty-three out of 47 lists had "The Thumper" in the top 10, with 26 of those being in the top five. It boggles the mind when you try to total up what his numbers would have looked like without the military time. At 60 years old he smacked a HR off of a pitcher at his old high school on an episode of "Greatest Sports Legends." Ted is the greatest left fielder ever according to this survey. Next at No. 3 just seven points ahead of Ted is another "Greatest Ever at His Position."

No. 3—WILLIE MAYS—1,913 points—47 mentions—The greatest ever in center field according to the survey, Willie was in the top five on 26 different lists. Fifteen different lists had him at No. 2 or No. 3. One voter actually had him outside the top 20. There's not much else to say about Mays. It's obvious that he belongs up here. Next at No. 2, the best ever at his position. . .

No. 2—HONUS WAGNER—2,000 points—46 mentions. Believe it or not, one guy left Honus off his list. I think it had to have been an oversight, but then again the same guy had Carl Furillo at No. 40. It didn't matter as Wagner easily outdistanced Mays and Ted to lock up the No. 2 spot. Thirty-eight of the lists had Honus in the top five including two first-place votes. Seventeen of the voters listed Wagner at No. 2 and that's where his final spot is. Curiously enough one list had him at No. 31. And now. . .

As if it's some kind of a surprise, the No. 1 spot belongs to. . .

No. 1—BABE RUTH—2,342 points—47 mentions—Babe was No. 1 on 43 lists and No. 2 on the other four lists. There really is not much of a contest when you consider everything he did, including his pitching, hitting, effect on a team, charisma, the fact that he won so much. When you watch a guy like Michael Jordan, you get a small idea of what a giant Babe was in his day. Babe once won a fungo contest by hitting a ball about 500 feet righthanded.

Here is a list of all the players who only got one mention on the survey and failed to make the final rankings. Obviously some of them had more total points that some of the players who did make the final list, but I didn't think one mention should get you on to the list no matter how high that one mention was.

Harry Heilmann—21 points

Eddie Plank—19

Al Spalding—14

Barry Larkin—13 (one of the greatest ever at shortstop)

Gabby Hartnett—13 (was hoping he'd get another mention, although I didn't list him)

Chief Bender—12

John Clarkson—10

Willie Stargell—10

Smokey Joe Williams—8

Sam Crawford—7

Bid McPhee—6

Carlton Fisk—6

Lou Brock—6 (glad he didn't make it)

Jesse Burkett—5

Billy Hamilton—4 (wish he had made it)

Sam Thompson—4

Bill Mazeroski—3

Gary Carter—3

Lee Smith—3

Robin Roberts—3

Ryne Sandberg—3

Bobby Grich—2

Cool Papa Bell—2

Dick Allen—2

Alex Rodriguez—1

Carl Furillo—1

Shigeo Nagashima—1

Obviously the last three names were listed by voters trying to make a point of some kind.

COOPERSON: People have spent time compiling a list which ranks Tim Raines ahead of Tony Gwynn. Would we call this time well spent? I guess the stolen-base disparity moves Raines ahead of that useless guy in San Diego.

JAMES: Ethan assumes that whoever doesn't agree with him is a waste of time. Raines has scored 1,475 runs in his career; Gwynn, 1,237. They're both great players, but I think it's a close call.

Jim Henzler's
"STATS Focus"

March 17, 1997—Power/Speed Numbers

Barry Bonds is arguably the best package of power and speed in major league history. Last year, for instance, Bonds slugged 42 homers while stealing 40 bases. He thus joined Jose Canseco as the only "40/40 players" of all time.

Bonds also led the majors in 1996 with a "power/speed number" of 41.0. The power/speed number was developed by Bill James in his *Baseball Abstracts*. It combines home runs and stolen bases using the following formula:

$$\frac{2 * HR * SB}{HR + SB} = \text{Power/Speed Number}$$

The formula is constructed in such a way as to emphasize proficiency in both home runs *and* stolen bases. A player must be adept in both areas in order to generate a high power/speed score. You'll get a sense of what that means by looking at the major league leaders last season:

1996 Power/Speed Leaders

Player, Team	HR	SB	Power/Speed
Barry Bonds, SF	42	40	41.0
Ellis Burks, Col	40	32	35.6
Barry Larkin, Cin	33	36	34.4
Dante Bichette, Col	31	31	31.0
Brady Anderson, Bal	50	21	29.6
Ray Lankford, StL	21	35	26.3
Andres Galarraga, Col	47	18	26.0
Steve Finley, SD	30	22	25.4
Marquis Grissom, Atl	23	28	25.3
Jeff Bagwell, Hou	31	21	25.0

As you can see, Brady Anderson parlayed his 50 homers and 21 stolen bases into a power/speed score 29.6. Meanwhile, the major league leader in home runs, Mark McGwire, laid a goose egg. His 52 homers couldn't compensate for *no* stolen bases, and McGwire's power/speed score was a big, fat zero.

Similarly, the major league leader in stolen bases, Kenny Lofton, doesn't appear in the top 10 with a power/speed number of 23.6. And the man who finished second in the majors in stolen bases, Tom Goodwin, mustered a score of just 2.0. Goodwin's 66 steals just couldn't balance his *one* home run.

Another interesting point to be made is the predominance of National Leaguers on the list. Anderson was the only American Leaguer in the top 10 last year. That only serves to illustrate the fact that Canseco was the last American Leaguer to reach the 30/30 mark in a season, when he hit 42 homers and stole 40 bases in 1988. Since then, a National Leaguer has attained the 30/30 mark 13 times!

But back to Bonds. Last year he led the majors in power/speed score for the fifth time in the last seven seasons. And he became just the fourth player in major league history to hit at least 300 career homers while stealing at least 300 bases. If he maintains his established pace, Bonds will pass Willie Mays' career power/speed figure sometime around the turn of the century. Of course by that time, Rickey Henderson may have already passed the Say Hey Kid:

Career Power/Speed Leaders

Player	HR	SB	Power/Speed
Willie Mays	660	338	447.1
Rickey Henderson	244	1186	404.7
Bobby Bonds	332	461	386.0
Joe Morgan	268	689	385.9
Andre Dawson	438	314	365.8
Hank Aaron	755	240	364.2
Barry Bonds	334	380	355.5
Reggie Jackson	563	228	324.6
Don Baylor	338	285	309.2
Frank Robinson	586	204	302.6

In a sense, the above list is a family affair. Bobby Bonds is Barry's father, of course. And Mays happens to be Barry Bonds' godfather. While Mays appears to be a few years away, Barry should reach, and possibly even pass, Bobby's figure by the end of 1997. Perhaps we should rename the category the "Bonds Number."

March 24, 1997—Isolated Power

If you ever wondered what it was like to enjoy baseball during the 1920s and '30s, you don't have to wonder any longer. The 1990s are turning into a pretty good imitation of that awesome hitters' era.

Over the last few seasons we've witnessed some of the gaudiest battings stats since those days of Ruth and Gehrig. Fifty home runs... 140 RBI... batting averages over .350... these are figures we didn't see very often in the not-too-distant past. But they've become relatively commonplace in the mid-'90s.

Need further proof that today's offense stacks up well when measured against any other era? Consider the highest single-season "isolated power" averages of all time. Isolated power has also been called "power percentage" in the past. It measures slugging percentage exclusive of singles, and can be calculated by starting with slugging percentage and subtracting batting average. But here's the technical formula:

$$\frac{2B + (2 * 3B) + (3 * HR)}{AB} = \textbf{Isolated Power}$$

Anyway, Mark McGwire clubbed 52 homers last season, and he needed just 423 at-bats to do so. He also mustered 21 doubles, producing an isolated power figure of .418. As you can see from the following chart, McGwire's mark (no pun intended) ranks as the third-highest single-season isolated power average of all time:

Highest Single-Season Isolated Power

Player	Year	AB	2B	3B	HR	Iso
Babe Ruth	1920	458	36	9	54	.472
Babe Ruth	1921	540	44	16	59	.469
Mark McGwire	1996	423	21	0	52	.418
Babe Ruth	1927	540	29	8	60	.417
Lou Gehrig	1927	584	52	18	47	.392
Babe Ruth	1928	536	29	8	54	.386
Jimmie Foxx	1932	585	33	9	58	.385
Jeff Bagwell	1994	400	32	2	39	.383
Albert Belle	1995	546	52	1	50	.374
Babe Ruth	1930	518	28	9	49	.373

(minimum 400 AB)

Anytime you're being measured against the likes of Ruth, Gehrig and Foxx, you've gotta figure you're doing something right. And McGwire certainly did a lot right in 1996. But check out who else appears on this list. Jeff Bagwell in 1994 and Albert Belle in 1995 both produced isolated power averages which ranked among the best ever. So that means we've now had three straight seasons with one of the top 10 isolated power scores in baseball history.

We are truly experiencing a special offensive period in the game's evolution. Bagwell, Belle and McGwire have produced seasons which even the Babe himself would be proud to call his own. Future generations of baseball fans may have a hard time distinguishing the accomplishments of this generation of ballplayers from those legends of the early lively-ball era.

April 8, 1997—Trade Value

How would you like to be Alex Rodriguez? To be 21 with his kind of ability? He appears to be the kind of player which comes along once in a generation.

But if you couldn't be Alex Rodriguez, who'd be the next-best choice? How about the Mariners' general manager? After all, he's actually living a rotisserie player's dream come true. . . to have Rodriguez play for him for as long as that GM can afford to retain Rodriguez' services. Or until that GM's own services are politely shown the door.

It's hard to dispute that Rodriguez is the most valuable commodity in baseball today. It becomes nearly impossible when you consider his many talents. How many shortstops can hit .358? Or accummulate 54 doubles? Or club 36 homers? Or slug .631? And how many can do all that at the tender age of 20? The scary thing is, Rodriguez figures to actually get *better*.

If you were the GM, would you ever trade a package like that? In today's baseball climate, where monetary factors determine many personnel decisions, the day may actually arrive when the Mariners consider just such a transaction.

But for now, Rodriguez sits on the top of this chart, which lists the players with the highest trade value in baseball. We'll explain more in a moment:

Players with Highest Trade Values

Player, Team	Pos	Age	Estab Value	Trade Value
Alex Rodriguez, Sea	SS	20	15.0	175.4
Frank Thomas, WSox	1B	28	17.7	154.0
Albert Belle, WSox	LF	29	18.0	153.9
Barry Bonds, SF	LF	31	18.7	152.5
Jim Thome, Cle	3B	25	16.0	141.0
Chuck Knoblauch, Min	2B	27	15.7	118.2
Mike Piazza, LA	C	27	15.7	118.2
Roberto Alomar, Bal	2B	28	15.5	107.9
Mo Vaughn, Bos	1B	28	15.5	107.9
Jeff Bagwell, Hou	1B	28	15.3	104.9

The chart is based upon a formula Bill James created. It determines a player's "established value" by weighting the player's "approximate value" over the past three years using several statistical categories. His age is then incorporated to estimate the length of his remaining playing career. A rather complex formula then combines the player's established value and estimated remaining career to generate his "trade value." The listed age is the player's seasonal age as of July 1, 1996. The program which generated the data uses the rounded age while employing the formula.

Anyway, Rodriguez clearly had the highest trade value at the end of last year. He didn't turn 21 years of age until July 27, and his offensive season was truly historic. It would have been a surprise had he not landed at the top of this list.

No other player in the top 10 was under age 24 as of July 1, 1996. The next-youngest player on the list is Jim Thome of the Cleveland Indians—Cleveland would actually boast three of the top five most valuable commodities in the game had Albert Belle not departed via free agency. But Belle now combines with Frank Thomas in Chicago to form one of the most imposing hearts of the order in baseball. Their White Sox figure to battle the Indians this summer for American League Central supremacy.

You might notice that no pitchers appeared on the above list. Part of the reason for that is that the formula penalizes them for simply being pitchers. It automatically deducts 30 percent from pitchers' computed scores, because they figure to break down physically more often and are otherwise more unpredictable than position players.

But that doesn't mean pitchers don't have value. Here are the hurlers with the highest computed trade values following last season:

Pitchers with Highest Trade Values

Pitcher, Team	Age	Estab Value	Trade Value
Greg Maddux, Atl	30	15.5	66.1
Mike Mussina, Bal	27	13.8	61.6
Ismael Valdes, LA	22	8.8	57.0
Pat Hentgen, Tor	27	12.8	52.6
Alex Fernandez, Fla	26	11.7	48.6
Andy Pettitte, Yanks	24	9.8	48.4
Pedro Martinez, Mon	24	9.7	48.0
Jose Rosado, KC	21	4.5	41.3
Brad Radke, Min	23	6.8	41.1
John Smoltz, Atl	29	12.2	39.1

Greg Maddux may have had his streak of four straight Cy Young Awards snapped by teammate John Smoltz, but the formula still considers him the pitcher teams would most love to acquire. Smoltz was able to move into the top 10, but he nevertheless ranks behind such lesser-known hurlers as Jose Rosado and Brad Radke, according to trade value.

Hmmm. . . I'm not sure if I'd be buying that. Yes, we all know that pitchers are unpredictable. And yes, Rosado and Radke are both appreciably younger than Smoltz and have each tasted success. But if I'm John Scheurholz, something tells me I wouldn't deal Smoltz for either of them.

Now if Alex Rodriguez was being offered, then I'd listen.

April 14, 1997—Cubs Losing Streak

Any optimism the Cubs may have had entering the 1997 season has already evaporated. The Cubs are as cold as the weather in Chicago, having lost their first 10 games of the campaign. Never mind that they've had to face probably the two best pitching staffs in baseball. The Baby Bears are threatening to "cave in" and hibernate before Memorial Day.

What does the Cubs' 0-10 start mean? Are they as bad as that distressing record would indicate? Well, we can actually determine the chances that a team of a certain "quality" would lose 10 games in a row. We'll substitute winning percentage as an estimate of quality. As parameters, let's say a pennant-winning team will finish with a .600 winning percentage, an average team .500, and a poor team .400. We can then compute their probabilities of losing 10 straight using the binomial distribution which students of statistics are familiar with.

Instead of getting bogged down in formulas, however, let's cut to the chase. Excluding factors such as momentum, opponent's ability, injuries, park factors and so forth, here are the chances that teams whose true levels of ability are the following winning percentages would actually lose 10 straight over any given stretch:

Pct	Probability	Chances
.700	.000006	1 in 169,351
.600	.000105	1 in 9,537
.500	.000977	1 in 1,024
.400	.006047	1 in 165
.300	.028248	1 in 35

It looks like we can write off the Cubs' chances of winning 100 games. A team whose true level of ability is a .600 (97-65) winning percentage—in other words, a pennant winner—would lose 10 straight games about once every 10,000th 10-game stretch. But a .300 ballclub (49-113) would have about a 1-in-35 chance of losing 10 in a row during any given period.

Now the Cubs are probably not *that* bad. Any team facing the likes of Greg Maddux, Kevin Brown, Tom Glavine, et al would have a difficult time maintaining success. But that doesn't make Chicago's 0-10 start any more palatable.

So where do they go from here? The Cubs have become just the sixth team since 1900 to lose their first 10 games in a season. Here are the other five, as well as their final records:

Year	Team	Start	Finish
1988	Baltimore Orioles	0-21	54-107
1904	Washington Senators	0-13	38-113
1920	Detroit Tigers	0-13	61-93
1968	Chicago White Sox	0-10	67-95
1988	Atlanta Braves	0-10	54-106
1997	Chicago Cubs	*0-10	??-??

Through 4/13/97

If the Cubs were looking for reassurance from that group, they're not going to find it. None of the other five teams played better than .440 baseball the rest of the season. Here's a capsule look at those teams:

1988 Orioles: After losing their first six games, the Orioles replaced Cal Ripken Sr. with Frank Robinson. As the record indicates, Robinson didn't have any more luck. But any manager would have had problems with a team which finished last in the majors in batting average, runs scored and ERA.

1904 Senators: One of the most dreadful teams of all time. Washington finished 23½ games out in 1904. Of seventh place. Only the 1916 A's (.235), 1935 Braves (.248) and the 1962 expansion Mets (.250) posted lower winning percentages than the Senators.

1920 Tigers: The Tigers actually recovered somewhat, finishing well ahead of the Philadelphia Athletics for seventh place. Detroit did have some talent on the team, including Harry Heilmann, the next year's batting champion, Bobby Veach (.307-11-113) and a 33-year-old Ty Cobb.

1968 White Sox: Just one year earlier, the White Sox led the American League for most of the summer. Those 1967 White Sox had finished just three games behind the Red Sox, but 1968 was a different story. In the Year of the Pitcher, check out some of the ERAs on the White Sox staff: Joe Horlen (1.87), Tommy John (1.98), Hoyt Wilhelm (1.72 in 72 games) and Wilbur Wood (1.87 in a league-leading 88 games). But the White Sox batted just .228 as a team and finished in ninth place.

1988 Braves: Looking back from 1997, it's amazing how far the Braves have come in such a relatively short time. But 1988 marked the first of three straight seasons that they posted the worst record in the National League. Dale Murphy started his decline (.226-24-77), and the Braves finished last in the NL in errors and runs scored.

One other thing to keep in mind—the 1920 Tigers were the only club on the above list to stay with the same manager all year. Every other team felt compelled to blame their skipper at some point. That's not exactly the kind of news Jim Riggleman would like to hear right now.

April 15, 1997—Jackie Robinson

Jackie Robinson obviously had a profound effect not only on major league baseball but on the nation's social conscience as well. His debut with the Dodgers 50 years ago this week (April 15) didn't necessarily correct a long overdue blight on the national pastime, but it was at least a step in the right direction.

It may be hard to believe now, in this age of $11 million ballplayers and $500 million franchises (reportedly the Dodgers' asking price), but there were many owners in 1947 who felt Robinson's presence would actually "devalue" baseball teams. That was far from what actually occurred that season. We prepared the following list for ESPN's baseball telecast this past Sunday night. We thank ESPN for asking us to research such a fascinating topic. The list summarizes National League attendance in 1947. Brooklyn's seven National League opponents are shown with their home attendance while facing the Dodgers, and then in all other home dates.

As you can see, Robinson's presence with the Dodgers was a *huge* marketing draw. Every National League franchise averaged at least 30 percent more fans against Brooklyn than in their other home dates:

National League Attendance—1947

Team	vs. Dodgers Total	Dates	Avg	vs. Others Total	Dates	Avg	Dodgers
Giants	412,763	10	41,276	1,188,030	51	23,295	+ 77.2%
Phillies	210,202	9	23,356	697,130	51	13,669	+ 70.9%
Cardinals	287,656	11	26,151	960,257	59	16,276	+ 60.7%
Cubs	301,970	11	27,452	1,062,069	59	18,001	+ 52.5%
Reds	166,407	9	18,490	733,568	54	13,585	+ 36.1%
Pirates	251,566	10	25,157	1,031,965	55	18,763	+ 34.1%
Braves	237,810	10	23,781	1,039,551	57	18,238	+ 30.4%
Total	1,868,374	70	26,691	6,712,570	386	17,390	+ 53.5%

Now there's probably more to these numbers than just Robinson's presence. After all, the Dodgers were the best team in the National League in 1947, winning the pennant by five games over the Cardinals. And there's probably something to the theory that teams from New York may have greater national appeal. And the Giants-Dodgers crosstown rivalry certainly contributed to the Giants' inflated numbers. But still, there can be no doubt that Robinson's human drama captured fans' interest. A 53.5 percent increase in attendance cannot be written off as coincidence.

One final note. While Robinson had a dramatic impact on National League attendance overall, he didn't have that large an effect on the *Dodgers'* home attendance. After drawing 1,796,824 fans in 1946, Brooklyn improved to just 1,807,526 in 1947. That's an increase of just 0.6 percent.

In any case, the fears of baseball's owners proved to be unfounded. Instead of having their franchises devalued, NL owners reaped huge dividends in 1947. Who knows how much baseball franchises would be worth today had Robinson not opened the major league door to a whole race of ballplayers? For that matter, how much would Robinson be worth?

May 19, 1997—Team Secondary Average

If you need another reason why the Indians have been averaging nearly six runs per game this season, check out their secondary average. The Indians have walked 192 times in 1,616 plate appearances. That's the highest rate in the majors. Likewise, the Indians' .214 team isolated power (slugging percentage minus batting average) ranks as baseball's best. And while the Indians aren't prolific basestealers, they haven't been thrown out a high percentage of the time, either.

Add it all up, and the Indians have compiled a .361 team secondary average. No other team is even close:

Team Secondary Average—1997

Team	Sec Avg
Indians	.361
Rockies	.315
Mariners	.305
Yankees	.299
Athletics	.295

As Bill James has pointed out, secondary average will tend to hover right around the same area as batting average. For instance, the major league's overall batting average this season is .264. Meanwhile, the overall secondary average is only marginally higher, at .267.

At the same time, the *spread* between the best and worst teams in secondary average will be much broader than for batting average. The Indians' .361 secondary average is 143 points better than the Phillies' .218. However, the difference between the highest (Rockies, .298) and lowest (Reds, .237) team *batting* averages is much narrower.

The Indians' current secondary average becomes really noteworthy when we put it in the context of history. I know it's still early, since Cleveland has only played 40 games, but the Indians' .361 mark easily ranks as the highest team rate since 1900:

Team Secondary Average—Since 1900

Year Team	Sec Avg
1997 Indians	.361
1994 Tigers	.324
1996 Mariners	.324
1938 Yankees	.322
1996 Indians	.320
1953 Dodgers	.319
1996 Orioles	.318
1936 Yankees	.316
1997 Rockies	.315
1995 Indians	.312

Here again, we see how special this era is for offense. Even if we exclude this year's Indians and Rockies, five of the top eight team secondary averages have occurred since 1994.

And we can also see that this year's performance is nothing new for the Indians. The '96 Tribe ranks fifth on the above list, while the '95 club ranks 10th. Still, they're no match for this year's team, which is on a pace for the ages.

May 26, 1997—Pythagorean Theorem

So far this season, the best three teams in baseball have been the Atlanta Braves, Baltimore Orioles and. . . the New York Mets?

You'll be forgiven if you did a double-take at the last team in that statement. While the Braves and Orioles have the records to justify that they truly are the top teams in their respective leagues, the Mets don't even have one of the top three records in their own *division* (entering Monday). And yet the Mets do indeed deserve consideration as one of the strongest teams in baseball, at least according to the Pythagorean Theorem.

For those of you unfamiliar with the concept, the number of runs scored and allowed by any team is closely related to that team's actual won-loss record. For instance, the Padres of 1996 scored 771 runs while allowing 682. The Pythagorean Theorem uses the following formula to estimate the number of wins the Padres should have thus produced:

Winning Percentage = $\dfrac{\text{Runs Scored}^2}{\text{Runs Scored}^2 + \text{Runs Allowed}^2}$

In San Diego's case, the number of wins that spits out is 91, which in fact matches the Padres' actual 1996 win total. The formula doesn't *always* do that, but its results are normally within two or three wins of the actual total.

Anyway, the Mets have scored 222 runs while allowing 172 this season. Based on a reasonable amount of luck, New York should be expected to be winning games at a .625 pace. Only the Braves and Orioles would be better:

Best Teams According to Pythagorean Theorem

Team	R	OR	Pct	Projected W-L	Actual W-L	Diff
Braves	231	153	.695	33-15	33-15	0
Orioles	253	176	.674	31-15	31-15	0
Mets	222	172	.625	30-18	26-22	-4
Yankees	265	206	.623	30-18	26-22	-4
Marlins	206	167	.603	28-19	29-18	1
Expos	250	228	.546	26-21	26-21	0

There are a couple of interesting points to be made about this list. First, four of the top six teams in baseball, at least according to the formula, reside in the NL East. And yet only two of them, if that many, will make it to the postseason.

Second, New York's teams have seriously underachieved their projected win totals. The Mets and Yankees have each fallen four games shy of what the Pythagorean Theorem would project. That matches the Cardinals, Tigers and Cubs for the largest deficit in baseball.

Which brings us to the Cubs. So far this season, the Cubs have also played four games *worse* than what would be expected using the Pythagorean Theorem. They've scored 202 runs while allowing 221, which translates to a projected record of 21-26 after 47 games. Instead, the Cubs are 17-30.

So what else is new? The Cubs played *five* games worse than their expected record last year (76-86), based on their 772-771 scoring differential. They were a little better in 1995, although they still fell one game shy of their projected win total.

I think we have a trend here. What do these last three Cub seasons have in common? I'll give you a hint. Take a look at the Padres of 1993-94:

Year	Proj	Actual	Diff
1993	71-91	61-101	-10
1994	53-64	47-70	-6

Jim Riggelman took over as Padres manager with only 12 games remaining in the 1992 season. Even in that short span, he managed to lead the Padres to one fewer victory (four) than what would have been expected based on San Diego's 35-40 scoring differential in those 12 games.

So let's see, in four-plus seasons Riggelman's teams have underachieved by a grand total of *27* games. Shouldn't he be starting to run out of chances?

June 2, 1997—Rey Ordonez

The New York Mets are starting to attract some attention as serious playoff contenders. They've gone 23-9 in their last 32 games, the best record in baseball since April 27. It's still awfully early to start talking about the postseason, but entering Monday's action the Mets are only one-half game behind the Marlins in the wild-card picture.

Part of the reason for the Mets' rejuvenation has been the performance of their starting rotation. Even without their much-ballyhooed Young Guns—Bill Pulsipher, Jason Isringhausen and Paul Wilson—the Met starters rank second in the majors with a 3.08 ERA.

And part of the reason for that unexpected development has to be the fielding brilliance of shortstop Rey Ordonez. Ordonez continues to make spectacular plays on a regular basis. And he consistently gets to more balls than almost any other shortstop in the game. Since Ordonez came into the league in 1996, only Alex Gonzalez has posted a better range factor:

Shortstop Range Factors—Since 1996

Player	Range
Alex Gonzalez	5.01
Rey Ordonez	4.99
Walt Weiss	4.91
Jose Valentin	4.91
Mike Bordick	4.88

(minimum 1000 innings)

So you can understand the concern many Met fans might be experiencing right now, after Ordonez broke his hand on Sunday and will be out of action for four to six weeks. However, while there's no doubt the Mets will miss his fielding ability, the same can't be said for his offense. Put a bat in his hands, and Ordonez is arguably the worst hitter in baseball. Even before the cast was applied.

His .256 batting average masks his overall weakness to some degree. But the man has almost no power, generating just 13 doubles, seven triples and one home run in 652 career at-bats. His isolated power mark of .046 ranks as the second-worst in baseball since 1996:

Worst Isolated Power—Since 1996

Player	Iso
Otis Nixon	.040
Rey Ordonez	.046
Tom Goodwin	.048
Jody Reed	.048
Jose Vizcaino	.066

(minimum 500 AB)

And he doesn't just hit with limited power. He doesn't get on base, either. He walked just 22 times in 502 at-bats in '96, and has actually *decreased* that rate in '97, coaxing just six walks in 150 at-bats. Because of his limited plate discipline, Ordonez will always have a hard time generating an on-base percentage above .300. His career mark is just .287.

So let's see now. He doesn't hit for power, and he doesn't get on base. No wonder his secondary average ranks as the poorest in baseball by a comfortable margin:

Lowest Secondary Average—Since 1996

Player	Sec Avg
Rey Ordonez	.095
Gary DiSarcina	.130
Ozzie Guillen	.138
Garret Anderson	.152
Carlos Baerga	.155
(minimum 500 AB)	

This is not to say the Mets won't miss Ordonez' presence. We'll get an opportunity to see just how much his defense means to the Mets' pitching staff while he's on the disabled list mending his broken hand. Furthermore, should Manny Alexander receive the bulk of the playing time in Ordonez' absence, it's not clear that he'll be an offensive improvement. However, based on the numbers, he can't be much worse.

June 9, 1997—Runs Created per 27 Outs

Sooner or later it had to happen.

One of these years we were bound to have a legitimate hitter post truly awesome numbers playing half his games at Coors Field. With all due respect to Dante Bichette, Andres Galarraga and Vinny Castilla, I wouldn't say they qualify as great hitters. But Larry Walker might. And he's enjoying an absolutely monster season.

Entering the games of June 9, Walker led the majors with a .416 batting average and a .781 slugging percentage. He's scored 61 runs in 59 games and is constantly reaching base, boasting a National League-leading on-base percentage of .511.

Add it all up, and Walker has created 91 runs according to the runs created formula. Furthermore, he's creating over *18* runs per 27 outs:

Runs Created per 27 Outs—1997

Player, Team	RC	RC/27
Larry Walker, Col	91	18.24
Frank Thomas, WSox	76	15.34
Dave Justice, Cle	64	13.19
Jeff Bagwell, Hou	70	11.74
Tony Gwynn, SD	59	10.21
(minimum 200 PA)		

For those of you unfamiliar with runs created, the stat is perhaps the best measurement of a player's offensive worth, combining a range of categories in one neat, concise package. Runs created per 27 outs (RC/27) takes the formula one step further, figuring the number of runs which a team consisting of nine such players would theoretically generate in a nine-inning game.

In Walker's case, a team consisting of nine players producing at his level would be expected to score over 18 runs per game. That's a phenomenal rate, and one which ranks among the best ever among players with at least 200 plate appearances in a season:

Highest Single-Season Runs Created Per 27 Outs

Year	Player	RC	RC/27
1920	Babe Ruth	220	19.47
1921	Babe Ruth	248	18.97
1941	Ted Williams	198	18.74
1923	Babe Ruth	233	18.44
1997	Larry Walker	92	18.24

(minimum 200 PA)

It's still early in the '97 season, so Walker could absolutely come back down to earth. But when you're listed among the likes of Ruth and Williams, you know you're doing something right. And considering only one other season in the top 10 occurred after World War II, you can see how historic Walker's season could turn out to be.

Still, there's little question that Walker has been helped by his home ballpark. As good as he is, it's likely that an even *better* hitter, such as Ken Griffey or Frank Thomas, might be posting even *stronger* numbers. What would Babe Ruth have done in 1920 had he played half his games at Coors? It's almost scary to imagine.

June 16, 1997—Toronto Blue Jays

It's not hard to see why the Toronto Blue Jays are in danger of falling out of contention in the American League East. Sure, Roger Clemens and Pat Hentgen have been pitching splendidly. In fact, they rank among the best 1-2 starters on any any staff in baseball. But the Blue Jays are nevertheless a sub-.500 ballclub, and for one specific reason: they can't generate any offense.

Check out some of Toronto's wretched numbers:

Toronto Blue Jays Offense

Category	Tor	AL Rank
Batting Average	.244	Last
Runs Scored	248	Last
Bases on Balls	183	Last
On-Base Percentage	.307	Last
Slugging Percentage	.389	Last

(entering June 16, 1997)

No matter how well Clemens and Hentgen pitch, they're not going to win any games if the Jays don't score any runs. And as the numbers indicate, runs have not been plentiful for Toronto this season.

The Blue Jays don't hit for average. They don't hit for power. And they don't walk. No wonder they've scored 43 fewer runs than Kansas City, the team with the next-lowest total in the American League. To put the Blue Jays in context, they've averaged only 3.9 runs per game. Meanwhile, the rest of the AL has averaged 31 percent more, at nearly 5.2 runs per game.

Fixing the dearth of offense is not going to be easy, either. There's not a single position or player the Blue Jays can point to and conclude "Aha! That's the problem." That's because almost *every* position is a problem. Toronto is deficient up and down its lineup.

In terms of runs created per 27 outs, the Blue Jays main position players have been woefully deficient:

Runs Created Per 27 Outs

Player	Pos	RC/27	MLB Avg
Benito Santiago	C	2.44	5.08
Joe Carter	1B	3.68	6.86
Carlos Garcia	2B	1.89	4.87
Ed Sprague	3B	5.84	5.21
Alex Gonzalez	SS	3.61	4.39
Ruben Sierra	LF	3.67	5.74
Otis Nixon	CF	4.40	5.43
Orlando Merced	RF	5.04	6.31
Carlos Delgado	DH	9.16	5.79

The averages for major league baseball are based upon the players with a minimum of 125 plate appearances at each respective position. As you can see, there are only two positions at which the Blue Jays have received better production than the MLB average.

The Blue Jays were a trendy choice to win the American League East this spring, following an offseason in which they signed Clemens to a big-bucks contract and completed the blockbuster trade with Pittsburgh in which they acquired Garcia and Merced. But now that we're in the middle of June, it's evident those predictions were vastly optimistic. Clemens has done his job. It's time for the hitters to start doing theirs.

June 30, 1997—Gary Sheffield

He may not be having the same kind of destructive offensive season that he enjoyed last year, but Gary Sheffield is still helping put runs on the board for the Florida Marlins. Sheffield posted an MVP-caliber season in 1996, when he hit .314 with 42 homers and 120 RBI. He' nowhere near those numbers in 1997, with his average hovering at .232 as we enter July. His power figures are also down, with only eight homers and 32 RBI.

But check out his on-base percentage, which, despite the lowly batting average, is still a remarkable .446. Only Larry Walker boasts a higher one in the National League. The reason for Sheffield's impressive mark is obvious—he's drawing walks in bucketloads, leading the majors with 71. In fact, since the beginning of the expansion era in 1961, Sheffield's current walk rate ranks among the single-season leaders:

Walk Percentage—Since 1961

Year	Player	Pct
1973	Dick Dietz	25.7
1987	Jack Clark	24.3
1962	Mickey Mantle	24.3
1997	Gary Sheffield	24.1
1990	Jack Clark	23.5
1985	Sixto Lezcano	22.9
1969	Jimmy Wynn	22.7
1996	Barry Bonds	22.4
1989	Jack Clark	22.2
1980	Gene Tenace	22.1

(minimum 150 PA)

Sheffield's outstanding walk rate in 1997 only extends a trend which has continued since his rookie season. Take a look at how his walk percentage has improved over the years:

Gary Sheffield's Walk Percentage

Year	Team	Pct
1988	Mil	7.9
1989	Mil	6.7
1990	Mil	8.0
1991	Mil	9.4
1992	SD	7.8
1993	SD/Fla	8.4
1994	Fla	13.3
1995	Fla	20.1
1996	Fla	21.0
1997	Fla	24.1

As is the case for many players, Sheffield has demonstrated much better plate discipline as he's aged. His command of the strike zone is roughly three times better today than it was as a rookie, at least in terms of walk percentage.

Another skill which improves for many players as they get older is power. **Sheffield looks** to be one of those guys. His home-run percentage has also been about **three times greater** since 1992 as it was before then:

Gary Sheffield's Home Run Percentage

Years	HR	PA	Pct
1988-91	21	1,244	1.7
1992-	146	2,804	5.2

Perhaps it's not a coincidence that Sheffield's power surge occurred after he left **Milwaukee** following the 1991 season. However, while San Diego's home stadium has historically been a better park for homers than Milwaukee's County Stadium, Florida's Pro Players Stadium actually *reduced* homers by 10 percent between 1994 and 1996. So Sheffield's improved home-run rate appears to be legitimate.

Home-run power and plate discipline have often been considered "old man's skills." And since he's only 28, Sheffield's home-run and walks rates might increase even **further as he** ages. If so, he figures to be special player for years to come.

July 14, 1997—First-Place in mid-July

With the All-Star Game now behind us, it's that time of year when the **pennant races are** really swinging into high gear. Teams are roughly eight games into the second half of their schedules, and the championship pretenders have long since fallen by the wayside. Clubs such as the Red Sox, Athletics and Phillies (especially the Phillies), though they may still pay lip service to wild-card possibilities, are now in positions of having to get ready for 1998.

At the other end of the spectrum, however, are clubs like the Orioles, **Mariners and Braves.** Those three teams, in addition to the Indians, Pirates and Giants, all rank first in their divisions. And if they're in first place 90 games into the season, it's obviously not unreasonable to consider them legitimate title contenders.

So what are the chances of these teams remaining number one come the end of September? If history is any guide, they're pretty good, and getting better.

For the purposes of this study, we'll go back to 1963, and take a look at whether the teams in first place entering July 14 in any given season ended up winning their league or division. We'll eliminate 1981 and 1994, two seasons gummed up or destroyed by ugly work stoppages.

So over the past 34 seasons (excluding 1981 and 1994), there have been 123 teams holding or sharing first place in a league or division entering games of July 14. Of those 123 teams, 80 ended up winning a league or division championship.

That rate of 65 percent isn't bad, but it appears to have gotten even *better* since major league baseball expanded to six divisions in 1995. Over the past two years, nearly 70 percent of teams in first place entering July 14 went on to finish first at the end of the regular season:

Teams in First Place Entering July 14

Years	Total Teams	Finished First	Pct
1963-68	12	7	58.3
1969-93	98	64	65.3
1995-96	13	9	69.2

As you can see, the current situation only increases the trend which may have started in the era between 1969 and 1993. Those were the years in which baseball had four divisions. In the six seasons before '69, only 58.3 percent of league leaders entering July 14 eventually became pennant winners.

Six years is a fairly small sample size on which to make a general statement, as is the two years since 1995. But it'll be interesting to see if the six teams currently residing in first place continue the trend.

July 21, 1997—Mickey Tettleton

Item from Bill James' *Baseball Book 1991*, regarding Mickey Tettleton:

"He's Gene Tenace all over again. . . My guess is that, like (Tenace), he will be extremely consistent at a level between 1989 and 1990—somewhere around .240 with 18 homers, 55 RBI."

Well, now that Tettleton has retired. . .

Most Similar Players to Mickey Tettleton

Player	Pos	AB	R	H	2B	HR	RBI	BB	Avg	Slg	Score
Mickey Tettleton	C	4698	711	1132	210	245	732	949	.241	.449	1000
Gene Tenace	C	4390	653	1060	179	201	674	984	.241	.429	927
Darrell Porter	C	5539	765	1369	237	188	826	905	.247	.409	859
Roy Campanella	C	4205	627	1161	178	242	856	533	.276	.500	847
Del Crandall	C	5026	585	1276	179	179	657	424	.254	.404	843
Bill Freehan	C	6073	706	1591	241	200	758	626	.262	.412	832
Walker Cooper	C	4702	573	1341	240	173	812	309	.285	.464	829
Andy Seminick	C	3921	495	953	139	164	556	582	.243	.417	827
Benito Santiago	C	4623	521	1200	203	154	613	283	.260	.414	826
Elston Howard	C	5363	619	1471	218	167	762	373	.274	.427	825
Rico Petrocelli	SS	5390	653	1352	237	210	773	661	.251	.420	820

Tettleton actually did a little better than Bill expected, averaging 28 homers and 82 RBI between 1991 and 1996. His batting average since 1991 was close, though, at .244.

But I'd say Tenace was a pretty good match, wouldn't you? Both players walked a ton. Both players had power—Tettleton's edge there could be due to the eras in which the two played. And both finished with exactly the same batting average.

Just one Hall of Famer appears among Tettleton's top 10 comps. Campanella, of course, had his career shortened by the exclusion of African-Americans, as well as his tragic car accident. I'm sure the Hall of Fame voters took that under consideration when electing Campy, and it's unlikely Tettleton will ever be considered for induction.

Benito Santiago is really the eighth-best comp to Tettleton? Here again, Bill was perspicacious. From his *Baseball Book 1990*:

"The most-comparable major league player: Benito Santiago. I didn't say he was comparable, mind you; I said he was the closest. . . "

Santiago is still active, so his similarity to Tettleton could shift as he completes his career. Somehow it just doesn't seem right that a player with Santiago's wretched plate discipline compares to Tettleton, one of the most patient hitters of this era.

Another player who recently retired stands a much better chance of earning a plaque in Cooperstown. By the time Lee Smith announced his retirement from the Montreal Expos last week, he had accumulated the most saves in major league history.

Not surprisingly, Smith's list of most comparable players includes some of the best relievers to ever pitch:

Most Similar Pitchers to Lee Smith

Pitcher	G	W	L	SV	IP	H	ER	BB	K	ERA	Score
Lee Smith	1022	71	92	478	1289.1	1133	434	486	1251	3.03	1000
Jeff Reardon	880	73	77	367	1132.1	1000	397	358	877	3.16	880
Rollie Fingers	944	114	118	341	1701.1	1474	549	492	1299	2.90	843
Gene Garber	931	96	113	218	1510.0	1464	560	445	940	3.34	820
Bruce Sutter	661	68	71	300	1042.1	879	328	309	861	2.83	818
Kent Tekulve	1050	94	90	184	1436.1	1305	455	491	779	2.85	811
Darold Knowles	765	66	74	143	1092.0	1006	378	480	681	3.12	805
Jesse Orosco	924	76	71	133	1106.2	885	365	482	995	2.97	803
Mike Marshall	723	97	112	188	1386.2	1281	484	514	880	3.14	803
Steve Bedrosian	732	76	79	184	1191.0	1026	447	518	921	3.38	799
Dave Righetti	718	82	79	252	1403.2	1287	540	591	1112	3.46	798

The art of relieving has evolved substantially over the past 20 years, so it shouldn't be a shock to see so many contemporaries among Smith's most-comparables. Remember, the majors didn't have a reliever save 30 games in a season until 1965, when Ted Abernathy saved 31. The first 40-save man didn't appear until 1983, when Dan Quisenberry saved 45.

That was also the year Smith began a string of 13 consecutive seasons with 25 or more saves. And he enjoyed his best seasons, at least in terms of totals, relatively late in his career. He waited until 1991, at age 33, to post his first 40-save campaign, with 47. He followed with 43 and 46 the next two years.

With so many relatively recent players listed among Smith's comparables, Fingers is the only one to as yet gain entrance to the Hall of Fame. Reardon, however, is a strong candidate. Sutter might be, too, considering not only his record but his role in helping to revolutionize the way modern relievers are used.

Still, Smith ranks a notch above either of them. It would be an upset if he doesn't eventually gain immortality in Cooperstown.

July 28, 1997—Curt Schilling

With baseball's trading deadline fast approaching, we can probably expect a flurry of deals in the next few days. This Thursday, July 31, is the last day general managers can swap players without first exposing them to waivers. If a team such as Cleveland is looking to upgrade its pitching rotation, it will almost surely have to make a move by Thursday. If not, it may never be able to fortify its staff for a stretch run this year.

One of the hurlers who now appears to be *off* the trading block is Phillies' righthander Curt Schilling. GM Lee Thomas, if he can be believed, says Schilling will finish the season in a Philadelphia uniform. In terms of Schilling's importance to the Phillies, the decision to retain him can be defended. After all, few pitchers in baseball have accounted for a greater percentage of his team's wins than Schilling has.

The following chart lists the pitchers whose winning percentage is most out of character from the rest of their team. For instance, the Phillies are 30-72 (.294) overall this season. However, if you take away Schilling's 11 wins and 10 losses (.524), the Phillies are an even more pathetic 19-62 (.235). So Schilling's winning percentage is 289 points above the rest of his team.

As good as that mark is, there are actually other pitchers with even better differentials (all lists are entering Monday, July 28):

Pitcher's Winning Percentage vs. Rest of Team

Player, Team	Record	Pct	Rest of Team	Diff
Roger Clemens, Tor	16-3	.842	.420	.422
Randy Johnson, Sea	14-2	.875	.523	.352
Brad Radke, Min	14-5	.737	.386	.351
Darryl Kile, Hou	14-3	.824	.489	.335
Curt Schilling, Phi	11-10	.524	.235	.289
Denny Neagle, Atl	13-2	.867	.589	.278
Willie Blair, Det	9-4	.692	.427	.265
Jeff Juden, Mon	11-4	.733	.471	.262
Shawn Estes, SF	13-4	.765	.506	.259
Kevin Foster, Cubs	10-6	.625	.371	.254

(minimum 12 decisions)

Another indicator of just how important Schilling has been to the Phillies is his ERA compared to the others on Philadelphia's staff. Schilling's ERA is nearly three runs better than his teammates:

Pitcher's ERA vs. Rest of Team

Player, Team	IP	ERA	Rest of Team	Diff
Randy Johnson, Sea	154.0	2.28	5.71	-3.43
Roger Clemens, Tor	163.1	1.54	4.29	-2.75
Pedro Martinez, Mon	146.0	1.91	4.63	-2.71
Curt Schilling, Phi	163.0	3.37	6.08	-2.71
Darryl Kile, Hou	176.1	1.94	4.17	-2.23
Justin Thompson, Det	138.1	3.06	5.05	-1.99
Roger Bailey, Col	129.2	3.82	5.79	-1.97
Kevin Appier, KC	157.0	3.15	4.97	-1.82
Wilson Alvarez, WSox	145.2	3.03	4.74	-1.71
Brad Radke, Min	158.1	3.58	5.24	-1.66

(minimum 75 IP)

Many of the pitchers on these last two lists are legitimate Cy Young candidates. One name perhaps conspicuous by its absence is Greg Maddux. But that's due more to the overall excellence of the Braves' staff than any failing of Maddux.

August 4, 1997—Ryne Sandberg/Streaks

Ryne Sandberg has announced he'll retire again at the end of this season. While we can't close the book yet on Sandberg's career, we can get a sense of how he compares to other players in baseball history.

In terms of similarity scores, the most comparable performer to Sandberg was Lou Whitaker. Although Whitaker couldn't quite match Sandberg's speed and home-run power, his raw totals were slightly better:

Most Similar Players to Ryne Sandberg

Player	Pos	AB	R	H	2B	HR	RBI	BB	SB	Avg	Slg	Score
Ryne Sandberg	2B	8263	1305	2351	396	278	1040	753	342	.285	.452	1000
Lou Whitaker	2B	8570	1386	2369	420	244	1084	1197	143	.276	.426	889
Ken Boyer	3B	7455	1104	2143	318	282	1141	713	105	.287	.462	851
Bobby Doerr	2B	7093	1094	2042	381	223	1247	809	54	.288	.461	847
Alan Trammell	SS	8288	1231	2365	412	185	1003	850	236	.285	.415	846
Ron Santo	3B	8143	1138	2254	365	342	1331	1108	35	.277	.464	807
Chili Davis	OF	7934	1143	2180	386	315	1253	1081	137	.275	.450	795
Gary Gaetti	3B	8066	1026	2067	397	327	1203	561	94	.256	.436	789
Joe Morgan	2B	9277	1650	2517	449	268	1133	1865	689	.271	.427	788
Joe Torre	C	7874	996	2342	344	252	1185	779	23	.297	.452	784
Buddy Bell	3B	8995	1151	2514	425	201	1106	836	55	.279	.406	782

Many observers, myself included, feel Sandberg deserves induction into the Hall of Fame. But if his list of comparables is any indication, his election may not necessarily be a sure thing. Of those players who are eligible, only Bobby Doerr and Joe Morgan currently have plaques in Cooperstown. And Doerr had to wait until the Veterans Committee finally elected him.

That's not to say that others on the list don't deserve induction. Ken Boyer, Ron Santo and Joe Torre all merit consideration. They've been championed as worthy candidates for quite some time now. And I personally feel Whitaker and Trammell should eventually be enshrined.

I was expecting a contemporary of Sandberg's to rank a little higher on Ryno's similarity list. Like Sandberg, Cal Ripken debuted in the majors in 1981. Both have posted identical .452 slugging percentages while playing most of their careers at a demanding middle-infield position.

But Ripken's durability, as well as Sandberg's 1½-year hiatus, has allowed Ripken to pull comfortably ahead of Ryno in most categories. As a result, Ripken ranks no higher than a tie for 34th on the list of Sandberg's most similar players. Of course, Ripken's position accounts for another part of the dissimilarity:

Player	Pos	AB	R	H	2B	HR	RBI	BB	SB	Avg	Slg	Score
Ryne Sandberg	2B	8263	1305	2351	396	278	1040	753	342	.285	.452	1000
Cal Ripken	SS	9646	1420	2667	508	366	1433	993	36	.276	.452	750

The scores presented above will likely shift somewhat as Sandberg and other active players complete their careers.

Streaks

You probably remember the 14-game losing streak with which Sandberg's Cubs opened the 1997 season. That streak ranks as the second-longest ever at the beginning of a campaign. Only the 1988 Baltimore Orioles, at 0-21, started a season more miserably.

The Cubs' streak this season was the third time since 1990 that a team had lost at least 14 straight games. In each case, the team broke the streak by winning the 15th contest.

You might get the impression, judging by that small sample size, that the probability of ending a losing streak increases as the streak gets longer. But according to the following chart, that suspicion would probably be wrong:

Losing Streaks Since 1990

Streak	Reached	Won Next Game	Lost Next Game	Pct
1	7861	3854	3951	.494
2	3951	1908	2015	.486
3	2015	969	1036	.483
4	1036	491	539	.477
5	539	261	277	.485
6	277	127	145	.467
7	145	69	75	.479
8	75	34	41	.453
9	41	16	24	.400
10	24	8	16	.333
11	16	6	10	.375
12	10	5	5	.500
13	5	2	3	.400
14	3	3	0	1.000

You'll notice the sum of wins and losses don't necessarily match the total number of games for each "streak" column. That's because carryover games from one season to the next are not included, nor are the current streaks for teams entering Monday's (August 4) action.

As you can see, since 1990, teams enduring a losing streak have been slightly more likely to *continue* their skids than to end them. For example, after losing one game, teams have posted a .494 winning percentage in Game 2. Of those losing streaks which reach two games, the winning percentage in the third game drops to .486. And so on.

In general terms, the likelihood of ending a losing streak has actually *decreased* as the streak increases. Only when the streak reaches 12 or 14 have teams been able to win over half the time, and the sample sizes for those two instances are so small that a conclusion would be rather speculative.

Consider this: While the chances that a team losing one game will eventually lose five in a row is roughly one in 14.6, the chances that a team which loses eight straight will then lose 12 straight increases to one in 7.5.

Keep in mind, the chances are one in 16 that an event with a 50/50 probability (i.e. having a coin land on tails) will occur four consecutive times (1/2 to the fourth power). So while going from one loss to five doesn't deviate far from that one in 16, going from eight to 12 straight losses is almost twice as likely.

Those statistics probably shouldn't be remarkable. After all, which teams are more likely to endure long losing streaks? Bad teams, of course. The better teams are more likely to stop losing streaks before they get too far. As they do, we're left with the "bad" teams reaching double-digit consecutive losses.

Intuitively, such a notion makes sense. And the above numbers would tend to support such a theory. After all, a .400 baseball club has a one in 7.7 probability of losing four straight games (assuming the losses are independent events). That roughly matches the earlier figures we calculated.

The reverse also appears to be true. As the following chart indicates, the winning percentage increases as *winning* streaks get longer:

Winning Streaks Since 1990

Streak	Reached	Won Next Game	Lost Next Game	Pct
1	7863	3950	3854	.506
2	3950	1996	1926	.509
3	1996	1049	934	.529
4	1049	539	508	.515
5	539	297	237	.556
6	297	149	145	.507
7	149	68	81	.456
8	68	40	28	.588
9	40	21	19	.525
10	21	11	10	.524
11	11	6	5	.545
12	6	5	1	.833
13	5	3	2	.600
14	3	1	2	.333
15	1	0	1	.000

Here too, it's likely that the teams posting the winning streaks have a considerable impact on the totals. Intuitively, good teams are more likely than bad teams to extend winning streaks. Following the previous logic, the above figures would therefore make sense.

August 11, 1997—Pitch Counts

Though it sometimes seems to evolve with the speed of a seasick snail, the game of baseball is constantly developing. The game today is different from the one played a decade ago, much less the one played at the turn of the century.

As a case in point, consider the way starting pitchers are used these days. The 130-pitch outing seems to be heading the way of the dinosaur. Rarely are hurlers asked to reach a pitch count of 130. In fact, through the first 3,256 contests of 1997, only 63 pitchers have thrown 130 or more pitches in a game, an average of 1.93 130-pitch outings per 100 starts.

This year's figures only continue the trend of the 1990s:

130-Pitch Starts

Year	Starts	130+	Per 100
1992	4,212	166	3.94
1993	4,536	171	3.77
1994	3,198	143	4.47
1995	4,032	141	3.50
1996	4,532	136	3.00
1997	3,256	63	1.93

As you can see, the rate of 130-pitch starts has decreased every year since 1992, with the exception of 1994. That, of course, was the year of the big strike. You have to wonder if management took a few liberties with its starters that year, knowing the season could end at any time.

Anyway, there's no denying the fact that high pitch counts appear to be getting rarer. It's likely that clubs have become more sensitive to a possible connection between pitcher injuries and overwork. Ineffectiveness is also a potential product of arm abuse.

Now, I'm not here to dispute the supposed relationship between high pitch counts and arm injuries or long-term ineffectiveness. However, I would like to present data which considers the *short-term* effects of various pitch counts. The following chart lists the results in the starts immediately *following* a certain number of pitches. We're looking at starts only; relief appearances are not included:

Starts After Throwing Certain Number of Pitches—Since 1990

Pitches	Gms	Pct	ERA	Pit	IP	Avg Allowed	BB/9	K/9
50 or less	1499	.459	4.55	89.6	5.62	.272	3.47	5.40
60-69	1279	.455	4.63	89.5	5.64	.275	3.32	5.42
70-79	2432	.481	4.25	90.3	5.80	.269	3.14	5.31
80-89	4104	.483	4.34	92.3	5.94	.269	3.07	5.43
90-99	5636	.491	4.33	95.1	6.08	.268	3.16	5.63
100-109	5811	.497	4.27	97.9	6.21	.267	3.16	5.78
110-119	4515	.518	4.11	101.1	6.40	.261	3.17	6.07
120-129	2560	.542	3.99	104.0	6.55	.256	3.21	6.49
130 or more	1110	.555	3.87	106.9	6.71	.252	3.12	6.77

Interestingly, the general trend is for better ratios in the games immediately following higher pitch counts. As you can see, the winning percentage generally improves, while the ERA and average allowed generally decreases.

Now, perhaps we shouldn't make too much of these numbers. After all, the poorer a pitcher is, the less likely he is of staying in a game and achieving high pitch counts. By extension, he would tend to be more strongly represented at the low end of the spectrum on the above chart. That is, in the games following relatively brief appearances.

It's also true that some of baseball's best pitchers have accumulated a large number of high-pitch outings. For example, take a look at Randy Johnson. His number of games pitched actually increases as the workload rises:

Randy Johnson's Starts After Throwing Certain Number of Pitches

Pitches	Gms	Pct	ERA	Pit	IP	Avg Allowed	BB/9	K/9
50 or less	6	.600	4.37	106.2	5.83	.246	4.11	11.06
60- 69	2	1.000	5.40	98.5	5.00	.318	2.70	11.70
70- 79	2	1.000	1.88	109.5	7.17	.245	3.14	8.16
80- 89	4	.000	9.56	83.5	4.00	.317	9.56	11.25
90- 99	15	.750	3.59	105.5	6.36	.195	5.38	10.20
100-109	28	.700	3.05	118.4	6.75	.203	4.71	10.19
110-119	36	.556	3.77	118.6	6.70	.210	5.37	10.70
120-129	50	.619	3.31	124.6	7.24	.209	4.45	10.81
130 or more	64	.792	2.80	123.6	7.33	.197	3.72	10.77

Johnson is a remarkable 38-10 (.792) in the starts following games in which he throws at least 130 pitches. But then, Johnson is a remarkable pitcher, period. For other hurlers, heavy workloads do not necessarily lead to greater effectiveness. A case in point is Chuck Finley:

Chuck Finley's Starts After Throwing Certain Number of Pitches

Pitches	Gms	Pct	ERA	Pit	IP	Avg Allowed	BB/9	K/9
50 or less	4	1.000	4.30	98.0	5.75	.239	5.09	6.65
60- 69	5	.800	2.45	121.8	8.07	.230	2.23	6.47
70- 79	10	.571	2.47	110.2	7.30	.211	3.95	5.92
80- 89	11	.667	2.54	112.6	7.09	.252	3.46	5.42
90- 99	16	.545	3.30	116.8	6.81	.247	3.96	8.26
100-109	49	.590	3.91	110.9	6.71	.252	3.72	7.82
110-119	49	.375	3.56	116.6	7.23	.248	3.33	7.16
120-129	48	.561	4.33	114.2	6.89	.264	3.78	7.81
130 or more	47	.659	3.56	112.4	6.88	.271	3.45	6.71

Finley's ERA has been over 3.30 in every range above 90 pitches. Meanwhile, it's generally been in the mid-2.00s in the starts after games in which he doesn't reach the 90-pitch plateau.

The results for other pitchers are somewhat mixed. High pitch-count outings haven't clearly affected hurlers such as David Cone, Roger Clemens, Ramon Martinez and Jack McDowell, at least in the *short-term*. Still, Cone and McDowell have suffered injuries which may be attributed in part to their relatively heavy workloads. While the data appears to indicate pitchers can absorb abuse temporarily, the tactic might not pay off in the long run. And today's managers seem to have taken note.

August 18, 1997—Offensive Winning Percentage

Larry Walker reached the 100-RBI plateau this past weekend, only adding luster to one of the best offensive campaigns of recent memory. Walker continues to pace the majors with a .380 batting average, leading Tony Gwynn by a single point entering Monday, August 18. He also leads the National League with 36 homers.

Despite his lofty Triple Crown numbers, it may be hard for Walker to convince voters that he deserves the MVP award. His Colorado Rockies are four games under .500 and seemingly out of postseason contention. Nevertheless, without Walker's performance, the Rockies would likely be buried even further in the National League West standings.

"Offensive winning percentage" (OWP) gives some indication of how valuable Walker has been. OWP tries to calculate the winning percentage a team composed of nine Larry Walkers (or anyone else) would compile against average pitching and defense. The formula compares the runs created per 27 outs (RC27) by an individual player to his league's runs-per-game average.

In Walker's case, he's created 13.74 runs per 27 outs. Meanwhile, the National League average is 4.52 runs per team per game. Crunching the numbers, Walker's OWP is calculated at .902:

$$OWP = \frac{(13.74/4.52) * (13.74/4.52)}{1 + ((13.74/4.52) * (13.74/4.52))}$$

Perhaps it's easier to explain using words. We're dividing Walker's RC27 by the league scoring average, squaring the result, and then dividing it by one plus itself.

Whether the word explanation is any easier is debatable. However, there's no denying Walker's perch at the top of the OWP leaders:

Offensive Winning Percentage Leaders—1997

Player, Team	Pos	RC/27	Win %
Larry Walker, Col	RF	13.74	.902
Frank Thomas, WSox	1B	10.98	.830
Mo Vaughn, Bos	1B	10.47	.817
Jeff Bagwell, Hou	1B	9.52	.816
Barry Bonds, SF	LF	9.51	.816

(minimum 250 PA for catchers, 300 for all others)

Now, one thing that should be clear is that Walker has definitely been helped by playing his home games at Coors Field. While the National League average is 4.52 runs per team per game, the average at Coors is almost 44 percent higher, at 6.48 runs per team per game.

You should also know that the runs-per-team game average is based upon the runs scored by a particular league in all of their games, including interleague contests. And when looking at a particular player who has changed leagues this season, we're only comparing his RC27 to his current league's runs-per-game average.

So much for the housekeeping. Let's take a look at more players. Here are the guys who've compiled the *lowest* OWP:

Offensive Winning Percentage Trailers—1997

Player, Team	Pos	RC/27	Win %
Deivi Cruz, Det	SS	2.23	.168
Mike Bordick, Bal	SS	2.39	.188
Carlos Garcia, Tor	2B	2.48	.200
Jorge Fabregas, WSox	C	2.53	.206
Mariano Duncan, Tor	2B	2.59	.214

(minimum 250 PA for catchers, 300 for all others)

Not surprisingly, this list is dominated by middle infielders and catchers.

August 25, 1997—Craig Biggio

With the St. Louis Cardinals playing so miserably recently, the pennant chase in the National League Central appears to have come down to a war of attrition between the Houston Astros and Pittsburgh Pirates. Entering action on Monday, August 25, the Astros led the pesky Pirates by three games, with 32 contests remaining on each team's docket.

Should the Astros hang on for the division title, it'll be interesting to see how MVP voters will rate the contributions of Houston's two best position players, Jeff Bagwell and Craig Biggio. Without Bagwell and Biggio, the Astros' postseason prospects would almost certainly appear much less bright.

Bagwell, who was named the National League's MVP once before, in 1994, is enjoying yet another stellar campaign. He ranks second in the league with 34 homers, 108 RBI and 102 walks. On a team not exactly packed with power, Bagwell has accounted for 33 percent of its home runs, the highest rate in baseball.

Still, it could be argued that Biggio is actually having the superior season. Like Bagwell, Biggio boasts an on-base percentage above .400. In addition, Biggio has stolen 30 bases and leads the majors with 118 runs scored. And consider Biggio's production compared to the other second basemen in baseball. In terms of runs created per 27 outs, Biggio's mark is roughly 16 percent higher than the next-best rate, and just about 68 percent better than the major league average at the position:

Runs Created per 27 Outs—Second Basemen

Player, Team	RC	RC/27
Craig Biggio, Hou	115	8.45
Chuck Knoblauch, Min	98	7.28
John Valentin, Bos	91	6.78
Joey Cora, Sea	85	6.60
Mike Lansing, Mon	81	6.36
Average at position with 240 PA: 5.03		

Bagwell is generating 9.08 runs per 27 outs, a very strong performance. However, consider the context. While Bagwell's RC/27 mark tops National League first basemen, it ranks no better than fourth in the majors.

And there's no denying the fact that Biggio plays the more demanding position. And plays it well. In fact, only one second baseman in baseball has a better range factor than Biggio:

Range Factor—Second Basemen

Player, Team	Range
Eric Young, Col/LA	6.03
Craig Biggio, Hou	5.61
John Valentin, Bos	5.60
Jeff Kent, SF	5.57
Tony Fernandez, Cle	5.39
(minimum 500 innings)	

Biggio's range factor could actually be considered even better than Young's, if we exclude team pitcher strikeouts from the formula. Since there's no defensive opportunity available when a strikeout is recorded, perhaps a closer approximation of range factor would involve the following formula:

Range Factor $= \dfrac{27 * \text{Successful Chances}}{\text{OOF} - (\text{Team K} * \text{OOF}) / \text{Team Outs}}$

where Successful Chances = Player's putouts plus assists, OOF = Outs on Field when the player is playing the position, and Team Outs = Total team pitcher outs recorded.

Utilizing that formula, Biggio jumps to the top of the pack among second basemen:

Range Factor (adjusted formula)—Second Basemen

Player, Team	Range
Craig Biggio, Hou	7.54
Eric Young, Col/LA	7.51
Jeff Kent	7.25
John Valentin, Bos	7.22
Mark Lemke, Atl	7.20
(minimum 500 innings)	

There are a number of strong MVP candidates in the National League this season, so it's unclear what kind of support Biggio will generate. His tally could be restricted if voters split their ballots between he and Bagwell. In addition, the Astros have another potential candidate in pitcher Darryl Kile, who shared the league lead with 17 wins entering Monday's action, and also ranked second with a 2.28 ERA.

For Biggio, the race for team MVP may be almost as tough as the race for league MVP.

Mat Olkin's
"Fantasy Baseball Advisor"

March 25, 1997—The Lofton Trade

Now *that* was some deal. To my mind, Atlanta undoubtedly got the better end of it. In fact, I have a hard time understanding why the Indians made the deal in the first place. I can't see how it helps their club in any respect.

All right, so Kenny Lofton's a free agent at the end of the year, and you have to get something back for him before he leaves. But this? What do you think you're getting, John Hart? I think you got screwed.

First, you got the guy who beat you in the seventh game of the '95 World Series, David Justice (I guess he won't be doing *that* to you again!). We all know that he didn't hit a lick this spring, the shoulder injury could recur, blah, blah, blah. . . but for the sake of argument, let's assume that he's good as new. Presto! Mr. Hart, you've just acquired yourself a brand-new, fully-operational David Justice. Go ahead and mark him down for a .290-30-100 season and forget about it. Now please tell us one thing: *what's the point?*

Well, sure, he can hit; that much is obvious. And yes, he is a lefthanded hitter as well, and we understand that you front-office types are often preoccupied with that sort of stuff. But what does he give you that you didn't already have? He isn't going to force Manny Ramirez to the bench. Julio Franco has to play, and even if he can handle second base a few times a week, you'll still need to keep the DH spot open for him. So who's left? Who has to sit?

Aha, Mr. Giles. Mr. Brian Giles. Perhaps you've forgotten the name in the afterglow of your big trade, so let me refresh you. When he batted .327 in Double-A in 1993, you told him, "Show me what you can do in Triple-A." So he went up to Triple-A the next year and batted .313 while doubling his home-run output. You eyed him suspiciously and said, "Hmm. Do that again." So he did—he went back to Triple-A and batted .310 while maintaining the power. You said, "Fair enough. Now let's see you hit major league pitching." You gave him nine at-bats, and he notched five hits, including a home run. You said, "That's nice, but you also made *four* outs. Looks like you've got some more learning to do." You shipped him back to Triple-A for the third straight year, and then he really started to push the envelope. He kept his average up while boosting his power even further. In 83 games, he had nearly as many home runs (20) as strikeouts (29). To keep him from embarrassing you any further, you finally called him up, and you even let him play a little bit. In 121 at-bats, he batted .355, although he wasn't able to match Albert Belle's slugging percentage—he missed by a whole 11 points.

When Belle fled to greener pastures, you were left with Giles to play left field, a possibility that absolutely terrified you. From the moment Belle shook Jerry Reinsdorf's hand, you vowed to find a way to prevent Brian Giles from becoming your full-time left fielder. First, you offered the ridiculous rationalization that Giles, a lefthanded hitter, needed a platoon partner.

Giles batted .364 against lefties last year. In the minors, he hit them at a .281 clip, with good power. The year before that, he hit .296 off southpaws. Anyway, you decided that he couldn't hit lefties, so you signed Kevin Mitchell, and even dropped broad (pun intended) hints that Mitch might wind up with the full-time job. The last time Mitchell played full-time, people still knew how to spell "Dukakis," but never mind. Anyway, as it turned out, the most demanding physical task that Mitchell was up to was signing on the dotted line.

That left you back where you started, so you went out and got Justice. That sealed it. "Take *that,* Mr. Giles," you whooped crazily. "That should fix *your* wagon!"

I'm sure that Mr. Giles' wagon has been properly fixed, his goat has been gotten, and his clock has been cleaned. And what, pray tell, has this accomplished for the Cleveland Indians?

"But Justice is going to *hit,*" you exclaim. "It's the *American League,* for goodness sake!" That it is, but if you're suggesting that Justice will suddenly turn into King Kong just because he's moving to the AL, I ain't buyin' it.

People love to say that it's easier to hit in the American League. They say it all the time. They must love to say it, because players move back and forth between the leagues all the time with no visible effect on their statistics, but people still keep saying it. Let's examine your theory, Mr. Hart. Here are some of the hitters who've moved from the NL to the AL in recent years: Joe Girardi, Will Clark, Gregg Jefferies, Otis Nixon, Jose Offerman, Paul O'Neill, Bobby Bonilla, Joe Carter and Eddie Murray.

You can crunch the numbers all you want, but I think you'll have to agree with me on one point: when these guys came over from the Senior Circuit, they just kept right on doing what they'd always done, more or less. O'Neill and Carter picked it up a bit, but that mostly resulted from moving into home parks that better accentuated their particular talents. Joe Girardi hit a little better than expected, Eddie Murray hit a little worse, and the rest of them did about the same. On what basis can you assert that the move to the AL will make Justice into a significantly more productive hitter?

If you take a look at the ballpark he's leaving and the one he's moving into, you'd have to conclude that he's more likely to be hurt than helped. Over the last three years, he's batted .322 with 29 homers in Atlanta, while batting .253 with 20 homers on the road. Jacobs Field, meanwhile, is hardly a haven for lefthanded hitters. Over the last three years, it's suppressed lefthanded hitters' home runs by around seven percent. Ever since you moved into the Jake, Jim Thome, your big lefthanded bat, has hit better on the road.

So your little theory doesn't sway me. You've replaced Giles, who could hit .300-20-80 with Justice, who could hit .290-30-100. To achieve that gain—if it is indeed a gain—you've taken on the final $12.5 million of Justice's contract, locking yourself into a two-year commitment to a player who's widely regarded as an overpaid injury risk. The Justice/Giles substitution has marginal value on the field, and it costs you millions. And we haven't even gotten to the Grissom/Lofton part yet.

There's simply no defending the Grissom end of it. Now, you might be able to get away with the assertion that Justice will help you. People may fall for that "AL ballparks" theory, and some less enlightened fans may not realize the talent you've wasted in Giles. But if there's even *one* person on this good earth who actually believes that Marquis Grissom is a better player than Kenny Lofton, then that person surely must be wearing your underwear at this very moment.

Lofton is a super basestealer, a tremendous defender and a top-flight leadoff man. Grissom is all of these things but one: as a leadoff man, he's unavoidably mediocre. Last year, the average NL leadoff man had a .337 on-base percentage and scored 109 runs in 162 games. Grissom, by way of comparison, logged a .349 OBP and scored 106 runs in 158 games. . . and this was the *best* year of his career.

Grissom's problem is simple: he doesn't walk, so he doesn't get on base, so he doesn't score runs. Let's take a look at your projected regulars and see how they ranked in OBP last year, compared to your new leadoff hitter: Jim Thome, .450; Justice, .409; Franco, .407; Ramirez, .399; Matt Williams, .367; Omar Vizquel, .362; *Grissom, .349;* Tony Fernandez, .339 (in '95); and Sandy Alomar, .299.

A leadoff man's primary function is to get on base so he can score runs. Don't you see what you've done? You've acquired a "leadoff" hitter who can't even do that! His ability to get on base is inferior to that of almost every other hitter in your batting order. Out of your nine projected hitters, the only one who would be a demonstrably *worse* leadoff man is Sandy Alomar.

That's why Lofton has always been—and will continue to be—a far superior leadoff man to Grissom. In each of the last four seasons, Lofton has had a much better on-base percentage, and as a result, he's outscored Grissom during each season. This year, Grissom should get on base about 33 fewer times over the course of the season. That will cost your team about 15 runs, which will add up to one or two extra losses.

Meanwhile, the Braves will be living large. Those 15 runs will be added to their bottom line, while Jermaine Dye will try to cover for Justice's loss. He probably won't be ready to do that, but on balance, they won't lose all that much offense. And they'll gain quite a bit in other areas.

First, they'll be out from under Justice's oppressive contract, which means that they've gained enough financial flexibility to think about keeping both Greg Maddux and Tom Glavine. They'll also be able to devote substantial playing time to Andruw Jones that much sooner. And finally, they get Alan Embree in the deal.

Embree—another talented youngster who couldn't get a fair audition in Cleveland—may prove to be a huge addition to the Braves' bullpen. He's a little lefty with a rebuilt arm and a fearsome fastball, a power pitcher in the mold of Ron Villone. He's hell on lefties, and he should finally give Atlanta a legitimate lefthanded one-out specialist to replace Pedro Borbon. Ah, if they'd only had him last October. . .

But enough about Atlanta, Mr. Hart. I'm sure you think they're going to plummet to the bottom of the standings with Lofton. We'll take a look back at this deal in two years and see who the real winner was. By then, the chances are that you'll still be shelling out million-dollar paychecks to David Justice, while insisting that Brian Giles is "too old" to be taken seriously as a prospect.

April 1, 1997—Opening Day

It's almost over. In 64 minutes, Pat Hentgen will throw a pitch, Tony Phillips will watch it pass, the fat man will sing, and the long, cold winter will finally be done. Amen.

With Opening Day comes opening-day rosters, and this year's collection contains more than a few surprises. Did you see who made the Rockies' squad? Darnell Coles. Yes, *that* Darnell Coles—the one who hasn't appeared in a professional game or the North American continent since 1995, when he batted .225 for the Cardinals to earn his release. After playing in Japan for all of 1996, Coles apparently has decided to test the theory that *anyone* can hit in Coors Field.

Reacquaint yourself with Oakland's Steve Karsay, who hasn't pitched in the majors in almost three years. He's taken a novel approach to his career, undergoing a few decades worth of elbow surgeries during his three-year sabbatical. Now, having gotten the requisite elbow reconstruction and resulting complications out of the way, he hopes to enjoy a successful career without further incident. His 2.50 spring ERA won him a spot in Oakland's starting rotation, and the A's expect their considerable investment in his rehabilitation to begin to pay dividends.

Carlos Perez is another hurler who's returned from the dark side of the moon (Money? Get back!). He looked great in '95 before arm and legal problems wiped out all of 1996 for him. Now Felipe Alou says he's all the way back, and he's been returned to the Expos' starting rotation. The southpaw, who's as predictable as your average Perez brother, should win somewhere between zero and 20 games.

Pittsburgh lefthander Steve Cooke was never as far gone as Carlos Perez, but he was out even longer, missing most of 1995 and 1996 with arm miseries. After going 3-1 with a 2.45 ERA this spring, the Pirates have decided that he's recaptured the impressive form he showed as a 23-year-old rookie in 1993. He usually can find the plate, and he always can find the ballpark.

During his long, distinguished career, Tommy Lasorda had occasion to "break in" many a talented pitcher, from Fernando Valenzuela to Orel Hershiser to Ramon Martinez. When Darren Dreifort made the big club in 1994, Lasorda handled him with no less timidity. Now that Dreifort's arm has been fully rehabilitated from that experience, he finally may be able to fulfill his early promise. This spring, he pitched so well that he was able to displace the formidable Antonio Osuna as the Dodgers' primary setup man.

As the returning warriors hope to recapture their past success, they are joined by a cast of precocious rookies that have arrived much sooner than anticipated. The Pirates' Jose Guillen has been the talk of the spring, making the jump from A-ball to the Pittsburgh roster. Such accelerated promotions are so infrequent that it's impossible to say what might happen as Guillen adjusts to a whole new brand of pitching. Still, the Pirates were so enchanted with his tools that they quickly shoved Trey Beamon out of the nest, although they did keep a safety net named Midre Cummings.

One of the most impressive pitchers in the Orioles' camp was Rule 5 draftee Mike Johnson. The 22-year-old righthander had a big year at Class-A in the Toronto system last year, and former Toronto GM Pat Gillick plucked him in the winter draft. Showing precise command of a respectable fastball and a good breaking pitch, Johnson posted a 2.95 ERA this spring and landed a spot on the roster. Now, Rocky Coppinger's arm injury leaves a hole in the Baltimore rotation that Johnson may be able to fill.

With Scott Brosius around, no one expected Oakland third-base prospect Scott Spiezio to see significant playing time this year. But the A's were so impressed with Spiezio that they went above and beyond the call to clear a spot for him. Second baseman Brent Gates was shown the door, and Spiezio, who'd played six games at second base in his professional career, was instructed to learn the double-play pivot and have it down cold in three weeks.

At first, the experiment had its skeptics, but Spiezio batted .303 and made only two errors all spring, so the A's decided to leave him there for the real games. Oakland manager Art Howe points out that he made the same conversion himself during his own major league career, moving from third to second base. At the keystone, Howe never did much with the leather, but Spiezio's got defensive tools that Howe never dreamed of having. Asking a rookie to learn an unfamiliar position at the major league level while adjusting to big-league pitching is a lot to ask, but it may end up working out. If it does, the A's may have themselves a fairly productive second baseman.

Down in Florida, Marlins' skipper Jim Leyland didn't have too many difficult decisions to make, but he made a gutsy call on his fifth starting pitcher. Passing over Rick Helling and Mark Hutton—who'd both pitched well for Florida last year—Leyland dipped down to Double-A and selected lefthander Tony Saunders. Helling and Hutton reacted like older siblings who were sent to bed before their little brother, but rest assured that Saunders can hold his own without a bib. After undergoing elbow surgery in '95, he returned with a dominant season at Double-A last year. Leyland never tries to get too much out of the back end of his rotation, but Saunders could make the decision pay off.

Down in Houston, Astros fans want to find out if Larry Dierker can do more than just call a good game. One of the first decisions he's made has been to add rookie Chris Holt to the starting rotation. While he lacks the outstanding stuff of, say, a young Larry Dierker, Holt possesses fine command of a variety of pitches. He's been an effective pitcher in tough parks in the minors, and he's thrown well this spring. Dierker seems to be betting that Holt can be this year's Donne Wall, and he may be right.

The Rangers have quietly added a kid pitcher named Danny Patterson. Actually, at age 26, he's not all that young for a rookie. It took him a while to convert to the bullpen and work his way back from elbow surgery. Since his return in late '95, he's developed what he calls a "Vulcan splitter," a pitch that he holds deep between his middle and ring finger. Featuring this bizarre offering, he fashioned a 1.68 ERA at Triple-A last year and threw 8.2 scoreless innings for Texas. He'll be setting up saves for John Wetteland this year, and both may live long and prosper.

We'll soon find out, anyway. The wheels have been set in motion, and by this time tomorrow, 12 guys will be batting .500. Someone will snap a ligament, someone else will get sent down, and next week, we'll marvel at the kaleidoscope once again.

April 8, 1997—That Clanging Sound Ain't Belle

When you lay out in front of you the year's first batting stats from today's *USA Today*, a few things may jump out at you. One is that the Tigers seem to be putting together a pretty decent lineup. Of course, the question of whether they're building a decent "team" is another issue entirely. To accept the idea that they may be on the road to respectability, you have to be able to completely overlook their pitching staff. If you're able to do that, *congratulations*—you may be qualified to work in Detroit's front office.

Yep, the Tigers are playing good, old-fashioned and/or new-fangled American League baseball, leading the league with 53 runs scored and a batting average of .317. Of course, all of that is completely negated by their sorry pitching staff: they've allowed 52 runs, the most in the league, and they have the highest opponent batting average in the loop, .310. It all adds up to a lot of exciting games, if not a lot of victories.

The White Sox have taken a similar approach, forsaking quality free-agent pitchers in favor of a big bat and a slick marketing campaign. If Albert Belle and Frank Thomas rattle enough rooftops, they reckon, perhaps Joe Magrane will be able to slip back into the rotation unnoticed.

Anyway, when the White Sox and Tigers met last Saturday, the question was, "What happens when two teams play each other, and neither one's pitching staff can get anybody out?" The answer, we discovered, was, "Everything."

The Tigers scored four in the first, the White Sox answered with three in the second, and Detroit came back with four in the top of the fourth to take an 8-3 lead. But the five-run cushion only lasted about as long as it took for the teams to change sides. In the bottom of the frame, Chicago erupted for seven runs to go on top, 10-8. Detroit responded with a run in the fifth to make it a "one-run game," as they say. The margin held for over one full inning, until the top of the seventh rolled around.

Tony Castillo came on to pitch for the White Sox. After allowing a hit to lead off the inning, he got a couple of quick outs. Then things really got started.

Castillo walked Bubba Trammell on four pitches. (In hindsight, we should have known that a guy named "Bubba" was likely to start some trouble.) Brian Johnson followed with an RBI single, and suddenly the lead was gone—it was now 10-10. There were still two outs. That brought up Deivi Cruz.

Cruz was selected by Detroit in the Rule 5 draft last winter. Before this season, he had never hit against anything even remotely resembling major league pitching. Last year, he played the entire year in the Midwest League, a low Class-A league. In other words, he was about four promotions away from the majors. He found his way into the Detroit spring training camp by way of the draft, and when Orlando Miller got hurt this spring, the Detroit people figured they had nothing to lose by sticking Cruz in the lineup, at least temporarily. He became their emergency/apathy shortstop.

On this afternoon, though, he had no problem hitting Tony Castillo. The lefty gave him something to hit and he jumped all over it, lashing a double to plate the go-ahead run for Detroit. Then came something even uglier. Brian Hunter lined a single into right-center to plate another run. As Cruz rounded third and looked to add to the lead, the throw came in from the outfield. It was a little off-line, but it looked like it would beat Cruz to the plate.

Suddenly, Castillo, who had been hanging around the middle of the diamond thinking about his stock portfolio or something, decided that he wanted to cut off the throw. He didn't, but he did manage to deflect it off-line. The throw bounced past catcher Ron Karkovice to the screen. If Castillo had been backing up the plate like he should have been, he would have been there to prevent the baserunner from advancing. But then again, if he'd been backing up the plate, he wouldn't have had the chance to kick the throw past Karkovice in the first place.

At any rate, Castillo did his best Eddie Cicotte impression, and Karkovice ended up having to chase the ball all the way to the backstop. For Karkovice—who runs well for a walrus—this took about as much time and effort as it took Dorothy to retrieve the witch's broomstick. By now, it was 13-10 Detroit.

The Sox were down and their own home crowd was booing them, but at least Damion Easley was up. He tapped an easy roller to third baseman Chris Snopek, who's normally a super fielder. The ball stayed down and rolled under Snopek's glove as Hunter came in to score the Tiger's 14th run.

Now, Castillo finally did something right—he picked Easley off first base. Easley was running, so Thomas took the throw, calmly took one step inside the baseline, and fired to second base. His throw sailed into left field for the Sox' third error of the inning, and all hands were safe. Finally, mercifully, Travis Fryman struck out.

That ended the inning, but the game continued, and both sides kept on scoring. By the time each squad had recorded 27 outs, the Tigers had tallied 15 runs and the White Sox had scored 12. Jerry Reinsdorf probably figured that if he'd just signed another hitter this winter, he could have won that game.

186

April 15, 1997—Age vs. Experience

So far, the Cardinals and the Astros have been two of the most surprising teams, each for different reasons. Most experts picked the Cardinals to repeat in the NL Central, while I (ever the contrarian) put my money on Houston. As of this morning, the Cardinals are the worst non-Cub team in the division, while the Astros sit atop the NL Central with an 8-5 mark.

I'm not gloating, mind you. It's still too early to attach much meaning to the standings, and anyone who requires proof of this should consider San Francisco's 8-3 record, or the fact that the Brewers, Royals and Twins are all ahead of both the White Sox and the Indians in the AL Central race. And to be fair, the Cardinals haven't had their best men on the field. They'll be a very different team when Ray Lankford, Delino DeShields and Andy Benes get healthy.

But I thought that Monday's Astros-Cardinals game provided an excellent illustration of one of the main differences between the two teams. The Cardinals got a couple of early runs off Darryl Kile, who eventually settled down to pitch eight strong innings. Meanwhile, Cardinal rookie Matt Morris matched him, allowing one run on his own throwing error, a pair of infield singles and a fielder's choice, and another run on a solo homer by Craig Biggio. Reincarnated Bolshevik sympathizer Mark Petkovsek pitched the seventh and the eighth, and the game went into the ninth, tied 2-2.

It's safe to say that by the end of the season, each team will find itself in familiar territory in the late innings of close games. Both the Cardinals and the Astros have strong starting pitching but lack the firepower to blow away the opposition. It will be especially important for each team to make the most of what it has in the bullpen.

On Monday, the Cardinals brought in lefthander Tony Fossas to pitch the top of the ninth. He got pinch-hitter Ray Montgomery and Craig Biggio but walked rookie Bob Abreu. Fossas picked him off, but Dmitri Young's error allowed Abreu to reach second. With Jeff Bagwell coming up and the go-ahead run on second base, La Russa was justifiably unwilling to let the righthanded-hitting Bagwell bat against Fossas, his lefthanded specialist. He had to go to Eckersley. Eck got Bagwell, and it went to the bottom of the ninth.

Then Astros manager Larry Dierker chose to play his ace, waving in lefthander Billy Wagner. Wagner fanned Gary Gaetti, Tom Lampkin and Steve Scarsone to send the game into extra innings.

By now, there's little doubt that Wagner is one of the premier closers in all of baseball. He throws mid-90s heat from an arm angle that makes the ball appear as if it's coming out of his shirtsleeve, and when you key in on the fastball, he'll drop over a curveball that batters seem to watch with a combination of resignation and disbelief. In 61.2 major league innings, he's allowed 33 hits while striking out 84 batters.

Anyway, the game went into the top of the 10th with Eckersley still on the mound. Derek Bell doubled to lead off the inning, and that was especially bad news for La Russa. Not only was the go-ahead run on second base with no one out, but the next batter Eckersley was going to have to face was the lefthanded-hitting Luis Gonzalez.

Let me explain what the problem was. When Eckersley was on top of his game, back in the late '80s and early '90s, getting lefthanded hitters out was not a huge problem for him. He made his living off the righties and held his own against everyone else well enough to be the best reliever in baseball.

When his effectiveness started to slip in 1993, it was the lefties who were beginning to get to him. They hit .328 against him that year, while righties still only hit .190 off him. The next year, it was the same: .322 for lefties and .231 for righties. In '95, it was more of the same: .347 and .145.

La Russa is an intelligent man, though. He knew that a pitcher who held righties to a sub-.200 batting average could still be an effective closer if he were given the right kind of protection. So when La Russa took Eck with him to St. Louis last year, he made sure to outfit his bullpen with not one, but *two* lefthanded one-out specialists, Tony Fossas and Rick Honeycutt. That way, he could neutralize the lefthanded bats in the opponent's batting order before bringing on Eck to close it out. And if Eckersley faltered, and the lefthanded bats came back around, he could still bring in another lefty to protect the Eck. It worked fine last year.

But now, in the top of the 10th, there were no more lefties in the pen. Forty-three-year-old Rick Honeycutt, the oldest player in the major leagues, was on the shelf with a broken walker or something, so Eck had to face Gonzalez. Eckersley found one way to keep Gonzalez from hitting him, though: he hit Gonzalez. The hit batsman brought up righthanded-hitting Tony Eusebio, who flied out. Then Larry Dierker pinch-hit for Billy Wagner, sending up lefthanded-hitting Billy Spiers.

We can't say for sure that La Russa would have brought in a lefty to pitch to Gonzalez if he'd had the choice, but Spiers was a different story. If La Russa hadn't made the move before, he almost certainly would have made it now. The Astros had no one left on their bench who could damage a lefthanded pitcher. Spiers, meanwhile, had gone 3-for-5 against Eckersley over the course of his career.

La Russa was caught. He was hamstrung because he'd been forced to construct a complex, multi-faceted bullpen committee to cover for his closer's fatal flaw. And the specialists he'd enlisted to execute the plan carried a lot of mileage. Now that one of them had gone down, the whole scheme had unraveled, and he was left with Eckersley facing a hitter who could beat him with the game on the line.

Spiers doubled into the right-field corner to score Bell and Gonzalez.

Then La Russa lifted Eckersley in favor of T.J. Mathews. Many think that Mathews has the stuff to be a closer, but La Russa's loyalty to Eckersley prevents that theory from being tested. Tonight, all Mathews could do was try to keep anything else from hitting the fan.

In the bottom of the inning, Dierker had to make a move himself. He'd pinch-hit for his closer, Wagner, but he still had *another* closer available—John Hudek. He used him, and Hudek retired the Cardinals in order to clinch the 4-2 win.

Again, I'm not trying to paint myself as Mr. Smart Guy, but this is one of the reasons I went with the Astros over the Cardinals. A bullpen where a bunch of octogenarians prop each other up is not my idea of a stable relief corps. Granted, Hudek isn't a model of durability himself, but he seems to be healthy, and as long as he is, the Astros will have two bona fide closers, one from each side. Even if he can't do it, I'll take my chances with Wagner alone.

A lot of you probably couldn't understand why I picked Houston over St. Louis. Monday's game explained it better than I ever could have myself.

April 23, 1997—Hermanson, Yes; Irabu, No

Felipe Alou has a proven track record as a genius. When he pulls a short reliever like Dustin Hermanson out of the bullpen and sticks him in the rotation, we have to give the idea the benefit of the doubt. If an alchemist like Buddy Bell wakes up in the morning and decides that he'd rather have Brian Williams or Doug Brocail work as a starter rather than as a closer, it's safe to say that his motivations have more to do with self-preservation than expertise. In other words, when things can't possibly get any worse, it's easy to make unconventional moves. If they work out, you get the credit, and if they fail, who's going to notice? Is Buddy Bell going to get fired because Doug Brocail blows a ninth-inning lead?

But Alou, on the other hand, makes odd role changes all the time, even with a team that's in the running more often than not. The amazing thing is that they almost always work out. The last time Alou moved a reliever into the rotation, it worked out so well that the lucky hurler ended up pricing himself out of the Montreal market. In mid-1993, Alou took a look at a 30-year-old middle reliever named Jeff Fassero and decided that he could handle a more challenging role. He gave him his first major league start on July 10 of 1993, and Fassero remained a cornerstone of the Montreal rotation until he left after the 1996 season.

Before the conversion from reliever to starter, Fassero was roughly comparable to, say, Mike Stanton or Scott Radinsky. After the move, he was one of the most effective and consistent lefthanded starters in baseball. In 100 starts from July 10, 1993 through the end of 1996, he went 43-35 with a 3.39 ERA. By way of comparison, John Smiley went 36-29 with a 3.65 ERA in 87 starts over the same span, and Wilson Alvarez went 42-33 with a 3.84 ERA in 103 starts. So by moving Fassero to the rotation, Alou came up with a John Smiley, virtually out of thin air.

Last year, he went the opposite way with young hurler Ugueth Urbina, who'd posted an 8-7 mark with a 4.51 ERA in 21 major league starts. Alou moved him to the pen in August of last season and began grooming him as the closer of the future. Since the conversion, Urbina's posted a 1.97 ERA in 24 games of relief, allowing 15 hits and nine walks while striking out 36 in 32 innings.

And we mustn't forget that it was Alou who came up with John Wetteland—the John Wetteland that we know today as one of the game's best closers. Before Alou got his hands on him, Wetteland was a washed-out starter who was pitching Triple-A relief in the Dodgers' organization. In 1992, Alou made him the closer and he immediately saved 37 games. That year, the Dodgers' save leader was Roger McDowell, who had 14. Under Alou, Wetteland saved 105 games in three years before leaving to become a millionaire. Then you have Ken Hill. In St. Louis, he went 23-32. Under Alou, he went 41-21. Since leaving Montreal, he's gone 27-20. You also have Butch Henry, who came to the Expos with a major league won-lost record of 8-17. In 37 starts over three years, he went 16-12 with a 2.74 ERA.

My point is this: if another manager had made Dustin Hermanson a starter, we might have had reason to give pause. After all, Hermanson—a hard-throwing short reliever who entered the year with a career ERA of 7.35—didn't look like a likely candidate to succeed as a starter. He'd never started a professional game in his life. His fastball/slider arsenal didn't seem particularly well-suited to the demands of starting. He was known for his live arm, but if the Padres or the Marlins had thought for one moment that he might have been able to use it in a more important role than middle relief, they probably wouldn't have traded him in the first place.

But Alou saw something that no one else did. He may yet be proven wrong, but so far it looks like he's still one step ahead of the rest of us. Hermanson's first start was a resounding success: five innings, four hits, one run, one walk and one win. Alou limited him to just 77 pitches, and he'll probably keep him under tight limits for the next few weeks as Hermanson's arm adjusts to the rigors of starting.

Like I said, the move could still bomb. Pitchers like Goose Gossage and Steve Bedrosian made similar bullpen-to-rotation conversions early in their careers, and the move didn't agree with either of them. Hermanson may ultimately end up like they did—back in the bullpen. However, you have to respect the fact that he just might end up like Jeff Fassero: a more successful starter than anyone had ever imagined.

Presently, people are expecting a heck of a lot more out of Hideki Irabu than Dustin Hermanson. While I have no reason to dispute the scouts' excitement about Irabu's reputed 99-MPH fastball and 90-MPH splitter, I remain somewhat skeptical about the Nomo-mania that's accompanied his signing.

Now, even if you're willing to believe that a pitcher could possibly have stuff that good, and that the Japanese team that held his rights would be willing to trade him for some American minor leaguers, you're still left with some unsettling questions. Like, "If he's that good, why don't the numbers confirm it?" His numbers from last year are attractive at first glance, but they hardly paint the portrait of a pitcher with unhittable stuff.

Last year, pitching for the Chiba Lotte Marines of the Japanese Pacific League, Irabu went 12-6, fanned over a man per inning and led the league with a 2.40 ERA. That looks great, until you consider who he barely edged out for the ERA crown. It seems that Irabu had a teammate who posted nearly identical stats, going 14-9 with a 2.40 ERA. You might remember this pitcher; his name is Eric Hillman.

Eric Hillman is a 30-year-old lefty who pitched for the New York Mets from 1992 through 1994, going 4-14 with a 4.85 ERA. At no point in his major league career was his stuff considered "unhittable." Several years ago, when he announced his intention to seek employment in Japan, not one American team attempted to dissuade him by offering him a seven-figure contract. But for last year at least, this lanky lefty of modest talents was able to pitch just as effectively as Irabu. How can that be?

Well, I'll be the first to say that Hillman was probably a much better pitcher than he appeared to be during his stay with the Mets, and he's likely a lot better now than he was then. But on the other hand, he probably hasn't transformed himself into a pitcher who could win big in the American major leagues. In all likelihood, he's effective enough to post superior numbers in Japan and decent ones here.

It wouldn't surprise me if Irabu turns out to be of the same general quality. During the past few years, a disproportionate number of Chiba Lotte pitchers have turned up on the Pacific League's ERA leader boards, while the team hasn't been tremendously successful in the won-loss column. This suggests to me that the Marines' ballpark may be one that favors their pitchers, helping them to compile numbers that make them out to be more effective than they actually are. If this is actually the case, it might help to explain why the Marines would dare to send their "overpowering" ace overseas.

May 20, 1997—The Lesser of Two Evils?

Tony Phillips and Terry Bevington could coexist no longer, so it was obvious that one of them had to go. The clubhouse was dividing itself into warring factions, publicly sniping at both the manager and each other. At first, it looked like Bevington would get the ax, but the White Sox came alive during a crucial homestand, and the front office publicly reaffirmed its commitment to Bevington. When the word came down, Phillips knew it was only a matter of time before they revoked his sox.

Last weekend, the Angels agreed to take Phillips off Bevington's hands, hoping that the switch-hitting multipositional leadoff hitter could jump-start their offense the way he had in '95. Although Phillips isn't the type of guy you'd invite to your kid's birthday party (his resume includes fistfights with fans, countless arguments with umpires, and a recent accusation of racism leveled at the AL president), he is a master of the underappreciated art of reaching base.

Most fans seemed to sense that he was worth quite a bit more than a bespectacled middle-reliever/wanna-be-first-baseman and a cryptogram catcher. Even the Sox players instantly realized that they'd been ripped off. Most of their "no comment" quotes translated rather easily into, "It's a sucker deal but the GM told me to keep my mouth shut about it."

Ron Schueler has yet to gag me, so I'll say it: Chicago dropped the ball on this one. Any time you have to consider giving away a player of Tony Phillips' caliber simply because your manager can't get along with him, you really have to ask yourself, "Isn't there any possible way I could just fire the manager instead?"

Now I might be singing a different tune if we were talking about a different manager. If it were Felipe Alou or Davey Johnson, I might say, "Show Phillips the door. The manager has to be in charge."

But we're talking about *Terry Bevington* here. The guy was *this* close to being fired two weeks ago. Did the Sox' strong play over the last two weeks really dispel all doubts about his managerial abilities? To my mind, there's ample justification to fire him before you even get halfway to the Phillips fiasco. I have grave doubts about this man's ability to ride out the summer in a White Sox uniform. Clearing out Phillips just to buy some more time for Bevington is like buying a new modem for a Commodore 64.

May 27, 1997: Generation Gap

Let's start today's column with a simple exercise. I'm going to describe two players to you, and when I'm done, I'd like you to choose one or the other. Before you start, let me assure you that the choice won't be all that difficult. Any competent major league manager would be able to make the right call without a second's hesitation.

First I'll give you "Player A." Player A is a 24-year-old lefthanded-hitting outfielder. He's a decent defender with a strong arm, capable of playing either left or right field. He's been a semi-regular for two years, compiling a .274 lifetime batting average with a .460 slugging percentage.

Now for the other guy. "Player B" is a 31-year-old switch-hitting outfielder. He used to be a good right fielder, but he's now become a liability in either right or left. He hates to DH, however. During an 11-year major league career, he's put up similar numbers to Player A—a .270 average and .453 slugging percentage.

Here's how each player has performed over the last two years:

Player A

Year	G	AB	HR	RBI	AVG	OBP	SLG
1995	121	379	15	54	.288	.326	.509
1996	132	422	11	45	.280	.342	.448

Player B

Year	G	AB	HR	RBI	AVG	OBP	SLG
1995	126	479	19	86	.263	.323	.449
1996	142	518	12	72	.247	.320	.375

OK, time's up. Who do you pick?

Come on—do I really need to ask? What sane person would take Player B? Player A is a better hitter and a better fielder. He's on the way up, while Player B is on the way down. As time goes by, the gap will only widen. I haven't told you *one* thing about Player B that would even *begin* to justify his selection.

There are quite a few things about Player B that I *haven't* told you, though. The first is that his name is Ruben Sierra (as you may have guessed by now). We've been comparing him to Player A, a.k.a. Shawn Green.

The reason I asked you to take part in this little exercise is to make you fully appreciate Cito Gaston's recent decision to replace Shawn Green with Sierra. You see, even if you *completely ignore* all of Sierra's other negatives, and focus only on the two players' ages, skills and recent performance, it's still *impossible* to make a case for Sierra.

And it doesn't get any easier when you begin to consider Sierra's troubled past. The guy's got enough baggage to sink an aircraft carrier.

Let's try to briefly sum up the last few years of Sierra's pitiful existence. In Oakland, Tony La Russa got fed up with him and referred to him in print as "the village idiot." Shortly thereafter, the A's traded him to the Yankees for an injured and overpaid Danny Tartabull. In New York, Sierra stomped and pouted when Joe Torre asked him to DH, and Torre decided that he had to be dumped at any cost. In exchange for Cecil Fielder's enormous contract, they were able to send him to the Tigers. Sierra hit one home run in 46 games for Detroit while committing five errors in only 23 games in the outfield. The Tigers agreed to pay almost all of his salary if he'd take his act to Cincinnati in 1997. After he batted .244 with two home runs and 21 strikeouts in 25 games for Cincinnati, the Reds decided that he wasn't even worth the minimum salary, and cut him.

That's when the Blue Jays got involved. Shawn Green wasn't hitting, and Cito Gaston apparently decided that it was time to do something. Something drastic. Green had to go.

It wasn't just a slump, Gaston decided. Green wouldn't come out of it and hit like he had for the past two years. He wouldn't follow the normal growth curve and improve upon his already respectable numbers. He wouldn't continue to develop over the next three years as he entered his physical prime. None of this would happen; Green had to be replaced, Gaston decided.

This decision was short-sighted, indefensible and reactionary, from my point of view. For a major league team to develop the nucleus of a winner, it must cultivate players like Shawn Green whenever the team is fortunate enough to have one come along. It cannot do that by seizing upon their slumps as opportunities to deprive them of their jobs.

But the follow-up to the decision was even more inexcusable—the signing of Ruben Sierra. Here, we see Cito Gaston's insecurity at its worst. Gaston is so uncertain of his own ability to judge young talent that he refuses to commit himself to a young player, no matter how obvious that player's talent may be. Even with young studs like Carlos Delgado and Alex Gonzalez, Gaston has remained acutely and publicly aware of their shortcomings, while exhibiting complete indifference to their exciting long-term potential. Gaston greatly prefers that his players spend the first half of their careers playing for some "other" major league team. That way, by the time he gets them, he doesn't have to bother trying to figure out how good they really are.

And when you put pressure on Gaston by burdening him with high-priced talent and pennant expectations, his patience for the youngsters grows even shorter. That's when he starts making panic moves like this one—moves that not only hurt the team in the long run, but in the short run, too.

Don't get me wrong; it's all right for a manager to express a general preference for veterans over youngsters. That goes against my way of thinking, and I wouldn't hire a man like that to manage *my* team, but a preference for established players isn't necessarily destructive. It can work, as long as finding *good* players takes priority over finding *veteran* players.

Gaston has lost sight of his goals. For years, his pathological pursuit of mediocre veterans has threatened to overwhelm his ability to field his best team. Now, can there be any doubt that the moment has finally arrived? *The man has benched Shawn Green to play Ruben Sierra.*

June 17, 1997—Why No One Throws 300 Innings Any More

Today's pitchers are wimps, any old-timer will tell you. Back when all was right with the world, pitchers would tirelessly throw inning after inning (like *real* men), piling up complete games by the dozens. Today's crybabies lack the guts to go the distance; they just work six or seven innings and leave the bullpen to finish their work.

Instinctively, I've always disagreed with that argument. By nature, just about every pitcher would rather throw nine good innings than seven. If modern pitchers were just as able to pitch complete games as their mound forefathers were, one suspects that pitchers would still be throwing 300 innings per season. They don't do that anymore, and it seems a little naive to conclude that a lack of proper masculinity is the critical difference.

Still, it's difficult to maintain that modern pitchers work just as hard when the conventional stats give the old-timers so much ammunition for their arguments. Before you can open your mouth, they shout, "Three-hundred innings! Show me a man alive who has *half* the guts that Eddie Plank did!"

Innings. It's their trump card; you can't beat it.

But to me, the whole argument is flawed. Where is it written that "innings" are the only proper way to measure a pitcher's workload? An inning is just a group of three outs. As a pitcher works, he accumulates innings, but those innings are an indirect and inherently flawed method of measuring the amount of work he's done.

In the course of obtaining a single out, a pitcher may throw any number of pitches, some of which will be taken, fouled off or batted for hits. Where is it written that the only pitches that take anything out of a pitcher's arm are the ones that result in outs?

Ideally, you'd measure a pitcher's workload based on the number of *pitches* rather than *innings thrown.* Unfortunately, pitch counts have only begun to be recorded over the last 10 years or so. Before 1987, we're left with the imperfect alternative, innings.

Let's get back to the question of the historic decline in innings thrown by starting pitchers. It's always been my feeling that the pitchers of the '90s throw just as many *pitches*—albeit in fewer innings—than the workhorses of long-ago. But in the absence of any conclusive proof one way or the other, that remains a mere theory.

Still, others have subscribed to the idea. In his book *The Diamond Appraised,* Craig Wright inferred indirectly (from two different sources) that pitchers from the dead ball era "threw significantly fewer pitches per batter than in modern times."

His analysis was intriguing in that it would explain how pitchers of that era were able to throw so many innings. If his conclusion was correct, it would also validate what I'd suspected: modern pitchers *aren't* wimps.

Then I stumbled upon something *extraordinary.* While doing some research for an unrelated project, I came across something in the *Spalding 1920 Base Ball Guide* that launched me into a state of pure sabermetric rapture.

There, along with the play-by-play of the 1919 World Series, was the baseball equivalent of the Rosetta Stone: *pitch counts* for each of the eight games of the Series. At long last, here was conclusive proof—if only a tantalizingly small sample—of the number of pitches per batter that were thrown in the dead ball era.

Incidentally, the *Guide* contains remarkably extensive breakdowns of the pitches each pitcher threw in the Series. The pitches are divided into "balls," "strikes," "fly balls," "ground balls," "foul hits," and "hit batsmen." It's too bad the chap who thought to record all of that isn't still alive; I'm sure STATS would love to hire him.

If you'll permit me one more digression, the pitch-count data sheds much additional light on the Big Fix. Take Lefty Williams' ill-fated outing in the Series' final game. After gamblers allegedly threatened to harm his wife the night before, Williams faced five batters, recording one out and allowing two singles and two doubles before being removed with a 1-0 count on the sixth hitter of the inning. Get this: he threw 15 pitches in that inning, and *13* of them were strikes. That doesn't paint the portrait of a nervous pitcher struggling with his control; rather, it tells the tale of a man who was laying batting-practice fastballs right over the plate.

But it's the raw pitch-count totals that teach us the most. In Game 1, the two teams threw 179 pitches *combined*—something that's well-near impossible to fathom today. No starter in the entire Series threw more than 130 pitches in a game. Even Dickie Kerr needed only 129 pitches to down the Reds in 10 innings in the sixth game. Here's the bottom line: the

White Sox and Reds' pitchers faced 580 hitters during the Series, and threw a total of 1,811 pitches. *That's only 3.12 pitches per batter.*

I cannot overemphasize the significance of that figure, 3.12, because it destroys the myth of the iron-man pitcher. Today's pitchers throw an average of 3.70 pitches to each batter, and that entirely explains the decrease in innings pitched since 1919. *Modern pitchers log fewer innings but throw just as many pitches as the old-time workhorses did.*

Why did old-timers throw so few pitches to each hitter? There are probably many reasons. First, there was a stronger expectation that starters would go nine innings back then. That pressure induced pitchers to take more care to pace themselves. Craig Wright offers quotes from Christy Mathewson from that period, explaining Matty's view of how important pacing was to effective pitching. It's also important to remember that every lineup from that period contained at least one hitter (the pitcher) and usually two or three hitters that were virtual non-threats. When a pitcher got to the bottom of the order, he could go right after the hitter with almost no fear of giving up a home run. Today's pitchers throw as hard as they can for as long as they can, and work carefully to each and every hitter. Few of us have ever seen the game played any differently, and it's easy to unconsciously assume that things have always been as they are.

But you don't necessarily need to understand *why* old-timers worked more efficiently; it's only important to understand that they *did*. Since they threw less pitches to each hitter, they could throw the same number of pitches as a modern hurler and wind up with about 18 percent more innings. If you make the proper adjustments to their innings-pitched totals, they suddenly seem quite reasonable by modern standards.

Take a look at the innings-pitched leaders from 1919. There was a three-way tie for the top spot between Bob Shaw, Eddie Cicotte and Hippo Vaughn. Each of them worked 306.2 frames, which translates into 258.1 modern innings. By comparison, the three leading pitchers in 1996 were Pat Hentgen (265.2 IP), Alex Fernandez (258) and John Smoltz (253.2).

Unfortunately, the idea of recording pitch counts was apparently too far ahead of its time. I went through most of the rest of the *Guides* for the early part of this century, and couldn't find another single instance where such data was published. It's a shame, too, because I really wanted to know what the heck was going on back in 1908, when Ed Walsh threw 464 innings.

But pitchers' efficiency has relevance apart from our historical concerns. Innings continues to be an imperfect and often-misunderstood yardstick for pitchers' workloads. In the 1992 edition of the since-renamed *Baseball Sabermetric,* Brock Hanke warned, "If a starter gets more than 250 innings and his name is not Roger Clemens, he's going to have a big collapse the next year."

As an example of a pitcher to stay away from, Hanke offered. . . *Greg Maddux.* "That idiot Don Zimmer gave [him] 263 innings last year. . . [he's] toast for 1992."

Two-hundred and sixty-three innings? Man, Zimmer must have a plate in his head.

Of course, it was during the 1992 season that Maddux became the best pitcher in baseball and has remained so, arguably, to the present day. He also led the league in innings pitched for five straight years. We're still waiting for the meltdown, and based on the last five years, it may be a while yet. It's far too easy to hammer on Hanke in hindsight (especially since the alliteration is so tempting), but I'm not trying to do that. Rather, I'm trying to show you how misleading innings-pitched totals can be if you ignore *efficiency.*

Maddux' key to surviving all those innings is that he's simply the most *efficient* pitcher in baseball. Last year, he finished second in the NL with 245 innings pitched, a total that might be destructive for others. But he also threw a league-low 3.10 pitches to each batter, enabling him to go the entire year without topping the 120-pitch mark.

With pitchers, half of the battle is minimizing injury risk. That's why when people ask me about trading for Maddux, I almost always recommend it. There's no one else who can give you the same number of innings without a significant injury risk. You can pay full value for Curt Schilling and possibly end up with a pitcher on the DL, but if you pay full value for Maddux, you're pretty much guaranteed to get full value out of him.

In the last couple of years, I've come to believe that efficiency is an important attribute to look for in a young pitcher. If a pitcher can't learn to economize on the number of pitches he throws to each hitter, the chances are that he'll eventually be asked to shoulder a burden that he can't handle. His manager will expect him to pitch into the seventh inning like other pitchers, without realizing the additional effort it takes for the inefficient hurler to get that far. Many, like Juan Guzman or Rocky Coppinger, will be set back by injury because they can't learn to economize.

Among the youngsters out there today, Chris Holt is one of the better bets around. He may not have the greatest stuff in the world, but he throws so few pitches per batter (3.42) that he'll probably remain healthy enough to have a Bob Tewksbury-like career. Two young Pirates, Francisco Cordova (3.32) and Esteban Loaiza (3.38) also have what it takes to survive. Roger Bailey has the right approach (3.24) but the wrong ballpark and no strikeout pitch. Brad Radke (3.57) needs to learn to keep the ball down, and Glendon Rusch (3.58) may need some time in the bullpen, but I expect each to have relatively long and surgery-free careers.

Chan Ho Park (3.93) worries me, but the Dodgers have been uncharacteristically careful with him. I love his stuff, and I expect him to continue to excel as long as he's handled carefully, but he's got a ways to go before he'll be safe at the 200-inning level. Shawn Estes (3.91) is an injury waiting to happen, and he'd better learn to make the most of what he throws. Alan Benes (3.98) may be able to survive, like his brother has. Jeff D'Amico (3.86) is lucky Phil Garner keeps him on a short leash (but he may get more slack with the way he's been pitching lately).

Anyway, that's my read on today's youngsters. Don't let anyone tell you they have no heart.

June 24, 1997—The Stolen-Base Counterrevolution

Remember the "stolen-base revolution" of the early '80s? It was an odd little detour in baseball's evolution, a momentary love affair with larceny, a misguided attempt to duplicate Whitey Herzog's success with the running game in St. Louis. Many clubs operated under the theory that the stolen base was a powerful weapon in a club's offensive arsenal. This mistaken belief led the Yankees to sign Dave Collins to play first base, for example. It also enabled players like Omar Moreno and Marvell Wynne to masquerade as legitimate major leaguers for years on end.

Thankfully, that era is over. Most of today's managers would take a real player over Tom Goodwin, and there's a reason for that: *natural selection.* If a manager devotes himself to obsolete strategies that put him at a disadvantage, in the long run he'll probably end up losing ballgames and, ultimately, his job. Through that process, managers like Chuck Tanner, Tom Trebelhorn, Hal McRae and Jeff Torborg are weeded out. The ones who figure out how to win today are the ones who survive to manage tomorrow.

Up in Montreal, Felipe Alou may be on the verge of starting a counterrevolution. He's pursuing a strategy that quite possibly hasn't been tried in 40 years. Alou has taken the central tenet of the stolen-base revolution and stood it on its head; rather than overemphasizing the value of the stolen base, Alou has dismissed it entirely.

By now, everyone knows that if you want to run on the Montreal Expos, just go ahead and lace up those cleats. Felipe has officially given you the green light until further notice. Run until your spikes get dull. The Expos have allowed the most stolen bases in the majors, 92, and they've also thrown out the fewest basestealers, 10. Elizabeth Taylor could run on the Expos, and she'd go in standing up.

Alou has made it clear—*in print, no less*—that he doesn't want his pitchers to bother trying to deter basestealers. In the June 3 issue of *Baseball America,* Alou explained, "Our pitchers aren't asked to hold runners because we have some more immediate worries with them."

In other words, Alou not only rejects the idea that the stolen base can hurt him, he also believes that it's not even worth trying to prevent it. The slide step, which has become so popular in recent years, isn't worth using, according to Alou. The quick-windup deliveries, the near-balk moves to first, the pitchouts—they're all irrelevant, Alou believes. The only thing that counts is getting the out *at the plate.* That's the "immediate worry" he mentions above. *Forget the baserunner and pitch.*

This is hardly a novel concept. Many great pitchers, including Jim Palmer and Nolan Ryan, were content to focus on the hitter and let the Bips fall where they may. But it's virtually unprecedented for a manager to adopt this approach as official team policy.

On the offensive side, Alou's been just as indifferent to the stolen base. The Expos have decent team speed and play in a large park with artificial turf, but they're still tied for next-to-last in the league with 44 steals.

For at least 15 years, the idea that you need to steal bases in a spacious, carpeted stadium has become an accepted truism. Now we have Alou gambling that it makes more sense to do the exact opposite. Is he winning?

Consider this. The Astros' and Expos' pitching staffs have compiled nearly identical opposition batting lines, with one exception:

Team	Avg	AB	R	H	2B	3B	HR	RBI	SB	CS	TBB	SO	OBP	SLG
Astros	.258	2559		660	124	12	62		46	32	248	510	.326	.388
Expos	.245	2419		592	123	21	61		92	10	268	478	.325	.389

The two teams have virtually identical numbers across the board. The Astros have allowed more hits, but the Expos have walked more men; on balance, their opponent on-base percentages are only one point apart, as are their opponent slugging percentages.

The only real difference comes in the opponent stolen-base department, where the two fall at opposite ends of the spectrum. As noted before, the Expos are the worst team in baseball at stopping the running game. Meanwhile, the Astros have allowed only 46 steals, half the number of the Expos, and the second-lowest total in the NL. The Astros also boast the second-best caught-stealing percentage in the league.

So the question is: all else being equal, how many runs can you save by stopping the running game? In the case of the Expos and Astros, all else *is* pretty much equal, and the answer, in this case, is: *one. The Expos have allowed one more run than the Astros.*

If the Expos remain in the hunt to the end, perhaps this aspect of Alou's game will receive the attention it deserves. It might even foster a new trend, where managers will shift their emphasis to using the word "run" as a noun instead of a verb. By then, the process of natural selection ought to have landed Ray Knight back in the broadcast booth.

July 8, 1997—Squeeze Me

Hello again, everybody. I just got back today from the honeymoon, so I hope you'll forgive me if I'm not up on all the events of the last couple of weeks. Since I've been gone, the only game I've had a chance to watch in its entirety was the Braves-Expos game last Friday night. My new wife Laura and I took in the game at the Big O in Montreal and, all things considered, it was one of the stranger events I've witnessed.

I was hanging out by the corner of the Expos' dugout during batting practice when a woodchuck suddenly popped out of the bat rack. He ambled lazily across the floor of the dugout and crawled through a hole in the wall behind the security guard.

At first, I wasn't sure if this was cause for alarm, but as a guest in their country, I didn't want to be accused of shirking my responsibilities. I managed to get the security guard's attention, but quickly realized that my eighth-grade French vocabulary didn't include the translation for "woodchuck." All I could do was gesture toward the hole and hope he'd get the point.

The guard didn't quite know what to make of my strange American sign language, but he dutifully knelt down and inspected the hole. Finding nothing, he looked at me, shrugged, got up and walked away.

Sometime around the fourth inning, the game was temporarily interrupted when the woodchuck wandered out onto the field. He sniffed around, oblivious to the impatient athletes around him, until something (Carlos Perez?) suddenly scared him and sent him running back into his hole. The security guard watched him scamper into the darkness but elected not to pursue the intruder.

During the game, a group of three seagulls flew from perch to perch high inside the dome. During pitching changes, they occasionally landed in the outfield. All in all, there seemed to be a tremendous amount of wildlife inside the supposedly enclosed stadium. It seems that not even a dome can ensure that the Dave Winfield seagull incident won't be repeated.

In the fourth inning, Atlanta rookie Chris Brock did something I'd never seen before. Mike Lansing was on second, and Brock was looking to pick him off. Out of the corner of his eye, he spotted daylight, and whirled and threw toward second. The only problem was that shortstop Jeff Blauser wasn't in on the play; he was standing flat-footed at his normal fielding position.

During the split second that Brock's arm was unwinding, his brain realized that the intended target was elsewhere. It was too late to abort, but Brock somehow managed to hold up just enough to keep from throwing the ball into center field. Instead, he managed a soft throw right to Blauser, who wasn't anywhere near second base. Blauser blew a bubble and lazily tossed the ball back to the rookie, as if he played catch with the pitchers during breaks in the ballgame all the time.

It's clear that a balk shall be called when the pitcher throws to an unoccupied base, but what happens when the pitcher just spins and tosses the ball to one of his fielders, who isn't even near any of the bases? Is that a balk? The umpires didn't call one, and Felipe Alou didn't press the issue.

One other thing I noticed is that Montreal fans aren't exactly what an American would call normal. Early in the game, it seemed like they weren't confident that they knew the appropriate moments to cheer. They maintained a constant low rumble, regardless of the game situation. With the orange faux-vinyl roof refracting and softening the din, if I closed my eyes, it was easy to imagine that I was lost in a faraway corner of the Home Depot.

Later, though, they found their tongues. By the end of the game, they were as loud as a bleacher crowd at Fenway; the only explanation I can come up with is the fact that they continue to sell beer after the seventh inning up there. It got so bad that in the ninth inning, a fan on the first-base side stood up and shouted four words at home-plate umpire Mark Hirschbeck. Three of the words I couldn't make out; the fourth was in English and will automatically get you ejected from any establishment where English is spoken.

Hirschbeck took off his mask, called over the security guards and fingered the offender, who was quickly led away. The whole incident seemed completely pointless to me; there hadn't been any calls worth complaining about. In all the games I've seen, it was the first time I'd ever seen a fan ejected from the ballpark. (However, friend and colleague Mike Wenz was once ejected from Riverfront Stadium by Eric Gregg for trying to give Gregg directions to Taco Bell. Mike now surmises that Gregg must have known the way already.)

My new wife Laura really impressed me in the top of the ninth. With the score tied 3-3, one out and a man on second, Felipe Alou elected to have his closer, Ugueth Urbina intentionally walk pinch-hitter Ryan Klesko and pitch to Mark Lemke. Laura said, "That's a bad move."

I said, "What are you talking about? Klesko kills righthanded pitchers. You don't want to give him a chance to drive in the go-ahead run. Lemke is a zero, especially from the left side. You'd much rather pitch to him instead. I'd think Alou was nuts if he *didn't* walk Klesko."

Laura said, "Bad move." Lemke immediately stepped in and lined a triple into the left-field corner, driving in both runners to give the Braves a 5-3 lead.

Maybe it was just a good move that backfired, but the fact was that she'd seen it coming and I hadn't, so I tipped my cap to her. But what happened next just floored me. The Expos brought in lefthander Omar Daal to pitch, and the Braves sent up Keith Lockhart to pinch-hit.

Let me digress for a moment. The best game I ever saw at Fenway Park was on June 4, 1995. I was there with a girl named Lisa, whom I was seeing at the time. At that point in the season, the Red Sox were just beginning to be taken seriously as contenders, and Tim Wakefield was pitching against the Mariners. As you may know, I am a huge Tim Wakefield fan.

For nine innings, Wakefield stymied the Mariners, mixing fastballs and knucklers to great effect, and picking runners off whenever he got into a jam. Tim Belcher was just as sharp, though, and after nine full innings, the game was still scoreless. Kevin Kennedy left Wakefield in to pitch the 10th.

Then Wakefield started to falter. A single and a hit batsman put runners on first and second with one out. That brought up Felix Fermin, which brought me great relief. Fermin tapped an apparent double-play ball right back to Wakefield. "Perfect," I thought. "We're out of it."

All Wakefield had to do was to turn and throw to second, which he did. I was already pondering the impressiveness of a 10-inning shutout when I saw the throw go to. . . *nobody.* The ball sailed into center field as Boston's shortstop and second baseman stood staring at each other, seemingly saying to each other, "I thought *you* were supposed to be covering the bag."

Wakefield should have been out of the inning, but a run scored on the play and the inning ended with the Sox trailing 1-0. Now he was going to get pinned with the loss; it was all so unfair. But in the bottom of the frame, Bill Haselman lined a one-out single, and Troy O'Leary followed with a monstrous blast into the net in left-center field. As the game-winning shot cleared the monster, the crowd broke into an ovation that didn't abate for at least 20 minutes.

When I finally grew exhausted of cheering, Lisa and I ambled out onto Yawkey Way. I turned to her wistfully and said, "You know, that must have been the best game I've ever seen here."

And she said: "What do you mean? *Nothing happened.*"

Lisa and I continued to see each other for a few more months, but right then, at that very moment, *I realized that we had absolutely no future together.*

Back to Montreal. One out, Lemke on third, lefthander on the mound, and the Braves have just gone up 5-3. As Daal goes into his windup, Laura turns and says to me, "It's a good time for a squeeze."

In the next split-second, a million thoughts went through my mind. The first one was, "Damn. She's right." The next million or so had to do with *why* she was right. For one, it was a perfect time for it. The Expos had fought hard all game, and now they'd been stuck with a two-run, ninth-inning deficit on one swing of the bat. They were down, and they were frustrated. Billy Martin used to love to employ the squeeze in this type of situation, to deliver a psychological knockout blow with a simple bunt.

Daal was a lefty, his back was to third base, and he was completely ignoring Lemke. The fact that he was a lefty would make it even harder for Daal to field the bunt and throw out Lockhart at first base.

The Braves had already laid down two bunts earlier in the game. Both had gone for singles on the fast turf when the balls got past the mound.

All of this and more went through my head, but before I could even respond, I saw Lemke coming down the line, well toward the plate. I saw Lockhart squaring around and laying down a perfect bunt. I saw Lemke score the sixth Braves run as Daal fumbled the ball and fell down, ultimately enabling Lockhart to reach second base.

I was speechless. I've watched a lot of games, often in the company of some very knowledgeable fans, but I *never* had witnessed anyone successfully predict a squeeze before. And here was Laura, calling it on the exact pitch.

If any of you out there feel that you and your spouse are a match made in heaven, I hope you're as lucky as I am. In other words, I hope that you've also been given proof.

July 29, 1997—One-Hit Woodard

You'd think I wouldn't be such a party-pooper.

Here I am, one of the last remaining Milwaukee Brewers fans on earth, suffering through the Brew Crew's annual injury epidemic. This season has turned out to be just another stale rerun of some other recent but forgettable year. They played their way onto the fringes of contention, only to suffer a rash of injuries that removed them from the race safely ahead of the trade deadline.

The ailments all sound the same after a while; only the victims' names change. This time, instead of Cal Eldred, Darryl Hamilton and Pat Listach, it's John Jaha, Marc Newfield and Ben McDonald. Watching the Brewers every year is like watching an endless series of Rocky sequels, with one small difference: the fighter defies long odds and hangs tough for most of the fight, but around the sixth or seventh round, he suddenly gets the holy crap beat out of him, every single time.

I'm sorry, but there aren't too many people who will pay to see that story played out for the ninth straight time. It doesn't matter how large your "market" may be, and it doesn't matter what kind of neat foldy-dome you stick on top of the stadium.

So, with my hopes lying inert on the canvas, you'd think I might take a little pleasure in the rare highlights I'm afforded—like Steve Woodard's spectacular debut last night. After giving up a double to Otis Nixon to open the game, Woodard didn't allow another hit. He fanned 12 over eight innings, beating his idol, Roger Clemens, 1-0. It was, without exaggeration, quite possibly the best debut by a rookie pitcher in the last 10 years. Exciting stuff, no?

Well, maybe. First, the good news. Woodard's only 22 years old, and he was leading the minor leagues with 15 victories when he got the call to the bigs. He'd gone 14-3 with a very respectable 3.17 ERA in an extreme hitter's park at Double-A El Paso, and his superb command was voted best in the league by *Baseball America*. Ready to trade Ismael Valdes for him yet? Well hold on, there's more to the story.

His dozen-K debut might make him look like a flamethrower in the boxscore, but that impression couldn't be further from the truth. In reality, the last time Woodard hit 90 MPH, he almost certainly must have been behind the wheel of a very expensive automobile. The majority of his 12 strikeouts came on perfectly placed curves and changeups. He deserves all due credit for that, but it also should be noted that his previous professional high was 10 strikeouts in a game.

And that's just the first of many "buts." As colleague Mike Mittleman hastens to point out, Woodard was facing the Toronto Blue Jays, rather than a lineup of competent major league hitters. Mike adds that the afternoon shadows at Milwaukee County Stadium didn't help the hitters to pick up Woodard's pitches, either. And then you have the generous strike zone of home-plate ump Dale Scott, something that Bob Uecker repeatedly mentioned on the radio that night before five innings were even in the books.

To sum up, a pretty decent pitcher made his major league debut under the most favorable conditions possible, and he delivered the best debut performance of the last 10 years. What, then, are we to make of that?

Well, we could take a look at the other pitchers who've made comparable debuts since '87 to see how they've done. I don't have the patience to comb through thousands of games to pick out the optimal candidates, but I am lucky enough to work with a gentleman named Jim Henzler. Somewhere along the way, he acquired the ability to command a computer to spit out a list of whatever you want; all Jim has to do is type a few lines of nonsense and the computer does the rest (this fascinates me, especially since computers just flat-out refuse to listen to me. Like dogs, they can sense fear, I believe. . .).

Anyway, Jim produced a list of the top 20 debuts by pitchers, 1987-1997, ranked by "game score," a concept developed by Bill James. The game score operates on a scale of around 100; the best game of the year might rate close to 100, and a very good game might rate about 70. Excluding Woodard, the 20th-best debut belonged to Jack McDowell, who got a 72 for throwing seven innings of shutout ball. He got the win, allowing four hits and no walks while striking out three. The rest of the games on the list were as good or better, so you know we're talking about Woodard-level quality. By the way, Woodard topped the charts with a game score of 91, although he wasn't included in the study, for obvious reasons.

The progression of these pitchers' careers may tell us a thing or two about what the future has in store for Steve Woodard. Some of them, like Mauro Gozzo, Kevin Morton and Sam Militello, hardly survived another dozen starts. Others, like Pedro Astacio, Tim Wakefield and Omar Olivares, achieved modest success. And finally, a couple of them—Jack McDowell and Roberto Hernandez (yes, *that* Roberto Hernandez)—later approached stardom.

But if you're thinking about picking up Woodard this week, you probably aren't consulting your tarot-card reader about whether he'll make the 2002 All-Star team. Your more immediate concern may be how he's going to perform in his next start. All right then, Mr. Astacio-Deficit Disorder, let's approach it *that* way.

How did the 20 pitchers do in their second start? Remember, in their first start, they combined to go 19-0 with an 0.28 ERA (Omar Olivares got a no-decision). In their next outing, they were—you might say—not quite as dominant: 6-7 with a 3.35 ERA. You want more? OK. In their third start they went 4-7, 3.89. Fourth start? Forget it. No. I'm not going to tell you. Because you *can't handle* the truth, that's why. Oh, all right, tough guy, try this: 5-5, 5.01. That's right: those 20 pitchers who each were so brilliant in their debuts combined to go 15-17 with a 4.04 ERA over their next three starts.

So does this mean I'm going to turn up my nose at Steve Woodard? Heck, no! I'm going to go after him with everything I've got. And if I get him, I'm going to trade him immediately.

August 12, 1997—Take A Walk

Imagine, if you will, a fictitious major league team. Let's call it the Beaverton Bips. Its front office is comprised entirely of men who lack the ability to comprehend the value of home runs. It's a stretch, I know, but bear with me.

These men are aware of the *existence* of home runs—they know that they happen from time to time, and that some players hit more than others—but as far as they're concerned, home runs are irrelevant to winning and losing. Although these men are perfectly competent to evaluate players' abilities in all other respects, the fact that Player A hits more home runs than Player B, in their eyes, has almost nothing to do with the two players' respective values on the field.

Now try to envision what kind of team the Bips might field in any given season. It wouldn't necessarily be a *bad* team; after all, they'd probably stumble across a power hitter or two without even realizing it. And they'd do their best to acquire players who could contribute in other areas.

Over a period of years, it's entirely possible that the Bips might even be able to field a winning team from time to time—perhaps once a decade or so. Every once in a while, they'd accidentally end up with enough power to contend, or they might build a club that would be strong enough in other areas to compensate for the glaring lack of clout in the lineup.

But in the great majority of seasons, the Bips wouldn't have a prayer. It would just be too easy for them to come up with an infield of Jose Offerman, Jeff Frye, Joe Randa and Jose Vizcaino and an outfield of Bip Roberts, Otis Nixon and Jose Herrera. And when they fielded that lineup and lost, the decision-makers would scratch their heads and say, "I don't get it. Everybody's hitting .290, and we're still losing." And so they'd go out and get Joe Girardi.

Simply put, this blind spot would handicap the team so severely that they wouldn't be able to remain competitive from year to year. It wouldn't be due to simple incompetence on the part of the men in the front office; rather, it would be due to their inability to appreciate one of the critical elements of a productive offense.

Sound too far-fetched to be true? Not really. Ladies and gentlemen, meet the Chicago Cubs. Please do your best to help them across the street; when the "Walk" sign blinks, they can't read it.

It is no exaggeration to say that the people who run the Cubs live in blissful ignorance of the value of walks. Home runs may show up on "SportsCenter" a million times more often, but walks are just as vital. Unless you plan on scoring all of your runs on dingers, you have to reach base before you can come around to score.

The Cubs like to get guys who can get on via singles and doubles, and they don't mind having a player or two who can run the bases swiftly. But when it comes to players who can also reach base by taking ball four, the Cubs have no interest whatsoever. And like the Bips, they end up losing, because they've cut off so many of their avenues to success before the race has even started.

Do the Cubs lack power? Yes, they do. But this problem is different, because they realize that it exists. They recently spent far, far too much money to lock up their only real power threat, Sammy Sosa. And they've already gone on record with their main target for next year:

a power-hitting left fielder. With Mark Grace and Kevin Orie holding down two of the corner spots, they may not be able to get enough true run-producers into the lineup, but at least they know that something has to be done.

The walks problem is another story. It is the end product of organization-wide ignorance of their importance.

Item: The Cubs are next-to-last in the NL in walks. They have finished last in the league three times this decade, and have never finished higher than ninth during the '90s.

Item: The Cubs' farm system produces players—virtually without exception—who hardly ever walk. Joe Girardi, Jerome Walton, Doug Dascenzo, Derrick May, Dwight Smith, Rey Sanchez and Jose Hernandez were schooled in the Cubs' system. The next ones to arrive—Brooks Kieschnick, Robin Jennings, Pedro Valdes and Brant Brown—will be no different.

Item: The Cubs' trade and free-agent acquisitions are all players who don't get on base. See, e.g., George Bell. They traded Bell for Sammy Sosa, which turned out to be a heck of a deal, but then Sosa walks about as often as Bell hit a cutoff man. They traded for Jose Vizcaino and made him a regular. They developed Shawon Dunston, let him get away, and signed him again when he became available. They signed Willie Wilson to be their leadoff hitter. They signed Brian McRae to be their leadoff hitter. They traded McRae for Lance Johnson, who's never walked more than 36 times in a season. Johnson is now their leadoff hitter.

Item: Manager Jim Riggleman has been quoted claiming that he urges his hitters to go after the first pitch, "because the stats show that hitters have the highest average on the first pitch." Admittedly, that's *technically* true—major league hitters are hitting .333 on the first pitch this year—but this is a classic case of a little knowledge being dangerous.

To look at that .333 average and conclude that hitters should go up there hacking is hopelessly simplistic. An average batter hits .333 on the first pitch *when he puts the ball in play;* if he swings and misses or fouls it off, the count goes to 0-1, and the average batter also hits .232 after starting 0-1.

You must also consider the fact that .333 represents not only the hitter's batting average but also his on-base percentage, since putting the ball in play usually eliminates the walk. When you consider all these other factors, it's clear that swinging at the first pitch won't give the hitter any special advantage. After all, if it did, everyone would do it, wouldn't they? Or is Jim Riggleman the only one who's been smart enough to discover the advantages of this approach?

And as a practical matter, when you announce in print that your team has been instructed to swing at the first pitch, you may encounter one additional drawback. Think about what would happen if Darryl Kile told the press, "Hitters hit only .178 against my curveball, so I'm going to junk all my other pitches and go with the curve exclusively." Right. Soon every hitter in the league would be sitting on Kile's curve, and even Rafael Belliard would be smacking Kile's bender into all parts of the ballpark. The same thing has been happening to the Cubs.

The pitchers all know better than to throw the Cubs a strike on the first pitch, and as a result, Cubs batters are hitting only .290 on the first pitch, which is *dead last* in the majors by a considerable margin.

Item: Now that the Cubs have officially given up on the 1997 season, they've fingered the two young players that they hope to build around: Doug Glanville and Manny Alexander.

That's the one that *really* gets me. That seals it: the Cubs don't get it and they never will.

Let's take a look at the Cubs' present lineup. Remember, the most important offensive skill is the ability to get on base. Let's see which Cubs, if any, are able to do that. Catcher: Scott Servais. OBP: .300. Ran well for a catcher, when he was 17. First base: Mark Grace. OBP: .423. His excellent on-base percentage is unique in the Cubs' lineup. Unfortunately, he lacks power, and runs like a newt with polio. Second base: Ryne Sandberg. OBP: .309. He may be replaced next year by Rey Sanchez, OBP .288. Third base: Kevin Orie. OBP: .352. Not bad, but shares Grace's weaknesses without sharing his strengths. Shortstop: Shawon Dunston. OBP: .305. Last walk: June 27. Number of at-bats since last walk: 147. Am I serious: hell, yes; damn serious. Left field: Doug Glanville. OBP: .346. I'll get to him in a minute. Center field: Lance Johnson. OBP: .380. Suddenly walking, perhaps because his shins hurt too much to run. Career OBP: .334. Right field: Sammy Sosa. OBP: .298.

So what have we got? We've got a team with a chronic, all-encompassing inability to reach base, and to fix the problem, we're going to build around. . . Manny Alexander and Doug Glanville.

You certainly must have heard how the scouts love Manny Alexander. I can only conclude that the player they scouted has been kidnapped and replaced by this sorry look-alike. If it turns out that Manny Alexander can indeed play shortstop in the major leagues, he'll be like Ray Oyler, but more annoying. He'll be like Rey Ordonez without the glove. He'll be like Rey Sanchez, except that the Cubs specifically dealt for him so that they could make him the cornerstone of their pathetic, last-place infield. Alexander has batted 464 times in the majors, drawing 32 walks for a .274 on-base percentage.

Glanville is a favorite of Jim Riggleman because he's fast and hits for a decent average. They'll be trying to unload Lance Johnson so they can hand over his center field/leadoff position to Glanville next year. Glanville has 416 major league at-bats, with 23 walks and a .330 on-base percentage.

Walks matter, and the Cubs' plans prove that they are no closer to comprehending this simple truth, even after decades of failure. You might wonder how they could remain blind to it. If one player walks before another one homers, the value of the homer is doubled. Instead, the Cubs plan to shell out big bucks for another power hitter, so they can try to hit twice as many homers. Oh, Manny.

August 26, 1997—Jimy Williams and I Are Not Crazy

It would be easy to see Tom Gordon's 1997 season as a failure. After posting a 6-9 record as a starter, he was moved to the bullpen by manager Jimy Williams. This move itself is *prima facie* evidence of stinkiness: starters are shifted to relief all the time, and it's no coincidence that the transition almost always follows a string of putrid starts. When the move is finally made, it's usually termed a "demotion."

Now, with this is mind, I'm going to tell you something that I don't expect you to believe right away: Tom Gordon has been one of the best starters in the American League this year. I'll let that sink in for a second.

Before I get to arguing about it, let me go even further. To do so, I'll need to ask you to suspend your disbelief. Suspend it, expel it, do whatever you need to do, but just hear me out. Because I'm here to tell you something very important: Gordon is going to be one of the game's best closers for the remainder of the season.

Gordon, a star closer? What, am I still delirious over the Ray Knight firing?

Well, yes, I am, but that's beside the point. Let's start with the assertion that Gordon has been one of the league's best starters.

We tend to evaluate starters mainly on the basis of their won-loss record and ERA. The reasons for this are self-evident: effective pitchers win games and prevent runs. Sometimes, a given pitcher's won-lost record or ERA will be misleading. The pitcher might win fewer games than he should have, or he might post an ERA higher than it should have been, given the quality of his work.

In Gordon's case, *both* numbers are skewed—abnormally so. As a starter, he went 6-9 with a 3.59 ERA. Neither measure even comes close to representing his true effectiveness.

First, his won-lost record was ruined by a complete lack of run support. You wouldn't expect that to happen in Boston—especially after Gordon received the *highest* run support in baseball last year—but it did. In 14 of his 25 starts, the Red Sox scored two runs or fewer while Gordon was on the mound. Technically, his run support is not the worst in baseball, but that's only because of a 15-run outburst that he received on August 5. Thanks to those mostly-useless runs, his run support per nine innings stands at 4.5. If he were given the same amount of support that his teammates have provided for Jeff Suppan (6.2), Steve Avery (6.7) or Aaron Sele (7.2), it's easy to imagine what Gordon's record might look like. After all, even Sele has been able to compile a winning record (12-10), despite having the highest ERA of any starter in baseball (5.90). With similar support, Gordon might easily be 10-5 or 11-4 instead of 6-9.

Then you have his 3.59 ERA, which isn't all that bad to begin with, considering the well-known effects of Fenway Park and the American League strike zone. Even so, this measure is equally misleading.

A pitcher's earned run average is almost always a reliable indicator of his effectiveness, but there are a few outside influences that can affect it. One major one is bullpen support. When a starter leaves the game with men on base, he relies on his bullpen to prevent those runners from scoring and inflating the starter's ERA. I trust that I don't need to explain how this applies to the Red Sox. I'll only say this: the Red Sox bullpen has allowed 87 of 231 inherited runners to score, the second-worst rate in the league.

In other words, Gordon has pitched a lot better than a guy who's supposed to have a 3.59 ERA, but his relievers have ruined it for him. We can see that by examining the stats that aren't as susceptible to outside interference, like Gordon's opponent batting average, on-base and slugging percentages.

Gordon's opponent batting average is .232, sixth-best in the AL. His opponent OBP is .305, 10th-best in the league. And his SLG is .326, third-best. How many other pitchers rate in the top 10 in each of those three categories? Only five: Kevin Appier, Justin Thompson, Wilson Alvarez, Randy Johnson and Roger Clemens. That ain't bad company, unless you're a hitter.

Truth be told, a pitcher with Gordon's opponent OBP and SLG ought to have an ERA around 3.08 (that's according to a handy little formula I use for predicting a pitcher's ERA: OBP x SLG x 31 = ERA). If Gordon's true ERA really was 3.08, he would rank sixth in the AL, tied with Andy Pettitte.

"All right, Mat," you say, "maybe you've convinced me he's a half-decent pitcher. So what if he is? What makes you think he can be a quality stopper?" Glad you asked—you saved me from an awkward segue.

First, Gordon is—and has always been—a tremendous one-inning pitcher. These are his opponent batting averages in the first inning he pitches, for each of his eight major league seasons: .251, .202, .177, .210, .191, .173, .288 and .206. For his entire career, he's been stronger in the first inning than at any other time in the game.

And second, Gordon *has* had success as a reliever in the major leagues. He's pitched almost 200 innings of relief in the majors, and based on the records he's compiled, a reasonable person might easily conclude that Gordon is cut out to be a reliever, rather than a starter.

In four different seasons (1989, 1991, 1992 and 1993) he split the year between the rotation and the bullpen. In three of those four seasons, he posted a lower ERA as a reliever. Over those four years, his cumulative record as a starter was 20-23 with a 4.34 ERA. Over the same span, he went 14-14 out of the bullpen with an ERA more than a full run lower, 3.30.

And still, even his 3.30 ERA in relief isn't properly reflective of his excellent relief work. Perhaps it was inflated for the same reason stated above (inherited runners allowed to score by other pitchers). Gordon was pitching middle relief, so he was probably exiting games in mid-inning far more often than other pitchers (after all, closers usually stay in the game until it's over). Anyhow, for whatever reason, his opponent OBP and SLG suggest that his ERA in relief should have been closer to 2.91.

So let's toss out his relief ERA and just deal with his opponent OBP and SLG as a reliever. For convenience's sake, we can add these two numbers together and call it Opponent Production (PRO). But don't let me lose you here. It doesn't matter what we call it. As Leo Durocher would say, you could call it a pen and pencil set and it wouldn't make a damn bit of difference. We're only doing it so we can compare Gordon to other top closers.

Gordon's Opp. PRO in relief was 613 (.309 OBP plus .304 SLG), which is excellent. The AL's average PRO has risen about seven percent since Gordon compiled those numbers, so for fairness' sake, we'll adjust that number upward seven percent, to 655. Now, how does that compare to today's best closers?

Quite favorably, thank you. He wouldn't displace this year's leader, Doug Jones (575—numbers don't lie, but liars can pitch). John Wetteland (580), John Franco (583) and Mark Wohlers (599) are safely out of reach. Then you've got the foursome of Randy Myers (614), Jeff Shaw (614), Rod Beck (619) and Billy Wagner (622). Still plenty of quality there. The next echelon includes Trevor Hoffman (637), Mariano Rivera (640) and Todd Jones (646). Then you get to the No.11 man, Gordon, and his hypothetical 655.

But look who comes *after* him. Remember, each of these pitchers rate *behind* Gordon in the ability to keep runs off the scoreboard: Dennis Eckersley (660), Troy Percival (662), Rich Loiselle (695), Ugueth Urbina (702) and Robb Nen (711). Rick Aguilera (738), Jose Mesa (745), Todd Worrell (753) and Ricky Bottalico (756) aren't even close.

To sum up, Gordon is 1) a good pitcher, 2) who's always pitched best in the first inning of an appearance, and 3) has pitched even better in relief when he's been given the chance, and 4) was more effective as a reliever than many of today's closers. He's already converted all three of his save opportunities so far; there will be many more before the summer's out.

September 9, 1997—Q & A

With the regular season winding down, the September callups having been announced, and the playoffs right around the corner, now is a good time for me to address some of the nagging questions I hear inside my head:

Q: Are you really going to write your whole column like this?

A: Well, I'm going to try. Of course, it would help if you'd ask some baseball questions.

Q: OK. What in tarnation has gotten into Matt Stairs?

A: Isn't that the Tigers' rookie outfielder? Juan In Tarnation? Oh, forget it. You asked about Stairs. . . he's certainly a good hitter, but he's not *this* good. It's not that uncommon for a player to play far over his head when he finally gets a chance to play after getting stuck in the high minors for several years. Perhaps it comes from being denied a chance to play for so many years, and having the maturity to take full advantage when the opportunity finally presents itself. If you think about it, it's not hard to come up with a list of players who had surprisingly good partial seasons as rookies in their late 20s. You can start with Dan Gladden,

Keith Lockhart, Dave Gallagher and Rich Amaral. The common thread is that they came up late and never hit as well again.

Q: The Mets sure helped themselves by picking up John Olerud, didn't they?

A: No, they didn't. That's not to say that Olerud hasn't played well. He's maintained his solid combination of average, power and walks, and he's certainly helped the Mets. The thing is that the Mets already had an Olerud-caliber first baseman, even before they acquired him. His name is Roberto Petagine. Like Olerud, he's a lefthanded first baseman with a good bat and great plate discipline. Last year he batted .318 with 12 homers and 65 RBI in 95 games at Triple-A. With the acquisition of Olerud (who's two years older), Petagine was forced back to Triple-A, where he batted .317-31-100 and drew 85 walks in 129 games. If the Mets had simply given Petagine the first-base job instead of Olerud, they might have gotten the same production out of Petagine for much less money.

Q: Well, at least Baerga has solidified the second-base position for them.

A: Actually, he's "solidified" it in the same way that leftover mac and cheese becomes "solidified" in the back of your fridge. Baerga used to give you three things: average, power and durability. Now all that's left is the average. Last year, Jose Vizcaino, Edgardo Alfonzo and the rest of the Mets' second basemen combined to hit .281-3-64. Baerga and friends in '97: .281-9-64.

Q: It looks like the Reds finally have some youngsters to build around. Since Jack McKeon has taken over, he's uncovered youngsters like Eduardo Perez, Chris Stynes, Jon Nunnally and Mike Kelly.

A: Again, I'm sorry, but *no*. Marge Schott never has understood what scouts were supposed to do, and by the time she was overthrown, she'd allowed the Reds' farm system to shrivel up and die. The pipeline is bone dry, so GM Jim Bowden is forced to scrounge for other teams' rejects, guys like the four you just mentioned. Perez has a little pop, but he's 27 years old and has no star potential. Stynes is a decent enough hitter to bat .290, but his lack of walks or power kill his value unless you can play him at second base. Nunnally has almost 30 homers in less than 600 major league at-bats, and may make a good platoon outfielder. He's going to be 26 next year, though. Kelly is 27 and has never played well until this year.

God, it must be hard to be the Reds' GM. There's no money and nothing in the minors, so the best marketing strategy you can use is: "Hey, our team is a mess, but look! We've got *Deion!* Lookit him dance! And here's Pete Rose Jr.! Just like his father, except on the field! Meet Eduardo Perez! Shh—don't tell him we fired his dad. Did we tell you we finally got the dog off the field? So come on out to 3Com Synergy Ballpark at Riverfront Yards!"

Sad, very sad.

Q: Hey, lighten up. At least they have Pokey Reese.

A: Look—if Reese is the best young player you can point to, that says enough right there. He may be a fantastic defensive shortstop, but it doesn't change my opinion one bit. Even if he's the best glove this side of Rey Ordonez, he's still using Darrell Chaney's bats. He couldn't possibly save as many runs with his glove as he gives away at the plate.

Q: What's the matter with you? Don't you like anybody?

A: Sure I do. I like Brett Tomko. He's the real thing. It's doubly amazing that he's been able to pitch so well despite all the upheaval around him.

Q: Isn't it true that you unlawfully removed the tags from your mattresses?

A: Objection—irrevelant.

Q: Overruled.

A: What!? You can't overrule me. I want a ruling by a neutral third party.

Q: Yeah, you and Scott Boras. Hey—has Scott Ruffcorn had the worst major league career in history?

A: Good question. Let's see. . . 30 games without a victory. . . an 0-8 record with an 8.57 ERA. . . 77 runs, 70 walks and 46 strikeouts in 70.1 innings. . . Yeah, I guess it really could be the worst ever. Even Terry Felton, who went 0-16, had a career ERA three full runs lower.

Q: I heard you're going to hang a big sign from the railing of the upper deck the next time you go to Comiskey Park. What's it going to say?

A: "Real Baseball: 1,864 Miles West."

Q: Cute. Tell me: what's wrong with John Smoltz?

A: Well, 13-11 with 200 strikeouts ain't too far wrong. On the whole, he hasn't pitched *that* much worse than he did last year, although it's a lot easier to see now that he isn't the pitcher Kevin Brown is.

But on the other hand, maybe there *is* something going on with Smoltz that we don't know about. He's tended to hit the wall around the 60-pitch mark: his opponent batting average through 60 pitches is .218, and from that point on, it's .285. Last year, he was dominant from start to finish, so he may be fighting a bit of fatigue at this point.

Q: What's wrong with Ryan Klesko?

A: His ballpark. Last year, the Launching Pad helped him a lot. This year, the Braves' new Park, Turner Field, has hurt him. The new field is a much tougher hitters' park, and it's hurt Klesko in particular. His road production has remained the same from last year to this year, believe it or not.

Q: Isn't it time for dinner yet?

A: Aha, glad you asked. Man cannot live on pontification alone. Off I go.

September 23, 1997—The Contract Drive

People always *say* that players perform better in their contract years, but is it really *true?* Using Peter Gammons' list of players who are going into free agency this winter, I began investigating.

First, I threw out all the guys who had an existing option for 1998. This was helpful for two reasons. First, it narrowed down the list to only the "pure" free agents—the guys who know they are heading into the open market this winter. And second, it shortened the list quite a bit. When you have a 3:00 deadline, that's a real plus.

Before I tell you what I turned up, let's take a minute to ask why the "contract-year" cliche arose in the first place. It seems to grow out of the theory that a player will be better motivated when he's about to enter free agency, because the promise of free-agent money will compel him to put out maximum effort.

I don't have a tremendous problem with this idea. Capitalism is built on the premise that people are greedy, and as far as I can tell, the system hasn't exactly disproven the idea. Besides, some of my best friends are greedy.

So I'm willing to concede that extra financial inducement *exists* in a player's contract year. The part that I'm *not* sold on is the assumption that this inducement will necessarily cause the player to be more productive.

We've already said that people are greedy, but I think we can make another generalization: people enjoy success. When Frank Thomas is at the plate, why is it that he wants to hit a home run? Wouldn't it require much less effort to simply pop up? Why waste energy with unnecessary baserunning? Tell me: when he sets himself in the box and glares out at the fool on the hill, why does Frank want to nail one off the light tower? Is it because he's thinking about how much that four-bagger will boost his value on the free-agent market when his contract is up?

C'mon. We both know the answer. Frank wants to hammer the ball because he *likes* to. It's fun. People will cheer for him. If he does it, he's succeeded, and if he doesn't, he's failed. Simply put, when he's on the ballfield, his failure and success is not measured in monetary terms.

But a strange myth has developed that holds that a player will play harder when he's about to hit the market. To buy into this, you have to believe not only that the player is greedy, but that the player is *so* greedy that he'll only give maximum effort when he's able to cash in on it immediately. The rest of the time, presumably, he only gives as much effort as necessary.

There are, without question, many people who are turned off by the high salaries of major league ballplayers. Many people, I'm sure, question whether a ballplayer's contribution to society justifies a multi-million-dollar salary. Someone predisposed to these views might even come to believe that ballplayers are motivated *only* by money.

But I'm not one of those people. As I've explained above, I believe that a player's motivation lies elsewhere.

But forget what anyone believes. Hundreds of years ago, many people believed the earth was flat. Today, many people believe that the earth is the only place in the universe where life has ever existed. Still, there is evidence to challenge both of those assertions. There also is evidence to discredit the idea that players play best in the last year of their contracts. Here it is.

First, the starting pitchers. I examined the 19 starters who will be free agents this winter, comparing their 1997 stats to last year's. As you might expect, there were individuals who improved markedly (Darryl Kile, Willie Blair and Scott Kamieniecki), but there were others who declined by similar amounts (Ken Hill, Bobby Witt and Terry Mulholland).

Did they pitch better in 1997 as free agency approached? Hardly. As a group, their winning percentage fell 14 points (.520-.506) and their win total dropped from 197 to 166, an average decline of 1.7 wins per pitcher.

"Well," I thought, "Maybe I'm just looking at it wrong." I wasn't sure if it was fair to do this, but I decided to remove the six pitchers who were hurt for a large portion of 1996 or 1997 (Mark Langston, Pete Schourek, Rheal Cormier, etc.), just to see what would happen.

Nothing happened, When you take the injury cases out, you get very similar results: winning percentage declines by seven points, and wins per pitcher declines by 0.7. Simply put, the starters didn't pitch any better in the last year of their contracts, on the whole. If anything, they pitched worse.

How about the closers? There were five of them. They averaged 35.6 saves in 1996, and 36.4 saves in 1997, and increase of 0.8 saves. Take it for what it's worth.

Finally, the hitters. This part is a little tougher, because there's no one stat that easily sums up a batter's worth. For example, the RBI column might tell you whether Dean Palmer had a better year or not, but it won't do justice to Mark Lemke's contributions. But what the heck, I figured; Lemke hasn't registered a complaint with me yet, and I've still got that 3:00 deadline.

So RBI it is. The list included 26 players who played regularly (more or less) in both seasons. Once again, some got better (Jay Bell, Jeff Blauser and John Olerud), and some got worse (Dean Palmer, Julio Franco and Brady Anderson). As a group, they declined by a total of 186 RBI, an average of 7.2 per player.

Now, I'll be the first to say that this study is far from conclusive. It's quite possible that players really do perform better in their contract year, and that this study somehow failed to reveal it. Perhaps last year's players were an exception to a long-term trend. Perhaps a group of similar players who *weren't* in their contract years would have declined even *more* steeply. Perhaps the small sample was overwhelmed by random fluctuations in the data.

But I'm partial to a much simpler conclusion—the "contract year" theory is a bunch of crap. I find the theory's underlying assumptions to be repugnant, and the evidence for its existence is, at best, wholly unconvincing. After the announcers are finished trying to brainwash your son, do the kid—and the world—a favor and tell him he's free to make up his own mind about it.

October 14, 1997—The Real Value of Postseason Experience

When Jaret Wright beat the Yankees in the fifth and final game of the AL Division Series last Monday, he may have started a trend. Now, hot on the heels of Livan Hernandez' stunning performance in Game 5 of the NL Championship Series, the Marlins will look to another rookie, Tony Saunders, should a seventh game become necessary.

Incredible. The World Series, as we know it, was first played in 1903. Since then, only eight rookies have been selected to start the deciding game of a postseason series. When Wright beat the Yanks, he became only the second rookie in history to win such a start. The last one was Babe Adams, who shut out the Tigers in the seventh game of the 1909 World Series.

Despite his moniker, Adams wasn't a full-bred rookie, in the conventional sense. He entered organized baseball relatively late, and enjoyed a few successful seasons in the minors before he was sold to Pittsburgh, where he spent his first full season in the majors at the age of 27. He went 12-3 with a 1.11 ERA that year, and ended up pitching complete-game victories in all three of his World Series starts against Detroit. One might infer that he wasn't quite quaking in his cleats as he put the finishing touches on the title-clinching whitewash.

Three years later, the Red Sox sent rookie Hugh Bedient to face the Giants' Christy Mathewson in Game 8 of the World Series (Game 2 had ended in a 6-6 tie when the sun went down and someone forgot to invent the lights). Bedient was only 23 years old, but he had gone 20-9 that year. He pitched well in Game 8, allowing one run over seven innings, but was lucky to escape with only a no-decision (Mathewson had bested him, 1-0, until the Sox tied it with a run in the bottom of the seventh). The Red Sox ultimately won it in the bottom of the 10th, in one of the greatest World Series finishes of all time. But that's a story for some other column.

After Bedient, there wasn't a single Game 7 rookie starter until after WWII. In the 1947 World Series, the Yankees' Spec Shea beat the Dodgers in the first and fifth games, and came back to start Game 7 on one day's rest. He was knocked out in the second inning, and left trailing 2-0 after allowing four hits and two runs in 1.1 innings. The Yanks came back to beat the Dodgers anyway, 5-2. Shea was 26, which is a little old for a rookie, usually. It wasn't all that uncommon in the late '40s, though, since a lot of men had their careers interrupted by WWII. Shea missed 3½ years in the service, himself.

The next one was Joe Black in 1952, and once again, there were extenuating circumstances. Black broke in with the Dodgers that year at age 28; he had been held back not by a lack of talent, but rather by a lack of whiteness. It was odd to see him start Game 7—or any World Series games at all—since he'd only started two games all season. Here's what happened: the Dodgers were playing the Yankees, and since it was a "Subway Series," they went straight through without any off days. That kind of scheduling can play hell with your pitching staff, and the Dodgers only had three starters they really trusted, anyway. Although Black had been their closer, he'd also been their most effective pitcher overall, leading the staff in wins and ERA, so they decided to go with their best. He won the first game of the Series, and lost Game 4 despite pitching well. He took the loss in Game 7, allowing three runs in 5.1 innings as the Yanks won, 4-2.

Twelve years later, Mel Stottlemyre took the mound to start the game that brought the Yanks' 45-year dynasty to a close. It was Game 7 of the '64 Series. Whitey Ford had gone down with an injury in the opener, leaving the bulk of the pitching chores to Jim Bouton and Stottlemyre. As a 22-year-old rookie, Stottlemyre had gone 9-3 in 12 starts down the stretch (of all the pitchers mentioned thus far, he is the only one who's truly comparable to Jaret Wright or Tony Saunders). Stottlemyre took on the Cardinals' Bob Gibson in the seventh game, but lost, 7-5, after allowing three runs in four innings. The Yanks dropped to sixth place in 1965, and didn't make it back to the Series until after being purchased by a Cleveland shipbuilder.

The next rookie to draw a deciding-game assignment in the postseason was Marty Bystrom in the fifth game of the 1980 NLCS. The Phillies and Astros were tied at two games apiece, and Phillies manager Dallas Green elected to start the 21-year-old Bystrom instead of Dick Ruthven, who'd pitched four days earlier. Bystrom was very young, but he had enjoyed one of the best September callups in years, going 5-0 with a 1.50 ERA in six games. He allowed only two runs in 5.1 innings in Game 5, and the Phillies prevailed, 8-7 in 10 innings. Ruthven worked the final two frames to notch the victory.

Before Jaret Wright, the last rookie to start a decisive postseason game was Joe Magrane, back in the '87 World Series. The 23-year-old southpaw had started Game 1, and was hit so hard (five runs in three innings) that when his turn came up again in Game 4, Whitey Herzog opted for Greg Mathews instead. But Mathews injured his thigh in that game, so when the Series went to the limit, Herzog had no choice but to start Magrane again. He started him, but he didn't necessarily trust him, mind you. Magrane took a 2-1 lead into the fourth. He got the first out of the inning, and the next batter beat Magrane to the bag for an infield hit. Herzog yanked Magrane right then and there; the next batter drove in Magrane's baserunner to tie the score, and the Cardinals ultimately lost the game to the Twins, 4-2.

All of this serves to illustrate just how seldom a manager will give the ball to a youngster in a big game. Jaret Wright and the seven pitchers listed above are the only rookies to start the final game of a postseason series, but all in all, they've acquitted themselves creditably, going 2-2 with a 3.02 ERA. Their teams have ended up winning five of the eight series in question.

There is still a prejudice against using rookie pitchers in the postseason, and perhaps it may be justified. As Wright prepared to take on the Yanks, the print media, the television announcers, and the rest of the English-speaking world repeatedly assured us that Wright would need to work hard to overcome the "jitters," a malady that apparently afflicts all players who have neglected to amass years upon years of postseason experience. When Wright actually won the game, it was interpreted *not* as an indication that his lack of experience had been irrelevant, but rather as a crowning achievement—a triumph in the face of a nearly insurmountable lack of seasoning.

Actually, I'm quite willing to believe that Wright was nervous, and if he was, I think I know why. Months before my wedding this summer, people began to ask me, "Are you nervous yet?" The first time I was asked this question, I thought about it for a second, and then replied, "What do I have to be nervous about? I made it through law school, and if I can do that, I surely can survive this. At least this time, when I say, 'I promise to honor and obey. . .' I know the Justice of the Peace isn't going to break in and ask me, 'Now, when you say 'honor,' would you define the term as broadly as the court did in *Alabaster v. Jones?*' This time, I'm going to know all of the answers going in, and I'm not even the one who has to wear the heels. So I guess the answer would be no, I'm not nervous."

The second time I was asked, I said, "No, I'm not nervous."

The 514th time I was asked, I said, "Oh, that's a real original one, you social wizard. And by the way, your shirt is ugly."

It wasn't the wedding; the only thing that was getting on my nerves was the unrelenting chore of assuring everyone that *I wasn't nervous.*

I suspect that Wright endured a similar plight. If it hadn't occurred to him that he ought to have been a quivering mass of ectoplasm, we can assume that he was duly reminded of that fact by game time. And I doubt that the thought served to relax him any.

I'm 28 years old myself, and I like to think I can remember what it felt like to be 21. Some things that shouldn't have scared the hell out of me, did (like voting machines. You're all alone in there!). And it took me years to develop a healthy fear of other things, like career planning or assurances that "it's a safe time of the month." In other words, it's hardly safe to assume that youth is a *dis*advantage. If you'd thrown *me* onto the mound for Game 7, I honestly don't know whether I would have laughed or cried.

At any rate, the empirical data doesn't quite confirm that rookies are postseason time bombs. In the 1990s, 16 postseason games have been started by rookies, and they've combined to go 7-3 with a 4.00 ERA, allowing only 89 hits in 96.2 innings. Meanwhile, the rookie relievers have worked in 83 games, posting a fine 2.91 ERA with a strikeout-to-walk ratio of almost two-to-one. All together, the rookies have gone 11-7 with a 3.49 ERA in the postseason this decade. Whether they were nervous or not was not recorded.

November 11, 1997—This May Sound A Little Crazy. . .

Last winter, when the Toronto Blue Jays became overnight media darlings by signing Roger Clemens and Benito Santiago and trading for Orlando Merced and Carlos Garcia, I refused to jump on the bandwagon. In fact, I did everything I could to shoot out its tires.

Clemens was a good addition, but I saw a lot of potential problems with the club:

(1) Replacing John Olerud with Orlando Merced didn't look like it would help (and it didn't);

(2) Carlos Garcia wasn't a good hitter and would hurt the team if he was used near the top of the order (he spent two months batting second and was worse than anyone could have imagined);

(3) Benito Santiago wasn't likely to repeat his big numbers from the year before (he didn't);

(4) The lineup contained three more hitters who were likely to decline—Joe Carter, Ed Sprague and Otis Nixon (all three dropped off), and;

(5) The starting rotation contained two pitchers with questionable arms who'd been worked heavily the year before, Juan Guzman and Erik Hanson (both got hurt).

Obviously, this is one of those prognostications that turned out well enough to bear repeating. I'm not here to pat myself on the back, though. God knows I've made enough bad predictions so that I'm not even tempted to start keeping track.

I just think it's funny that the media and I have switched sides on this issue. The Blue Jays have been widely written off, and unless something truly dramatic transpires in the next two months, I doubt anyone would view them as a challenger to the Yankees and Orioles going into next season. Anyone besides me, that is.

Yes, I'm willing to test this limb. In fact, if things remain pretty much as they are in the AL East, I'm picking Toronto to win the division. And you can hold me to that.

Why? Because few teams are more ripe to be shaped into a winner than the Blue Jays are right now. Let's take it position-by-position:

Catcher: Benito Santiago. Yes, Benny bit the big one last year, but tell me—why was that? I'll tell you why. It was because he had a season-long battle with Charlie O'Brien for the affections of the pitching staff. Santiago handled the pitchers just as well as—and possibly *better* than—O'Brien, and received zero credit for it from the pitchers, the press or anyone else. Naturally, he was frustrated by it, and his hitting suffered. This year, O'Brien is gone, and Santiago should rebound as he assumes the full-time job.

First base: Carlos Delgado. Last season, in his first year of full-time play, he finally began learning to hit lefties. This year, if he starts hitting them *hard,* he could bust out with a monster year. His slugging percentage against righties made the AL top 10 last year, so he doesn't have far to go to become one of the league's premier sluggers. At age 26, he's poised to do just that.

Second base: Nobody. I'll get back to this.

Third base: Ed Sprague. He played with a bad shoulder last year and his homers and RBI dropped by more than half. He should rebound.

Shortstop: Alex Gonzalez. He stepped up his defense last year, but his bat has stagnated for the past three years. He was one of the Jays' young players who suffered the most under Cito Gaston, a man who seemed to be opposed to youth as a matter of principle. Gonzalez is only 25 this year, and he still has good offensive potential. He may finally realize it now that Gaston is gone.

Left field: Jose Cruz Jr. I trust you've heard of him.

Center field: Shannon Stewart. As a leadoff man, he should be comparable to the dear departed Otis Nixon, except Stewart will contribute more doubles and triples.

Right field: Shawn Green. Green is another young player who somehow managed to swim after Gaston threw him in the lake. Still, Gaston never let him do anything more than platoon, and every once in a while, Cito would put him in his place by benching him in favor of a guy like Ruben Sierra. Green just might be a valuable full-time player, and it may help him to play for a manager who's interested in finding out.

DH: Currently vacant, but decent DHs are not a scarce commodity.

Now let's put it all together:

CF Stewart

2B

LF Cruz

1B Delgado

DH

3B Sprague

RF Green

C Santiago

SS Gonzalez

A few questions:

Does the lineup have players who get on base? Yes. Stewart should get on base more than Nixon did. Cruz was a very patient hitter in the minors and should draw more walks as he matures. Delgado is already very selective. If they can find a second baseman to bat second and get on base, they will have four guys at the top of the lineup who can get on.

Does the lineup have power? Yes. Cruz, Delgado and Sprague are all either actual or potential 30-HR men. Shawn Green has a career slugging percentage of .463, and some combination of Ivan Cruzes and Roberto Petagines will hit close to 30 homers from the DH spot.

Are these players on the way up or the way down? As a group, they're definitely on the way up. Of the seven regulars listed above, five are still approaching their peak. That's a sharp contrast to last year's lineup, which featured six of nine players on the way down.

I think they can field a pretty fair offensive team, especially if they can acquire one more player: Chuck Knoblauch. Why not? He's available, he's exactly what they need, and they've got both the money and the prospects to get him. Look at the high-salaried players they've shed over the last few months: Joe Carter, Otis Nixon, Orlando Merced, Charlie O'Brien and Mike Timlin. Put all that money in a pile and dump it at Chuck Knoblauch's feet, and let *him* decide whether it's enough. I usually don't speculate so freely, but in this case, the player and the team's needs match up so well that I just can't help myself. If Knoblauch is batting second, that's a good lineup. Now on to the pitching staff.

First, you've got Roger Clemens and Pat Hentgen. Each one has been worked hard in recent years, but neither has shown any signs of wear. I think Hentgen can handle it, but I'm less certain about Clemens. Still, Roger could take a few steps down and still be quite a pitcher.

Then you have the two injury cases, Juan Guzman and Erik Hanson. What these guys need is a manager who can recognize their limits and prevent them from exceeding them. Whoever the new manager turns out to be, he couldn't possibly be any worse in this regard than Gaston was.

There are some other promising starters around to fill out the rotation: Woody Williams, Chris Carpenter, Marty Janzen and Robert Person. All have quality arms.

The bullpen is a bit more unsettled. Kelvim Escobar comes in as the Armando Benitez of the crew, a wild young flamethrower with little experience and a history of minor injuries. Dan Plesac should be able to do a reasonable impersonation of Jesse Orosco, if he can stop smiling so much. Paul Quantrill's ERA last year was a blatant lie, but he's got a rubber arm and should remain a useful setup man. Carlos Almanzar and Kenny Robinson are potential contributors.

I'm telling you, keep an eye on 'em.

November 18, 1997—Give That Trophy Back

Perhaps I should be embarrassed to admit this, but I just can't make sense of the National League Most Valuable Player balloting. Am I all alone on this one? Can someone help me out here?

As best I can understand it, the argument for Larry Walker goes something like this: his home numbers were no better than his road numbers, therefore Coors Field didn't inflate his numbers at all. Since his numbers should be taken at face value, and those numbers are the best in the league, he therefore deserves to be MVP. That's pretty much it, isn't it? If there's a better explanation of his selection, I haven't heard it.

Understand this: I need a better explanation than *that*. To me, the idea that 22 out of 28 voters would be swayed by the meager argument above is baffling, disheartening and, quite frankly, frightening. The possibility that people would be persuaded by such feeble reasoning does irreparable harm to the notion that humans are the most intelligent race in the universe.

All right, enough false dramatics. Believe me, it would be very easy for me to just repeat Walker's numbers to myself and try to accept the voting. Forty-nine home runs. A .366 batting average, the highest for a 40-homer hitter since Babe Ruth. More than 400 total bases, the first National Leaguer to break the 400 barrier since Hank Aaron. Thirty-three stolen bases. A .720 slugging percentage. His numbers just *sound* like MVP numbers. If you can't give the MVP to a guy who hits .366 with 49 homers, people seem to say, then you must be stupid or something.

As I noted above, the rationalization that holds the whole Walker argument together is the notion that his road stats somehow "legitimize" his overall numbers. People seem to think that just because his road numbers are as good as his home numbers, we are free to conclude that his home stats *haven't been inflated by Coors Field.* Let's take a closer look at that.

Ever since the Rockies entered the league, their hitters have dominated the NL leader boards. And right from the start, people have used those same hitters' home-road splits to show that their superiority was due to their home field rather than actual talent. Every year, Dante Bichette has put up huge numbers at home and quite ordinary ones on the road. People have seized on the difference, and in an apparent effort to pin down Dante's "real" talent level, they've decided that his road stats are more representative of his ability. Is this a valid approach? Absolutely—to a point.

In any other park, Bichette would hit around .260 with 15 home runs, at a guess. But you can't simply ignore what he does at Coors Field, even if it is horribly skewed. Somehow, Bichette is able to take better advantage of Coors than most other hitters. Should this count *against* him? Hell, no. If he's better able to exploit Coors than the opposing team's left fielder, that's going to result in real wins for the Rockies. In other words, the fact that Bichette hits so well at Coors makes him *more* valuable, not less. That's not to say that he's as valuable as a guy who hits .300 in a real park, but he's not as useless as your average .260 hitter, either.

Of course, there's still the issue of how to put his home stats into proper context. They obviously can't be taken at face value, but since they reflect a large part of Bichette's value, they shouldn't be ignored, either. The proper approach might be to compare his Coors production to the average hitter's production at Coors. Without doing the math, you might find that Bichette is 10 runs better than the average hitter in 81 games at Coors. If you found that he was 10 runs worse than the average hitter in 81 road games, then you might properly conclude that his overall production over a full season was dead average. (You might get different results than that, of course, but that's one way to approach it.)

The point is that you can get a realistic assessment of Bichette's production at Coors if you compare it to other hitters' production there. Comparing Bichette's home stats to his road stats can give you an idea of how much his home stats are inflated, but to get an idea of the actual *value* of his home stats, the relevant line of inquiry is to consider them within the context in which they were compiled. To put it another way, Bichette might really be a .260 hitter, but he's more valuable to the Rockies than a .260-hitting left fielder would be to another team, because he has an ability to take better advantage of his home park than most hitters do.

But few people seem to approach it that way. Given Bichette's home-road splits, most people seem to take them as an "either-or" proposition. Since Coors skews the home numbers, people simply reject them and concentrate entirely on the road stats. This has gotten to be standard procedure when analyzing a Colorado hitter—if you want to know how good he "really" is, just ignore the home stats and look at the road stats. And the result is always the same—the road stats are inferior, and you're left to assume that he's not as good as his stats would have you believe. That's been the case every time, until Larry Walker came along and messed things up.

Walker hit just as well on the road last year; now what are we to make of this? Like I said, many people just used the same logic in reverse, and concluded that he *really was* as good as the number showed. Is this acceptable reasoning? Not necessarily.

Over a period of years, home-road splits do tend to reveal whether a hitter is helped or hurt by his home park. But in any given season, the splits can go the wrong way. A Houston hitter can hit better at home for a season or two. If you give him a few more seasons, his numbers will eventually settle back in where they ought to be, but 81 games is not a long enough time to wash out all of the random fluctucations. To paraphrase Mark Twain, if you think Fenway doesn't help John Valentin, wait a season.

In most cases, if you use a large enough sample, you can get a pretty good read on a hitter by just looking at his road stats. But if you limit yourself to a single season, you might wind up drawing some bizarre conclusions. In the case of Larry Walker, people looked at his '97 splits and decided that he *really was* that good, because he hit just as well on the road.

This led to an even more ridiculous conclusion—the assertion that Coors didn't help Walker at all last year. This is patently absurd. *Of course* Coors helped Walker. The Rockies and their opponents batted .317 at Coors last year. That's with the pitchers' hitting included. It's an inescapable fact: Coors makes an average batsman into a .317 hitter. It helped Larry Walker last year, no matter what he hit on the road.

If Walker's road average for a given season really holds the key to his true ability, how do you explain the fact that he batted .142 on the road in '96? Did his batting skill really double in one year? Of course not; these are just the blips and bumps that turn up in the data sometimes. If you wait long enough, they smooth out. Over the last three years, Walker has batted .371 at Coors and .275 on the road. The park helps him.

At this point, it might be wise to narrow the scope of our inquiry. Rather than trying to puzzle out the murky, abstract question of how *good* a hitter Walker is, let's focus on something more concrete: his *value*. After all, we're not talking about the "Most *Good* Player Award."

How valuable was Larry Walker last year? Let me tell you how I would approach the question.

First, I would look at his home stats:

	G	AB	R	H	2B	3B	HR	RBI	BB	SO	AVG	OBP	SLG
Home	78	302	82	116	30	4	20	68	36	34	.384	.460	.709

Those are tremendous, without a doubt, but what was their *value?* What were they worth at Coors, where everyone hits a ton?

We can get a better idea of what they're worth if we take out the Coors effect. If you compare the Rockies' and Rockies' opponents' numbers last year at home and on the road, you'll find that Coors inflated these stats by the following percentages:

Runs	+33.3 %
Singles	+26.6 %
Doubles	+23.1 %
Triples	+ 20.6 %
Home Runs	+26.9 %

If you reduce Walker's runs and RBI by 33.3 percent, his singles by 26.6 percent, etc., you get the following batting line, "adjusted" downward to cancel out the Coors influence:

	G	AB	R	H	2B	3B	HR	RBI	BB	SO	AVG	OBP	SLG
Home (adj)	78	278	62	92	24	3	16	51	36	34	.331	.418	.612

To put it a different way, Walker's production at Coors last year was equivalent to hitting .331 with 16 homers in a neutral park. This is an accurate reflection of the value of Walker's home stats.

His road stats need no adjustment. Let's add them together with his adjusted home stats. These are Larry Walker's '97 numbers, minus the help from Coors:

	G	AB	R	H	2B	3B	HR	RBI	BB	SO	AVG	OBP	SLG
Total (adj)	153	544	123	184	40	3	45	113	78	90	.338	.431	.671

Are these still MVP-caliber numbers? Yes, possibly. Unless there's a better candidate, of course. . . which there is:

	G	AB	R	H	2B	3B	HR	RBI	BB	SO	AVG	OBP	SLG
Walker (adj)	153	544	123	184	40	3	45	113	78	90	.338	.431	.671
Piazza (raw)	152	556	104	201	32	1	40	124	69	77	.362	.431	.638

I think it's fair to say that when you remove Coors Field from the equation, it puts Larry Walker about even with Mike Piazza, at least in terms of raw numbers. But then you have to consider two factors that weigh heavily in Piazza's favor.

First, Piazza played in Dodger Stadium, the most pitcher-friendly park in the National League. Over the last three years, Dodger Stadium has depressed scoring and batting average more than any other park in the league. The Astrodome is the only NL park that's taken away more home runs.

Obviously, if you make the appropriate ballpark adjustments for Piazza, he comes out significantly ahead of Walker. I'd do it myself, but I don't want to belabor the point any more than I already have.

I can still hear some of you in the background arguing that Walker's a better hitter because his road stats were better than Piazza's last year. But I would maintain that their road production is not the end of the story.

Piazza hit well at home, too: he hit .355 with 22 home runs at Dodger Stadium, in a park where all hitters combined to bat .245, and the Dodgers and their opponents combined to score only 7.7 runs per game. Piazza's home production had *tremendous* value—far more than Walker's home production did. And Piazza's road production wasn't that far behind Walker's either; Piazza hit .368 and slugged .643 on the road. On balance, it was no contest, if you consider the parks.

Then you have the question of Piazza's and Walker's respective positions. Piazza is a catcher and Walker is an outfielder. This matters, a *lot*. It matters because good-hitting catchers are so hard to find. This gives the Dodgers a tremendous edge against everyone else, because there's only one Mike Piazza. Walker is good, but compared to everyone else's right fielder, the Rockies don't have nearly as big an edge. Think of it this way: the Rockies don't have a Mike Piazza, so they have to play a zero like Kirt Manwaring. The Dodgers don't have a Larry Walker, but they do have a pretty decent right fielder. And if they didn't have Raul Mondesi, they'd have someone else who would hit about 15 more home runs a year than Manwaring, because there are always decent-hitting outfielders around waiting for a job. (Ask Billy Ashley.)

And how good was Piazza's season, for a catcher? Simply put, it was *the best of all time* hands-down. Make a list of all the players who've ever caught 100 games in a season, and you'll discover that Piazza's totals rank at or near the top in *all* the major categories.

You want hits? He's the only catcher in history to get 200 hits; he had 201. No one else has ever recorded more than 193 in a season. Batting average? His .362 mark is the second-best ever, two-tenths of a point behind Bill Dickey's all-time record. OK, you want average *and* power? Fine. Piazza tied for fourth all-time with 40 longballs. RBI? His 124 RBI tied for eighth. Dickey hit for a slightly higher average one year, and Johnny Bench and Roy Campanella had better power numbers in their single best seasons, but no catcher has ever come close to matching Piazza's across-the-board domination of the all-time leader boards in a single season.

And again, he did this in Dodger Stadium.

You say you want to argue about defense. OK, but tell me: do you really think people voted for Walker because of his glove? If they did, how come he's never gotten more than 11 points in the MVP balloting before?

Anyway, if you want to argue, we'll argue. Walker's Gold Glove is a given. Piazza has a bad rep, but his throwing improved a lot last year. He threw out 28 percent of enemy basestealers; the league average was 32 percent. In addition, the Dodgers' staff ERA was 0.69 lower with him behind the plate (which is no fluke—in the previous four seasons, the staff ERA with Piazza has been substantially lower three times: -0.50, -1.59, +0.02 and -1.05). If you want to argue that Walker's defense was worth more than Piazza's last year, fine, go ahead, but if you want to say that it made up for Piazza's superiority on offense, I'm not nearly convinced.

From the virtually universal acceptance that greeted Walker's MVP selection, I take it that I may be standing alone on this one. If that's the case, so be it. I'd rather stand alone with the truth than be surrounded by sheep. Piazza was robbed. If you've got an argument with that, bring it on.

Steve Moyer's
"Baseball Babble-On"

3/14/97

Sorry, I do slip once in a while, but, today's going to be: *a useful column by Steve Moyer*.

Jay Payton's gonzo with injury for 1997. No more a sleeper he.

Boy, first Brent Gates is released, then Mark Johnson gets sent down. Just kidding. Mark Johnson, the White Sox no-name catcher was sent down.

Did you see who's leading the Red Sox in spring hitting? Why it's right fielder Ethan Faggett, of course. (And folks wonder why children axe-murder their parents.)

I can tell Kirt Manwaring reads my column. He's hitting .316 now, up from .000 a week ago. He just needed a little push from me.

All right, time for the useful stuff. I can stall no longer. What I'm going to give you below is a list of guys to take a crack at when your draft hits the "No Man's Land" portion. You know, when names like "Manny Alexander" and "Rafael Belliard" inevitably start being mentioned. Every guy in my list has a great chance to be tons better than those guys, mostly because each is having a good spring, some for other reasons. Many of these guys will be worthless, but what have you got to lose for a buck or two when you can't think of anybody and you want to say "Rudy Seanez"? One final note: I *don't* think spring performance means a guy is a lot better or worse than he was before, in most cases. I *do* think spring performance can open the door for an opportunity that may not have existed before. Well, here goes. I'll just list guys, and if I still have time, I'll add some comments. See you next week with LABR league inside dirt.

BALTIMORE: Jeff Reboulet, Jerome Walton, Mike Johnson, Scott Kamieniecki

BOSTON: Tim Spehr, Butch Henry, Ricky Trlicek, Jim Corsi

ANAHEIM: Jack Howell, Luis Alicea

No WHITE SOX

CLEVELAND: Casey Candaele, Herbert Perry

DETROIT: Deivi Cruz, Vince Coleman, Pedro Munoz

KANSAS CITY: Joe Vitiello

MILWAUKEE: Todd Dunn, Kelly Stinnett

MINNESOTA: Matt Lawton

YANKEES: Jorge Posada

OAKLAND: Dave Magadan, Brian Lesher, Patrick Lennon, Frank Catalanotto, Steve Karsay, Richie Lewis, Chuck Ricci

SEATTLE: Dave Silvestri, Lee Tinsley

TEXAS: Lee Stevens, Jerry Browne, Tom O'Malley

TORONTO: Felipe Crespo, Robert Perez

ATLANTA: Wes Helms, Hensley Meulens, Kevin Rogers, Mike Bielecki, Yorkis Perez

CUBS: Dave Hansen, Dave Clark

CINCINNATI: Curtis Goodwin, Mike Morgan

HOUSTON: Richard Hidalgo, Russ Johnson, Tommy Greene, Chris Holt

LOS ANGELES: Darren Hall

No EXPOS

METS: Roberto Petagine, Andy Tomberlin, Juan Acevedo

PHILADELPHIA: Derrick May, Mark Parent, Kevin Sefcik, Jerry Spradlin, Ron Blazier

PITTSBURGH: Emil Brown, Keith Mitchell, Dale Sveum

ST. LOUIS: Miguel Mejia, Andy Van Slyke

SAN DIEGO: Terry Shumpert

SAN FRANCISCO: David McCarty, Julian Tavarez, Doug Henry

COLORADO: Darnell Coles, Angel Echevarria

FLORIDA: Ralph Milliard, John Cangelosi, Pat Rapp

3/28/97

Buy the new *STATS Diamond Chronicles* now. Just do it.

Example #327 of why players should just play the game, collect their money, and keep their mouths shut when it comes to making player decisions. Steve Finley, on the Jody Reed trade, giving Quilvio Veras the Padres every day 2B job: "Jody's the better second baseman, period." Boy, now there's a future front-office guy if I ever saw one. Jody Reed slugged .297 last season. What can you possibly do to make yourself valuable when you slug .297? Rey Ordonez slugged .303 last year, for heaven's sake. Maybe he gave out diamond rings in the clubhouse. Jody Reed is finished as a worthwhile ballplayer. His last good year was 1994 and the last good one before that was 1990.

Isn't it funny how with all the preseason gab about the Royals' Macfarlane/Sweeney/Fasano catching decisions, the Royal catchers entering the season will be Macfarlane and Tim Spehr?

I wish they'd pass a United States law saying that anyone who pays by check in a long checkout line could be shot. And people who pay by check for items totalling less than $10 anytime could be skinned alive.

If J.T. Snow isn't ready to start the season, darned if I'd use Stan Javier at first, like the Giants seem to be planning. I've heard really bad things about the state of Javier's speed, which accounted for much of his value in previous seasons. I hate to say it, but I'd give David McCarty his million-and-first chance, on the basis of his hot spring. Despite the fact that he's blown opportunity after opportunity and his numbers are .224/.281/.316 (notice he's still not down to Jody Reed slugging level) in 731 career at-bats, he's still only 27. He's in the minors now, though.

So where were you when you heard the news about the Kenny Lofton trade?

I'd like to spend the rest of this column analyzing (fancy word for criticizing) what others said about the trade:

Rod Beaton (how did you know I'd start here?): "Lofton for Grissom is a fairly even exchange: one great, 29-year-old leadoff hitter and Gold Glove center fielder for another." Hmm. Fairly even, eh? Kenny Lofton's OBP last year was .372. His career OBP is .379. That's pretty good. Marquis Grissom's OBP last year, hitting a career-high .308, was .349. One point more and that's satisfactory, in my book, for a leadoff hitter. His career OBP is an unsatisfactory .332. So, I guess the 47-point difference in career OBP (even the 23-point difference in last year's) doesn't mean much? Let me explain that difference in sixth-grade terms. What if you had one batter who hit for a .279 batting average and another who hit for a .232 batting average. Otherwise, their skills were about on the level, the .279 guys steals more bases, but the .232 guy might hit for a bit more power. Would you say that trade was "a fairly even exchange"?

John Hart: "Baseball in the '90s is extremely apparent in this trade, and we had to make it." Yep, John, wouldn't it be so much better if we all could go back to the days where the owners made all the money and the players were basically slaves.

Frank Thomas: "It was a good trade for Cleveland. They picked up two All-Stars for one." But the Braves made room for a guy who will kick Justice's butt (more definitely if Justice plays as much as usual) in Andruw Jones. And Jones doesn't command quite the salary of Justice.

Mo Vaughn: "There aren't too many Kenny Loftons and Marquis Grissoms out there. We need a guy who could occupy a base, not necessarily steal bases." I'm not sure exactly what this quote means, but it may mean that a major league player recognizes the value of OBP. If that's what you meant, Mo, you didn't want Grissom anyway. Have you been talking to Duquette or something?

Sandy Alomar, Jr.: "With the way salaries are going these days, baseball is kind of like a Monopoly game. It's like a Rotisserie league." This is my favorite. Explain that Monopoly analogy to me in more detail, Sandy. Does that mean if Kenny Lofton is Boardwalk, then Marquis Grissom is Marvin Gardens? If Grissom is a house, then Lofton is a hotel? If Lofton is the hat, does that make Grissom the thimble? Who's the dog? Alan Embree? And the Rotisserie league thing. When major league people are playing the biggest derogatory card in the deck, it's always the "real baseball's getting like Rotisserie" thing. God forbid. Maybe you wouldn't be so overrated in Monopoly, Sandy.

My opinion is that it was a great trade for the Braves. They've got the best leadoff hitter they've had since maybe ever and they've got room for both Jones and Klesko now. I'm not sure I like the Dodgers to win the NL anymore.

I lied about Lofton/Grissom-Justice ending my column.

Now, the Babble-On Oscars. There's only one category:

Movie Term That Was Clever Maybe The First Two Times You Heard It And Now Makes You Want To Vomit When Heard Or Seen In Print:

1) "Jerry McGuire" —"Show me the money."

2) "Donnie Brasco" (yeah, I know it's 1997 against 1996)—"Fuhgeddaboudit."

4/18/97

I know I'll be the only columnist to say this, but I think I've had enough Jackie Robinson and Tiger Woods for a while.

This in last week from former STATS programmer/Spin Doctor/New Waver/Alternative Dude-Man Dave Mundo:

"Harry made the following astute observations during today's Cub game:

'Now pitch-hitting for Atlanta, Audrey Jones.'

But it was no match for:

'Harry Caray back with you at Sportsman's Park. . .'

You know, I include the preceding only because it's just plain funny, not because I plan to rag on Harry. You come to expect that stuff after about two WGN Cub telecasts and it actually creates a game within the game trying to catch all that kind of stuff. The guys who bother me are the ones who are supposed to know what they're doing.

I just happened to pull out my Willie Hernandez 1985 Sporting News *Baseball Register* to verify the spelling of Kent Tekulve and guess whose listing I ran into a few pages earlier? Dale Curtis Sveum. I kid you not.

Do you think Troy Aikman really wears Brut? Yeah, and Deion Sanders wears Old Spice.

Lance Johnson now has 11 walks in 58 at-bats. Last season he had a grand total of 33 in 682. Combined with his current batting average of .293, that gives him a very Rickey-Henderson-like .406 OBP. Now I'm no Don Zminda or Neil Munro, but I can't think of anybody else who ever spent 10 major league seasons swinging at anything close only to turn into a patient hitter in the eleventh. I know guys like Julio Franco and Lonnie Smith were free swingers early in their careers and gradually developed into patient hitters, but this isn't close to the same. Maybe this whole phenomenon is simply an early-season freak occurrence. Nonetheless, I do have to warn Mr. Johnson that if he ups his walk total to 70 from his usual 30, he'd better watch out, because he's going to make himself a damn good offensive player.

I dare you. Go ahead. Acquire Pat Rapp and his current 1.83 ERA for your fantasy team. I dare you. Go ahead.

The hockey preseason is over now. The games count.

How about Phil Nevin coming back from injury so soon? I thought he was out for the season. It makes me wonder just how supposedly wimpy and un-tough these players of today are. I can think of Nevin and Mark Lewis real recently, Mark McGwire last season, and Fred Barnett in football, just off the top of my head as examples of guys who came back way earlier than expected from major injuries. Is this due to simply my impression or medical advances or maybe are there still some tough guys around?

Paul Konerko watch: .423 (11-for-26), with three homers, seven RBI, and five walks, which add up to a .515 OBP and .769 SLG. The Dodgers *will* regret that big Eric Karros contract (unless they *can* make Konerko even a mediocre glove at third).

Finally, a little story that I ran out of room for last week. The other week, as most of you know, Alex Fernandez carried a no-hitter into the ninth inning. I watched that ninth inning on STATS' online live-action thing. I was pulling for Fernandez' no-hitter, not only because it's hard not to pull for a no-hitter by anyone, but because I paid big bucks for him in LABR. So, first batter up is Dave Clark, another LABR guy of mine, and Clark whiffs. Great, two more outs to go. Then, Dave Hansen, another LABR guy of mine (you can see the price I paid by paying big bucks for Fernandez), comes up. A few pitches into the at-bat, Hansen singles and the no-no's over. My first thought is, like most: "Crap, no no-hitter." Then, I thought: "Wait a minute, from a Rotisserie angle, Hansen's single probably means more than Fernandez' no-hitter." And I could feel better. The twisted joys of fantasy baseball.

5/2/97

Sorry, but there's going to be waaay too much baseball in this week's column. Everybody slips sometimes.

My favorite *USA Today* headline of last week, you don't ask? "Head lice show signs of resisting usual treatments." Talk about journalism that hits home.

Yes, I'm one of those guys who gets all excited when Phil Plantier gets called up. He's 0-for-4 so far.

Have you been swallowing all this media crap about the Braves being so good because now they're speed-oriented instead of power-oriented? Let me tell you what the difference is in the Braves this season, from an offensive standpoint:

1) Michael Tucker is out of his skull.

2) Jeff Blauser is hitting way above his level of ability and nine years out of 10 he's way below.

3) Kenny Lofton is the first good leadoff hitter the Braves have had in years.

4) Javy Lopez isn't exactly piddling around with a .700 SLG.

So, have you been swallowing all the media crap about Deion Sanders all of a sudden turning the corner? Well, right now Deion's at .369-.412-.495. Now anybody's a pretty good hitter when he's hitting .369. Do you believe Deion will hit .369 for the season? Right now, Deion has seven walks in 111 at-bats. Let's just say Deion was hitting .300 (we'll say .306 for math purposes). What would his OBP be? .347. That's *almost* adequate for a leadoff hitter. Now, what if Deion were hitting .280, which is probably pretty realistic (.279 to be exact)? His OBP would be a leadoff-stinky .322, which sounds about right for Deion. The thing that always intrigued me about Sanders is his often-high slugging percentages. I've always said he'd be better-suited as a No. 6 hitter and I still firmly believe that. Of course, no one else does.

Mr. Excitement-Sparkplug-Make-Things-Happen, Tom Goodwin's at .159-.221-.193.

So have you been swallowing all the media crap about the Rockies turning things around on the road? In reality, they're hitting .377-.448-.571 at home and .255-.332-.456 on the road. Those road numbers really aren't terrible, but I'm sure they'll fade. And they're nowhere near the home numbers.

And, yes, now it's been proven that *anyone* can hit at Coors. Kirt Manwaring is hitting .317-.382-.417, including .348-.415-.457 at Coors. But it's not Coors. It's that he's never been around a bunch of players with a winning attitude like he is this season with the Rockies.

The sabermetricians have to bow to the scouts for Mike Lieberthal's seven homers. But we don't have to bow for his .219 batting average.

Speaking of the scout-players, did you notice there wasn't one stat in Rod Beaton's Thursday article about how well Josh Booty is coming along? That's because he's hitting .221.

The only thing better than being on the "Oprah" show is being banned from it.

I really intended to rag on Rickey Henderson and his .173 batting average, since he's gotten more playing time than expected so far. However, what I didn't realize was that his OBP is .394 (17 walks) and he's tied for third on the team in runs scored with 14. And the three guys he's competing with have no fewer than 35 more at-bats than Rickey has. But don't worry. He's on the bench now. For Chris Jones.

Bill James' new book is finally out, so go get it. However, I have yet to see the book I consider somewhat my first literary venture, the *STATS Diamond Chronicles* in any bookstore. It must be a conspiracy.

I saw the Detroit Lions have an offensive tackle named Juan Roque in camp, which brought to mind early-'70s Cardinal outfielder Jorge Roque. Boy, the pronunciation jobs my friends and I did on that guy.

5/9/97

My wife and daughter have been visiting the in-laws in Illinois this past week, so I've had waaay too much opportunity to blast loud music in the house like I'm 18 years old again or something. This column will suffer for it.

I like this guy Matt Beech the Phillies just brought up. Ignore his ERA at Triple-A this year. He's a lot better than that. And he throws a lot of strikeouts, if that counts in your fantasy league. I'm not sure I'd want him in a just-this-year league, but if you can pick him up and hide him in reserve for a year or two in a keeper league, I'd do it.

You know, here's a radio slogan for a rock station that would have me listening all day— "Any Boston is too much Boston."

But later on I decided, if you strip out all the crappy stuff about Boston and trade whomever their crappy lead singer is for Eric Carmen, you'd almost have The Raspberries, who are one of my faves.

I saw the Angels promoted Frank Bolick from Double-A to Triple-A last week. Frank Bolick. Now there's a blast from the past.

So far, my favorite paragraph from Bill James' new book, you don't ask? "But for now, this discussion has two groups. On the one hand, you have the barroom experts, the traditional sportswriters, the couch potatoes, and the call-in show regulars, all of whom believe that batting orders are important. And then, on the other hand, you have a few of us who have actually studied the issue, and who have been forced to draw the conclusion that it doesn't make much difference what order you put the hitters in, they're going to score just as many runs one way as another. You can believe whoever you want to; it's up to you."

Babble-On fans, be sure to cast your vote for Albert Belle as an AL All-Star starting outfielder when they pass out those ballots at the game. I can't wait to read all the p-ed off media articles. Don't forget Barry Bonds too.

Have you ever wondered what controversial-to-the-max Dan Duquette consultant Mike Gimbel looks like? Well, I happened to catch an MTV video by the rock band the Foo

Fighters and the lead singer/guitarist looks a heckuva lot like a 20-year younger, less maniacal version of Mike.

Over the past few years, my West Coast correspondent buddy and I have had this award we talk about every year. It's called the "El Diablo" award and it's given to the player who most likely sold his soul to "El Diablo" prior to the season, based on the uncharacteristically fantastic year he's having. I don't know if we ever get around to actually giving the award, but we always discuss the contestants throughout the year. Prior contestants were guys like Mike Kingery—1994 (although it's hard to make it to the "El Diablo" list if you hit for the Rockies anymore), Gary DiSarcina—1995, and Fernando Valenzuela last year. (It's always better when given to a Hispanic player, of course. It is the "El Diablo" award, after all.) This year, there's one guy who's just absolutely blowing away the competition, and he's even Hispanic. By now you probably know I'm talking about the Expos' Pedro Martinez. 0.50 ERA, 36.1 IP, 17 H, 2 ER, 10 BB, 42 K. Holy smokes. That looks like a whole family's worth of souls to me.

I know what it's like to be a bitter, grizzled old vet now. I returned to my old fastpitch softball team this spring after a five-year Illinois absence. And now, instead of being in the lineup every game, at least to begin with, I have to come off the bench. And as I watch those college kids who are a lot quicker and stronger than me, even though I have to hope for the team, I secretly hope for them all to look bad, so I can get back. Quite the team player, huh? The other thing I noticed is when I left I was like one of probably three guys in the entire league who wears an earring and the only guy who wears two. Now, it's like every other guy. The late 90s—earrings, tattoos, goatees and cigars.

5/21/97

Have you ever noticed the Nike swoosh is the same as the Newport cigarette swoosh only upside down?

Like I said a column or two ago, Pedro Martinez probably has the NL and major league El Diablo award locked up already for 1997. However, Scott Erickson is sure making a strong bid for the AL award.

So, just how long are the Phillies going to live with Wendell Magee (.200/.254/.261) and Mike Lieberthal (.181/.235/.386) every day?

If the Cubs were smart, they'd realize they have a real nice platoon combo in Jose Hernandez and Dave Hansen at third and they'd get Dave Clark, who could easily hit 25 dingers at Wrigley Field, into the lineup a lot more often. The silly high draft pick/scout darling/media darling guys they're trying to force-feed into the majors and onto the fans just ain't gonna cut it, I'm sorry to say:

Kevin Orie—Had a good 296 at-bats at Double-A last season and still only slugged .480 there. Nothing else in his past shows me that he's anything special. He is 24. That's not real real young, but he could improve.

Tyler Houston—Gosh darn it, we'll make something out of this guy yet. We'll play him out of position, whatever. We need that sub-.300 OBP in our lineup everyday.

Brooks Kieschnick—In the top 10 of all pretender prospects in baseball today.

Doug Glanville—In the top three of all pretender prospects in baseball today. (Kimera Bartee is the current number one, but I think even his army of believers is starting to dwindle. Pokey Reese is two.)

My West Coast correspondent wanted you to know that Ken Ramos, the recent Astro call-up, had 23 walks and five strikeouts at Triple-A New Orleans prior to his major league debut. I've always liked Ramos (career .302/.391/.399 in the minors), but, quite frankly, I didn't think he'd ever have a major league debut anymore, now that he's almost 30, but you never know. Hey, like I said last column, Warren Newson is leading off every day for the Rangers. Will wonders never cease? (They'll probably cease when speedy sparkplug Mark McLemore returns.)

Speaking of speedy sparkplugs, Tony Womack's developing nicely into one of those leadoff guys that everyone loves. You know—subpar .332 OBP, but 15 flashy steals. He's going to get worse before he gets better, too.

Thank goodness for a wonderful *USA Today* today, a nice surprise for a guy who has to write his weekly column two days early:

"Indians sign trio of stars for $81.1M" -

David Justice—four years, $28 mil—That's wonderful if he stays healthy and keeps hitting .428. Talk about the right place at the right time.

Marquis Grissom—five years, $25 mil—Ouch. Unless Grissom gets hurt, the Indians are stuck with a crappy leadoff hitter for five years. Ask the Braves what it means to have a real leadoff hitter. And no one can afford Rickey Henderson.

Jim Thome—three years, $24.5 mil—Brilliant. I'd sign this to-be superstar for as many years as he'd let me. Somebody's gotta hit solo homers when Grissom's not on base.

5/29/97

GQ magazine strikes again this month with a fantastic diary by New Jersey Net Jayson Williams. The issue I'm referring to has Will Smith on the cover, by the way. It may be my imagination, but they sure seem to be sneaking in more and more sports the past couple of years. And that's great as far as I'm concerned. There's no better deed that a man can do for himself than to go out and purchase a subscription to that magazine. It's so good and so good for you. The articles are great (the non-sports ones too) and you can't help but pick up on some fashion tips that will prevent you from ever being mistaken for a newspaper beat writer.

With this ESPN fill-in work I'm doing during these two weeks, I haven't had a lot of time to think about Babble-On material. So I'm going to rip off Stefan Kretschmann for a few neat charts that lucky STATS employees get in a mail message, updated daily.

Players Who Can't Hit Their Weight

Player	Avg	WT
Scott Brosius	.157	185
Greg Vaughn	.190	202
Carlos Garcia	.199	205
Eddie Murray	.216	220

Murray will soon have trouble hitting his age.

Players Who Are Still Looking For A 1997 Hit (15 AB min)

Player	AB
Mark Clark	23
Don Slaught	20
Ismael Valdes	19
Shawn Estes	16
Osvaldo Fernandez	16

There's my genius $1 LABR league minor league catcher (with the .285 lifetime BA) showing the pitchers how to do it.

Chance For More RBI Than Hits (min: 25 H, H-RBI)

Player	H	RBI
Jeff Kent	41	44
Juan Gonzalez	28	29
Jay Buhner	39	35
Ken Griffey	65	61
Todd Hundley	41	37
Tony Clark	54	49
Reggie Sanders	25	20

Sorry, can't think of a snide remark for this one.

Pitchers With A Higher BA (*10) Than ERA (5 AB min)

Pitcher	Avg	ERA
John Smoltz	.440	2.60
Armando Reynoso	.333	3.00
Rick Reed	.190	1.70
Garrett Stephenson	.143	1.33

Ahhh. Lots to say about this one. Rick Reed shows me just how pathetic many of those replacement players really were. And how Rob Dibble said something like those guys playing was on the order of beer-game level. Who's playing the beer game now? And who the heck does Garrett Stephenson think he is? The three ERAs he posted thus far in his career above A-ball are 5.15, 3.64, and 4.81. His ERA at Scranton prior to his call-up was over six. His career minor league ERA is 3.94. In six innings with the Orioles last season he was smoked to the tune of 12.79. So, what does he do in the bigs for the Phils? Only quality outing after quality outing. Well I'm not convinced. El Diablo competition for Pedro, perhaps?

Last 162 Games

Player	Avg	OBP	SLG	R	2B	HR	RBI	BB
Mark McGwire	.309	.450	.732	120	27	67	143	135
Albert Belle	.289	.382	.560	113	38	42	147	90
Juan Gonzalez	.311	.365	.635	107	41	55	176	55
Ken Griffey	.316	.395	.667	148	32	64	183	81
Edgar Martinez	.326	.456	.550	129	54	26	120	134
Kevin Mitchell	.305	.418	.587	82	31	37	115	101
Larry Walker	.332	.409	.655	129	42	40	127	57
Bill Mueller	.309	.384	.389	42	21	0	27	38

Don't ask me what Bill Mueller's doing in there either. It's Stefan's chart and I needed something funny for this column.

6/6/97

Let's open this week's back-to-normal Friday column with a quote from 86-year-old Maureen O'Sullivan, who used to play Jane to Johnny Weissmuller's Tarzan. The *USA Today* asked her about working with the chimps: "They're nice when young, but after age seven they get mean. But Johnny, they loved him. I think the Cheetas were all homosexuals." And you thought "Ellen" got the TV ball rolling.

Now onto a piece of fan mail I got this week from a guy who got my personal e-mail without my approval. That's not so bad, though, because I sort of knew him from before. That's actually a fairly funny story in itself. Apparently he had his hair real long in college and half-heartedly decided to get it cut for his STATS interview. Well, guess who his first interviewer was? Anyway, here's David Milstead's e-mail that he graciously gave me permission to reprint here:

Now you know why it's godawful font time again. Pick your favorite closer:

	ERA	W	L	Sv	SvOp	IP	H	BB
Mel Rojas	5.60	0	2	5	9	27.1	25	17
Jose Mesa	7.45	0	3	3	5	19.1	35	10
Heath Slocumb	8.34	0	3	6	9	22.2	35	23

The spring stats siren's song is haunting me already in the person of Mark Johnson. Now, I would've been the first one to tell you back in January that Mark Johnson was as worthless as big, white first basemen get. Then came spring. And, even though I told you, dear readers, that spring stats can be useful in creating an opportunity for a guy who needs one, I warned you that less than 100 at-bats does not a new player make. Did I listen to myself? Nada.

Mark Johnson

	Avg	AB	R	2B	HR	RBI	SLG
Spring	.398	83	15	10	7	20	.795
Now	.231	156	24	7	3	20	.333

His on-base percentage is an impressive (for him, at least) .363, which pretty much accounts for those 24 runs scored. However, that's not exactly what one is looking for from one's 6-4/230-pound first baseman. So now that Kevin Young's taking advantage of his 61st chance at a major league job, I'm stuck with Johnson playing every other game against righties.

Here's a hard, fast rule for next spring that I promise to follow: No bidding more than $5 on a guy on the basis of his spring stats. I will follow it. I will. I will. I will. (Until Chuck Carr steals 10 bases.)

6/13/97

The Pirates' Tony Womack: "The same people who keep waiting for us to fold are the ones who said we wouldn't do anything all season." What I'd like to know is, who are the *other* people?

Sorry to write about the same thing everyone else is writing about this weekend, but I have to speak my peace on this interleague baseball thang. At first I hated it, then I decided maybe it wasn't so bad, but now that it's here, I hate it more than ever. Yeah, it's curious or interesting or queer or whatever you want to call it alright (I'm going to the Phils and Blue Jays tomorrow night), but, all in all, I just wish it would've gone away before it ever started. You see, baseball is all about patience, and interleague games ruin a lot of that. Now, instead of a Yankees/Mets or Dodgers/Angels or White Sox/Cubs World Series being something really really special if it ever were to happen, the whole thing will be cheapened and watered-down. But the average fan and his kids love interleague play and it's going to bring all kinds of people back to baseball, you say. Well, I could give a rat's about the average fan and his kids. The average fan and his kids would probably love seeing all the players dressed as Lost World dinosaurs too (I can't say I'd mind that so much myself, actually), but do we have to do it? And as far as bringing fans back to baseball, as Don Zminda has pointed out about a trillion times, even though baseball isn't quite back to the pre-strike days, it's way better off than any other time in baseball, except for those pre-strike days. I hate it. It just wrecks so much that's great and unique about baseball. First the wild cards, then this. Closer and closer we creep to basketball and hockey. Ugh.

Todd Hollandsworth in the minors and Karim Garcia in the majors. Isn't that the way it was supposed to be all along?

Mike Devereaux in the minors. Isn't that the way it was supposed to be all along?

I happened to pick up a few old '70s *Street and Smith's* and *Baseball Digests* along the way over the past few weeks. There are a couple of really cool ads that I wanted to remind you of/point out to you in case you're interested or you happen to remember them. The first is on the last page of the 1971 *Street and Smith's*:

"Next Time A Loudmouth Says: I'LL BEAT THE H--- OUT OF YOU! Which of these 3 vital decisions will you make?

- COWARD'S DECISION—Slink away like a whipped dog bringing shame upon yourself and your loved ones.

- FOOL'S DECISION—Rush in and get beat up because you don't have the fighting Know How.

- WISE DECISION—Unleash a whirlwind attack and utterly destroy the loudmouth because you had the good sense to send for my FREE Terror Fighting Self-Defense course and learn my self-defense TERROR TACTICS.

Well I'd say my life's been about 90% COWARD'S DECISION and about 10% FOOL'S DECISION. I'm kind of glad I never chose WISE DECISION, because I'd probably be writing this column from state prison.

Here's the other one, from the October 1979 *Baseball Digest*:

What Would Pete Rose Hit in the Year 2001? Find out with TIME TRAVEL. Travel through time with your favorite ballplayers! TIME TRAVEL—the patented new table baseball game—lets you manage your favorite stars in any era—from the turn of the century to the distant future. Imagine Babe Ruth facing Tom Seaver... or Pete Rose at bat in the year 2001. TIME TRAVEL automatically compensates for artificial turf, the dead ball or rabbit ball, futuristic equipment.

Did any of you ever buy this game? Boy, I would love to get ahold of one. This is honestly fascinating to me. Sure, the old players versus new players thing has been done up, down, backwards, and sideways, but it's the other concept that's really fascinating. I wonder if the guy who invented this game realized that in the year 2001 there would be hardly any artificial turf left? But the two words "futuristic equipment" are the most intriguing. Like what? Roger Bresnahan in a hockey-style catcher's mask? Ted Kluszewski on steroids? Jackie Robinson with earrings and tattoos? Ah, for the opportunity to TIME TRAVEL back to 1979. How quickly I would send off my $8.95 to East Pittsburgh to play TIME TRAVEL BASEBALL GAME.

According to a transaction I read this past week, the Mets signed an OF they drafted named Jose Rijo-Berger. I'm not kidding. Is that guy a ready-made marketing campaign or what?

Rod Beaton writes last week about the Dodgers' interleague plans: "Mike Piazza gets a break for his achy knees, and Tom Prince catches. It won't provide an offensive boost. Prince hits little." That's where you're wrong, Rod. Prince can hit. He just never gets the chance to play regularly. His last couple of minor league seasons are monsters. I'll bet Prince would be no worse than middle of the pack offensively, if he got the opportunity to play every day. I hope he becomes a regular expansion catcher. He'd be a perfect choice. And besides (yes, I know, even Manny Alexander can hit for a few games), he went 2-for-3 last night in the first Dodger interleaguer.

Keep your pants on, all those of you (including me) who figured Kirt Manwaring has conclusively proven that *anyone* can hit with the Rockies. Manwaring is now down to .264/.329/.331. That includes .293/.341/.390 at home and .227/.316/.258 on the road. And if you're thinking that .390 slugging percentage ain't too bad, consider that it puts Manwaring last in home slugging percentage among teammates with more than 50 home at-bats. And next-to-last is Walt Weiss, almost 40 points higher at .429. And next-to-next-to-last is Eric Young, over a hundred points higher at .492.

And finally, Todd Van Poppel signs with the Rangers, for his 20th team tryout in the past two years. I got to thinking, isn't it the case with most, if not almost all, failed pitching prospects, that they either come to the table with problems that they never work out, like Bill Bene, or they wreck their arms, like Brien Taylor? Neither of those happened to Todd Van Poppel. So what the heck happened? What does it say for all those scouts who thought he was the greatest thing since whomever-you- want-to-name? Now, in all fairness, I must point out that the guy doesn't turn 26 until December, even though it seems like he's about 34. That means he could still screw around for a couple of years and have a fine career. Or he could still screw around for five years and have *a* career. But he sure doesn't seem anywhere close at this point.

6/20/97

Minor league mastermind John Sickels replied to my Todd Van Poppel piece last week and I got his permission to reprint it:

"When Todd Van Poppel was in high school, he could throw 95 MPH. Now, he's lucky to break 87. Why? Good question. For some reason, a lot of guys who can break the radar guns in high school lose velocity as they move up the pro ladder, even if they don't get hurt. Willie Banks is another example. He could hit 95 in high school and was once clocked at 100 in the low minors. But by the time he reached the majors, he was only hitting 91 consistently, and he soon lost even that.

"It seems to happen to a lot of high school guys, even if they don't have some sort of obvious catastrophic injury."

241

I'll infer that the scouts probably expect these high-schoolers to mature and *add* velocity (no wonder they get so excited), when in fact many *lose* velocity. Fascinating. It just goes to show, even a guy who knows everything about baseball like me can still learn a lot from John.

Continuing on a John Sickels roll, the Rangers just called up a shortstop named Hanley Frias. I knew nothing about him, so I checked out his minor league numbers and they looked pretty good, which led me to further check out my favorite STATS publication, *STATS Minor League Scouting Notebook*. Some highlights (I'm reprinting this without John's permission—nah, nah, nah-nah, nah):

"Hanley Frias has received zero heed from the prospect press, but if I needed a shortstop, I'd think about picking him up. His MLEs suggest he can hit .270 in the majors; there are shortstops who can't do that, you know. If Kevin Elster comes back to earth and if Benji Gil continues to stink, Frias could get a shot at the shortstop job. I would like to see what he could do with it."

Well, Kevin Elster came back to earth alright. And Benji Gil has continued to stink. And the new Cal Ripken, Billy Ripken, is out for four to six. So maybe we should all keep an eye on Mr. Frias.

I hear the Brewers are interested in Kevin Mitchell. Is that a match made in hell or what? Maybe things have changed, but remember how perceived-loafer-minority Gary Sheffield was treated there?

Go ahead. Pick up LaTroy Hawkins. I dare you.

I was watching the Angels/Dodgers on ESPN the other night and I couldn't help but notice the new Angel uniforms. Is it my imagination or are they a lot more reminiscent of those wonderful tasteless 1970s uniforms than the recent barrage of plain, drab, "classy" 1950s-styles? Could this be the birth of a new trend? I sure hope so. What comes around always goes around.

I've been collecting old *TSN Baseball Guides* and *Registers*. What I didn't realize before is that prior to 1972, the *Registers* include player head-shots. These books are great. They're almost like a combination *TSN Register* and *Who's Who In Baseball*. Also, up until somewhere in the 1970s, the *Registers* have wacky nicknames for many players, sometimes with detailed descriptions of how the nicknames stuck. I'll probably do a column sometime on the best ones. If you have an opportunity to pick up any of these, from the '70s back, you should. If you don't like them, give them to me. And if *TSN* was smart, they'd start re-including head-shots and wacky nicknames in their current *Registers*. What comes around always goes around.

6/27/97

Pat Hentgen, meet the hapless Red Sox.

Hey, did you catch those amazing Boone brothers? Bret's hitting .200 and Aaron was hitting .125 before he was sent down. That's a combined .194. Maybe I should give my brother a call and see what he's been up to lately. By the way, Aaron really is a pretender, not a contender. He would outhit Pokey Reese eventually though.

I caught *USA Today*'s "Commentary" guy Mike Lopresti's team analysis at this almost-half-way point. He says this about the Expos:

"The usual. No payroll. No names. Ten games above .500. Felipe Alou could make a decent team out of nine shoe salesmen."

And that got me to thinking, why the heck is every ounce of credit for the Expos always given to Felipe Alou? How about some for the farm system, the players, etc.? I swear, I haven't looked at the Expos and felt they were doomed going into any of the past several seasons. Just because Joe Average Fan doesn't know their players doesn't mean they can't be good.

And speaking of the Felipe's, I (and surely you) have heard they're trying real hard to trade David Segui to make room for Ryan McGuire. Wow. I don't care what he's done in 25 at-bats, he's a pretender too. His high end is Segui and that's not what I'd be looking for in my young first baseman's potential. His low end is Tim Hyers.

Here's a great big *who cares*? to the WNBA from me.

Time for a Brady Anderson check, say you? He's got seven homers and we're almost halfway home. Not that he's having a bad year, as his .313/.430/.465 attests to. But I guess all that talk of bulking up and new whatever-he-was-doing last season was all the bunch of hooey that it usually is. Sometimes, the ball just does things off the bat over the course of one season that it never did before and never will again. Ask Wally Joyner about his 34 dingers in 1987.

And maybe for the first time in his career, Sandy Alomar is playing like the All-Star he's frequently been.

The *New York Post*'s Phil Mushnick offered this last week about Yankee radio broadcaster John Sterling:

"Sterling has recently filed with the U.S. Patent and Trademark Office for a patent on his 'It is high. . . It is far. . . It is gone!' home-run call, which Sterling eagerly begins on all sorts of occasions—doubles off the wall, deep flyball outs, line drives that barely clear the wall and the occasional home run that actually meets Sterling's description."

Well, hooray. I have a buddy on this one too. There should be an electric shock system built into all announcer chairs to be activated at every "bek-bek-bek" or "Goodbye Mr. Spalding."

Go ahead. Pick up Kevin Gross. I dare you.

The Orioles have a couple of good-looking young starters at Triple-A, just waiting for the call. Rick Krivda sports a 3.01 ERA and a sensational 16 walk to 84 K ratio in 95.2 IP. I heard he'll be the first. Jimmy Haynes (remember him?) is at 3.44 with 113 Ks (and 55 walks) in 102 IP. Meanwhile the O's are trying to unload Shawn Boskie to make room. Good luck. I wouldn't want him either.

And a personal fave of mine, Matt Dunbar, retired. Too bad. Dunbar's troubles were the epitome of a problem I believe is responsible for many younger pitchers' failures, yet I don't ever hear this talked about—not believing in the stuff that got you there. I see these guys every once in a while. They pitch great in the minors. Great ERAs and few walks. They come to the majors and they can't throw a strike. Why? The physical conditions are no different. The mound's the same, the pitching distance is the same. I believe it's the pitcher thinking, "Gosh, I'm in the majors now. Every pitch has got to be perfect or they'll smoke me." Dunbar was great in the Yankee farm system for years. He won a spot with the Marlins in 1995. In his minor league career through last season he walked 199 in 474.2 IP. In 1995 with the Marlins, he walked 11 in seven innings. This spring, the A's basically handed him the one-out lefty job at the beginning of spring training. He totally sucked in spring. Listen up, Reggie Harris, Scott Ruffcorn, Jason Grimsley, Matt Beech, etc. If they couldn't hit you in the minors, chances are they won't hit you in the majors, either. They may hit you a little harder, but you'll adjust. But, believe me, you ain't gonna last long walking a guy an inning.

And what has happened to two pitchers I had tabbed as great sleepers for 1997, Richie Lewis and Chuck Ricci? Both opened the season with the A's. And with Billy Taylor playing Billy Bullinger, there was plenty of opportunity for anyone who stepped up in the pen. Richie Lewis was far-and-away the best Tiger pitcher last season, finishing with a 4.18 ERA while the staff ERA was 6.38. So he moves from hitter-happy Tiger Stadium to more pitcher-friendly Alameda and what happens? A 9.64 ERA. He goes down to Edmonton for a tune-up and tunes up a 5.85 ERA. At least now he's ended up at Triple-A Indianapolis for the Reds and has thrown five scoreless innings. Ricci has, to me anyway, always deserved a shot. He's been excellent in the minors since 1994, including 10 innings of 1.80 for the Phillies in 1995. He begins spring with the A's collecting the first couple saves of the spring. But he's a surprise cut, to me anyway, and starts off at Edmonton. What happens? 16.88 ERA. He gets cut and moves to the Expos' Triple-A Ottawa. What happens? 13.50 ERA. Now he hasn't pitched in a while and I don't know what's become of him. Maybe he's hurt. Maybe he's released. Maybe he's opening a pizza shop with Matt Dunbar. Go figure.

7/4/97

I recently bought a 1919 *Reach Baseball Guide* and boy is it neat. I wanted to reprint this blurb for all you folks out there who crab about the length of today's ballgames:

"The 1 to 0 game that went 18 innings on May 15th was the second 18-inning 1 to 0 game in major league history, the other being in 1882 between Providence and Detroit in the National League. The 1918 game between Washington and Chicago had many remarkable features. Neither team made a change in its lineup and 139 chances were accepted without an error. The game was played in 2 hours and 47 minutes, not a great deal longer than it frequently has taken to play nine-inning games."

The other thing that struck me about the *Guide* is the "Deaths" section. There are 10 pages of the book focusing on over two full pages in fine print of guys who died over the past year. They're separated into "Major Deaths" and "Minor Deaths." Lots of pneumonias, with quite a few tuberculoses and Spanish Influenzas thrown in. One guy "drowned in some mysterious manner" and Oliver Tebeau "committed suicide by shooting himself in his cafe." (That must hurt to get shot in the cafe.)

7/18/97

Hi. I hope you missed me as much as I miss the vacation I had last week.

Do you remember Deion Sanders? You know, the guy whom the media told us had skipped a year and was now one of the greatest leadoff hitters of all time. That was when he was hitting like .370. Do you want to know what his current OBP is? He just crossed the Steve-Moyer-acceptable-for-a-leadoff-hitter line into unacceptability at .349. And that won't go up either. Big surprise.

Speaking of greatest leadoff hitters of all time, do you want to know what Rickey Henderson's done since the Padres went against everything everyone else does and benched Greg Vaughn's trillion-dollar waste butt and started playing Rickey every day on May 25? How does .325 (49-for-151) sound, with 34 runs scored, four homers, and 15 RBI? Not bad for an old man whom nobody wants.

Fun story of the week, from ESPNet SportsZone:

"Upon being told he was the first player to have a homer reach the upper deck at Veteran's Stadium in Philadelphia since Mike Schmidt did it 22 years ago, Atlanta Braves outfielder Andruw Jones didn't know how to respond. 'I never heard of that name,' Jones said. 'I'm just starting to hear of players in the '80s and '90s.'"

Rich Robertson's numbers sure make him look a lot like a lefthanded Ricky Bones. You know, lots of hits allowed, a bunch of walks, and never as many strikeouts as walks. It has never hurt Bones, though. There's always another team that seems willing to give him a chance over someone in their farm system who might be able to pitch.

Frank Castillo at Coors Field. Woo hoo.

The *USA Today* shouts "Is Major League Baseball Fan-Friendly?" as their top sports page feature the other day. You know what I say? Who cares. I look at baseball like beer and women—necessary evils. No matter how crappy I feel the next morning, I'm still going to let loose once in a while. No matter how bad women kick me around, I'll be back for more. And I don't give a rat's whether Major League Baseball gives a rat's about me or not. I'm still going to watch on TV and follow the boxscores and enjoy myself to high heaven when I'm at the ballpark. So there.

I think all of us sabermetrician-types need to bow to the scout-types for the season Tino Martinez is having. I know that Yankee Stadium's right field fence is tailor-made for a lefty slugger and I still don't think he's really that good, but, gosh golly, he sure is beating the petunias out of the ball in 1997.

8/1/97

Two more reasons I love baseball:

1) Jason Grimsley was traded for Jamie Brewington last week.

2) Greg Cadaret is back.

By the way, STATS memory photographer Ethan Cooperson reminded us all that Jason Grimsley was once traded even-up for Curt Schilling.

Closers closers everywhere. Who will close in San Fran with big Rod and big Roberto? Who will close in Seattle with big Heathcliff and big Mike Timlin? Then there's always stinky Norm Charlton and stinky Bobby Ayala still around. Who will close in Boston? Who will close on the south side of Chicago? (Karchner already got a save last night.) Will whomever closes out the season as closer in either of those places stick as closer for next season? I love baseball.

I've gotta say I think the Mariners were crazy to let Cruz Jr. go for some late-season pitching. And I also gotta say that I'd love to see nothing more than the Giants fade and the White Sox surge now (except to see the Red Sox continue their little surge). Why? Because for years now, I've suspected this urgency to throw prospects to the wind to borrow a bunch of "proven" veteran ballplayers for the stretch run fails as often as it works. I'd love to see a real study done on this and I'll ask again this year at *Scoreboard* time. Again, the always overlooked luck factor is the key. How much more chance does an expensive acquisition have of stumbling into a hot streak for a couple of months than an unproven guy? How much less chance does an expensive acquisition have of going ice-cold for a couple of months than an unproven guy? Are these differences (if they, in fact, are at all significant—which I'll bet they might not even be) worth throwing a chunk of the team's future away for? Let me put it this way, in terms of the Giants/Sox trade. Here's how the Giants win the trade:

1) Alvarez and/or Hernandez and/or Darwin step up and carry the Giants to the division crown.

2) All six guys the White Sox got never amount to anything.

Here's how the Giants lose the trade:

1) No. 2 above doesn't happen and the Giants don't win the division.

2) No. 2 above doesn't happen and Alvarez and Hernandez and Darwin really don't make a significant contribution.

If I had to bet, I know where I'd place my money. Yet there's the media, heaping praise on the Giants and ridiculing the White Sox. And the teams that stand pat always seem to get knocked too. Could the White Sox have given Cleveland a better run for the money with the three guys they gave up (I guess four with Baines)? Maybe. Were they in danger of getting absolutely nothing for Alvarez and Hernandez come year end? Definitely. Are the Giants as smart and the White Sox as stupid as the media would have you believe? I don't think so.

Who is this 10-4, 4.27 ERA Willie Blair guy the Tigers have? He can't be the same cruddy Rockie/Padre guy I remember, can he?

I happened to notice that everyone's favorite breakout sleeper for 1997, Alex Gonzalez, is puttering along at .227/.284/.376.

8/8/97

There's only one thing that could be better than "Greg Cadaret is back:"

Scott Bailes is back.

This column's probably going to be a shorty this week because:

A) I have to do it a day early because I'm going to my in-laws' family reunion in West Virginia. (That's not a joke. This here river don't go to Aintree.)

B) I still have a ton of real work to get done today before I go.

Sorry. I'll have to put an exciting, misleading title on this in the Baseball News section so people read it anyway.

I watched a bunch of the Rangers/Yankees on ESPN last night and found out you really do learn something new every day. The Rangers' new third baseman Fernando's last name is pronounced "Tah-TEECE" not "TAY-tis" like I'll bet you (me and every other ignorant fantasy baseball geeko) were calling him. And he's got really big ears too, in case that helps you make a decision on him.

Why do the Cubs insist on finding time for Tyler Houston (.232/.260/.312) and Kevin Orie (.271/.351/.445) at the expense of Dave Hansen (.297/.429/.390) and Jose Hernandez (.279/.325/.450)? All right, I guess youth is the answer. But, let's face it, the best Tyler Houston is ever going to be is what Jose Hernandez is now. And although Orie has surprised me with decent but unspectacular numbers, the Cubs sure could use that .429 OBP of Hansen's in the lineup every day. Or at least every day they face a righty. The Cubs, playing in one of the finest hitters' parks in baseball, are, as usual, second-to-last to only the Reds' .318 in OBP at a miserable .320. Some year their guys upstairs (surely not *these* guys upstairs) will finally realize that the team pitching will never look pretty after a full season at Wrigley. They need to *get on base* to win. (Where's that on-base superstar Andre Dawson when you need him?)

Speaking of on-base superstars, my favorite *USA Today* clip from last week is this one:

"Deion Sanders has lost interest in Cincinnati, and that's a big reason for his slump."

Oh, really? I kind of thought it was the fact that he had no business doing what he was doing at the beginning of the year and he'd come back to earth sooner or later. I hate to say I told you so, but Deion's now down to a .280 batting average and a bordering-on-crappy-for-a-leadoff-hitter .338 OBP. About exactly where I told you in May he'd be about now. But, gosh golly, aren't those 52 steals pretty? (Yeah, pretty useless, except in fantasy baseball.)

But my favorite *USA Today* entire article, maybe for the whole season, has got to be Wednesday's "The Lost Arts—From bunting to base running, baseball lacks basics" Whose idea is it for this crapola, anyway?

Yup, baseball just ain't what it used to be.

"Like hitting the cutoff man and fundamental base running, bunting is a baseball nuance many see slipping away. And the dough goes to the power hitters."

Yup, baseball just ain't what it used to be.

"Just a failure to move up 90 feet or take advantage of a ball in the dirt or get a double on a ball in the gap because you don't run hard."

Yup, baseball just blah blah blah blah blah.

"It's lack of awareness."

Yup, blah blah blah blah blah blah blah.

"When Jackie would get on first and Pee Wee would bunt to the third baseman. . ."

Blah blah f-ing blah blah blah. Who cares????? Do you think I could find this same article written 10 years ago? Yes. 20 years ago? Yes. In 1920? Yes. Did you ever read things Ty Cobb said about Babe Ruth? To paraphrase, it was always something like, "That big, fat SOB, he stands there and belts the ball out of the park. What's that? He don't know nuthin' about buntin' and base stealin' and slidin' hard and scorin' runs the way they're suppose to be scored." Yup, blah blah f-ing blah blah blah. The more things change, the more they stay the same.

And guess who the two big player spokesmen are in the article? Tom Goodwin and Tony Womack. Stink and Stink-O. Give me Mickey Tettleton (retired or not) any day.

The closer myth is something else I've been giving a lot of thought to lately. The Mariners throw Jose Cruz Jr. plus a bunch of other prospects to the wind for a couple of guys, simply because they have that flashing "*closer*" halo above their heads. It doesn't matter if their ERAs are five, not one bit. They're *closer*s and *closer*s are a rare breed. Ask Kelvim Escobar. It took him his entire four-year minor league career as an exclusive starter to learn what it takes to be a top-notch closer. The Jays would've been much better off trading their whole farm system for Rickey Bottalico or Doug Jones or Norm Charlton than to just hand Escobar the ball. What were they thinking? If I were a GM (ha ha ho ho), I'd get guys 20 saves and sell them off as fast as you can say DeWayne Buice. I'd have me a regular *closer* factory, you might say, I reckon.

Just thought I'd mention, there's a Superdeedooperdee (my daughter's been Barney-ized too) article on Rickey Henderson in the August 4 *TSN*. There's a fantasy sleeper if I've ever seen one for the next few years. Rickey wants Cobb's runs scored record and Ruth's walks record, both of which he's about five seasons away from. And if anyone can do it (and if some team is gracious enough to let him and his .400 OBP play) Rickey can.

The ticklers for this new "Keenan" show promise "talk with attitude." Wow, now there's an original concept. Let's go one better. How about "extreme talk"?

8/15/97

A tale of two leadoff hitters:

	Avg	AB	R	H	OBP
Player A	.344	352	63	121	.409
Player B	.270	293	63	79	.416

Who would you say is the better leadoff hitter? One of these guys has lost a large chunk of his season to injury. The other has lost a large chunk of his season sitting behind a waste-of-free-agent-money load. One of these guys is considered, pretty much uncontested, the premier leadoff hitter in baseball. The other is considered an old man who is now a good but not great player anymore. One of these guys will make gobs of money next season. The other is always considered to be too expensive to keep and, in fact, is usually the first guy to be unloaded by any team he's with, to cut costs. Now look at those at-bat and runs scored totals and tell me, honestly, who the better leadoff man is. I don't really have to tell you who those two players are, now do I?

I think my Lance Johnson as early-season walk-monster suspicions were true. Remember, Lance, after refusing to take a walk his entire career, was all of a sudden walking like mad in April? I had hoped Johnson had seen the light. I suspected he might be walking only because his shin splints prevented him from feeling good enough to swing at everything. Here are the numbers:

	Avg	G	AB	R	H	BB
Shin Splint Lance	.296	26	98	20	29	19
Healthy Lance	.304	52	191	25	58	15

Now, which leadoff hitter do you want, the Lance who scores 20 runs in 26 games, or the Lance who scores 25 runs in 52 games? I know which the Cubs would rather have. They probably put a provision in his contract with a fine attached for every base on balls.

Yeah, yeah, it's chart day and I might as well get the last one out of the way. Did you notice when James Mouton batted cleanup for the Astros last week? (He went 2-for-4 with three ribs, but that's beside the point.) It got me to thinking about the MVP-type year Jeff Bagwell's having and the wonderful protection (load of crap) that he must be getting from the cleanup and No. 5 spots in the Houston order, if James Mouton's getting a chance. Well, here it is:

	AB	R	H	2B	HR	RBI	SB	BB	Avg	OBP	SLG
Bagwell	435	85	128	31	33	105	22	93	.294	.425	.598
Cleanup	476	57	125	26	7	61	7	55	.263	.342	.361
#5	469	60	117	31	11	52	8	45	.249	.319	.390

By the way, 433 of Bagwell's 435 at-bats are from the No. 3 spot. Geez. To hear the media and "baseball" people tell it, it would be impossible to have a season like Bagwell's having with those kind of numbers coming up behind him. It just goes to show you what hogwash protection is. But, then again, like Rob Neyer told me, inevitably, talk turns to, "Just imagine the season Bagwell would be having *with* good protection." (Like what, 60 homers and 200 RBI?)

Kenny Lofton, can you steal a base this year? *Pleeaase*?

My third-favorite minor leaguer, behind Paul Konerko and Ron Wright, Ethan Faggett, was promoted to Double-A yesterday. I looked at his numbers today and he'll probably never make the majors. And his name surely is pronounced "fah-JET" or "FAJE-wah" or something. I don't care. He's fun to have around anyway.

Ivan Rodriguez, where is that 25-30 HR power we've been expecting you to develop since you were about 11? Last time I checked, you had 12 homers and it's August 15. Oh well, maybe when you're 32 in the year 2003.

Tony Phillips. Do you remember a few months ago when the White Sox just *had* to get rid of Tony Phillips? Yes, there was all this talk of too much fire in the clubhouse and a potential dynamite keg with him and Belle and all. But it sure did seem curious to me that all this talk occurred *before* any incidents actually happened, at least that we, the stupid fans, ever heard about. Now, however, a new development. Do you get the feeling that the White Sox knew something a long time ago that we finally know now?

8/22/97

Goodbye to Eric Young as a good hitter. And goodbye to Pedro Astacio as a good pitcher. It was nice knowin' ya, guys.

Otis Nixon, can you get a friggin' hit for the Dodgers? *Pleeaase*???

Whatever happened to Kevin Elster? I heard he'd be back in September, but that was like in May. Rod Beaton, help me out here.

Are all you fantasy Jason Bere owners out there dusting him off about now?

Best *USA Today* note of the week:

"The Marlins have called up right-hander Antonio Alfonseca, who has six fingers on his throwing hand."

That's fascinating to me and I wonder if there's ever been a six-fingered major leaguer prior to Alfonseca. I will refrain from making my own stupid quip to go along with the ones you'll be seeing from everyone else.

There were a couple of real pretty pitching outings, within a couple of days of each other, put on for our entertainment by David Wells and Robert Person. Let's take a last look at them for all of you fantasy owners (I have Person in a couple of leagues) out there:

	IP	H	ER
Wells	3.0	10	11
Person	3.2	9	9

But then again, nothing can shock a Ken Hill owner anymore.

Do you remember making Strat-O-Matic or Statis-Pro or APBA batting lineups up as a kid? This is how I used to do mine:

#1—Guy with a high batting average and lots of steals but not much power.

#2—Guy who could bunt well. Often couldn't hit at all.

#3—Best overall hitter on the team.

#4—Guy with lots of homers and usually at least a decent batting average. Often the runner-up to #3.

#5—Guy with lots of homers and often not much else.

#6 through #9—Best guy left.

I noticed Cito Gaston batting Mariano Duncan (.263 OBP this season, .250 for the Jays) second every day since his acquisition and I wondered if Cito still does his lineup like I did when I was 11. Then, I looked at the Blue Jays. Did you realize there's currently no active player on the team with 100 at-bats and even a .350 OBP? Maybe I'd bat Duncan second too (just kidding). The Jays should thank God for Shannon Stewart.

I was all set to do my Red Sox commercial by running post-All-Star standings. But here they are:

American League

East		Central		West	
Yankees	28-13	Brewers	23-20	Angels	25-17
Orioles	25-14	White Sox	20-22	Mariners	22-18
Red Sox	26-16	Indians	21-23	Rangers	17-25
Blue Jays	20-23	Twins	15-25	A's	14-25
Tigers	18-23	Royals	16-26		

National League

East		Central		West	
Marlins	23-16	Astros	24-15	Dodgers	24-16
Phillies	21-15	Pirates	20-21	Padres	23-17
Braves	21-19	Reds	17-21	Giants	20-20
Mets	20-20	Cards	17-23	Rockies	18-21
Expos	15-24	Cubs	13-27		

There goes the Red Sox commercial. The Yankees have been so hot and the Orioles have been so lucky (they haven't won a game by more than three runs since August 12 and they've won a grand total of one game by more than three since that time), that Boston isn't any higher in these standings than they are in the real ones. But what struck me, as it does about a million times a season, is the magnifying glass on early-season play. Imagine if the above chunk of the season began on Opening Day instead of at the All-Star break. Some sample feature headlines we'd be seeing:

"Phrancona's Phantastic Phils"

"World Champs Look Unbeatable Again"

"Can Garner's Surprising Brew Crew Keep It Up?"

"Poor Felipe Alou"

"What's The Problem In Atlanta?"

"Pirates, Giants Still At .500 In May"

Etc. Like I say every year, keep this stuff in mind next May.

8/27/97

Get ready for the shortest Babble-On you've seen in a long time. I'm off to ESPN tomorrow and I just ain't got the time, man.

Jason Isringhausen looks like he's at about the Pete Harnisch stage in his comeback.

Scott Karl looks like he's got about the quietest seven-game win streak of all time.

Ethan Cooperson looks like John Smoltz. But apparently everyone but me knew that already.

252

Dave Pinto pointed out Aunt Fritzi's bikini to me on Tuesday. (He also mentioned that he prefers her nightgown with the one strap falling off.)

Allan Spear pointed out "What Rey Sanchez Brings To The Yankees" to me yesterday:

a. Bad attitude
b. Hypochondria
c. Abysmal baserunning
d. Flashy but inconsistent fielding
e. No power
f. No patience at the plate
g. No clutch hitting
h. Silly spelling of first name

You can tell I didn't make that list up because I don't know what hypochondria and abysmal mean.

Mike Grace returned from his long vacation to show that he's still Mike Grace—I'll take the ball five times a season but when I do, it's gonna be damn good. Is there a Steve Ontiveros in the house?

Speaking of the Phillies, what the heck has happened to Ricky Bottalico lately?

Speaking of the Phillies, guess who has more double-digit K outings this year, Curt Carlton or Randy Johnson? That's right, Curt has 15 to Randy's 13.

Speaking of the Phillies, I feel sorry for Phillie fans because Midre Cummings has decided to hit .346 since he's arrived in Philadelphia. Terry Francona thinks he's good. Too bad. Someone needs to get the tools out of Francona's eyes. They already have one Derrick May and they sent him to the minors.

Speaking of the Phillies, Billy McMillon. Now there's a player.

Speaking of the Phillies, Matt Stairs is having about the quietest butt-kicking season of all time. (Yeah, I know he has nothing to do with the Phillies. I figured continuity might help make up for length this week. That's what she said, I guess.) He has 22 homers and 16 doubles in 254 at-bats. He's hitting .331/.418/.654 with 51 runs scored and 61 RBI. For goodness sake, he's having Pat Lennon's season (what I thought, anyway). Not that I'd toot my own horn, but back in the 1992 *Baseball Scoreboard* there's an article written by a timid, green STATS employee entering his second STATS baseball season that touts Stairs as a longshot prospect to keep an eye on. Never mind that he was an Expo second baseman and that two of the other guys I wrote about were Luis Mercedes and Juan Guerrero. Chad Curtis was another and he's not been doing too bad lately either.

Finally, keep this in mind the next time *USA Today* tells you to be happy because your team has pillaged the farm for a pennant-stretch-proven closer. Oscar Palacios points out that Matt

Karchner's numbers look like 0.00 ERA, 10 saves, 10 ops, 10.2 IP, five hits allowed, and nine Ks since the trade that obviously doomed the White Sox.

9/4/97

I've talked to a former major league basestealer and a current major league consultant about the biggest mystery, in my mind, of the 1997 baseball season. Kenny Lofton now has 21 stolen bases and 20 caughts. His previous full-season stolen-base low prior to this year is 54. His previous full-season caught-stealing high prior to this year is 17 (last year, when he stole 75 bases). Both experts I spoke to felt his injury troubles this year are his major problem. One of the experts feels that it's clear that Lofton has lost a step. He also told me that many basestealers survive early in their careers on pure speed and then they must go through a transition period of learning to use their heads as much as their feet. Lofton is likely at that point. His almost total failure as a stolen-base threat this season has to make him the most interesting fantasy player going into 1998. Let's face it, what's kept him afloat as a good player this season is his astronomical batting average that he somehow continues to maintain. But I guarantee, he ain't gonna hit .350 next year.

Hensley "Bam Bam" Meulens is back in the major leagues. Woo hoo. If he'd have hit a homer for every fantasy article written about him in the late '80s, he probably would have had a career.

If you can still latch onto Todd Helton in your fantasy league, do it. I think you've gotta make room for him next year if you're in a keeper league. Also pick up Paul Konerko now if you're in a league that only allows major leaguers, now that he is one. He'll be a little harder to hang onto, but if you have the room, do it. From everything I hear, he's the Dodger 3B next year. And if he can hit half of what he has hit in the minors, what a fine fantasy 3B he'll be.

Todd Worrell. There can't be any two sweeter words to Dodger opponents in the late innings recently. Hey, don't the Mariners need another closer?

Pete Rose Jr. Who cares? Why does he deserve the call-up when so many better guys don't get it? You know why as well as I do. While his daddy deserves reinstatement at this point, Petey Jr. doesn't deserve squat. He's gotta be the only former replacement player that everyone seems to have totally forgiven and forgotten about. This nepotism crap has gone too far. It's definitely been responsible for some way-overrated prospects the past few years. Do Eduardo Perez and the Boone brothers ring a David Bell? Rose Jr. is almost 28 years old and couldn't hit at Triple-A for heaven's sake. Don't believe the hype. Pete Rose Jr. is neither a prospect nor a major league-caliber ballplayer.

By the way, I'm off this weekend to a midwest baseball extravaganza. Saturday, I'll be at my first Tiger Stadium game ever, to see two of my faves, Rickey and Tony, take on the Tigers. Then, Sunday at Wrigley and Monday night at Comiskey. I can't wait. If you're going to be at one of those games, look for me and my dad (it's his birthday present) and m three buddies. We'll be the obnoxious beer drinkers (not my dad) talking like we know everything about baseball (I do). I'm sure I'll have lots of stories for next week.

9/12/97

Now, for what you've all been waiting for:

My Late-Summer Vacation
by Steve Moyer

Friday, September 5—My dad and I get up early and wait for Jerry and Jim to pick us up. They get to my place at 7:30. We leave. Our first stop is at a Denny's somewhere along PA Route 80 for breakfast. I get a fiesta omelette. Jim and I break down and spend the extra 59 cents for a hologram baseball card, because if either of us get Frank Thomas, our meal is free. Jim gets someone whom I don't remember, but it's not Frank Thomas. My pack is a freak in that it contains two cards, Jason Kendall and Dante Bichette (boo), neither of which are Frank Thomas. We're on our way. Route 80 is boring as all get-out. At 3:20 eastern time, somewhere in Ohio, we start trying at half-hour intervals to pull in the Cub game on the radio. We finally get it in about in time to hear Harry say, "Let's Get Some *Runs*," in the seventh, something I haven't heard in over a year. The Cubs end up rallying late in the game to beat the Mets. We arrive at John's house in South Bend at about 6:30. We proceed to the Catfish Lounge (John's basement, filled with all kinds of baseball stuff hanging on the wall) for beers. Jason Bere turns human on TV against the Indians. Greg Maddux is his usual non-human self against the Padres. We go to bed.

Saturday, September 6—Up early for Blueberry Morning breakfast and into the car at 8:00 for the trip to Detroit. I've never been to a game at Tiger Stadium, so this is the day I've looked forward to the most. However, going back on I-80 for three and a half hours from where we came yesterday is kind of driving me crazy. We get there eventually. Our seats are fantastic. To me, Tiger Stadium is what old-time stadiums are all about. You need that musty cement smell around the concession stands. You need those visible girders and stuff. You need that totally-enclosed-by-metal feeling that I just don't get at Wrigley Field. I loved it. I cheered extra loud for Rickey Henderson (one of my faves, as all of you should obviously know) and Tony Phillips (just to tick—I'm not sure the "p" word works on AOL—everyone off). One of my players, Bobby Higginson, hits a grand slam. We saw Juan Encarnacion ("Encarnation" on our league's roster sheet) hit his first major league homer. Jim calls him Juanster Jr. now. I was only disappointed in the fact that Bob Hamelin didn't play. We drove home later and watched more baseball on TV that night. It was, all in all, a very fine day.

Side Note—Tiger Stadium was great. The Tiger mascot, "Paws," however, was probably the most pathetic mascot I've ever seen. For those of you who don't know, he's just a plain old guy in a Tiger suit, maybe with a baseball hat on. He's not clever or funny or anything really. And his suit. . . *aye caramba*. It looked all ratty and moth-eaten and about 25 years old. Believe me, there were plenty of "Paws" jokes during the rest of the trip.

Sunday, September 7—We boarded the train at South Bend at about 8:30 for the el in Chicago and, eventually, Wrigley Field. We did have enough time to stop in at the Cubby Bear for lunch and the beginning of football's Week 2, in all its glory on the million Cubby Bear TV screens. I hadn't had a Goose Island beer in over a year, which I thoroughly enjoyed. The weather was gloomy, which kind of spoiled the day a bit, as did Steve Trachsel, from whom I really needed a LABR win. Trachsel pitched great the first couple of innings, started getting behind batters around the third, after which they'd smash the ball right at a Cub fielder. A couple of innings later, the smashes were no longer at the Cub fielders. I followed Tony Saunders getting the bejeezuz pounded out of him, Andy Benes mysteriously leaving a superb 2-2 performance in Coors Field early (later that night I learned the disastrous news), and the beginning of Denny Neagle's usual wonderful pitching against the Padres, all on the Cub scoreboard. Bobby Jones got his first victory since about 1993 to beat Trachsel for the Mets. The highlight of the Cub game was a guy sitting a row in front of us, who, to me, epitomizes what's wrong with Wrigley Field. He wanted to talk baseball constantly with my group even though he really had no clue about this season. He scored the game (one of those guys, obviously, who thinks it makes him a real baseball fan because he scores) even though he didn't know who most of the players were. (And he'd write 8X for a flyout to center—whatever that's supposed to mean.) He announced to us very early on that he doesn't like the Cubs, or even baseball very much, for that matter (believe me, it wasn't hard to tell), he was here mostly for the atmosphere. (I did notice he had "Let's get a team" written on his scorecard at the very beginning of the game. I wondered what the heck that was for. Well, when Harry had gotten done singing, he started frantically yelling, "Let's get a *team*" about four times. At this point, even I felt kind of bad for the guy. Apparently, he dreamed this up and was so excited about it, he wrote it on his scorecard so he wouldn't forget to yell it during the seventh-inning stretch. I think he fantasized that all the fans around him would start cracking up when he yelled. Needless to say, no one did.) Anyway, back to the subject. I've always felt Wrigley was filled with too many atmosphere seekers and partiers and people who just don't really give a crap about baseball. And I don't need 'em. Go to the park and feed the birds or something. Enough lecture. We went home, figured out how our football players had done, and went to bed.

Monday, September 8—We didn't have a ballgame to go to until the evening, so I spent Monday afternoon farting around at the South Bend mall and Value City (where I bought my wife a Vikings winter coat—that's Minnesota Vikings, not like a big piece of bear fur and watching a super 1975 show on Bigfoot. We left in the car for Comiskey about 5:00 Jerry's brother-in-law had corporate seats right behind the White Sox dugout. It was great I had never sat that close before. I even got on the JumboTron. Former STATSer Dave Munde saw me and sent me a mail message about it the next day. Current STATSer Peter Woelflei didn't see me though, because I looked up at him in the press box and he was just looking down at his computer. The game was probably the best game for a game's sake we saw al weekend as the Sox and Brewers battled back and forth until Matt Karchner had his first ba outing since the Giant trade. In the bottom of the ninth, with the score tied, Frank Thoma led off with a walk. Albert Belle followed. We argued back and forth about what Bevingto should have done with Belle. Shockingly enough, I almost think you need a bunt in that situation, where you absolutely need one run and no more. It sure is difficult to take the bat out of the hands of an extra-base threat like Belle's hands, though. Bevington let Belle hit, he lined out to right, the White Sox didn't score, and lost the game in the 10th. Oh well. What do you think of people who leave a tie game in the seventh inning? There was a pretty big swarm of them. Why come to the game at all? They should hang out with my buddy from Wrigley. (By the way, I forgot to mention above, we did talk about inviting that guy into our Rotisserie league, so that after the expansion draft we could immediately rape all his good players from him.) Finally, someone in our group reminded the rest of us that if we had been sitting behind the dugout at Tiger Stadium, "Paws" would've been dancing in front of us and we could've tripped him.

Tuesday, September 9—Back in the car at 7:30 for the nightmare trek along I-80 home. I got home to my wife and daughter, who couldn't stop saying, "Dadadadada" all evening. It's nice to know someone misses you.

(I just realized in spell-checking this that Blurb spelled incorrectly is Blubr.)

I know it's awfully cliché about now, but I'll miss you a lot, Rich Ashburn, wherever you may be.

9/18/97

It's about time to conclude that, contrary to previous notion, not everyone can hit at Coors Field. Kirt Manwaring is hitting .229/.296/.281 in 327 at-bats with only a couple weeks of the season left. That includes .253/.306/.329 at Coors. Without doing any research whatsoever, I'll state that Manwaring's 1997 is the worst Rockie hitter season put up at Coors Field with any decent at-bat total in history. I happened to notice something else interesting about Manwaring's 1997 along the way. Of those 327 at-bats, 301 came as the No. 7 hitter in the Rockie order. Which got me to thinking, why the heck would you let anyone (besides maybe the pitcher) hit behind Kirt Manwaring? Manwaring is conclusively the worst Rockie hitter of all time. For 1997, the only guys who've had a worse year are John Vander Wal at .163/.250/.221 in less than 100 at-bats (don't ask me what happened there) and Craig Counsell at 0-for-1. Most of the No. 8 Rockie at-bats were put up by Walt Weiss, who at least gets on base, and Neifi Perez, who at least hits with some pop. What was Don Baylor thinking all year? Don't ask me.

Speaking of Rockies, I think Pedro Astacio is on a personal mission to prove me wrong by saying bye-bye to him when he moved to Coors. To his credit, he has been pitching his butt off lately. However, as Bill James pointed out in an e-mail discussion this past week, Astacio has managed to avoid Coors in all but two of his outings thus far and in those two outings his ERA is over four. I think if you're in a fantasy league that holds onto a lot of players from season to season, now's the time to unload Pedro Astacio. You'll be glad you did when his ERA's at about five and a half next All-Star break.

Go ahead, get Willie Banks. I dare you.

Over at the little corner store by my house, I noticed a pack of 1997 Pinnacle baseball cards the other day. Guess who is pictured on the wrapper? Andruw Jones. Now I like Andruw Jones as much as the next guy, but, boy, has the state of baseball cards changed. Do you think in 1975 you would've seen a rookie who hadn't done much of anything yet on the wrapper? (Actually, back then, I don't even think they put actual players on the wrapper, just hokey cartoon pictures of generic players.) The whole modern baseball card industry is perverse anyway. I stay away from that nonsense.

You've probably seen this quote from Ozzie Guillen already, whining about his fear that he won't get re-signed by the White Sox, concerning his age:

"It's not important. I see players who are 25 and can't play this game."

I see one who's 33 and can't either. When baseball wins can be attributed to walking the fewest amount of times, Ozzie will be a gem. That's when the White Sox (or anyone else) would be smart to sign him. Makes me think of a lame movie for a lame player: "Look Who's Talking."

Why doesn't Bud Selig just go away? Who likes this wienerschnitzel? Anybody? The stupid six divisions and ultra-stupid wild-card crap wasn't enough. Now, we've gotta put every other National League team in the American League and vice versa. Go back to selling cars, Bud, a subject you might know something about. I'll go follow soccer or something. (Just kidding. No one could make baseball bad enough to justify following soccer.)

I was going to warn you about getting excited about 31-year-old Phillie rookie Darrin Winston until I looked more closely at his numbers. He's a strange case in that he had been a reliever almost exclusively during his minor league career and now comes to the majors as a starter. We've seen the reverse over and over again, but this is kind of weird. And, with the exception of his last season before this one, 1995—he quit baseball in 1996 altogether— his ERAs have been acceptable to excellent. In fact, I'll bet he's a player whom the scouts never really liked very much and, therefore, never got all the chances he probably deserved. You might want to take a flyer on this guy even though he's 31. (He's almost three years older than Willie Banks, for example.)

A guy who I'm really excited about is the reverse case I talked about in the previous paragraph —the Astros' Jose Cabrera. Here's a guy who middled along as a minor league starter and has really kicked in out of the pen. His combined Triple-A 1997 numbers, you ask? 8-2, 7 IP, 47 H, 27 BB, 70 K, 2.01 ERA. His 1997 numbers in his cup o' coffee so far? 10.1 IP, H, 3 BB, 12 K, 0.87 ERA. I know 10 innings don't mean much of anything, but I'd take thi guy at the end of my draft next spring if I were you.

My daughter (who will turn one this Saturday) said her first word this past week, "I". Yo can tell she's a daddy's girl. (Actually, the word she says is "eye" because her mom's bee pointing eye, nose, mouth with her for weeks, but, heck, that would ruin my stupid littl closer.)

10/3/97

Sorry about last week. I was at ESPN Thursday, got home Friday afternoon, and just ran out of Babble-On time. I hope I didn't ruin too many of your weekends for lack of silly sports journalism. I had so much good stuff to say that's too outdated for now, too. Too bad.

I told you before and I'll tell you again, the Dodgers are still going to catch the Giants. (And the Red Sox are going to be the World Champs, too.)

Wasn't it kind of strange to see former center-field rookie of the year Jerome Walton at first base during playoff Game 1? Walton's story is a funny one in that he's gone from being a speedster-type guy to a patience-and-power-type guy over the years. The only guy I can ever remember doing that was Lonnie Smith. I think Walton's a more valuable player now than he was years ago and I like him.

Last year, I gave you the order of how much I'd like to see each team win the World Series and, even though the whole thing's well on its way already, I'll tell you again. From most to least:

1. Giants—Barry needs a ring.
2. Astros—Just for the helluvit.
3. Yankees—Because so many people hate them and I got to go to a game (details later).
4. Mariners—Randy, Alex. They have an injured guy named Moyer, even though I don't really like him.
5. Indians—Thome. I kind of feel sorry for them because their dynasty fell apart before it happened.
6. Orioles—I like Davey Johnson. I don't like a lot of their other guys (Ripken especially).
7. Braves—Pitching, defense, and timely hitting again. B-O-R-I-N-G.
8. Marlins—We'd never hear the end of Leyland's genius.

Oh, before I forget. Remember, playoff experience is everything. Ask Randy Johnson, Andy Pettitte, Jaret Wright, David Cone, Edgar Renteria, Gary Sheffield, Orel Hershiser, etc. etc. etc. etc.

Important News Bulletin—"Pete Rose Jr. likely will be removed from the Reds' 40-man roster soon," Rose's agent, Brian Goldberg, said.

OK, raise your hands, all of you who thought Pete Rose Jr. was a good player, deserving of a 40-man roster spot. Fools. The guy's almost 28 years old and was about the biggest charity-publicity-nepotism case of a major league cup o' coffee I've ever seen. His best hope is to be the 40th man on the Devil Ray roster or something.

Speaking of Pete Rose, here's what I think about his reinstatement. It's like some crummy former Eagles guy (not those Eagles, THOSE Eagles) once wrote:

"Forgiveness. Forgiveness. Even if, even if, you don't love me anymore."

259

(Yeah, the love part doesn't really make sense, but who cares?)

It's good to be back east. Because, for my money, last night is what baseball is all about.

It's my birthday tomorrow. Keep those cards and letters coming.

10/10/97

As things are getting back to normal after last season's fluke, when a team I was actually hoping for won the World Series, you may have noticed that the four bottom teams in the order I gave you last week of who I was hoping for, are now left. And it just so happens that the Indians, the team I'd like to see win the most, are given about a snowball's chance in hell from everyone I've read. Wouldn't it be kind of neat to see David Justice and Marquis Grissom on TV in October in a different uniform, *against* the Braves? I sure hope the AL wins, though, even if it has to be the sacred holy almighty Cal Ripken and the Orioles. I wish both NL teams could lose. I guess I like the so-full-of-what-it-takes-to-win-in- the-playoffs-pitching-and-defense-and-playoff-experience-loaded-that-they've-won-all-of-one-World-Series-even-though-they're-in-the-playoffs-every-year Braves just a little better than the see-I-told-you-Leyland-is-such-a- genius-now-that-he-has-five-trillion-dollars-worth-of-players-to-work-with-and-it's-too-bad-the-poor-thing-best-manager-in-baseball-had-to-spend-all-those-years-whining-about-how-he-had-nothing-to-work-with-with-the-Pirates-they-sure-missed-him-this-year-didn't-they Marlins.

Speaking of playoff experience, our little STATS e-mail baseball discussion group talked at length about it last week. To make a long story short, I think it's all hooey. Bill James said he thinks I'm wrong, that he thinks a study would reveal that a team that was in the playoffs the season before beats a team that wasn't probably 55% of the time. Someone else replied questioning how much 55% means anyway. Don Zminda said we'd do it as a *Scoreboard* essay this year and, until that's accomplished, we're all just talking. And he's right. However, I don't know if *that* particular study, even if it shows the last-year team beats the new team 80% of the time, would shut me up anyway. There's so much dire importance given to playoff experience that study doesn't take into account. Some questions I'd like answered about the oh-so-important playoff experience factor:

1) Is it a team thing or an individual player thing, or both?

2) When does it go away? If you miss the playoffs one year, do you start from scratch? If you were in the playoffs 10 years ago, but not since, does it still count?

3) Rafael Belliard is now participating in his sixth playoffs in the past seven years. Gary Sheffield's never been in the playoffs before. You know what my next question's going to be. And, the answer is, of course not. But, if playoff experience is so important, there must be an answer to the question. How many more years of playoff experience make Rafael Belliard more dangerous than Gary Sheffield in the playoffs?

4) What stats, exactly, does playoff experience help? As with my previous question, if I took any other winning ingredient and asked the same two questions, the answers would be easy. If Rafael Belliard had Mark McGwire's power, you might say he'd be as dangerous as Gary Sheffield. If Rafael Belliard had Deion Sanders' speed, he wouldn't be as dangerous as Sheffield, but he'd be a helluva lot more valuable than he is. So what does Rafael Belliard's vast playoff experience buy him? Well, I say it buys him nothing. That's my story and I'm stickin' to it.

Yes, he was talked about quite a bit during the season, but did you take a look at the final 1997 numbers Rick Reed put up? 13-9 record is OK, 2.89 ERA is nice. 208.1 IP is nothing to scoff at. But a 113-to-31 strikeout-to-walk ratio is pretty special. A ratio like that tells me this is no fluke we're talking about here. And the funny thing is that this guy was a scrub, a replacement player whom all the world had a jolly good time laughing and joking about a few short springs ago. He looked good to me back then and he looks better now. Don't believe what *they* tell you. Figure it out for yourself.

You know, I even felt a little bit sorry for the Orioles when they lost on Grissom's dinger last night. Jim Thome's two-out check-swing ball four sure looked like a check-swing strike three from the overhead camera angle. Oh, well.

Did you catch that missed defensive DP opportunity by the Orioles late in the game, when Alomar handled the pivot throw at second base kind of funky-like and threw the ball over Palmeiro's head? It made me laugh and think at the same time. (Sort of like walk and chew gum.) If that would've been Wilton Guerrero or Luis Castillo in there, how the announcers would have gone on and on about a rookie mistake, the kind a veteran guy just wouldn't make. Since it was Alomar, they just kind of glossed over it.

The Dodger chokage still fascinates me. I've been wanting to blame Darren Lewis in the lineup everyday down the stretch so badly. But in the end, I guess I have to go along with the fact that it was a pitching collapse. This past week I was talking to a good friend/baseball consultant of mine. He said the Dodger fall was due to two factors:

1) Todd Worrell.

2) The San Francisco Giants were the biggest overachievers of all time, due to the fact that they were the first team ever to win a division while being outscored. (I think that's the fact. If it's not exactly, it's close.) Nice people say they were overachievers. I'd call them lucky. Don't bet a Rey Ordonez rookie card on them next year.

The Todd Worrell thing was really interesting to me. Looking back, he's 100% correct. Worrell blew two games in particular that didn't seem nearly as significant at the time as they do now:

On August 25, the Dodgers enter the ninth inning three outs away from taking a doubleheader from the Pirates, with a 3-1 lead. Worrell comes in. Walk, homer, homer, and it's a split.

On September 2, Worrell enters a slugfest with the Rangers, intending to bail out Scott Radinsky. The score's 12-8, the bases are loaded, and nobody's out. Just the stuff a veteran closer like Worrell's made of. A walk and two singles and a bunt fly out later, the game is tied (the subsequent reliever made a loser out of Worrell), and Worrell's in the showers.

After both of these games, the Dodgers still held slim division leads and everybody, like me, figured, no big deal, they'd prevail. They didn't. Hello, 1998. Hello, Antonio Osuna.

10/17/97

Anyone remember Andujar Cedeno?

It's official. The Tiger Brian Hunter is now the real Brian Hunter. The sleepy-eyed original Brian Hunter is now the other Brian Hunter. The laws of nature say both of them cannot spend an entire season in the major leagues at the same time.

My big discovery of this week is that Juicy Fruit gum really tastes a lot like bubble gum, but you never think so because it isn't pink.

For a guy who, number-wise, seems to be a real solid ballplayer, after watching Omar Vizquel on TV, one wonders how he manages to hit his way out of a paper bag. I think the guy would be thinking about laying down a bunt with the bases loaded and two outs. Can he leave the bat in a friggin' vertical position for an entire postseason at-bat? (You know what I mean, I think. I got this funny picture in my head of Vizquel chopping at the ball like a tomahawk, which, I guess was what coaches were trying to teach Vince Coleman to the bitter end.)

Just when people were really starting to believe that Sandy Alomar was the most overrated player in baseball, he has to go out and have a career year and personally be responsible for like seven of the Indian postseason wins. Now we'll have to start all over. (Maybe he was beginning to believe he was overrated too.)

Last weekend we did some yardwork and I was burning leaves and the stuff we cut down and having a few beers at the same time. Let me tell you, nothing will make you feel more like a man than burning stuff and drinking beer in your backyard. Testosterone city.

So now they've done it. A stinkin' unbelonging wild-card team has made the World Series —already. What did the Braves get for the best record in baseball? The right to get beat in a short series by a team that finished behind them over the grueling 162-game schedule. The NHL and NBA would be proud. You know, STATS' Oscar Palacios mentioned in a recent baseball e-mail that, the fact is, as soon as you go to a playoff system, any system at all, there's a chance that the best team won't win. Logic follows that the more teams you let in, the more chance the best one won't win. And, I know this is sick, but, for my tastes and an a world of order, they could make me much happier by eliminating the playoffs altogether. Just start with a 162-game schedule and all the teams in one big group. Keep playing until either the 162 games has run out or every team but one is mathematically eliminated. Then you're done. Viwolla! (I don't know how to spell that word, so I picked the most ridiculousl easy way to pronounce it.) You've got a true champion every year. You'd better hope they never make me commissioner.

I actually hate to even suggest it, but, if I were an expansion team, I think I'd take a flyer on Dave McCarty. (Suckerrrrr.) He punished Triple-A pitching again for about the ninth year in a row.

So how did it work out for all you folks who thought Pat Listach was on the comeback trail as the new Astro shortstop at the beginning of the season? Did he do well for you?

I was going to tell you how although Marquis Grissom is a crappy leadoff hitter, he's a really good No. 9 hitter. But, unfortunately, after looking at the AL average No. 9 hitter, he's only a little above average (thanks Kevin Fullam for pointing that out). That should teach me for trying to build up Grissom.

10/24/97

Your homework assignment for next week: Explain in detail how pitching, defense, and postseason experience win championships within the context of the 1997 World Series.

In umpteen years of NFL playoffs, I think I'm correct in saying there's been one wild-card champion. It looks a whole lot like major league baseball is going to have one in exactly its second season of diluted playoffs. Is everyone happy now?

And one more thing. If they can change this (dilute the playoffs) and change that (realignment) and change every other thing (interleague play), why can't they change what really needs changing and give the teams with the better record home-field playoff advantage over the others? I don't have a problem with the World Series home team being predetermined, but every round of playoffs leading up to it should have the home team determined by record. Don't you think that makes sense? But why don't I hear any motions to change that?

My wife and I got into this mentoring program at church for the teenagers in cat class. We have a boy in eighth grade. I'm glad to say he's into sports and we talked a little football and World Series last Sunday. Guess who his favorite baseball player is? Yup, Cal Ripken. That makes two kids I know from church who like baseball and both like Cal Ripken as their favorite. Argh. I gotta start steering these kids right.

Do you believe all the bad press Kenny Lofton is getting all of a sudden? Years ago, before he had done anything, I thought Lofton was way overrated as a prospect. Just to show you I'm not *always* right (hope I don't lose any readers there), I have to embarrassingly admit I thought the Astros would eventually be better off with Eddie Taubensee than with Lofton. But after five successful seasons and constant media drumming in my head about how Lofton was baseball's premier sparkplug, I was coming around to the fact that Lofton was really a pretty decent player. Now, after one subpar but certainly not horrible season, and a bad postseason (where three lucky hits can mean a huge batting average difference), I'm hearing nothing but how Lofton's a choker, losing it on defense, selfish, a bad guy to have around on the team, etc. How this can happen in one season is what I want to know. I think Lofton is definitely baseball's biggest, most interesting individual player puzzle for 1998.

You know, with all this "No. 32" Marlin reverence and all, you'd think Alex Fernandez was dead or something. From what I heard, he might be back at the All-Star break already.

My one-year-old daughter has led me to the realization at 37 years of age that "Twinkle, Twinkle Little Star" and the "A-B-C-D-E-F-G" song are really the same song in disguise. Who is behind this conspiracy to fool the youth of America? Which song was the original and which one copied? Lawsuits need to be filed. Immediately.

I've been quite intrigued by the discussion I hear over and over again about sliding into first. The general consensus is that it's not a helpful thing to do and it actually slows the runner down. Tim McCarver, I believe, said what made the most sense to me in that, "you never see a sprinter dive for the finish line." The only thing that doesn't make sense to me is, why do runners continue to do it so often if it hurts the runner's chances of reaching safely? Why don't coaching staffs crack down on the guys who do it and break them of this bad habit? I have no answers on this (what a surprise), just questions.

11/7/97

Au pair has now replaced paparazzi as our new media word of the month.

Deion Sanders turned down his $2.5 million option to stay with the Reds next season. I certainly hope it's for reasons other than he thinks he's worth more. God help the silly team that pays him more. God help the silly team that pays him at all. He would be valuable as a minimum-wage pinch-runner/defensive sub.

It's too late now to rant about how sad it is to see baseball get its first second-place champion. I'll try to be positive. I'm happy for Darren Daulton. I'm happy for Jim Eisenreich. I'm happy for John Cangelosi. I'm happy for Gary Sheffield. I'm a little happy for Bobby Bonilla. I guess I can stop now.

Please, please, please, you fantasy geeks out there, beware of the Arizona Fall League. Each time the new *Baseball Weekly* comes out, say to yourself:

Fifty at-bats mean nothing. 100 at-bats mean nothing. 150 at-bats mean little.

Then say:

Ten innings pitched mean nothing. 25 innings pitched mean nothing. 50 innings pitched mean little.

If I can refresh your memories for a second, Donnie Sadler was Alex Rodriguez about this time last year and Paul Konerko was J.R. Phillips. Don't make the same mistakes again Remind *me* to repeat my own mantra during spring training games.

Speaking of *BBW*, I like their cover blurb this week: "Philadelphia's Scott Rolen and Boston's Nomar Garciaparra are our choices for Rookies of the Year." Talk about out on a limb. If I can refresh your memories for a second, last spring I picked Frank Catalanotto, then of the Oakland A's, as my AL Rookie of the Year. Now that's a real man's pick.

Last too-late World Series comment: Why are big baseball scores viewed as bad and small scores viewed as good? Why is it that if the pitchers are failing it's a bad thing, but if the hitters are failing, that's OK? I swear, it's another after-effect of this "purist" "little ball" "real baseball" nonsense that has existed since Babe Ruth started knocking the crap out of all those little scrubby hit-'em-where-they-ain't-and-run-real-fast guys back in the 1920s.

I read somewhere that the Cubs are considering Eric Karros for Mark Grace. That same somewhere said that Karros would be just what the Cubs need. Yeah, substituting a career .319 OBP for a career .384 OBP on a team that tied for second-to-last in the most important hitting stat there is would be just the ticket.

Raise your hand if you knew Jeff Reed hit 17 homers last year? That's tied for eighth-best in the majors in only 256 at-bats. Now, guess how many were at home and how many on the road? Wrong. He hit eight on the road. He is more fuel for my theory that catcher hitting skills often develop way later than other position players. My theory on this theory is that catching is such a demanding defensive position that it takes longer to get the hang of it and, when catchers finally do, sometimes the hitting starts to blossom post-30.

I picked up a 1980 *Street & Smith's* for a couple bucks at a flea market the other weekend. Get a load of this, in an article written by Phil Collier, "new president of the Baseball Writers Association of America":

"However, Kuhn is hopeful the NL might look favorably on his proposal for a 'wild card' DH. Here's how it would work:

"A 'wild card' DH could be substituted for any hitter in the lineup and could be used three or four times a game, at the manager's choosing.

"The possibilities have to be frightening from a pitcher's point of view. Any time he got himself into a bases-loaded jam, a pitcher could be certain of having to face the other team's 'wild card' DH."

Yee hah. And you thought our friend Bud had wild ideas. Wild-card DH. I don't like the idea, but I love the term. Chew on that, Bob Costas.

The new STATS *Handbooks* are out and Christmas is here, as far as I'm concerned. These are the best books around, no doubt. Until the *Minor League Scouting Notebook* comes out, that is. You know what's best about the *Handbooks*? No dumb ass like me telling you what to think. It's pure numbers. Read 'em and weep. Find your own sleepers. Make up your own theories. Stay awake in bed until the sun rises. Better than sex. Yes sirreeee. From here on out, my comments are from my first run through these annual masterpieces:

Does your major league team need a closer? Try Paul Abbott. Yes, he's the now-30-year-old former Twin phenom prospect. He's not reared his head in the majors since 1993, and back then, it was pretty ugly whenever his head reared. (And probably really ugly when his rear headed.) (I'm not even sure what that means exactly.) Anyway, since then he's learned control. Last year, he walked 29 and K'ed 117 in 93.2 IP. The last season he didn't K more guys than IP was 1994. He must be a real chucker. He started for most of last year, but that matters little. He's with the Mariners, or at least he was at the end of last season. If you still have him, M's, I double-dog dare you. Tell Heathcliff to hike. Tell Timlin to transfer. Tell Norm to nock it off. Give Paul Abbott a shot and your troubles will be over. Trust me.

The Jose Tolentino fan club here at STATS Pennsylvania was happy that Jose slugged .544 in 305 at-bats for Triple-A Calgary last season at age 37. Do you think he showed Mark Johnson anything on what hitting is about?

There's one Molina in the *Major League Handbook*. You probably know about him. His name is Izzy. There are two Molinas in the big part of the *Minor League Handbook*. Their names are Ben and Jose. What's my point? They're all catchers. Isn't that special?

I'll give you a quarter for all your Kevin Maas rookie cards. Last year he hit .219 in 260 at-bats for the Triple-A Reds and the Triple-A Astros. He's still only 32. Maas only possesses the two skills I like best —walking and hitting for power—but baseball purists hate. Too bad he never had those other "Deion Sanders" skills. Then he'd be turning down $2.5 mil instead of probably contemplating retirement.

Wikleman Gonzalez. I love baseball.

11/14/97

I was thinking about Tim Scott and Jeff Shaw the other day. (What a life.) A few years ago, when they were both Expos, I starting getting them mixed up. They were both innings-eating middle relievers. Shortly thereafter, Tim Scott had a couple of good years and was all of a sudden considered a premier setup man. Jeff Shaw had a mediocre-to-poor couple of years and was considered a fringe player. Since then, Scott's career has pretty much gone into the toilet, while Shaw first latched onto a Scott-like premier setup-man role with the Reds and then, when Jeff Brantley got hurt, managed to take advantage and is now considered a fine closer. How do you like that? I swear, middle relief and especially closing is so often mostly a matter of a little luck and being in the right place at the right time. Tim Scott's 15 minutes came and went. Jeff Shaw's time is now.

The main thing I wanted to talk about today is the expansion draft. I'm really excited. I can't wait. I hope your work or vacation situation is such that you can watch the whole thing as it happens or at least join in ASAP. It sure seems to me that there are a lot more quality players available this time than ever before. I don't know if the rules changed (I probably should know if I'm writing this column or I should look it up, but I don't feel like it) or if it's just the salary structure of teams trying to unload high-priced players so they leave them unprotected. As the last draft the field was filled with half-baked players and half-baked prospects, in this draft, although most of the prospects are still half-baked, the established player selection is pretty darn good. But I've seen all the mock drafts and the strategies there are totally what's been used in the past and, if for no other reason *than* the past, those strategies are all wrong. A guy named Marc Topkin, who drafted for the Devil Rays in the *Baseball America* draft, said: "We wanted tools and upsides, not necessarily middle-of-the-road guys where you know what you're getting. We took high risk/high return players." And do you know what that kind of strategy gets you? Take a look at the first round of Marlins picks in the 1992 draft—Nigel Wilson, Jose Martinez, Darrell Whitmore, Kip Yaughn, Jesus Tavarez—to name all the guys who support my argument. Yeah, the Marlins won the World Series. But it had nothing to do with the players they picked back in 1992. If you look at all the players picked in all the expansion drafts throughout history, the bottom line is this— these guys aren't going to have much at all to do with the future of your team. However, the popular, often praised by the critics (I clearly remember the consensus being that the Marlins had outdrafted the Rockies back in 1992) strategy of drafting is that same "Draft For Tomorrow, Not Today" method. Why not try something new? Here's what I'd do:

Let's make our first assumption that hitting is fairly predictable, pitching is not. If a guy has hit well for the past three years at any level above Class-A, there's a really, really, really good chance he'll hit in the majors. Maybe not the first month of the season. Maybe not the first half of the season. But, eventually he will hit. Pitching is much more unpredictable. Some guys wow 'em in the minors and just can't do it in the majors. Many guys wow 'em in the majors for one or more years and still can't do it the next year or ever again. Put it this way, let's make a bet. I'll throw out Frank Thomas and Mike Piazza and I'll pick five other hitters who I'll bet will have a great 1998. You throw out Greg Maddux and Randy Johnson and you pick five other pitchers who you'll bet will have a great 1998. Would you make that bet?

So, concentrate on putting proven-record hitters into a scenario where they can produce their career year. Then, sell them off for guys with *real* futures. Some suggestions? Try Roberto Petagine and Frankie Menechino and Arqui Pozo and Brian Raabe and (I cringe as I type this) David McCarty. None of these guys are blazing hot 19 year-old wonders of the minors, but try finding one of those amongst the guys offered. Heck, maybe even give a big old moose like Pat Lennon or Dan Rohrmeier or Russ Morman a try. Or maybe a little old moose like Keith Mitchell. No, they're not flashy names, but they'll play the pants off Josh Booty and Nigel Wilson and Alex Ochoa if they're given the chance. I guarantee it.

What about pitching? The best I can think of is to take guys with major league proven records. Don't bother about age. Maybe even try the old rotating-three-innings with no real starters or relievers approach that no one seems to be willing to try for more than a game or two. Some suggestions? Jon Lieber, Tom Candiotti, Mike Trombley, Steve Reed, Jim Corsi, Doug Jones. Pick one of those guys and trot him out there all year for 30+ saves. Somebody will pay you a big prospect for him come August.

By the way, don't assume anything for Rockies. Don't assume the hitters will hit at your park and don't assume the pitchers will get shelled. Whatever you do, please don't take Dante

Bichette, especially Arizona, where he may continue to put up his wonderful string of hocus-pocus home-park batting totals.

So there you have it, the secret to successful expansion drafting. Next week I'll evaluate. And don't forget to think of me groaning when the first pick is some guy who hit .130 at A-ball last year but has "all the tools."

11/21/97

The Braves' signing of Andres Galarraga is just flat-out unbelievably silly. Reasons:

1) Galarraga turns 37 in June.

2) Galarraga has hit .334-.396-.644 at Coors and .268-.324-.490 on the road the past three seasons (that's .334, 71, 247 and .268, 48, 149 for you dinosaurs who still don't understand on-base and slugging). Turner Field ain't no Launching Pad either. It's a pitchers' park.

3) Ryan Klesko can't play left field.

4) Money.

When Andres Galarraga hits .268 next season, who won't be at all surprised? Aaaah, that would be me.

Did you know?

1) Jack Howell hit 14 homers last year.

2) Tony Clark walked 93 times in 1997 after walking 29 times in 1996. (Psst. That means he's becoming a better hitter.)

3) Jacob Brumfield will turn 33 in May.

I'm not kidding, I was at the store magazine rack the other night and I noticed a wrestling magazine that had "For Mature Fans" on the cover. Really.

OK, here's the deal on the expansion draft. First I'll do the amusing stuff. Then, I'll give you my opinion on each player drafted. I'll probably just do one team today, since I have to crank out another column Wednesday already due to turkey day week. Here we go.

Final notes:

1) They should call him David Dot-lucci.

2) Did you get the feeling that the young black guy they had announcing the third-round picks was nothing more than a lame display of MLB trying to show how non-racist they are by proving to us that, see, black guys with funny names really can speak and pronounce words articulately?

Here are the goods on the Tampa Bay Devil Rays:

Tony Saunders—A real good first pick. Saunders did prove to me that mock protected lists and drafts are about as useful as WWF magazines "For Mature Fans." Every list I saw had Saunders protected.

Quinton McCracken—Should do OK. He was helped more by Coors than you might think. A Luis Castillo nosedive is not out of the question.

Bob Abroowoowoo—Not as good as everyone seems to think, but not bad either. Off to the Phillies for steady but unspectacular shortstop Kevin Stocker.

Miguel Cairo—Doesn't get on base, but steals bases. Could be another (way overrated) Tony Womack.

Rich Butler—A little speed, a little more power. Might be OK. Last season was his only real good one in the minors, however. He either developed or fluked.

Bobby Smith—If someone would challenge me to name a more overrated minor league infielder not named Booty, I'd have a tough time.

Jason Johnson—Consistently good K-to-walk ratios. He might be OK. At least he isn't a middle reliever.

Dmitri Young—I thought he was a nice pick until I found out he was definitely going back to the Reds. Would you trade Dmitri Young for Mike Kelly? I wouldn't. I would've told the Reds I don't care, I'm not giving him back.

Esteban Yan—I've always heard he has great stuff. Had a nice year at Triple-A last year. Might turn out.

Mike Difelice—Stinks. There're probably 25 catchers whom nobody cares about right now in the minors who are just as good or better.

Bubba Trammell—Can really blast the ball. Will be a star if the Tampa park isn't too tough on hitters.

Andy Sheets—Everyone seemed all excited about him, too, for some unknown reason. Traded for stinky John Flaherty.

Dennis Springer—Will give the Rays tons of (poor quality) innings, which is just what they need (according to everyone on TV). Mike Moore, where are you?

Dan Carlson—Let's start the parade of faceless middle relievers. (Dennis Springer is at least interesting because he's a knuckleballer. Not good, mind you, interesting.) I cannot believe the Giants didn't have something better to offer than this.

Brian Boehringer—Pitched a good 48 innings last year out of nowhere. Traded for stinky John Flaherty.

Mike Duvall—Faceless middle reliever No. 2.

John LeRoy—Had a 5.03 ERA for the Braves Double-A team. Does that mean he's somehow a pitcher? (The keyword is Braves. Tell that to David Nied.)

Jim Mecir—FMR No. 3.

Bryan Rekar—I'm really interested to see if he develops now that he's away from Pitcher's Nightmare. A genuinely "high ceiling."

Rick Gorecki—Somewhat promising. Not a bad guy to take a chance on.

Ramon Tatis—FMR No. 4. Let me throw in "way overrated" also.

Kerry Robinson—Won't do anything that stinky Chuck Carr can't do already. Oh, besides bat lefthanded all the time, that is.

Steve Cox—Think lefthanded Randy Milligan. That's not too bad, but no one (except Tampa, I guess) seems to like him.

Albie Lopez—Never began to do anything "they" said he would. Maybe he's a change of scenery guy. He probably just needs to be a closer or something.

Jose Paniagua—Why does everyone think he's so great? Pitched 51 lucky 1996 major league innings. Big deal.

Carlos Mendoza—Promising. Of course I don't know his weird things though.

Ryan Karp—FMR No. 5.

Santos Hernandez—I thought he was FMR No. 6 until I looked at his numbers. The big point on TV was that he'd first tasted Double-A this season at age 24. The big question is why? Were his ERAs too low? Were his K-to-walk ratios too impressive? Was he having an affair with the GM's wife? May be nothing at higher levels, but I like him better than FMRs 1-5.

Randy Winn—Another "high ceiling" of Chuck Carr. This guy even switch hits. (I don't mean that in a "weird-thing" way either.)

Terrell Wade—Hooray, hoorah. Does one bad, injury-filled season take a guy from Mr. Hotshot Prospect to bum? Apparently so. They said he might not be healthy enough to start 1998, but I'd take a chance on his future anyway.

Aaron Ledesma—"High ceiling" of Rene Gonzales.

Brooks Kieschnick—May have been one of the most overrated prospects ever to walk the planet in his time. He has managed to make unbelievers out of many.

Luke Wilcox—The Devil Rays should have just said "pass." The best thing about him was that you could tell whomever was doing that bottom of the screen stuff at ESPN was using our *Minor League Handbook*. He's in our book as Chris Wilcox. If you noticed, when he was first picked, the announcers kept saying Luke, while the bottom thing said Chris. They

270

changed it eventually. That's probably the most you'll ever remember about Luke/Chris Wilcox.

Herbert Perry - Was ready to mash before a spring injury last season. Sure, I'd take a chance.

Vaughn Eshelman - Still living off those first couple of major league outings. He stinks.

12/5/97

I'm so so so so sorry for not getting time to write the day before Thanksgiving as I had said I would. What's been taking up my time has been this CybrCard programming project I've been working on. It's over soon so I don't anticipate any more skipped columns anytime soon. But get out and buy those friggin' CybrCards when they come out. Why?

1) I busted my butt getting them done on time.

2) My name's in the credits (at least it was on last year's).

3) They really are the coolest thing in the world. Just buy one. I'll bet you'll want them all after you look at it.

I'm going to try to write more this week to make everything up to you. So, instead of doing the nonsense first, I'm going to do what I promised first, critique the Arizona Diamondback draft picks (yeah, I know that's pretty old and tired at this point, but remember, you haven't seen *my* views yet), then I'll add as much nonsense as time will allow at the end. I'll try to make that lots and lots of nonsense.

1) *Brian Anderson*—Everyone seems to think he has such a great future, but I'm just not real sure why. He is young (25) with a bunch of MLB experience already behind him, although I don't think this is as big a deal for a pitcher as it would be for a young hitter. His walk totals are good, but he gets hit hard and doesn't throw very many Ks. They've gotta pitch somebody, but I wouldn't want him (or any other Diamondback starters) on my fantasy team.

2) *Jeff Suppan*—You could say almost the same things for Suppan as I already said for Anderson, but Suppan's K totals were good until last season. I already traded him off the team I had him on.

3) *Gabe Alvarez*—Looks about like Kevin Orie to me. It's up to you whether you think that's good or bad. Traded to Detroit anyway. Matt Williams is a lot better than Kevin Orie, in case you weren't sure.

4) *Jorge Fabregas*—The worst pick of the draft. Fabregas has this rap as a bad defensive catcher with pop in his bat. Here's a question —where's the pop? Tell me Carlos Delgado, tell me Francisco Cabrera, tell me Hector Villanueva, tell me Earl Williams for heaven's sake, but don't tell me Jorge Fabregas. A bad defensive catcher who can hit but really can't hit is a bad proposition.

271

5) *Karim Garcia*—May be the best pick of the draft. Should be a monster if they don't expect him to be a monster after 50 at-bats.

6) *Edwin Diaz*—Solid defensive middle infielder who *does* have some pop, but never walks. I'm not crazy about him. He could turn out to be Vinny Castilla, though, I guess.

7) *Cory Lidle*—Here come the Arizona faceless middle relievers. He did start his last couple of years in the minors, so his ERA could get even higher.

8) *Joel Adamson*—Good K-to-walk ratios. I'd like him a lot more if he were pitching somewhere else. Will either be a fairly-hammered FMR or a totally-hammered starter.

9) *Ben Ford*—FMR No. 3. Boy, weren't the Yankees lucky.

10) *Yamil Benitez*—Sort of like Edwin Diaz playing the outfield. Yuck.

11) *Neil Weber*—Would be an OK young lefty starting prospect, again, if he were elsewhere. Should be toasted in Arizona.

12) *Jason Boyd*—Must be a scout's player, because I'll bet I could find 50 24-year-old minor league middle relievers with better numbers.

13) *Brent Brede*—Like Garcia, this guy should cook too, if given a fair opportunity. A fine choice.

14) *Tony Batista*—I like him too. A real good bet to do a whole heckuva lot better in his second chance at a starting job.

15) *Tom Martin*—What was the big deal? I don't know, but anyone who helped reel in Matt Williams goes down as a good choice in my book.

16) *Omar Daal*—I liked him a lot too about last year at this time, but he'll probably be cannon fodder in AZ.

17) *Scott Winchester*—About as promising as Felix Rodriguez, who'll learn to dread pitching in Arizona, just like Winchester would have, had he not gotten sent back to the Reds.

18) *Clint Sodowsky*—Enough about Diamondback pitchers. The starters will get pasted, except maybe one or possibly two (roll the dice for which one(s)). The middle relievers will get pasted, except maybe one to three of them (get out the dice again). The closer will be good. I wouldn't bet more than a few cents right now that that closer's going to be Hector Carrasco.

19) *Danny Klassen*—Before you start thinking he's the next Alex Rodriguez, remember, that's El Paso. John Jaha hit like 80 homers with a .777 batting average there one year. I have a feeling by the time Jay Bell is ready to be moved as the Diamondback shortstop, we'll hardly remember who Klassen is anymore (or he won't be a shortstop).

20) *Matt Drews*—Wouldn't touch him with a 6'8" pole.

21) *Todd Erdos*—I didn't make clear exactly who the FMRs were above, so I can't number them. Let's just call Todd Erdos—FMR.

22) *Chris Clemons*—What's exciting about this? I don't know. Go ask some scout.

23) *David Dellucci*—What's exciting about this? A lot. This guy can really play. Again, he may not if they don't give him a fair shot (at least 150 at-bats). But he will if they do.

24) *Damian Miller*—Another bad defensive catcher who can hit, but can't really. Would be just as bad as Fabregas, but at least he's not a high pick.

25) *Hector Carrasco*—Looks good for now as the Diamondback closer. But a lot can change. Carrasco's pitching has been inconsistent, to say the least. He could lose the job when someone else is signed, in spring, in May—you pick. He may keep the job and get 40 saves. I just wouldn't go trading Trevor Hoffman to get him.

26) *Hanley Frias*—Mediocre backup shortstop at best. Klassen has an outside shot. Frias isn't ever going to be anything exciting.

27) *Bob Wolcott*—Are they still saying how great his potential is because of that one lucky postseason start? I didn't think so.

28) *Mike Bell*—Didn't David prove that the Bell surname isn't a free ticket? I guess not.

29) *Joe Randa*—I don't know why the Tigers want him, but I'll plead the Tom Martin evaluation rule.

30) *Jesus Martinez*—I like him a lot more with the Marlins than with the Snakes. I don't like him very much anywhere. He does have the best first name of the Martinez brothers.

31) *Russ Springer*—The "good" Springer. He'll have a tough time keeping that label.

32) *Bryan Corey*—FMR number something.

33) *Kelly Stinnett*—Sleeper city. Given the chance, he'll shoosh those other catchers away like flies. I think he'll kick butt in that light Arizona air—again, given the chance.

34) *Chuck McElroy*—Went to Colorado, where he'll get smeared as bad as he would've here, for Harvey Pulliam. Pulliam's interesting, but I'm not sure how interesting you can be when you're 30 and have 187 MLB at-bats.

35) *Marty Janzen*—His 1998 ERA will look more like his 1997 minor league ERA (7.20) than his major league ERA (3.60).

Whew. Thank God that's over. Now for the nonsense:

Top Five Non-Simpson "Simpsons" Characters

5. Mean kid who says "Ah-hah." I forget his name. (*Editor's note: Nelson*)

4. Mr. Burns—He'd score a lot higher if he was naked all the time.

3. Sailor guy who talks like a pirate. His appearance is usually fairly out of context, but always entertaining.

2. Willy The Janitor.

1. Millhouse.

Don't tell me Smithers. He's way overrated.

Jon Nunnally will have a bone removed from his right foot, just like he had a bone removed from his left foot earlier this offseason. Is that weird or what? Do you think he found out he can run faster without bones in his feet? Do you think his feet will flop around, like a penguin?

Sung to the tune of "Goodnight, Ladies" (you have to sing "Darryl Kile" really fast):

"Goodbye, Darryl Kile, goodbye, Darryl Kile, goodbye Darryl Kile, hello to a five ERA."

Don't tell me Pedro Astacio either. He lucked out by not having to pitch at Coors very often last season. Talk to me about him around the All-Star break.

What the heck ever happened to Julian Lennon?

Dave Martinez going to the Rays means the White Sox are serious about Mike Cameron. I like him.

Doug Creek and Mark Acre signed to play in Japan yesterday. Creek could be the next big thing in Japan. He threw a ton of Ks last year. I was keeping an eye on him with the White Sox. Acre to me was the definition of why you should get out that old grain of salt when you hear the term "closer of the future."

Did you know?

A) Rafael Belliard hit his second career homer last year. The first one came in 1987. George Bell and Andre Dawson were the MVPs that year. Steve Bedrosian and Roger Clemens (yes, that Roger Clemens) won the Cys.

B) Raul Mondesi put together about the most unnoticed 30/30 season I've ever seen last year. Didn't that used to be a big deal?

From my local newspaper, sometime before last Wednesday, when I wanted to relate it:

"A drunken Philadelphia Phillies mascot crashed a Phanatic Bandwagon into a utility pole Thursday, then fled to his home, police said."

That wacky Phillie Phanatic. Anything for a laugh.

One of my favorite things about the expansion draft is the amount of players who were definitely going to an expansion team, who are still where they were before. Todd Zeile and/or Eric Karros? Still there. Tom Pagnozzi? Still there. How about George Arias? I think he was a Diamondback before they existed. So much for the media.

How long do you think it'll be before Jim Leyland's whining like a lost puppy about how the new Marlins can't compete due to lack of funds? But, rest assured, once the Marlins put together their first three-game win streak, that old "Genius" light above his head will be shining bright and clear. I'm still waiting for him to succeed with a real challenge. Then I'll call him a genius.

OK, that's it. I hope I wrote enough to make up for all my recent failures. I'm home alone on a Friday night and there's too much beer to drink and too many 1970s board games to be played and too many unviewed Ultimate Fighting tapes at the Blockbuster to write one more than one more word. Goodbye.

12/12/97

I was going to tell you about the guys I picked in my league's big winter free agent draft on Thanksgiving Saturday. However, I've accumulated quite a load of nonsense to write about and maybe I'll save the draft stuff until next week. I'll play it by ear.

A guy named Jerry Storch (no relation to Larry I suppose—bet he's never heard that before) e-mailed me. He wanted me to ask in his behalf about what ever happened to Brian Turang? Last he's been seen in our system is on the 1996 Triple-A Syracuse (Blue Jays) team. More interestingly, he's the boss of Sindee's Fantasy Stats (yes, *that* Sindee's Fantasy Stats). He said the story of how the Sindee ad came to be was a good one and he'd tell it to me if I wanted to know. I said I'd love to (ahwuluvto) and I'd love to use it here if he'd let me. But I never heard back from him. Oh, well. Maybe he's busy with Sindee.

Carlos Garcia designated for assignment. Can we stop waiting for his big breakout season now?

You know, I sometimes rag really hard on the decisions baseball people make. So, now for something completely different. Amidst all this talk of clutch and playing big in big games and attitude and clubhouse and all that other happy horse excrement, the Cleveland Indians were smart enough to know that, even though Kenny Lofton didn't play the pants off Marquis Grissom last season, nine seasons out of 10, Lofton will. So they therefore signed Lofton for less than they would've had to a year ago and sent Grissom packing. And they ended up trading Lofton's subpar season for a year's worth of Grissom and David Justice for Alan Embree. And all I have to say about the whole thing is good for the Indians. It makes my heart happy to see a team do something that really and truly makes sense. (See, I'm not really that bad of a guy.)

Paul Sorrento to the Rays. How many DH/1B guys do they feel they need? Let's see, they've now got:

1. Fred McGriff 2. Paul Sorrento 3. Bubba Trammell 4. Herbert Perry 5. Steve Cox

I guess that makes Cox a minor leaguer and Perry a definite sub. Maybe they'll let Trammell stumble around in the outfield like Ryan "We Needed Galarraga Like A Hole In The Head" Klesko.

Everyone's upset about the Pedro Martinez deal. I'm a lot more upset about the Willie Blair deal. As far as I'm concerned, it's one thing to throw a house full of money at one of baseball's top pitchers. It's another to throw a truck full of money at a guy who's had one good year out of eight in the majors. Yeah, that year happened to be last year. So what? Anyone who plays for a carbon copy of what happened last year is going to lose almost every time. Ask the Padres about Greg Vaughn.

Hey, *TSN*, I think your new *Rolling Stone/Spin* type format is pretty good. I especially like the new color-coded sport sections so I don't have to guess whether the baseball will be in the front, back or middle from issue to issue. I don't like the following two notes:

As I've mentioned before here, I like to collect old baseball magazines, books, etc. Last weekend I picked up a 1974 *Street & Smith's*. It's fascinating. The ads alone are worth the three bucks I paid for it. How about this one?:

"Irwin Kosewski, winner of over 50 trophies for 'Most Muscular Waist' (in 50 narrow victories over me) in various 'Mr. America' contests, says, 'You wouldn't think that a guy like me would wear the SLIM GUARD, but I do. Every day if possible. It keeps my waist and middle trim while I wear it. I swear by it. You chubby guys will, too."

You talkin' to me? You talkin' to *me*??

Here's another:

"I'll show you how to. . . . . . Cut any bully down to size with a deadly five-second trick developed by the 'Suicide Squad' of the Orient! (Wait a minute here. Wouldn't the 'Suicide Squad' be dead if they were so good at it?)

. . . 'Wipe-Out' any kill-crazy goon with one jab of your finger in the right place! (Good fantasy team or band name there -- the Kill-crazy Goons.)

. . . Put POWER into your fist for 'demolishing' a thug's skull and ribs!

. . . Smash down, 2, 3, or more attackers AT ONCE!

. . . Disarm gun-toting, knife-wielding creeps and 'put them away' quick as a flash!

. . . Use an attacker's own clothing and body to annihilate him in an INSTANT!"

If I wrote my whole column like that, would it make it more exciting and interesting? Let's try it:

. . . The guy from Sindee's e-mailed me but I never got THE WHOLE STORY!

. . . Carlos Garcia, 'designed for ASSIGNMENT'!

. . . Indians sign Kenny Lofton and dump Grissom—GREAT MOVE!

. . . Devil Rays—too many gosh darn 1B/DHs!

Nah, it's not really that exciting.

Finally, there's an article entitled, "Mod Managers For Mod Players." I kid you not. Of course, it's the same article you could find any year from now back to 1902 about how the old managers were tough but the new guys have to be soft and squishy in order to get along with "today's ballplayer." That's not the point. The point is the word "Mod." With all the bell-bottom jeans and stretchy ring-zipper shirts and platform shoes, I don't hear anyone using the word "Mod" anymore even though it's totally appropriate. Well, from now on, I'm going to be baseball's Mod columnist. There.

Well, no draft stuff today. I didn't even get to all the nonsense. That'll probably serve me well since I have to write again Thursday because I'm heading out Route 80 to Illinois for the holidays with the in-laws next Friday. Yee. Hah.

12/18/97

This has got to be the best transaction listing I've ever seen, and it was from today:

New York Mets—Signed pitcher Jae Weong Seo and infielder/outfielder Jae Hwan Seo.

And you thought you couldn't keep the Valentins and the Kevin Browns and the St. Louis A. Beneses straight.

I don't know how many of you do the internet auctions, but I do and it's a lot of fun. Last week, I saw a Chito Martinez game-used bat and I almost had to cry. I was like the biggest Chito Martinez fan in the world. As far as I'm concerned, if there was ever a guy who could've been a real good player with a chance, maybe not a superstar or anything, but a real good player, Chito was the man. He walked a ton and hit for power a ton and that's quite a start in my book. But when he really had the chance to bust loose, Johnny Oates insisted on giving the PT to Joe Orsulak in the Oriole outfield. Why? I don't know. You tell me. But I hadn't thought about Chito in a long time. The bat, by the way, was already at 15-something (maybe I'm not the biggest Chito fan in the world), so I didn't bid, in case you were wondering.

Speaking of those auctions, let me tell you something. When a seller puts "LOOK" in the short description, it makes me not want to look and when he or she puts "L@@K" in the description, it *really* makes me not want to look.

Pat Lennon gets released and Bob Hamelin gets designated for assignment. Now, maybe these moves were those kind that teams make for 40-man roster or waiver or some other kind of reason where they really intend to keep the guy, and they have to do this, but, geez. I think I could find a place for a guy who hit .293 and OBPed .374 in a little bit of the majors and has been hammering the minors for years or a guy who put up .270/.366/.487 with 18 homers. But that's not how teams think. They need room for guys like Kimera Bartee, who hit .218/.294/.289 last year in 501 Triple-A at-bats. But boy is he fast.

Did you take any notice to the Rule 5 draft? Were you intimidated by that list of tons of names in this week's *Weekly*? I'm gonna do you a big favor. I've already done the research and here are the only guys you have to worry about. Anyone not included here, you can pitch into that big trash barrel where you put all your leaves last fall. Because they ain't goin' nowhere. (Wow, that's two uses of "ain't" in the same column.)

Mark Deschenes—picked by the Dodgers from the Indians—This guy was Cleveland's minor league pitcher of the year. So what the heck is he doing getting let go in the Rule V draft? Well, obviously those old liver-spotted scouts don't like him that much. Obviously, he doesn't possess a 95-mph fastball. And maybe he lacks "makeup" or something. (He should hang around Rodman for a while.) But that doesn't make the fact that he just totally blew away everyone he faced last season as a closer at Class-A and high-A go away. And guess who's going to get a real shot to make the major league roster this spring? And guess who needs a closer? Now, do I think it's reasonable to think that Deschenes leaps over Antonio Osuna and Darren Dreifort and Scott Radinsky and Darren Hall during spring training and trots out of the pen in the ninth inning of the Dodger opener as the closer? No. Do I think it's within the realm of possibility that Deschenes has a good spring and makes the club and Osuna/Dreifort/Radinsky/Hall are ineffective/get hurt/get traded sometime during the season and Deschenes gets a shot as closer? Yes. Do I think it's within the realm of reason that Deschenes has a good spring and makes the club and picks up a save here and there as a middle reliever during the 1998 season? Yes. Do I think it's within the realm of reason that Deschenes gets totally smoked against the big boys during the spring and gets sent back to liver-spot hell in the Indian system where it's obvious they don't like him that much? Yes. I'm not advocating using a first-round fantasy pick on this guy. What I am advocating is, if it's time for your last pick and the only pitcher you can think of is Rudy Seanez, take Marc Deschenes. He's got a small chance to be the baseball story of the year.

Frank Lankford—picked by the Dodgers from the Yankees—Lankford is one of those guys that the liver-spotters just hate and I'm not even real crazy about. Since he's pitched at upper levels, he couldn't strike out a blindfolded Rob Deer. (I don't like that grammar either, but that's not the point.) But he gets guys out everywhere. His worst ERA in five years was 3.34 —his first season back in 1993. And last year it looks like they successfully converted him from middle reliever to starter. Frank Lankford might be Jim Corsi, at best. He might be Dave Eiland, at best. But there's a slight chance he might be Bob Tewksbury, at best. I like Bob Tewksbury pitching in Chavez Ravine. Again, he'd have to jump over Dennis Reyes and Mike Judd and maybe Darren Dreifort (plus whomever the Dodgers might yet acquire) to get a starting shot. It would take a miracle for Lankford to start the season in the Dodger rotation. But it would take a much smaller miracle for this to lead to that and, before you know it, Lankford's in the rotation in July.

Brian Edmondson—picked by the Braves from the Mets—My hopes for Edmondson are a lot more tempered than for Deschenes and even Lankford. Brian Edmondson ain't (that's three) gonna close or start for the Braves. No way. But he might pitch middle relief and, for the Braves, one could do worse. Edmondson was bumbling along as a very mediocre starter, until last year, when they made him a middle reliever, he became lots more effective. I'd say high end for Edmondson is low-three ERA and three saves. Low end is never sees the major leagues. He's better than Rudy Seanez.

That's it for the major league phase. There are three guys I wanted you to keep an eye on from the Triple-A and Double-A drafts. Two guys are real, real longshots and one guy's just a plain old longshot.

Real, real longshot No. 1—Ray Brown —picked by the Royals from the Padres—Brown put up great numbers in 1996 with the Double-A Reds, then somehow ended up with the Padres for 1997. He stumbled at Triple-A, but crushed the ball at Double-A for the second straight season. This would be fine if your last name was Booty, but it apparently doesn't cut it if your name is Ray Brown. Just keep the name in the back of your mind. Jeff King isn't getting any younger or better.

Real, real longshot No. 2—Antuan Bunkley—picked by the Tigers from the Brewers— Forgive me. I just can't look at .381/.450/.656 and not get at least a little bit excited. Yes, it's rookie league. Yes, Tony Clark isn't getting younger, but he might get better (and he's pretty friggin' good now). Put this guy on your back, back burner. His name, in and of itself, is worth remembering.

Plain, old longshot—Frank Menechino—picked by the A's from the White Sox—This guy's numbers make a lonely (remember, my wife's been gone for over two weeks now) sabermetrician like myself get downright excited. Just look at those OBPs: .443, ooh, .403, aah, .427, ooh, .391, aah, .391, a little more to the left, .391, aaah, .397, aaaaah, .447, uhngh. (Where is that tissue box?) This guy's *career* OBP is .411. I know a team that doesn't have a steady third baseman right now. I like Mark Bellhorn as much as the next guy. (Hmm, that doesn't sound too good right about now.) Anyway, Menechino doesn't get the major league shot like the guys in the major league phase. And the A's already goofed up giving their 2B job to Scott Spiezio last spring when they could've given it to Rule 5'er Frank Catalanotto. So don't expect anything, but keep an eye out anyway.

Lastly on the Rule 5 draft, I like this guy Arizona took named Ynocencio DeLaCruz. I'm sure his name can be properly pronounced any way but this, but we'll call him "Wino."

Speaking of wino, I noticed Kareem Abdul-Jabbar in my morning paper advertising Coors' new non-alcoholic (is it Coors Cutter with a new name or is it totally new?) beer called, drum roll please. . . Coors Non-Alcoholic. So, if Coors' non-alcoholic beer is called Coors Non-Alcoholic, shouldn't their regular beer be called (you catch on fast) Coors Alcoholic? And what a great marketing campaign that could be. . .

I'd better say first that this is *not* Kareem Abdul-Jabbar talking. He doesn't touch the stuff. Instead, just imagine some grubby looking guy.

"You know, as an alcoholic, I drink a *lot* of beer. And the beer I drink most is new Coors Alcoholic. Try it. You'll be hooked."

Sorry, I wanted to review all the movies I've seen since my wife left and I ran out of Ultimate Fighting tapes to rent. (What happened to them anyway? The newest one at my Blockbuster is "Ultimate Ultimate 2" and that's from 1996. Where did they go?) However, all this darn baseball stuff got in the way. And I still have to tell you about my league draft sometime. It's always good to have lots of material, I guess. And, by the way, I'll be heading out to Illinois tomorrow. So if you're planning on going to that company Christmas party and ingesting large amounts of Coors Alcoholic, please stay off Route 80.

1/9/98

Don Zminda, Zee-Man to you, was oh so kind enough to print out a copy of the new *Minor League Scouting Notebook* for me to edit (yeah right, as if I wouldn't be dying to read it anyway) to go over while I was out in Illinois. All I can tell you is, if you're in a league like I am, in which you have a big roster, can draft players from anywhere, and basically keep them as long as you want, this book is *the most important* non-totally-statistical source you can buy. If you need to be told that Mark McGwire hits lots of homers and Mark Grace doesn't, go spend $6 on a magazine. If you want to hear, verbatim, what all those baggy old scouts are saying, like "Luis Ordaz is great with the glove now and eventually is going to become a hitter" (sure, just like Pokey Reese and Rey Ordonez and Eddie Zosky and Robert Eenhoorn before him), listen to Gammons and Beaton and *Baseball America* and all those guys. (If you don't know who Luis Ordaz is, you'd better go back to the $6 magazine.) The difference between John Sickels and those guys is he knows the players *and* he knows how to evaluate. That's a deadly combination.

The important parts of the new *Minor League Scouting Notebook* you can read for yourself when it comes out. I'll get straight to the nonsense. Just before the nonsense, I have to tell you the my favorite serious sentence in the whole book: "The kind of guy expansion is supposed to benefit but often doesn't." As usual, John hits the nail right on the head.

Minor League Scouting Notebook Name Nonsense:

1) I can't wait to see Garrick Haltiwanger pitching to Radhames Dykhoff in the majors.

2) If you like Chip Glass as a prospect, you should see his cousin, Dishwasher Safe.

3) I can picture some GM saying this to Tiger GM Randy Smith: "Look, it's Mike Drumright or the deal's off. And don't give me any Nick Skuses either."

Just a little prospect humor there. I'm going to debut those jokes at a local comedy club's open mike night. Speaking of humor, my local newspaper started a contest asking how readers think "Seinfeld" should end. I sent in my e-mail suggesting all the characters get their heads severed and stuck on poles. That would finally make the show funny to me. Maybe.

Don Zminda's
"Zee-Man Reports"

March 27, 1997—Spring Training

I'm back from spring training, where the weather was gorgeous and I got to see four games: Orioles-White Sox, Cardinals-Pirates, Rangers-Cardinals and Yankees-Cardinals. Seeing the Cardinals three times was kind of a fluke; I normally get to watch my favorite club, the White Sox, several times each spring, but for most of last week the Sox were either on the road or playing home night games, which I try to avoid. So instead I went to Bradenton, where the Pirates train, or up to St. Petersburg to see the Cards. Some random thoughts:

1. The Cards looked pretty good, even though they lost two of the three games I watched. I was particularly impressed with Dmitri Young and think he'll continue to hit well once the bell rings. With Ray Lankford out of the lineup, Young should have a few weeks to show people what he can do.

2. While Young is young and promising, that Cardinal bullpen is just *old*. The Redbirds aren't exactly torturing their aging firemen this spring. Dennis Eckersley came into one of the games I watched in the fourth inning, and two days later, they brought him in for the seventh (he left after working to four hitters). He's even started one game this spring. What's with that? "Eck needs to get in a round of golf before it gets dark," one writer told me.

3. Speaking of "old," my favorite moment of the spring was the eighth inning of the Cardinal-Pirate game: Dale Sveum, Cory Snyder and Gary Gaetti were all in the game at the same time. Two days later, Andy Van Slyke (currently hitting over .500) got a pinch-single for the Redbirds, and Snyder ran for him. Holy 1987, Batman!

4. The Lou Gehrig of spring training, thus far, has been Mark Johnson of the Pirates. Johnson hit his sixth homer of the spring in the Cardinal-Pirate game I watched, and he also had four RBI in that contest. Johnson is currently hitting .415 with a .908 slugging average, and he seems a perfect fit for the title that Willie Upshaw used to have 15-20 years ago: "Mr. March." To put it mildly, there are grave doubts that Johnson can continue this kind of thing once the season begins.

5. Dwight Gooden started for the Yankees against the Cardinals, and looked awful—even Donovan Osborne got a line single off him. But Gooden's pitched pretty well this spring, as have the Yankees starters overall. I don't think the Yanks will do it this year, however; third place seems about right, after which they'll fire Bob Watson and Joe Torre. Naturally.

6. In the Oriole-White Sox game, Sox pitcher Danny Darwin gave up a king-sized home run to Brady Anderson. The ball soared into the parking lot and smashed the windshield of the car belonging to Mike Pazik, the Sox pitching coach. Nothing like making a good impression on your boss, Danny.

7. I wasn't in Sarasota to see Robin Ventura's ghastly leg and ankle fracture, but people who were there told me it was awful. It now looks like Ventura may miss the entire 1997 season, and the injury was so bad that you have to wonder if he'll *ever* completely recover. For veteran fans, this injury had an eerie similarity to the serious ankle fracture suffered by the

Cincinnati Reds' third baseman, Gene Freese, in spring training 1962. Freese, who was 28 years old and coming off the best season of his career (.277-26-87 for a pennant-winning club), got into only 18 games in 1962 and never played regularly again after the injury. Let's hope Ventura is more fortunate.

It's been an interesting spring, and there's a lot more we could talk about: the Brave-Indian trade (I didn't like it from Cleveland's point of view. . . why would you want David Justice, when Brian Giles is a better hitter?), the shocking demotion of Jose Cruz Jr. (boo, Lou!), where Rickey Henderson will end up, a lot of other stuff. But we'll get into subjects like that over the next few weeks. For now, it's only five days until Opening Day, and that's a heck of a nice feeling.

April 3, 1997—The Big Trade

The regular season has begun, but people are still talking about the big Indians-Braves trade that took place over a week ago. Here at STATS, the general consensus (though it's hardly unanimous) is that the Braves got the better of the deal. Which is weird, because outside these walls, most people seem to feel just the opposite, that the Indians made out better.

Why would we say that the Indians made a bad deal? You could summarize it in two words: Brian Giles. As most of you probably know, Giles is a 26-year-old outfielder who has been waiting his turn to break into the Cleveland outfield for several years now. What you may not know is how good a player Brian Giles is.

One thing we've learned over the years is that a hitter's minor league performance is a reliable indicator of how he's going to perform in the majors. So, for that matter, is a hitter's recent *major* league performance. With the help of Bill James, who invented this stuff, we've been producing "major league equivalencies" in the *STATS Minor League Handbook* for several years now, and "major league player projections" in various publications including the *Major League Handbook* for even longer. Here are our 1997 projections for both Giles and Justice, based on the assumption that each will play full-time for Cleveland this year:

	AB	R	H	2B	3B	HR	RBI	BB	SO	Avg	OBP	SLG
Giles	549	93	166	26	5	21	81	69	62	.302	.380	.483
Justice	547	94	155	24	2	31	103	100	82	.283	.394	.505

Justice, as you can see, has a definite edge, especially in the home-run and RBI categories. But there's not *that* much difference, and anyway, it's based on the assumption that Justice can come all the way back from last season's serious shoulder injury. . . something that isn't guaranteed to happen. We're a little bit more certain that Giles could post the kind of numbers shown here than we are about Justice; after all, Giles has had three straight terrific years of Triple-A ball, and last year he batted .355 with a .612 slugging percentage in a 121 at-bat trial with the Tribe. The fellow can hit.

It's pretty clear to most baseball people that Marquis Grissom, as fine a player as he is, isn't as good as Kenny Lofton is. So Cleveland ends up with Grissom & Justice instead of Giles & Lofton. . . and they've also given up Alan Embree, a hard-throwing lefty who could break through this year. Is the Tribe really better off for 1997 than they were before? It's hard to see how they are, though clearly they can now trade Giles for help on the mound or at second base. But if they wanted a pitcher or a second baseman, why didn't they trade Lofton for *that*? Why deal for a commodity—a hard-hitting outfielder—they already had in Giles? Hence our frustration.

There's been a lot of complaining in Atlanta over this deal, but the Braves did one thing the Tribe *didn't* do: they showed faith in a young player, Andruw Jones. Perhaps the Braves will lose Lofton—whose impending free agency prompted the deal in the first place—when the season ends. Perhaps they'll wish they'd held on to Grissom. But we have a strong feeling that if the Indians let Giles get away, they'll regret it just as much in a year or two.

April 10, 1997—Offense, AL vs. NL

Has the National League had it with all this slugging? I monitor the level of offense in baseball on a regular basis over the course of each season, and something weird has been happening thus far this year. Basically it's 1996 in the American League all over again, while the National League numbers look like those of the low-scoring mid-1960s. Here's an AL/NL comparison for the first week of 1997:

	Avg	R/G	HR/G
AL	.283	11.70	2.55
NL	.242	7.67	1.51

This is a *huge* difference, one that's virtually off the map. The American League has been the higher-scoring league for some time, mostly because of the DH, but the difference is never this profound; it's usually on the order of about 15 batting average points, a run and a half per game and about half a home run per contest. The league difference for early '97 is more than twice that.

I will point out up front that one factor which lowers the NL numbers somewhat is that they include only one game at Colorado's hitting paradise, Coors Field. But the games at Coors generally add only about half a run to the NL's overall level of scoring. So Coors or no Coors, we're looking at a sharp decline in the level of offense in the Senior Circuit. Meanwhile, it's still bombs away in the American League—to say the least. If the AL continues to score runs at the early '97 pace through the rest of the season, it'll be a new league record.

I also compared the offensive figures for the first week of '97 with the first seven days of every season going back to 1987. Over the 11-year period, the highest-scoring first week for an individual league was the '97 AL. The *lowest*-scoring first week, by contrast, was the '9 NL. Again, that's just weird.

One week's worth of data isn't much to go on, and these numbers don't mean a whole lot yet. But they're fascinating nonetheless. Has the National League decided there's "too much hitting in baseball" and done some subtle things to bring the game more into balance—maybe expanding the strike zone or something? Maybe they're freezing the baseballs, the way Eddie Stanky used to do with the White Sox in the late '60s. Whatever the case, we'll be monitoring the figures and updating this study from time to time over the course of the year.

April 17, 1997—Peak Age

John Hunt of *Baseball Weekly* created quite a stir last week when he devoted his "Fantasy Insider" column to the question of when players have their career years. Studies going back to Bill James have always said that players as a group tend to peak at age 26 or 27. But according to statistician Roger Anderson, who was quoted in Hunt's article, the most common age for a career year is in the 30-to-32 range.

Anderson's analysis contained a number of flaws, and Hunt was man enough to acknowledge that in this week's issue. He even presented a counter-argument from Keith Law of the *Baseball Prospectus*. I decided to do a little bit of analysis of my own. I began by dividing modern baseball history into five different eras, beginning with 1901. Then I picked the 10 best offensive players of each era; you could quibble about some of the choices, but the big picture is what we're looking for. I next used Bill James' runs-created formula to pick the peak season for each player. And finally I noted the player's age (as of July 1) during his peak season. Players whose careers spanned different eras were put into the era in which they had their best season.

Here's a rundown of each era.

1901-1919			
Player	**Year**	**RC**	**Age**
Ty Cobb	1911	207	24
Nap Lajoie	1901	179	26
Tris Speaker	1912	175	24
Joe Jackson	1911	175	21
Honus Wagner	1908	148	34
Sam Crawford	1911	147	31
Home Run Baker	1912	140	26
Sherry Magee	1910	139	25
Eddie Collins	1912	136	25
Elmer Flick	1901	124	25

In choosing the players of this era, I left out guys like Ed Delahanty and Jesse Burkett who'd had their best years in the 19th century. Another difficulty is that the 1911-12 seasons—big hitters' years, by deadball-era standards—wound up being over-represented. But this is still a very useful list. The significant things are the average age of the group in their peak seasons—26.1—and the fact that only two players had their best year after their 30th birthday.

1920-1945

Player	Year	RC	Age
Babe Ruth	1921	238	26
Lou Gehrig	1927	208	24
Jimmie Foxx	1932	207	24
Ted Williams	1941	202	22
Rogers Hornsby	1922	200	26
Hank Greenberg	1937	178	26
Al Simmons	1930	163	28
Johnny Mize	1939	162	26
Harry Heilmann	1923	159	28
Mel Ott	1929	157	20

This group is younger than the first one. No player had his best year past the age of 28, and the average age of the group was a peach-fuzzy 25.0. I *might* have included Bill Terry, who had his best year at age 33 in 1930. But Terry was clearly an exception to this pre-WWII rule that the great players tended to have their best seasons in their 20s.

1946-60

Player	Year	RC	Age
Stan Musial	1948	191	27
Mickey Mantle	1956	188	24
Ralph Kiner	1951	165	28
Duke Snider	1954	162	27
Willie Mays	1955	157	24
Eddie Mathews	1953	157	21
Hank Aaron	1959	157	25
Jackie Robinson	1949	135	30
Al Kaline	1955	135	20
Ernie Banks	1958	135	27

Only one player over 30 in this group—Jackie Robinson, who of course was banned from the major leagues until he finally broke in at age 28. The average age of the group is again very young at 25.3; adding Roy Campanella (best year at age 31 in 1953) instead of, say, Al Kaline, would have raised the average by a year, but the group is still quite youthful.

Player	Year	RC	Age
Frank Robinson	1962	160	26
Carl Yastrzemski	1970	157	30
Willie McCovey	1969	151	31
Billy Williams	1970	147	32
Harmon Killebrew	1969	146	33
Joe Morgan	1975	145	31
Reggie Jackson	1969	144	23
Pete Rose	1969	138	28
Willie Stargell	1973	136	33
Roberto Clemente	1967	137	32

Wow. . . what a difference. Could Roger Anderson be right? There are seven players on this list who had their best years at age 30 or above, and the average age of the group is 29.9. This period, we should point out, is biased a bit by the fact that it includes the "big strike zone" years of 1963-68, when pitchers dominated and it was hard to create a lot of runs. So you could easily pick 1967 as Carl Yastrzemski's best year, or '67 for Harmon Killebrew. Even so, it appears that the superstars of the 1960s and '70s were having their best years a little later than the stars of previous eras. Does the trend continue into the most recent era? Let's see.

1977-96

Player	Year	RC	Age
Barry Bonds	1993	172	28
Rod Carew	1977	160	31
Wade Boggs	1987	154	29
Mark McGwire	1996	149	32
Jim Rice	1978	147	25
George Brett	1980	135	27
Rickey Henderson	1985	138	26
Mike Schmidt	1980	137	30
Robin Yount	1982	137	26
Tony Gwynn	1994	104	34

The current era is much harder to study because there are so many great players in mid-career—Frank Thomas, Albert Belle and Mo Vaughn, to name just three—and who knows whether they've had their career years yet or not? In addition, there were three seasons significantly shortened by work stoppages during the period, making it difficult to pick a career year using runs simply runs created. Then there's George Brett, whose career year was clearly 1980, when he batted .390, not 1985, the year he had his most runs created. I somewhat arbitrarily decided to leave anyone who was still under 30 in 1996 off the list, and to credit 1980 as Brett's career year, as well as 1994 for Tony Gwynn.

Given all that, it's hard to draw any firm conclusions about this list; the average age, in particularly, is pretty meaningless. But it's interesting that, as in the 1961-76 list, there are a high number of great players whose best years happened at age 30 or later: Gwynn, Mark McGwire, Rod Carew, Mike Schmidt. This is something that was almost unheard-of prior to World War II.

We're only looking at superstars here, and I can't yet answer the question of whether or not most players still peak at 26 or 27. Perhaps we'll get into that in the next *Baseball Scoreboard*. But Anderson may be right about one thing: today's great players seem a little more likely than in the past to have there best seasons after they turn 30.

May 8, 1997—Losers Rarely Rebound

Here in the Chicago area, it's been a gloomy spring for baseball fans. The White Sox are 10-19, the Cubs 8-23. Only the Phillies, at 10-21, are in the same class, and people expected *them* to be bad. But is there any hope for the local nines, and the Phillies as well? Does a horrible start like this always bury a club for the rest of the season?

I asked Jim Henzler to go back to 1951 and find all the teams which got off to really bad starts—records of 10-20 or worse for their first 30 games. From 1951 through 1996, there were 93 of those teams, or just about two per year. Here's how the teams performed overall:

	W-L	Pct
First 30 Games	854-1936	.306
Remainder of Season	5097-6455	.441
Final Record	5951-8391	.415

As you can see, the teams tended to play much better after their lousy start. But a .441 winning percentage is still pretty bad, and overall the clubs wound up playing .415 ball for the season as a whole. Over a 162-game schedule, that would produce a final record of 67-95—the sort of record that you find at the bottom of most standings boards.

Since the Sox could still be 11-19 after 30 games, I also asked Jim to to look at teams which were 11-19 after 30 games. There were 52 teams which started the year 11-19, and those 52 clubs finished the year with an overall winning percentage of .425. That works out to a final record of 69-93 in a 162-game season. Not much hope for the White Sox there.

But is there *any* room for hope when a club starts out this badly? Only the barest glimmer. Here is a list of all the teams since 1951 which recovered from a bad start (11-19 or worse after 30 games) to finish at .500 or better:

Year Team	After 30	Final
1987 Tigers	11-19	*98-64
1963 Twins	11-19	91-70
1965 Pirates	9-21	90-72
1989 Blue Jays	10-20	*89-73
1974 Pirates	10-20	*88-74
1986 Reds	9-21	86-76
1990 Giants	11-19	85-77
1996 Red Sox	10-20	85-77
1988 Padres	10-20	83-78
1979 Indians	10-20	81-80
1973 Cardinals	8-22	81-81
1955 Phillies	9-21	77-77
1969 Astros	9-21	81-81

* Division winner

Only 13 teams in 46 years recovered to finish at .500 or better. But three of them managed to win division titles: the 1974 Pirates, the 1987 Tigers and the 1989 Blue Jays. Another club, the 1973 Cardinals, started out 8-22 but came within an eyelash of winning the National League East. The Redbirds wound up 81-81, a game and a half behind the Mets, who took the division with a modest 82-79 record.

Perhaps the most amazing team on the list was the 1987 Tigers, who started out 11-19 but went 87-45 the rest of the way to win the American League East title on the last day of the season. But those Tigers were eliminated in the LCS, as were the 1974 Pirates and 1989 Blue Jays. So there *is* some hope for the White Sox, Cubs and Phillies. But not much.

May 15, 1997—Relief Wins

I finally got to see the movie "Shine" last night. About 20 minutes into the film, I started thinking, "Gee, this story seems familiar." In case you aren't familiar with it, "Shine" is a true story based on the life of a gifted young pianist who was emotionally abused by his demanding, manipulative father; suffered a nervous breakdown just when he was about to make it big; underwent institutionalization and some hideous shock treatment; and then came back after years of struggle to perform again on stage (although not very well, according to most reviews I've read). If you're a baseball fan, you'll recognize this story immediately: yes, it's "Fear Strikes Out," the Jimmy Piersall story! In one movie, it was having to play Rachmaninoff that drove the hero over the edge; in the other, it was having to play shortstop. I know which one *I* think is harder. . .

But actually, I'm here to talk about something else: a now-extinct breed of relief pitcher. Those of us who started following baseball in the 1950s and '60s got used to relievers who worked a ton of innings, posted great ERAs and—most distinctively—won a lot of games.

There have been 25 occasions in baseball history in which a pitcher has won 14 or more games in a season without starting a game. *All* of those seasons happened in the years from 1950 (Jim Konstanty) to 1986 (Mark Eichhorn and Roger McDowell). A few of these guys were middle relievers, but the vast majority were closers, although that term didn't exist yet. Often they had more relief victories than they had saves.

You simply don't see this any more. The pitcher with the most saves in baseball history, Lee Smith, has never won more than nine games in a season, and since 1986, he's never won more than *six* in any year. Since becoming a relief pitcher in 1987, Dennis Eckersley has never posted more than six wins in any campaign. This is typical; closers *never* post high win totals any more.

Why did the relievers of 10 or more years ago post so many wins in comparison with the relievers of today? There's a common misconception that it's because they really weren't very good. . . that they got most of their wins after they'd blown a save, then got bailed out by their hitters. But I don't think that was the case at all. Here is a list of all the relief seasons in history with the following traits:

1. No games started
2. At least 14 wins in relief
3. At least 10 saves
4. An ERA under 3.00
5. At least 90 innings pitched in relief

Pitcher	Year	W-L	Sv	ERA	Gm	IP
Jim Konstanty	1950	16-7	22	2.66	74	152.0
Hoyt Wilhelm	1952	15-3	11	2.43	71	159.1
Roy Face	1959	18-1	10	2.70	57	93.1
Luis Arroyo	1961	15-5	29	2.19	65	119.0
Stu Miller	1961	14-5	17	2.66	63	122.0
Ron Perranoski	1963	16-3	21	1.67	69	129.0
Dick Radatz	1963	15-6	25	1.97	66	132.1
Dick Radatz	1964	16-9	29	2.29	79	157.0
Eddie Fisher	1965	15-7	24	2.40	82	165.1
Phil Regan	1966	14-1	21	1.62	65	116.2
Mike Marshall	1972	14-8	18	1.78	66	116.0
Mike Marshall	1974	15-12	21	2.42	106	208.1
John Hiller	1974	17-14	13	2.64	59	150.0
Mark Eichhorn	1986	14-6	10	1.72	69	157.0

There are some superb seasons here, among the best any reliever ever had. As for the notion that they got most of those wins after blowing saves, Bill James did a detailed study of Elroy Face's 18-1 season in his wonderful new book, *The Bill James Guide to Baseball Manager*. Bill discovered that only three of Face's wins came when he entered a game with a lead blew it, and then got the victory when the Pirates rallied. Two more of Face's wins came after he'd entered games with the Pirates trailing. But a whopping 13 of them came when he entered the game *with the score tied*. So Face's 18-1 record wasn't bogus at all; it was fantastic, given that he had numerous opportunities to wind up with a loss.

Most of the pitchers on the list were as good, if not better, than Face was in 1959. Look at the innings totals: everybody but Face worked at least 115 innings. Obviously these guys entered many games in the seventh and eighth innings, and it's also obvious that, like Face, they came into numerous contests with the score tied. Current-day closers aren't used like that; they seldom enter the game unless their club is leading and it's a save situation. In addition, they seldom enter a game before the ninth inning. As a result, their opportunities to record a win are much more limited. By the same token, the relievers of the past had far fewer opportunities to record saves—especially with complete games being much more common back then.

In case you're worried, this is not another diatribe about how today's pitchers are wimps, and relievers were real men in the good old days. There's no right or wrong here; it's just a difference in the way the pitchers are used. But I have to say that I, personally, miss the days when you could see a Dick Radatz fire his fastball for three innings. Could a pitcher be used like that nowadays and remain free from injury? Our own studies from the last 15 years or so indicate that relievers who have worked a lot a lot of innings (100 or more) have tended to break down. But I miss "The Monster," all the same.

Let's go ice down our arms.

May 22, 1997—Relievers & 1967

My column last week on relievers' wins generated a lot of mail, and I wanted to add one last note on how much relievers' usage has changed over the last generation.

In Game 3 of the 1977 ALCS—just 20 years ago—Billy Martin of the Yankees brought in his closer, Sparky Lyle, in the sixth inning of a game the Yanks were losing. Lyle worked 2.1 innings as the Yankees lost, 6-2.

In Game 4 the next day, with the Yankees needing a win to stay alive in the best-of-five series, Martin brought in Lyle in the *fourth* inning of a close game. That's right, the fourth. Lyle worked 5.1 scoreless innings as the Yanks won, 6-4, to force a deciding fifth game.

Game 5 was played the very next day, and though Lyle had worked 7.2 innings over the previous two days, Martin didn't hesitate to bring him in again in the eighth inning. . . even though the Yanks were trailing at the time. This time Sparky got the final four outs as the Yanks rallied to win the series with three runs in the ninth, 5-3. (This sort of usage, bringing the ace reliever in with his team trailing, was one reason why the relievers of the past posted so many more victories.)

The Yankees had one day off; then they began the World Series against the Los Angeles Dodgers. Game 1 lasted 12 innings, and sure enough, there was Lyle again, working the final three-and-a-third innings and allowing no runs and only one hit before the Yankees pulled it out, 4-3. In five days, Lyle had pitched in four games and worked 12 and two-thirds, giving up only one run. . . and that came in the first of the four games. Pretty incredible pitching. Not to mention pretty incredible managing.

No one would ever work a reliever that hard any more, and I'm not advocating that they should. And Martin's use of pitchers was extreme even in the late 1970s. But that's how much the game has changed in 20 years.

On to other another topic. For the last several years, an amazing group of volunteers known as Retrosheet has been attempting to obtain and computerize play-by-play scoresheets for all major league games prior to 1984. You can't find this sort of data in the official records at the Hall of Fame, because—rather incredibly—no one bothered to save and compile play-by-play information until the very recent past. Retrosheet has received the cooperation of a number of major league teams in its efforts, but even the teams' information is incomplete. So the project will almost certainly never be complete, but the group has already compiled a very impressive array of information. And it keeps on growing.

One of the members of the group, a fellow named Luke Kraemer, has taken the Retrosheet data from the 1967 American League season and produced two absolutely fascinating books. One is called *The 1967 American League Boxscore Book*, and it contains the most detailed compilation of box scores for a season that you're ever likely to see. The other book, *The American League Complete Player Reference*, is even more fascinating. It's a book very much like the *STATS Player Profiles*, with detailed splits in numerous categories for both players and teams. Some nuggets from the book:

1. Fenway was still Fenway in 1967. The pennant-winning Red Sox batted .273 with 90 homers and .440 slugging in their home games, .238 with 68 homers and .352 slugging in their road games.
2. Carl Yastremski, who won the triple crown and the American League MVP Award that year, was definitely helped by Fenway, but he was no slouch on the road, either. Yaz was .332-27-74 (.678 SLG) at Fenway, .321-17-47 (.567 SLG) on the road.
3. In the heat of one of the great pennant races of all time, Yaz batted .417 with nine homer and .760 slugging from September 1 on.
4. Jim Lonborg, the American League Cy Young winner in '67, was definitely hurt by Fenway. Lonborg was 9-5, 4.39 at home, vs. 13-4, 2.22 on the road.
5. The Red Sox pitching staff had a 3.86 ERA at Fenway, a 2.85 ERA on the road.
6. Throughout the '67 season, there were rumors that the White Sox were freezing the baseballs at Comiskey Park in order to deaden the ball. There appears to be something to the story. The Sox batted .208 and slugged .291 at Comiskey, vs. .241/.349 on the road. The opponents batted .206 and slugged .284 at Comiskey, vs. .234/.329 in Sox road games. Those are some slugging percentages!
7. The White Sox didn't win the pennant in '67, but don't blame their ace, Joel Horlen.

eight starts from September 1 on, Horlen was 5-1 with an 0.84 ERA.

8. And don't blame Mickey Lolich for the Tigers not winning. From August 1 to the end of the year, Lolich went 9-1 with a 1.31 ERA, and limited opposing hitters to a .162 average with one home run in 308 at-bats. Wow.

9. I don't know whether the lights were lousy in 1967, or whether this is just a fluke, but AL pitchers had a 3.43 ERA in day games in 1967 (686 games) vs. a 3.09 ERA in night games (934 games). I'd forgotten how many more day games they played back then.

10. Plagued by injuries and winding down his career, Mickey Mantle batted .287 as a righthanded hitter, .216 as a lefty. But Mantle hit for more power from the left side: one homer every 15 at-bats as a lefty (17/259), one homer every 36 AB as a righty (5/181).

I could go on and on, but you get the picture. If you're interested in the 1967 books, you can order them directly from Luke Kraemer for $17.95 each postpaid, or $33.95 for both. You can reach Luke at:

Pastime Press
625 NW Waterhouse Ave.
Beaverton, OR 97006
(503) 645-3550
lkraemer@europa.com

I'm sure he'll appreciate the order.

If you're interested in helping out the Retrosheet project, they're always looking for volunteers. You can write the president, David Smith, at:

Retrosheet
David Smith
6 Penncross Circle
Newark DE 19702
Dwsmith@strauss.udel.edu

May 29, 1997—Frank Thomas

I can't resist asking the trivia question they used on the White Sox broadcast last night: What pitcher won at least 14 games for five consecutive seasons, pitching for a different team each year? Answer at the end of the column.

When the White Sox signed Albert Belle prior to this season, at least a couple of sportswriters predicted that Frank Thomas would break Roger Maris' record. The reason? With Belle hitting behind him, opposing teams wouldn't be able to pitch around Thomas as much. He'd get fewer walks, better pitches to hit, and as a result, more home runs.

Thus far in the '97 season, this hasn't been what's happened at all. Thomas' walk rate is up, not down; his home-run rate, on the other hand, is lower, not higher.

	Thomas BB	Thomas HR
1996	109 BB in 141 G	1 HR each 13.2 AB
1997	48 BB in 48 G	1 HR each 15.1 AB

The home-run rate is only marginally lower, and Thomas could easily equal or surpass his 1996 rate by the time the season is over. But the walk rate is a puzzle, at least at first. Actually, there's one sense in which the opposing moundsmen aren't pitching around Thomas as much: he's getting far fewer intentional walks than he did in 1996. Thomas was given 26 IBB during the '96 season; with the '97 campaign nearly a third over, he has only seven IBB. But he's still drawing unintentional walks at a far greater rate than he was in 1996. Why would the pitchers be putting him on more often, despite the presence of Belle behind him?

The answer is that they aren't, at least not deliberately. Thomas has always been one of the most selective hitters in the majors; like Ted Williams, he generally feels that he's doing pitchers a favor when he swings at pitches out of the strike zone. But even Thomas puts some limits on his selectivity. The White Sox had some excellent hitters coming up behind Thomas in 1996, but face it, Harold Baines and Robin Ventura aren't Albert Belle. . . and they aren't Frank Thomas, either. As a result, Thomas sometimes grew impatient with men on base. He appeared to feel that if he didn't expand his strike zone a little, his team would be missing a chance to have its best hitter swing the bat. You could easily argue that he was doing the pitchers a favor by doing this, but Thomas is human like everybody else; when he keeps reading that he's supposed to be his team's "big RBI guy," he's apt to give in to the temptation to swing the bat a little more.

In 1997, though, he feels under no such pressure. People have this "protection" stuff all wrong, I think; just because Albert Belle is in the on-deck circle, they're not going to start throwing fastballs down the middle to Frank Thomas in order to avoid walking him. They will continue to work the corners out of respect for Thomas, trying to throw strikes but not always succeeding. Thomas' 1997 mindset probably goes something like this:

1. I don't have to be the "big RBI guy" any more; we've got Albert Belle now.
2. Because of that, I'm not going to swing at pitches out of the strike zone any more.
3. If they miss the plate and walk me, that's fine. Albert can drive the runs in.

For the most part, Thomas has always had this philosophy, which is one of the reasons why he drew a lot of walks even in 1996. But in 1997, he feels more inclined than ever to stick to his guns. As a result, he's an even more valuable hitter. Thomas is currently hitting .373, 24 points better than he hit last year. His on-base percentage is a whopping .507. How good is that? No hitter has had an OBP over .500 since Ted Williams and Mickey Mantle did it in 1957, and Mantle and Williams (who also topped .500 in 1954) are the only hitters since 1926 to have OBPs over .500.

Studies have always indicated that this "protection" stuff is overrated, but an article we did in the *Baseball Scoreboard* a few years ago indicated that it does make a little difference when you have two superstars hitting back-to-back. Having Albert Belle hitting behind him seems to be helping Thomas be a better offensive player than ever. . . though not in the way that people thought.

Trivia question answer: Mike Torrez. He went 15-8 for the '74 Expos, 20-9 for the '75 Orioles, 16-12 for the '76 A's, 14-12 for the '77 Yankees (he was also 3-1 for the A's at the start of that year) and 16-13 for the '78 Red Sox. Torrez also won 10 games for both the '69 Cardinals and the '83 Mets, giving him double figures in wins for seven different teams. And as Mat Olkin points out, he was the guy who hit Dickie (Thon) and got hit by Bucky (Dent). One of the more unique careers ever.

But we're sure you knew that. See you next week.

June 5, 1997—Questions & Answers

Burning questions of the day:

1. Will anyone hit .400?

Currently there are two players over the .400 mark (Larry Walker and Tony Gwynn) and two more over .390 (Frank Thomas and Will Clark). For all the talk you hear about Maris' record, we've had players come a lot closer to hitting .400 in recent times than anyone's come to hitting 61 homers. Since 1977, three players have hit between .388 and .394 (Rod Carew, George Brett and Tony Gwynn). That's only a few hits short of .400.

So it could happen; I just don't think it will. To put it simply, I believe that the pressure to keep grinding out those two-hit games you need to hit .400 would be too intense. Gwynn, who gets hurt a lot, probably has the best chance because it's a lot easier to hit .400 in 450 at-bats than it is in 550. You also have to consider that Walker has Coors Field going for him. I wish both of them well, and the other guys as well. But I don't think anyone will hit .400 this year.

2. Will anyone challenge Hack Wilson's RBI record?

No way. Scoring is down more than half a run a game in each league thus far this year, and nobody came close last year. But you could certainly see somebody—Griffey or Galarraga, most likely—knock in 160 or more. The last time anyone topped 160 ribbies was in 1938 (Jimmie Foxx). I think that'll change this year.

3. How about Maris' record, then?

The pressure is going to be really tough, but I still think Junior's going to do it. The best thing would be if both he and McGwire were challenging the record in September; that means people won't be hounding one guy so much.

I think Griffey is the one player who could handle that sort of pressure. He loves this sort of thing. McGwire's a possibility, also, but I don't see him staying healthy enough.

4. What's wrong with the Dodgers?

They're just very overrated, is all. Even their pitchers aren't as good as most people think; the L.A. team ERA in road games is 3.90, sixth-best in the league. They have a good staff, but Dodger Stadium makes them look better than they really are. As for their hitters, the Dodgers currently have a team OBP of .313, second-worst in the league. You can't win unless you put people on base. The Dodgers have had Wilton Guerrero (a "corkin' good" ballplayer) hitting first or second most of the year. The guy's got three walks in 50 games!

5. So what's happened to all those "great young prospects": Andruw Jones, Todd Walker, Dmitri Young, to name three?

They haven't done much so far (and Walker got sent back to the minors). They should all be OK, eventually. People forget that even great players often take a little time to adjust to the majors. Carl Yastrzemski batted .266 as a rookie, Pete Rose .273, Willie Stargell .243 with 11 homers in 108 games. Sometimes you just need a little patience. I think the Braves are bringing Jones along just right, spotting him here and there and breaking him in gradually. He's going to be a great player, and I think Walker and Young will be very good also.

June 12, 1997—Swinging at First Pitches

One of our readers, Jim Petty, was watching an Indians-Red Sox game recently, and the announcers were criticizing Nomar Garciaparra for consistently swinging at the first pitch. According to Jim, the broadcasters said that it was important to "make the pitcher throw a strike before you start swinging." Jim wondered if this was really true, and whether our data could shed any light on the subject. He points out the example of Tom Glavine, a pitcher with great control. "If Glavine is going to get the first pitch over," notes Jim, "you're working yourself into a hole."

Let's look at some numbers. First of all, here's how National League hitters (AL numbers are very similar) have fared this year when they put the first pitch in play:

	AVG	HR Rate
1st Pitch in Play	.316	1 HR each 34.8 AB

This looks great; wow, a .316 hitter! However, there are several other factors to consider:

1. The hitter will often swing at the first pitch and *not* put it in play. He'll swing and miss or hit a foul ball. That puts him behind in the count. This happens *a lot*: in the major leagues thus far this year, only 41 percent of first-pitch swings have resulted in the ball actually being put into play.

2. Even if the hitter succeeds in getting the first pitch in play, he's forfeiting his chance to draw a walk. So that .316 average is also his on-base percentage, and a .316 OBP is nothing to rave about.

3. By putting the first pitch in play, the hitter also forfeits his chance to get a fat pitch on an even more favorable count: 2-and-0 or 3-and-1, for example.

To demonstrate No. 3, here are the NL figures for the other favorable counts along with 0-0:

	AVG	HR Rate
1st Pitch in Play	.316	1 HR each 34.8 AB
2-0 Pitch in Play	.329	1 HR each 23.3 AB
3-1 Pitch in Play	.333	1 HR each 20.0 AB

You can see that both the batting average and home-run rates are even better on 2-0 and 3-1 counts. . . which suggests that the hitter should *never* swing at a first pitch.

Of course, that's silly. If a hitter never goes after a first pitch, the pitcher will simply throw the ball down the middle to get a strike, and starting out 0-1 puts virtually every hitter at a major disadvantage. So the hitter has to swing at enough first pitches to keep the pitchers honest.

More importantly, there's Jim Petty's question about Tom Glavine. A pitcher with great control is unlikely to get behind in the count, so isn't the hitter doing him a favor by laying off the first pitch?

Here are some figures for Glavine, based on 1994-96 data:

	AB	HR	BB	AVG	OBP	SLG
1st Pitch in Play	340	9	—	.353	.353	.497
1st Pitch Strike	983	10	40	.226	.258	.305
1st Pitch Ball	953	14	170	.247	.359	.353

Hitters who swing at Glavine's first pitch and put it into play fare very well. He remains a tough pitcher even after a first-pitch ball, so it would probably be a good idea for hitters to go after a Glavine first pitch more often than they would against an average hurler. And in fact they do; thus far in '97, hitters have swung at Glavine's first pitch 34 percent of the time, vs. 32 percent vs. NL pitchers overall. Remember, though, that these are figures based on putting the first pitch in play; more often than not, a hitter will go after a Glavine first offering and come up empty.

How about Greg Maddux? Here are the same breakdowns for Maddux, again based on 1994-96 data:

	AB	HR	BB	AVG	OBP	SLG
1st Pitch in Play	446	3	—	.251	.275	.307
1st Pitch Strike	1249	10	28	.185	.205	.250
1st Pitch Ball	713	10	41	.251	.291	.346

Maddux has even better control than Glavine, so hitters are even more tempted to go after the first pitch with him on the mound. Thus far in '97, they've swung at 39 percent of Maddux first-pitches, which is much higher than the overall NL rate of 32 percent. Swinging at those first pitches doesn't do them much good, but they at least fare substantially better than if they lay off the pitch and it gets called a strike. Their best hope is if Maddux' first pitch misses the strike zone; trouble is, it doesn't happen very often.

What the numbers show is that, overall, patience pays off: hitters who resist the urge to jump at the first pitch tend to wind up with greater rewards than hitters who don't. But you have to swing at *some* first pitches, and when you're facing a guy with pinpoint control, it's probably a good idea to pull the trigger a little more often.

June 26, 1997—The SABR Convention

I spent last weekend doing one of my favorite things: attending the annual SABR convention. SABR is short for the Society for American Baseball Research, and if you're an avid fan of the game, I'd recommend joining as soon as possible (the address is at the end of this article). Along with getting the opportunity to interact with people who really love baseball, you'll receive a monthly newsletter and several outstanding publications over the course of the year. The books alone are well worth the annual membership fee, which is $35.

For me, the convention is a sort of baseball reunion. I see people there I never see anywhere else over the course of the year, and the convention gives me a chance to talk baseball with them, virtually nonstop, for three-plus days. Other highlights of this year's convention, which was held in Louisville, Ky.:

1. A tour of the Louisville Slugger factory and museum. This was really neat. They took us through the whole plant, which isn't very big, and you could watch major leaguers' bats being made. There were stacks of bats everywhere, including a pile for Ken Griffey Jr. Naturally my friends and I couldn't resist picking up one of Junior's bats and swinging it. Who knows? We might have swung the bat that'll belt No. 62.

2. Several player panels featuring former major leaguers, minor leaguers and Negro Leaguers. Panels this year included Pee Wee Reese, Carl Erskine, Mel Parnell, Paul Foytack and Connie Johnson, among others. There was also a special session with former St. Louis Brown pitcher Ned Garver, and a keynote address by Hall of Famer Jim Bunning. All the sessions included a lengthy Q and A period afterward. These were often very revealing. For instance Bunning defended Gene Mauch's much-maligned use of the Phillies' starting rotation late in the disastrous 1964 season; according to Jim, "You had to be in the clubhouse. Nobody else (apart from Bunning and Chris Short) wanted the ball." And Ed Stevens, the Dodge first baseman who lost his job to Jackie Robinson in 1947, refused to take the politically correct route of praising the Dodgers for promoting Robinson. On the contrary, Stevens— who posted some pretty good stats as a 21-year-old rookie in 1946—is still bitter about Branch Rickey's treatment of him. According to Stevens, Rickey told him to be patient, keep his yap shut and go back to the minors for a year; at the end of the year, Rickey said he would trade Dodger second baseman Eddie Stanky, move Robinson to second, and then give Stevens his old job back. Stevens said he went along with the plan and had a good year

Montreal, but Rickey then double-crossed him by trading him to the Pirates when the season was over. He's still mad about it.

3. An outing to a minor league game between the Iowa Cubs and the Louisville Redbirds. Miguel Batista of the Cubs threw a two-hit shutout *and* hit a home run! Wrigley Field, here we come. . .

4. A number of excellent research presentations. My favorite was a video produced by a Philadelphia university professor on the Phillies' first ballpark back in the 1880s, the precursor to Baker Bowl. The guy had computer-animated drawings of the park which showed the layout in great detail. Outstanding.

5. A memorabilia room where you could buy books (new and old), media guides, videos and things. My favorite purchase was a book written by Joseph J. Dittmar and published by the McFarland Publishing Co. in 1990, entitled *Baseball's Benchmark Boxscores*. The book has both box scores and articles about 105 record-setting games from baseball history—everything from the 26-23 game between the Cubs and Phillies in 1922 to Harvey Haddix' 12-perfect-inning game in 1959, and more. Great stuff.

6. A viewing of the complete original NBC broadcast of Game 1 of the 1955 World Series between the Dodgers and Yankees. Mel Allen does the first four-and-a-half innings, Vin Scully the last four and a half. The '55 World Series was the first one I remember watching as a child, so naturally I really got into it. One of the more fascinating things about the game was that there were *two* attempted steals of home—not the front end of double steals, but outright swipe attempts by a runner on third, which is something you never see any more. Billy Martin was out; Jackie Robinson was safe. Or so said umpire Bill Summers.

7. The annual SABR Trivia competition, which is the mother of all trivia contests. There are both individual and team (four people) competitions, and everybody knows their stuff. Sample question: Name the player in major league history who had the most 30-homer seasons (six) in his career without hitting more than 300 homers. Answer: Hank Sauer. But of course you knew that. I was lucky enough to be on the winning team this year, though my contributions were about equal to Charlie Hayes' contribution to the Yankees' World Series win last season. My teammates Eddie Gold, Richard Klein and Mark Kanter were awesome, and it was great to be part of a winner. Pete Palmer, the *Total Baseball* guy, won the individual competition.

Every time I go to this convention, I come away stunned by how many people there are who are totally into baseball and the history of the game—both on and off the field. There was a guy who gave a research talk on the umpiring back in 1908, for instance. Another toured Hall of Famers' gravesites and came back with a plea for baseball to take better care of them. A third talked about how different the American League might have been had Herb Score not been injured back in 1957. Still another talked about train wrecks involving major league players. And on and on. Whatever problems baseball has—and we know it has plenty—it certainly doesn't lack for dedicated fans. No other sport comes close to matching it.

If you're interested in finding out about SABR, you can contact the organization at:

Society for American Baseball Research
P.O. Box 93183
Cleveland OH, 44101
Phone: 216-574-0500
E-mail: info@sabr.org
Website: www.sabr.org

July 3, 1997—Interleague Play

I hate to admit it, but I like interleague play a lot more than I thought I would. In a word, the games have been *fun*. The last three nights, the White Sox played the Pirates in one of those series everybody was making fun of ("Yeah, White Sox vs. Cubs'll draw some interest, but how about when the Sox play the Pirates?"). That shows how wrong people were (including me). The series drew about 25,000 fans per game—big crowds by Three Rivers standards— and the fans went nuts when Pittsburgh took all three games. Albert Belle makes more than the entire Pittsburgh roster, so naturally everybody booed their heads off every time Albert stuck his head out of the dugout. Great stuff. . . even if my team got swept.

Not every series was great, of course, but a lot of them were terrific, and there were some real gems, particularly the matches involving really good teams like the Orioles and Braves. But will it be like this next year? A lot of the old grumps—baseball has more of these than any sport ever ought to—are sniffing that "interleague play is a novelty" and attendance is sure to plummet at these games next year. Well, maybe attendance *will* drop a little, but I'm betting that interleague play will still be a big hit. As for the "novelty" thing, people said the exact same thing about night baseball when it first came in.

It's not all perfect, of course; what is? One problem interleague play has created is the schedule—way too many two-game series. So apparently they're going to switch to an unbalanced schedule next year, like this:

vs. division opponents	14 games vs. each (total 56)
vs. other divisions in league	9 games vs. each (total 90)
interleague games	16 games total vs. 1 division

That works out to 162; remember that with expansion, there will be three five-team divisions next year. I'm glad they're finally going to more games against division opponents, but I personally don't think 14 games is quite enough. Here's a plan I like better:

vs. division opponents	18 games vs. each (total 72)
vs. other divisions in league	7 games vs. each (total 70)
interleague games	4 games each vs. 1 division (total 20)

This puts much more emphasis on divisional play, which is the way it ought to be anyway. Sure, teams would be giving up a couple of games with the Yankees or whoever, but I'm convinced that they'd make up for that, and then some, with the added emphasis this setup would give to the divisional races. Rivalries such as Yankees-Orioles, Mariners-Rangers and Braves-Marlins would be better than ever thanks to the additional head-to-head matchups.

Even 14 games vs. division opponents is a step in the right direction, though. I'm glad to see it happening.

On to other stuff. The level of offense in baseball has dropped significantly this year compared to '96. Here's a comparison of the '97 figures with the numbers at the same point last year (first 93 days of each season):

	Avg	Runs/G	HR/G
AL 1996	.279	10.98	2.46
AL 1997	.273	10.03	2.17
NL 1996	.261	9.44	2.06
NL 1997	.263	8.99	1.79
MLB 1996	.270	10.21	2.27
MLB 1997	.268	9.51	1.98

One result of the drop in offense is that several pitchers are putting together really great seasons: Roger Clemens, Randy Johnson and Pedro Martinez, to name three. Yet things are still favorable enough for hitting to have guys batting .400 and challenging Maris' home-run record. I personally like a lot of hitting, but last year's season-long slugfest was a little extreme to be enjoyable *every* year. It's good to see a little balance return to the game.

July 10, 1997—World Series, 1952 Style

As many of you know, I love old sports movies and newsreel clips, and I also collect tapes of radio and TV broadcasts of major sporting events. I recently obtained videotapes of the NBC broadcasts of Games 6 and 7 of the 1952 World Series, which are said to be the oldest complete-game broadcasts known to still exist. The tapes—and the games themselves—are so fascinating that I decided to devote a column to them.

I was well aware that baseball broadcasting was much different back then, but it was a shock to discover *how* different. There were two announcers for the '52 Series games, Mel Allen and Red Barber, but they hardly interacted at all: one guy would do the first four-and-a-half innings by himself, then the other one would take over. (You'd be surprised—well, maybe not—about how little you miss all that endless yakking.) There was only one sponsor, Gillette, and they pretty much kept things to a minimum, also. There were a few rather lengthy commercials with ballplayers shaving (Alvin Dark, Gene Hermanski, Birdie Tebbetts... wonderful stuff), but usually they'd just show a short cartoon with the Gillette parrot singing "How are you fixed for blades?" (Boy, did *that* take me back.) Sometimes they'd do nothing but flash the Gillette logo between half-innings, and sometimes they wouldn't even do that. There were no replays, naturally, and only a small number of cameras, but the NBC boys did a very nice job of covering the action, all things considered.

While the broadcasts themselves were fascinating, it's the way the games were played, and managed, that I really want to focus on. This Series was one of the many Dodger-Yankee classics of that period, and the Dodgers entered Game 6 with a three-games-to-two lead. The starting pitchers were veteran righthander Vic Raschi, for the Yankees, and 22-year-old rookie righty Billy Loes for the Dodgers. Raschi, who was working on three days' rest, had started and thrown a complete-game three-hitter in Game 2 (the '52 Series was played on seven consecutive days). Loes' only previous appearance in the Series was a two-inning relief stint in Game 2.

The Yankees won the game, 3-2, with all but one run scoring on home runs; Yogi Berra and Mickey Mantle homered for the Yankees, and Duke Snider hit two home runs for the Dodgers. But three things really stuck out in watching the broadcast:

1. The wild swings some of the players were taking. I don't mean scrubbeenies, either, I mean guys like Roy Campanella and Gil Hodges. They were spinning around, practically falling into the dugout on a few of their roundhouse swings. With all due respect to the players of the past, it looked like a sandlot game at times.

2. Watching the young Mickey Mantle in action. More than anyone on either team, the Mick looked like a 1997 superstar: graceful, athletic, muscular... and he could really *move* on the bases.

3. The way the managers used the pitchers. This was the biggest thing. I kept a pitch count for both sides, and Dodger manager Chuck Dressen let Loes—just 22, remember, and considered a prize prospect—throw 147 pitches before he finally took him out with one out in the top of the ninth. As was still fairly typical in that era, Dressen replaced Loes with one of his starting pitchers, Preacher Roe; Roe had thrown a complete-game six-hitter in Game 3 three days earlier. On the Yankee side, Raschi threw 118 pitches, which isn't excessive, before Casey Stengel lifted him in the eighth. Like Dressen, Stengel replaced Raschi with a starting pitcher, Allie Reynolds. The Chief had already worked seven innings as the starting pitcher in Game 1 and nine more in a complete-game win in Game 4 three days later. Now here he was again, on one day's rest. Reynolds worked an inning and a third, threw 21 pitches, and recorded the save.

Game 7 was played the next day. Dressen's starter was rookie righty Joe Black, who despite the lack of off-days, was making his third start of the Series... and his second straight start on two days' rest. Funny thing was, Black had been Dressen's *relief ace* during the regular season. Can you imagine the 1997 Orioles making it to the World Series, and then starting Randy Myers in Game 1? Of course you can't... but baseball was much different in 1952.

So here was Black, who'd tossed a complete-game victory in Game 1 and then worked seven innings in Game 4, toeing the rubber for his third start in seven days.

Talking near the end of the Game 6 broadcast, Mel Allen had suggested, with a straight face, that the Yankees would probably start Reynolds the next day—this despite Allie's relief appearance in Game 6 along with his two earlier starting assignments. Instead Stengel chose Eddie Lopat, who'd worked 8.1 tough innings (10 hits, four walks) in Game 3, on three days' rest. Casey had something in mind for Reynolds, though—and apparently a plan for getting through Game 7 with several different pitchers.

Lopat breezed through the first three innings, using only 27 pitches, then gave up a single to Duke Snider to lead off the fourth. Jackie Robinson then laid down a bunt and beat it out for a hit. Roy Campanella was next, and he too, bunted to move the runners over. . . only the bunt was so good that Campy also beat it out for a hit. The bases were loaded with nobody out and Gil Hodges up, but Lopat hadn't given up a run, he was still pitching effectively, and Hodges was 0-for-19 in the Series (he would wind up 0-for-21). No matter; Stengel wanted a new pitcher. He wanted Allie Reynolds.

The bionic-armed Allie got out of the jam with only one run scoring, then worked two more innings before Stengel finally took him out. My tape was missing a little bit of the action during Reynolds' stint, but he definitely threw at least 30 pitches while he was in there. Even Stengel didn't want to push it too far with Allie, so when the Dodgers came up in the bottom of the seventh with the Yanks leading 3-2, Casey lifted Reynolds. . . and brought in the man who had started and thrown 118 pitches the previous afternoon, Vic Raschi.

Raschi didn't have a thing, which didn't surprise *me* any. He gave up a walk to Carl Furillo, got pinch hitter Rocky Nelson on a popout, gave up a line single to Billy Cox and then walked Pee Wee Reese. That loaded the bases with one out and the Dodgers' most dangerous hitter, Duke Snider, due up. If they had let him, Casey would have probably put Reynolds back in there, or maybe Lopat, but that was against the rules, so he finally (finally!) brought in a guy who was mostly a relief pitcher, lefthander Bob Kuzava. Naturally Kuzava was making his first appearance of the Series.

To make this long story just a little shorter, Kuzava got out of the jam with some major help from Billy Martin, who made a brilliant catch on a Jackie Robinson pop fly near the pitchers' mound that seemed fated to drop in. Kuzava finished the game—though I swear I saw Allie Reynolds warming up in the bullpen in the ninth—with no further damage, and the Yankees won yet another championship, 4-2. On the Dodger side, Black worked 5.1 so-so innings; he was succeeded, naturally, by two pitchers who were normally starters, Roe and Carl Erskine.

Looking at the action, I got a much deeper appreciation for how much baseball has changed in 45 years. Sure, there were relief aces back then, and the Yankees had won a couple of championships with heavy reliance on a star fireman, Joe Page. But that was still unusual, and when Page wore out in 1950, the Yanks got through their most important games by using their starters in relief whenever they thought it necessary. The Dodgers, on the other hand, *did* have a bona fide relief ace in Joe Black. . . but they felt that in a short series, they were better off using Black as a starter.

The other thing that occurred to me, as it must to any thoughtful person who observes the way pitchers were used in 1952, is that

a) either the pitchers of two generations ago were real men, while the pitchers of 1997 are wimps (take that, Randy and Roger!), or
b) those 1952 pitchers knew some secret physiological tricks that enabled them to perform truly amazing feats of durabilty, or
c) maybe they just weren't throwing very hard on a lot of their pitches, compared to the moundsmen of today.

Unlike many of you, I was alive in 1952, and the romantic in me would like to think that men were men back then, and just as there will never be another Jimmy Stewart, there'll never be another Allie Reynolds. But I just can't buy it. The players of today are better athletes, as they are in every sport, and the pitchers throw harder than they did back then. Period.

But the game sure was fun back in 1952.

July 17, 1997—Flukes

Back when I was just getting into sportswriting, one of the first baseball articles I had published was a piece called "The Unlikely Heroes of 1970." It was a rundown of some of the once-in-a-lifetime seasons which took place that year. A few examples:

1. Luis Aparicio, who was 36 years old and in his 15th major league season, batted .313 in 1970—a career best by 33 points and 51 points higher than his eventual lifetime average of .262.

2. Bert Campaneris, another veteran shortstop who would eventually play 19 major league seasons, hit 22 homers in '70. In his other 18 years, Campy had a *total* of 57 homers, and he never hit more than eight in any other year.

3. Jim Hickman, another vet who was in his ninth major league year, batted .315 with 32 homers and 115 RBI. Prior to that, Hickman's career bests were a .257 average, 21 homers and 57 RBI.

4. Wes Parker, who was in his seventh season, hit .319 with 47 doubles and 111 RBI. Parker lasted two more years, and apart from 1970, his career highs were a .279 average, 24 doubles and 68 ribbies.

5. Billy Grabarkewitz, who hit .236 with 28 homers and 141 RBI in his seven-year career, produced more than half his homer and RBI total (17 HR, 84 RBI), along with a .289 average and an on-base percentage of .403, in 1970.

6. Cito Gaston batted .318 with 29 homers and 91 RBI in 1970. In the rest of his 11-year career, Gaston never hit more than 17 homers, never drove in more than 61 runs, and never batted higher than .269 in a season in which he had more than 150 AB.

Weird stuff, most of it basically unexplainable. Ever since then, I've been fascinated by fluke hitting seasons. Not surprisingly, most of them happen in big-hitting years, and it looks like we're going to have a good number of them in 1997. Of course, you can't *really* tell if these are true fluke seasons yet, since a) there's a lot of the year still left to play and b) sometimes players improve dramatically from one year to the next, and then maintain some semblance of that level. Anyway, here are my candidates.

MATT STAIRS. You gotta love this guy. Stairs is 29 years old, and while he hasn't had much chance to play in the majors prior to 1996 (263 AB), he's been a consistent .300 hitter with a little bit of power during his minor league career. But nothing he's done either in the minors or the majors could prepare us for what he's done thus far in '97: .367 average, .733 slugging, 15 homers and 42 RBI in only 150 at-bats. Stairs just isn't going to keep hitting like this, but his home-run power is legitimate: counting 1996, he has 25 homers in his last 287 major league at-bats. If he got 400 AB in a season against righties, he could hit around 30 homers.

SANDY ALOMAR JR. Currently hitting .363 with 11 homers (and .587 slugging) in 259 AB. A lot of dumb people have been saying, "He's always been good, the only difference is that he's healthy now." That's ridiculous, of course; except for seasons where he's had a handful of at-bats, Alomar has never hit higher than .307 in his professional career prior to this. . . and that includes two seasons in the Pacific Coast League. The average is bogus and he'll start sinking like a stone soon; the power numbers, though, are not out of line with what he's done the last few years.

JOEY CORA. Future member of the "Bogus All-Star Hall of Fame." Cora's not a bad hitter—he batted .297 and .291 the last few years—but a .331 average with .513 slugging? And the power numbers. Last year Cora hit a career-high six homers in 530 at-bats; he's already got nine this year in only 335 AB. I'd suspect cork, but Joey's too nice a guy to do something like that, isn't he? Whatever, this a fluke.

RAY LANKFORD. Always a pretty good player, but he's gone through the roof this year, hitting .327 (previous high .291), slugging .662 (previous high .513) and hitting 22 homers in only 269 at-bats (career high is 25, but in 483 AB). Clearly he's playing over his head, but I wouldn't be surprised if Lankford continues to perform at a higher level than he did prior to 1997.

TINO MARTINEZ. He's not Joey Cora, but how can Tino Martinez be threatening to hit 61 homers? Previous best was 31 homers in 519 AB; now he has 33 in 356 AB. I guess after Brady Anderson hit 50 last year, we should have been ready for anything. Tino's a good guy, works his ass off, handles the New York pressure without a sweat. Roger Maris was an unlikely candidate to hit 61 dingers, also; I don't think Tino will come close to that, but if he does, I'll be happy for him.

This is *not* a fluke, but did you know that since the start of the 1993, Tony Gwynn has batted .372 with 83 strikeouts in 2,257 at-bats? Blows me away.

What a strange and wonderful game baseball is.

July 24, 1997—The Prospect Game

I thought I'd devote today's column to the subject of "prospects." STATS has been rating prospects for several years now, and we've devoted an entire book, the *Minor League Scouting Notebook*, to the subject for the last three. Others have been around longer, particularly *Baseball America*. I thought it would be fun to review how *BA* and STATS have fared in rating the top prospects over the last few years. We'll go back to 1991, using *Baseball America's* Top 100 Prospects issues; the STATS ratings began in 1995. I'll list the top 15 per year in each ranking system.

1991 *Baseball America* Top Prospects

1. Todd Van Poppel
2. Andujar Cedeno
3. Ryan Klesko
4. Jose Offerman
5. Roger Salkeld
6. Arthur Rhodes
7. Ivan Rodriguez
8. Reggie Sanders
9. Mark Lewis
10. Mo Vaughn
11. Bernie Williams
12. Wil Cordero
13. Rondell White
14. Raul Mondesi
15. Willie Banks

COMMENT: One of the telling stories about the prospect game came in the came in the 1990 amateur draft. The Braves, with the first overall pick, reluctlanctly passed on the consensus No. 1 prospect, the "unsignable" (for them) Todd Van Poppel. . . and settled for a guy named Chipper Jones. Back in 1991, that seemed like the Braves' loss, but people found out otherwise soon enough. They would also find out how hard it is to rate pitchers as top prospects. Among the four pitchers on the 1991 top 15 list, only Arthur Rhodes has made any impact at the major league level, and he's still only a middle reliever. Yeah, I know, guys get hurt, but that's the big problem with pitchers. . . they get hurt much more than hitters do, so it's risky to build your hopes around them. As for the hitters, Andujar Cedeno at No. 2 turned out to be pretty embarrassing, but *BA* did fine with Klesko, Rodriguez, Sanders, Vaughn, Williams and Mondesi. They also had Tino Martinez at No. 18 (higher than I would have ranked him back then), and a guy who did turn out to be a legitimate pitching star, Mike Mussina, at No. 19.

1992 *Baseball America* Top Prospects

1. Brien Taylor
2. Todd Van Poppel
3. Roger Salkeld
4. Chipper Jones
5. Arthur Rhodes
6. Royce Clayton
7. Wil Cordero
8. Ryan Klesko
9. Frank Rodriguez
10. Pedro Martinez
11. Reggie Sanders
12. Rondell White
13. Mark Wohlers
14. Kurt Miller
15. Derek Bell

COMMENT: Taylor, Van Poppel and Salkeld at 1-2-3. . . three crap-outs, as it turned out. This time BA hit on Pedro Martinez and Mark Wohlers, at least. The only really big star among the hitters, as it turned out, was Chipper, but the rest of the hitters in the top 15 have all had impact at the major league level. You can't say that about the pitchers.

1993 *Baseball America* Top Prospects

1. Chipper Jones
2. Brien Taylor
3. Cliff Floyd
4. Carlos Delgado
5. Tim Salmon
6. Wil Cordero
7. Todd Van Poppel
8. Jason Bere
9. Allen Watson
10. Tyrone Hill
11. Kurt Miller
12. Dmitri Young
13. Manny Ramirez
14. Ray McDavid
15. Rondell White

COMMENT: The same routine. For every Cliff Floyd who falls by the wayside, you can find about five pitchers who've done the same. The only pitcher here who has really made an impact at the major league level was Jason Bere, and he hit the skids after a couple of years.

BA Managing Editor Jim Callis probably wouldn't want me to point this out, but *BA* had Mike Piazza, who would be the NL Rookie of the Year in '93, down at No. 38, one spot behind Nigel Wilson and three behind Mike Kelly. Take if from a guy who's made his share of mistakes: it's easy to look dumb in this prospect-rating business.

1994 *Baseball America* Top Prospects

1. Cliff Floyd
2. Chipper Jones
3. Jeffrey Hammonds
4. Alex Gonzalez
5. Carlos Delgado
6. Alex Rodriguez
7. Manny Ramirez
8. James Baldwin
9. Rondell White
10. Jose Silva
11. Darren Dreifort
12. Steve Karsay
13. Trot Nixon
14. Chan Ho Park
15. Ryan Klesko

COMMENT: Poor Cliff Floyd. He's had a career that would make you think he was a pitcher: first he was overrated, then he got hurt. There's plenty of hitting gems on this list, however, headed by Chipper, Alex Rodriguez and Manny Ramirez. Among the pitchers, James Baldwin, Chan Ho Park and Darren Dreifort could still turn out to be really good, but that's another problem with pitchers: even when they're legitimately good, it usually takes them longer to develop. And often they get sidetracked by injury, as Dreifort did.

1995 *Baseball America* Top Prospects

1. Alex Rodriguez
2. Ruben Rivera
3. Chipper Jones
4. Derek Jeter
5. Brian Hunter
6. Shawn Green
7. Charles Johnson
8. Alex Gonzalez
9. Johnny Damon
10. Ben Grieve
11. Armando Benitez

12. Bill Pulsipher
13. Todd Hollandsworth
14. Alan Benes
15. Antonio Osuna

COMMENT: It starts getting harder to evaluate the lists now, because some of these players are still developing. But again, the only pitcher on the list who could become a big star is Alan Benes; meanwhile, three of the top four hitters are *already* stars.

1995 STATS Top Prospects

1. Alex Rodriguez
2. Derek Jeter
3. Carlos Delgado
4. Alex Gonzalez
5. Charles Johnson
6. Scott Ruffcorn
7. Alan Benes
8. Jimmy Haynes
9. Johnny Damon
10. Jim Pittsley
11. Jose Malave
12. LaTroy Hawkins
13. Bob Abreu
14. Rich Becker
15. Ray Durham

COMMENT: I can hear a few of you saying, "OK, big mouth, you're so smart, let's see *your* list!" Here's the first, from the 1995 *MLSN*. After the top three, we look as bad as *Baseball America* ever did. We've got five pitchers in the top 12, and only Benes looks like a star. You'd think we'd have learned from the other guys' mistakes, but no. . .

1996 *Baseball America* Top Prospects 1. Andruw Jones 2. Paul Wilson 3. Ruben Rivera 4. Darin Erstad 5. Alan Benes 6. Derek Jeter 7. Karim Garcia 8. Livan Hernandez 9. Vladimir Guerrero 10. Ben Davis 11. Jason Schmidt 12. Matt Drews 13. Derrick Gibson 14. Billy Wagner 15. Bartolo Colon

COMMENT: Ben Davis? Now, *that's* embarrassing. Too early to tell about many of these, but for once there's two pitchers who are *already* good in Benes and Wagner, with hopes for some of the others. For now, anyway.

1996 STATS Top Prospects

1. Johnny Damon
2. Paul Wilson
3. Andruw Jones

4. Derek Jeter
5. Ruben Rivera
6. Billy Wagner
7. Jason Schmidt
8. Karim Garcia
9. Scott Rolen
10. Bob Abreu
11. Jimmy Haynes
12. Javier Valentin
13. Steve Gibralter
14. Todd Walker
15. Shannon Stewart

COMMENT: Johnny, Johnny, we know you can do it. We know you can be a superstar. Johnny, don't make us look bad! Like the *Baseball America* list, this one has its share of hits and misses. They had Vladimir Guerrero a year ahead of us; we had Scott Rolen a year ahead of them. We've both come up empty thus far on Paul Wilson and Ruben Rivera, but we're not the only ones. A savage game, this prospect-rating business.

1997 *Baseball America* Top Prospects

1. Andruw Jones
2. Vladimir Guerrero
3. Kerry Wood
4. Matt White
5. Travis Lee
6. Miguel Tejada
7. Todd Walker
8. Kris Benson
9. Ruben Rivera
10. Nomar Garciaparra
11. Paul Konerko
12. Jose Cruz Jr.
13. Scott Rolen
14. Bartolo Colon
15. Derrek Lee

Too early to say much, but the top two are looking good, as are Garciaparra, Cruz and Rolen. The only thing you can say about the pitchers is that nobody's turned into Todd Van Poppel yet.

1997 STATS Top Prospects

1. Andruw Jones
2. Vladimir Guerrero
3. Nomar Garciaparra

4. Scott Rolen
5. Paul Konerko
6. Ruben Rivera
7. Edgard Velazquez
8. Todd Walker
9. Todd Helton
10. Mike Sweeney
11. Jaret Wright
12. Kerry Wood
13. Miguel Tejada
14. Adrian Beltre
15. Dmitri Young

Four gems at the top; after that, who knows? We're getting smarter in one way, however: no pitchers in the top 10.

Summing up, we think we know our stuff, and ditto for the people at *BaseballAmerica*. When it comes to hitters, we've both picked our share of lemons, but there aren't many great players we've missed the boat on. Rating the top pitchers, though, is really, really hard. . . for just about everybody. Good fantasy players have known this for a long time, but isn't it amazing how major league clubs will risk high draft picks and shell out millions of dollars for some high-school pitching phenom? History shows that this is a risk that's simply not worth taking. Yet take it they do.

July 31, 1997—Baines, Managers, & Realignment

Got a problem with Norway? Move to baseball.

White Sox fan that I am, I'm still mystified about the Harold Baines deal. How can a team so close to first place (albeit in the pathetic AL Central) justify unloading one of its best hitters? This isn't the time of year for a contender to unload a Harold Baines. . . this is the time to *acquire* a Harold Baines. It's kind of like they're punishing the Sox fans for not coming out in big enough numbers—like they're saying, "You guys haven't done enough to pay for Albert's contract, so we're not going to bother trying to win." Great way to build the old fan base, eh?

The silliest thing about the whole Baines deal was the Sox announcing that they're going to have another ceremony to retire Harold's uniform number again. Well, *that'll* pack the fans in, won't it? Right about now, I'd rank "We're Retiring Harold's Number Again Night" with that other great Sox promotion, "Senior Citizens Run the Bases Day" (they really have this, honest. Danny Darwin always gets in line).

On to other news. Jack McKeon's back! Where do they dig these guys up? I keep getting this image of the "Old Managers Retirement Home," with all the geezers sitting around, swappin' baseball stories ("Yeah, old Greg Cadaret. Now there was a pitcher!"). Once a year the phone rings, with some desperate GM on the line, looking for a fill-in skipper. First old coot to grab the phone gets the job. Last year Johnny McNamara won the race, this year it was Trader Jack. Gene Mauch, your turn is coming; maybe you should run the bases at Comiskey a few times to get yourself in shape.

And speaking of Greg Cadaret: he's back, too. Even earned his first hold since 1994 last night. I wept for joy; so did Dan Schatzeder and all the other guys at the "Old Lefties Rehabilitation Home (Retire? Never!)."

I've been looking at these realignment plans, and call me an old fogey, but I just can't buy the notion of reshuffling the leagues completely to create more geographic rivalries. It's a noble idea, but one of the strengths of baseball is its long history and tradition, and while it's important not to live in the past, it's also important to *respect* the past. Look at this from a White Sox fan's perspective: under a plan that seems to be seriously under consideration, the Sox would no longer be in the same league with the Orioles, Red Sox, Yankees, Indians and Tigers. The Sox have been playing those teams since around 1901, and those are real rivalries, geographic or not. I'm sorry, but picking up a few games against the Cubs and Cardinals isn't going to make up for the loss of the Sox vs. the Yankees. This is a *terrible* idea. I personally prefer the simplest realignment plan, which involves only the Astros and Royals switching leagues; that improves things geographically, and as Bill James said to me last week, "The Royals think they're a National League team, anyway." We'll still have the Central-vs.-Central interleague games, which I (and most fans) like. That's enough messing around with things.

The dumbness of labeling people as "good managers" or "bad managers" is really high-lighted by the Terry Collins situation. Last year the Astros fired Collins because he was "too intense," then the Angels hired him for the very same reason, because they *wanted* an intense manager. In Houston, Collins' in-your-face personality just didn't mesh with guys like Jeff Bagwell and Craig Biggio, and the Astros seem to be doing better without him. Meanwhile Collins has fit in perfectly with all the intense players on the Angel roster. To be honest, he's got the team playing way over its head. Of course, the season ain't over yet. If the 'Stros die in September this year like they did in '96, we'll know something about *them*. But no matter what the Halos do from here on out, Collins has been a success.

I was watching the Cubs play the Rockies at Coors last week, and Mark Grace and Larry Walker (who was filling in at first for Colorado), spent the whole game spelling out messages to each other in the dirt ("You Won't Hit .400" and stuff like that). Did this offend anybody besides me? I don't know Walker that well, but he's known as a blood-and-guts kind of player, and anyway, *his* team was winning the game and killing the Cubs in the series. So I'll give him a pass. But as for Grace, I personally thought this was typical Cub behavior: "Yeah, we're getting our brains beat out, but who cares? We play in Wrigley and the fans love us, so who needs to concentrate on the game? Let's screw around a little." I don't know, maybe I'm overreacting, but I found myself wishing the Cubbies had a Terry Collins who would yank Grace off the field and scream, "Cut this crap out! We got a game to win!"

It sure doesn't look like anybody's going to challenge Maris' record, does it? I'm really disappointed. And nobody's going to hit .400, either. I guess Mark Grace was right.

August 7, 1997—A Classic Game

I was lucky enough to be at the Dodger-Cub game last Sunday night, and if you didn't get a chance to see it either in person or on ESPN, you really missed something. Peter Pascarelli, who works with the ESPN television crew, wasn't exaggerating a bit when he came over to me after the game and said, "If they'd played this game in October, people would be talking about it for 20 years." Here's a rundown of the action:

1. Thanks to a home run by Raul Mondesi, the Dodgers grabbed a 1-0 lead in the top of the second.

2. LA threatened again in the top of the fourth, putting two men on with two out. Greg Gagne then singled to left. I was just about to about to mark down another run for the Dodgers when Cub left fielder Doug Glanville unleashed a beautiful throw to the plate. Mike Piazza, who was trying to score from second, was a surprisingly easy out.

3. Good as Glanville's play was, the Cubs made an even better one an inning later. Brett Butler hit a scorching liner that looked like a sure double, but Mark Grace somehow jumped up and caught it. . . even though the ball was already by him. How he did that—and how he held onto it—I'll never know.

4. Cub starting pitcher Steve Trachsel, who was 3-for-42 on the year as a hitter, led of the bottom of the sixth with a long double off Dodger starter Ismael Valdes. Three batters later, he scored the tying run on a single by Mark Grace. . . on a 3-and-0 pitch. (At this point I want to take back all the bad things I said last week about Mark Grace. The man can *play*.)

5. The tie score didn't last long: Mondesi led off the seventh with another homer to put L.A. ahead again, 2-1.

6. The Cubs looked certain to tie it up when Shawon Dunston led off the bottom of the seventh with a triple. But Valdes struck out Ryne Sandberg on three pitches, and then Scott Radinsky came in and retired pinch hitters Kevin Orie (foulout to third) and Jose Hernandez (strikeout).

7. Shrugging that off, the Cubbies did tie the game in the eighth against Darren Dreifort. . . with an assist from first-base umpire Charlie Reliford. With Doug Glanville on first, Reliford called a balk on Dreifort for no reason apparent to anybody in the press box. Glanville eventually scored on a double by Sammy Sosa. . . on *another* 3-and-0 pitch. Thanks, Charlie.

8. It was still 2-2 entering the bottom of the ninth, with Ryne Sandberg leading off for the Cubbies. Sandberg, who had announced his retirement a day earlier and then celebrated by hitting two home runs, now got hold of another one. It might be, it could be, it isn't. . . the ball came within a foot of landing in the basket in deep center field, but instead hit high off the vines for a double. Kevin Orie moved Sandberg to third with a sacrifice; then Cub manager Jim Riggleman sent up his best pinch hitter, Dave Clark. All Clark needed to do

was hit a fly ball and the Cubs would win. Instead he hit a ground ball right back to Dreifort. Sandberg, who was running on contact, was retired in a rundown, and the Cubs failed to score. They had now come up empty on two opportunities in three innings with a runner on third and less than two out.

9. This was now a game the Dodgers seemed destined to win, and sure enough, Roger Cedeno led off the 10th with a bunt single off the Cubs' shaky closer, Mel Rojas. Nelson Liriano bunted Cedeno over to second and Butler followed with a walk, but Rojas was able to work out of the jam.

10. The Cubs had yet another opportunity when that man Grace led off the bottom of the 10th with a single off Antonio Osuna. But Osuna, throwing smoke, pitched out of it.

11. Neither team threatened in the 11th, but in the top of the 12th, with Rojas still out there, Gagne crushed a homer into the left-field bleachers. The Bleacher Bums threw it back, then let Rojas have it.

12. Leading, 3-2, the Dodgers turned the game over to *their* shaky closer, Todd Worrell. Worrell quickly got Glanville for the first out. He then must have heaved a sigh of relief when Jim Riggleman, out of position players, had to send up a pitcher, Kevin Foster, to pinch hit. Foster swings a decent stick, but Worrell handled him easily, striking him out on five pitches.

13. With two out and nobody on, Grace came to the plate. Grace isn't a home-run hitter, but he'd been killing the Dodgers all night, and he'd been killing everybody for more than a month. Worrell wanted no part of him, and walked him on four pitches.

14. Sammy Sosa was next. A couple of weeks prior to this, I was listening to a Chicago sports-talk show, and the announcer was laying into Sammy, going on and on about how "all his homers are meaningless" and "he never does anything in the clutch." If I'd had a cell phone, I would have called up and pointed out that in 1996, Sosa had ended *three* different games with game-winning homers in the final inning. Dodger manager Bill Russell must have known that, too, because he called time out and slowly walked to the mound to talk to Worrell. Everybody in the ballpark knew what he was telling Worrell: "Don't give him anything good to hit, especially on the first pitch." Sosa is notorious for swinging at everything, and had already struck out twice in this game—each time on three pitches. So Worrell listened patiently to Russell, nodded his head. . .

15. . . . and gave Sammy a good pitch to hit. Sosa crushed it out of the ballpark. Cubs win—no make that "CUBS WIN!!! CUBS WIN!!! CUBS WIN!!!" 4-3.

If the Dodgers don't win the National League West, they're going to remember this game. A lot of other people will remember this game, whether the Dodgers win it or not. I'll be one of them.

Gee, I love baseball.

August 14, 1997—White Sox, Rookies & More

Thoughts about the game:

My White Sox, defying all expectations, are creeping closer and closer to first place in the AL Central. Does this mean Jerry Reinsdorf will now trade off even *more* good players, to make it absolutely certain his team won't win? Wouldn't surprise me a bit. What a nutsy franchise this is; by comparison, the crosstown Cubbies now seem like a totally sane franchise. And *that's* saying something.

You never really know about these things for some time, but this seems like one of the best rookie crops in many years. Look at the players who have broken in this year, beginning with Nomar Garciaparra, Andruw Jones, Vladimir Guerrero and Scott Rolen. That's four players with superstar potential. Plus there are other guys like Todd Greene and Mike Cameron and Brian Giles and Jose Cruz Jr. and Neifi Perez and Todd Helton with tons of promise. So this *could* be one of the best groups ever, but we won't really know the answer to that for at least five years. And maybe more.

Rickey Henderson got traded again yesterday in one of those July/August deals that are becoming increasingly prevalent: star player's team falls out of pennant race, star player's team deals him to club which is *in* pennant race. In this case the Padres had been talking about trading Henderson for months, and the Angels will be his fifth major league club. Including his three stints with the A's, Rickey has now been traded four times, and moved to another team via free agency twice. . . with his old club not making much of an effort to re-sign him on either occasion. The economics of baseball have had a lot to do with his constant movement. In addition, Henderson's personality has undoubtedly helped him wear out his welcome a few times. Still, I can't help thinking there's another factor: even after all these years, baseball people still greatly underestimate the value of a leadoff man who can get on base. When they talk about good leadoff men, many baseball people still think "speed" and "stolen bases" first. How else can you explain the ridiculous overrated-ness of players like Deion Sanders, Brian Hunter and Tom Goodwin? While Henderson is still very fast and an excellent percentage basestealer, he doesn't steal sacks the way he used to. So people think his skills are declining when the skill that always made him *most* valuable—his ability to reach base—hasn't declined much at all.

I'm among the many who consider Henderson the greatest leadoff man of all time, but his constant movement from team to team begs a question: can a player who constantly changes teams be truly considered a great player? I think he can, but you have to take this into consideration when you do your evaluation. For instance, Bill James refused to rank Rogers Hornsby as the best second baseman of all time, in large part because Hornsby wore out his welcome on so many teams. I think Bill's assessment is probably an accurate one, and I'd rate both Joe Morgan and Eddie Collins ahead of Hornsby, as Bill does. As for Rickey, I would guess that when he becomes eligible for the Hall of Fame, Henderson will meet a little resistance from some writers because of the way he's drifted from club to club. . . that and his personality, which has often been described as "me first." But he'll make it; his record is simply too impressive.

The Angels, of course, wanted Henderson primarily because of the uncertainty over whether Tony Phillips will be available down the stretch. I'm not going to prejudge Phillips, but whether he has a drug habit or not, the man has some real personality problems that ought to be dealt with. He's a great player, without question, but it's just not healthy for a team when a player is exploding like that all the time. . . not to mention what it's doing to the player himself. I wish Phillips well, but he's one ex-White Sox player I *don't* miss.

If you had any remaining doubts that baseball is a game played and managed by people who think like 12-year-olds, consider the big flap in Tuesday's Orioles-A's game. The A's didn't like it that Jeff Reboulet stole second in the sixth inning with the O's up, 7- 0. . . so the next time Reboulet came to bat, they threw at him (actually, behind him, which is considered even more dangerous). Both benches emptied, of course. Well, if the A's were incapable of overcoming a seven-run lead, why didn't they save everybody some time and just give up then and there? I'm sorry, but in the 1997 American League, a seven-run lead is *not* insurmountable, even for the Oakland A's. So what's the big deal about Baltimore continuing to try to score? I still like Whitey Herzog's response when people complained about his teams stealing with a (fill-in-the-blank)-run lead: "I'll promise not to steal any more bases," he'd say, "if you promise not to get any more hits."

Nobody ever took him up on it.

September 4, 1997—Realignment, The DH & Interleague Play

Random thoughts:

REALIGNMENT. No matter what Bud Selig says, the so-called "radical" realignment plan is dead; too many teams are against it. But I still think a few teams will switch leagues, especially since some of them want to. The consensus is that we'll have one 16-team league and one 14-team league; the format I'd most like to see would be to have two divisions in each league. The schedule would go something like this:

16-Team League
14 games each vs. teams in own division (98 games)
6 games each vs. teams in other division (48 games)
14 total interleague games

14-Team League
16 games each vs. teams in own division (96 games)
7 games each vs. teams in other division (49 games)
16 total interleague games

This gives the 16-team league 160 games, the 14-team league 161; undoubtedly they'd add a game or two to get up to 162.

I, personally, could live with this, since it offers two advantages. First, it puts more emphasis on games within the division, which is something nearly everyone agrees needs to be done. In addition, it eliminates those NFL-style four- and five-team divisions which can easily lead to teams with vastly inferior records finishing first (for further references, consult the Houston Astros). It also retains interleague play on basically the same basis as the hugely successful format we've had in 1997.

Will this happen? I think the 16/14 league split is a given, from everything I've heard. But the latest word is that the magnates are considering splitting the 16-team league in *four* divisions, each with four teams. The other league would have three divisions. I would hate that. . . but I don't think they're going to be asking for my opinion.

THE DH. Whether you like it or not, it's almost certainly going to stay, but only in the American League. Think the Players Association is going to happily go along with eliminating those multi-million-dollar jobs for Harold Baines, Paul Molitor, etc.? Never gonna happen. The National League will never accept the DH, so it appears we're stuck with the different-rules-for-each-league scenario for the foreseeable future.

Actually, there is a way the players might go along with eliminating the DH. The scenario would go like this:

1. Players agree to eliminate the DH at some point in the future, like five years from now. Thus careers aren't drastically affected overnight without any preparation.

2. Owners offer the players some sort of compensation in exchange for the elimination of these often high-paying jobs: a 26th roster spot (this is already being discussed), maybe a payment to the players of X million dollars.

But this won't eliminate the DH for 1998, and I don't think it's going to happen, even in five years. Every poll I ever see says that American League fans like the DH, while National League fans don't want any part of it. Fine by me. We've lived with this situation for 25 years now; what's the urgency about changing it?

The only tricky thing here would be what would happen to the DHs if several teams switch leagues, which is possible. My hunch is that they'll find some way to deal with that (maybe give Chili Davis a gold watch if the Royals move to the NL?), but the solution *won't* involve getting rid of the DH for 1998.

INTERLEAGUE PLAY. The second round of games is over, and I have to admit it: I wound up liking this a lot more than I ever thought I would. My own favorite team, the White Sox, just got through playing the Astros and the Cardinals, and I found both series totally fascinating. What was really interesting was the clash in styles of play between the leagues. Sunday's Sox-Astros game ended when Houston, down two runs with two out in the bottom of the ninth and their cleanup hitter, Derek Bell, at the plate, tried a double steal. This is something an American League team would *never* do, and I'm sure the 'Stros were depending on the element of surprise. The Sox were ready, though, and Jorge Fabregas threw out Craig Biggio at third to end the game. Fabulous. . . or maybe just Fabregas.

The very next day, the Cardinals, down a run, tried *another* ninth-inning double steal, this time with one out. This time Fabregas tossed out Delino DeShields, and the game ended shortly thereafter. Great stuff again, and definitely not the sort of thing a Sox fan sees every day. As long as interleague play is limited enough to make games and moments like this special, I'm all for it.

September 18, 1997—Big Mac

Some notes about Mark McGwire:

1. Yes, he can hit eight or nine homers in 11 games. Following up on last week's column, there have been five separate 11-game stretches in McGwire's career in which he's hit eight home runs, and another stretch (in May of 1987) in which he's hit nine. The odds are against him, of course, but he's done this sort of thing in the past. He could do it again.

2. It would really help McGwire if he could start those final 11 games by knocking another homer or two out of Wrigley Field this afternoon. As I write this, it's about 20 minutes before game time, and conditions are perfect: temperature in the 80s, brisk wind blowing out. . . and gopher ball-prone Steve Trachsel (a National League-leading 29 HR allowed) on the mound for the Cubbies. Who could ask for anything more?

3. It won't happen this year, of course, but do you think those dumb fans in the Wrigley Field bleachers would "throw it back" if McGwire hit No. 61 or 62 there? Stupidest tradition in baseball next to The Wave, if you ask me.

4. Through Tuesday, McGwire had 33 hits for the Cardinals, 19 of them home runs. In fact, he had nearly twice as many home runs (19) as singles (11)! Definitely a unique combination. Overall this year, McGwire has 53 homers, 57 singles, but this sort of pattern is not unusual for him. In 1995, he had 39 homers, 35 singles.

5. McGwire, who will turn 34 on October 1, has 382 homers, an outstanding total for a player his age. Through age 33 (with age figured as of July 1 of each season), only 11 players in history have hit more than 382 homers. Ten of those 11 wound up with more than 500 home runs—the only one who missed was Lou Gehrig, who hit 493 before his career was ended by ALS—and all 11 are in the Hall of Fame. The two players right behind McGwire on the list, Ernie Banks (376 homers through age 33) and Willie McCovey (370), also wound up with both 500-plus homers and a berth in the Hall of Fame. Nice company.

6. Great as McGwire has been, his career would have been much, much greater had he not missed so much time with injuries in the years from 1992 through 1996. Over those five seasons, he missed a total of 297 games, nearly two seasons worth, because of injuries. We calculated in the *Baseball Scoreboard* last year that the missed playing time cost him over 80 home runs (84 to be exact), and that's *not* counting the time he missed due to the strike in 1994-95. With full health McGwire most likely would have had over 460 homers by now—a figure topped only by Jimmie Foxx (519), Hank Aaron (481), Eddie Mathews (477) Mickey Mantle (473) and Babe Ruth (470) through age 33. Given continued health and his recent level of performance, he quite possibly would have had a shot at 700 homers, maybe even Aaron's record total of 755.

Well, he did miss that time, and we'll never know whether McGwire might have challenged Aaron and Ruth. What he has done is remarkable enough. This is truly one of the most awesome sluggers of all time.

I can't leave this column without mentioning the owners' latest screwy realignment plan. This one has:

- "Only" seven teams switching leagues.

- Four four-team divisions and no wild-card in the NL, three divisions of four or five teams, plus a wild-card, in the AL.

- No American League teams west of Texas.

- The White Sox and Brewers, one of the better geographic rivalries currently around, in different American League divisions.

- The Braves and Marlins, another hot geographic rivalry that's just starting to rev up, in different *leagues*.

- The A's and Giants in the same league but different divisions—apparently because Giants owner Peter Magowan wants no part of the Athletics.

- The Brewers in the same division with the Marlins, Expos, Blue Jays and Devil Rays. The Brewers have about as much proximity to those teams as they would to a team from Moscow. One thing you have to give Bud Selig credit for: if this plan goes through, he'll be screwing his own team even worse than he's screwing the rest of us.

All is I can is: They're going to have seven teams switch leagues to give us *this*?

September 25, 1997—Exploring the Issues

Issues of the day:

THE HOME RUN RACE. It's over, barring a miracle finish: McGwire and Griffey probably aren't going to catch Maris. But it sure has been fun, and it points out how vulnerable the home-run record is in an era of slugging. Someone will hit 62, it says here, quite possibly as early as next year.

I liked what Lou Piniella did last night, DH-ing Griffey and batting him leadoff. Give the man all the chances he can get to go after the record, I say.

THE WILD-CARD. I'm not a die-hard traditionalist, so I can live with the three-division setup. But as Bob Costas pointed out in *The Sporting News* a few weeks ago, one of the things the wild-card has done is to dramatically lessen the chances of being able to enjoy a down-to-the-wire pennant race between two really good teams. Most of the great races in baseball history involved two outstanding clubs: for example, Dodgers-Giants 1951 and

1962, Yankees-Red Sox 1978 and Braves-Giants 1993. Under the current scenario, both teams would be wild-cards, and instead of producing the sort of late-season drama we all vividly remember, the teams would be coasting down the stretch like the Orioles and Yankees did this year.

That's a loss of one of the things that made baseball really special. Sure, there's some possible compensation from the longer postseason, but a postseason series doesn't go on for weeks and months, the way a great pennant race does. Baseball has lost something truly great here.

THE DODGER-GIANT RACE. Though they're hardly great teams, this *is* a good race. A couple of weeks ago, the Dodgers seemed to have everything under control, but they're 7-13 in September and on the verge of elimination heading into the final weekend. Meanwhile the Giants have risen from the dead. Who woulda thunk it? This is everything I love about baseball.

Not to gloat or anything, but one thing the Dodgers' El Foldo has done has been to shut up all those people who thought the key to victory was having Otis Nixon and Eric Young at the top of your lineup. Speed is nice, but when you're hitting .205 with a .287 OBP—Young's September stats—it doesn't matter if you're Carl Lewis.

THE NL MVP RACE. I'm hearing more and more support these days for Jeff Bagwell and Craig Biggio, two guys who are "leading the Astros to a title." Both are worthy candidates, but how much credit should you get for finishing a few games over .500 while holding off those mighty Pittsburgh Pirates? The same people boosting Bagwell and Biggio seem to be dismissing Larry Walker, whose team has virtually the same record as the 'Stros, along with Mike Piazza, whose club has a *much* better record than Houston. Walker and (presumably) Piazza "didn't win," the critics will say, while Bagwell and Biggio did. This argument makes no sense at all to me.

I think the race should come down to Bagwell, Walker, Piazza and Barry Bonds, who's been on fire down the stretch while having another typically great season. Bonds won't make it (not enough RBI to impress the voters), but I'd have a hard time choosing among the other three. If I had to vote today, I would go Piazza, Walker, Bagwell, in that order. But I wouldn't argue much with ranking those three in *any* order.

One thing I like about Piazza: despite the Dodgers' slump and the wear and tear of a season behind the plate, he's been heroic in September, hitting .385 with 19 RBI in 20 games. Since the All-Star break, he has 21 homers and 65 ribbies in 65 games. This is probably the best offensive season any catcher has ever had.

NL CY YOUNG. Another tough race. Four viable candidates here in Pedro Martinez, Greg Maddux, Denny Neagle and Curt Schilling. Toss out Neagle first: some of his numbers are a lot like Maddux', but most of them just aren't as good. Schilling's been pretty incredible pitching for a crappy team, but even after granting him that, his credentials just don't measure up to Maddux and Martinez.

So in my mind at least, it comes down to the M&M boys. Martinez has the best ERA in the league, he's 17-8 despite some of the worst run support in baseball, he's held opposing hitters to a .184 average—the lowest in either league among ERA qualifiers—and he's about to join Schilling in the 300-K club. Those are fabulous credentials. Maddux, meanwhile, is second in ERA, his record is 19-4, and he's allowed 20 walks in 33 starts—six of them intentional. Hard to argue with either one, but if I had to pick, I'd go with Martinez.

What a great season. And now, the playoffs. Wild-card or not, I'm gonna love 'em.

October 2, 1997—Did You Know?

We'll get into the playoffs next week. In the meantime, here are a few stat notes you might have missed about this wild and crazy season:

NOMAR GARCIAPARRA of the Red Sox had 209 hits, the fifth-highest total ever recorded by a rookie. The top four: Lloyd Waner (223 in 1927), Jimmy Williams (219 in 1899), Tony Oliva (217 in 1964) and Dale Alexander (215 in 1929). Harvey Kuenn also had 209 hits as a rookie with the 1953 Tigers. Interestingly, only one member of this group is in the Hall of Fame: Waner. And he's generally considered one of the weaker members. We still believe in you, Nomar!

CRAIG BIGGIO of the Astros scored 146 runs, the most by a National League player since Chuck Klein of the Phillies crossed the plate 152 times in 1932. When you consider that Klein played in Baker Bowl while Biggio labors in the Astrodome. . . well, Biggio's performance is even more impressive.

BIGGIO scored those runs the hard way, getting hit by 34 pitches in 1997. In this century, only Ron Hunt (an incredible 50 times for the 1971 Expos) and Don Baylor (35 times for the 1986 Red Sox) have been plunked by more pitches. Biggio and JASON KENDALL of the Pirates (31 HBP) were sort of the McGwire and Griffey of the HBP in 1997; only Hunt, Baylor and Biggio have exceeded Kendall's HBP total among 20th century players.

MARK GRUDZIELANEK of the Expos had 54 doubles, a record for National League shortstops and the most by an NL player since Joe Medwick had 56 two-baggers in 1937.

JUAN GONZALEZ of the Rangers drove in 131 runs in 133 games, giving him a two-year total of 275 ribbies in 267 games in 1996- 97. The last time a player averaged more than an RBI a game over a two-year stretch while playing at least 125 games in each season was way back in 1937-38, when both Hank Greenberg (329 RBI/309 G) and Jimmie Foxx (302 RBI/299 G) turned the trick.

LARRY WALKER (49 HR), ANDRES GALARRAGA (41) and VINNY CASTILLA (40) of the Rockies combined for 130 home runs, the highest total ever by three National League teammates. They were also the third trio of teammates in history with 40-plus homers; the others were Davey Johnson, Hank Aaron and Darrell Evans of the 1973 Braves and Galarraga, Castilla and Ellis Burks of the '96 Rockies. Ah, Coors.

MIKE PIAZZA of the Dodgers batted .362, tying Bill Dickey (1936 Yankees) for the highest average ever recorded by a catcher. Dickey has the edge if you take the figures out another percentage point (.3617 to .3615), but since Dickey wouldn't have qualified for the batting title under modern-day rules, we'll call this one even.

JULIAN TAVAREZ of the Giants worked in 89 games, the most by any major league pitcher in a decade. Kent Tekulve of the 1987 Phillies is the last pitcher to work in 90 games in a season.

The OAKLAND A'S had only two complete games all year, the fewest ever by one team in a season. The A's CGs both came in June: Mike Oquist went the distance on June 6 vs. the Blue Jays, and Don Wengert matched him two weeks later against the Angels. The A's then went through their final 89 games without a CG; was this their personal tribute to Mark McGwire?

The ANAHEIM ANGELS and CLEVELAND INDIANS each went without a 20-game winner for the 23rd straight year, extending a somewhat dubious American League record they share jointly. The last pitchers to win 20 for each club? Nolan Ryan (Angels) and Gaylord Perry (Indians), both in 1974. Seems like only yesterday. . .

SEATTLE MARINERS pitchers fanned 1,207 batters, breaking the league record of 1,189 Ks set by the 1967 Indians. So how did the M's end up with a 4.78 team ERA?

October 9, 1997—Postseason & Awards

Current events:

THE DIVISION SERIES. Only one of them was really good—Indians/Yankees—but that's OK. . . not every series is going to be great, and anyway, both the Orioles/Mariners and Giants/Marlins series had their moments. The problem I have with the Division Series is simply that it's too much baseball in too short a time, even for a fanatic like me. How can you possibly absorb everything that's going on? The games go by like that, and suddenly four teams are gone.

Television, I'm sure, has the same problem with this round of games, which is one reason why they don't do well in the ratings. Do you think that if the NFL tried to broadcast its playoff games in prime time seven nights a week, the ratings would be as high as they are for Monday Night Football? Not on your life. I suspect that if the Division Series sticks around—and it certainly looks like it will whether we like it or not—most of the weeknight games will be broadcast on ESPN or some other cable outlet, the way the first two rounds of the NBA playoffs are. When and if that happens, the "baseball-is-doomed" crowd will have another field day, citing this as still more evidence that the game is dying. But that' not the case: they're simply trying to do too much here. The market is over-saturated with too many games.

On to the LCS.

BRAVES/MARLINS. We've been having this endless argument on our office e-mail network about the value of "postseason experience." Some people think it means everything, other people think it means next to nothing. I hope to do a serious study on this subject in the next *STATS Baseball Scoreboard*, but for now I tend to be in the this-stuff-is-overrated category. Look at Greg Maddux in Game 1 of this series: despite all of his years of playoff experience, he was clearly not on his game, and pitching like a guy who was feeling some postseason pressure. Whereas Jaret Wright, pitching the decisive game of the Indian-Yankee Division Series, looked as calm as could be. This sort of thing happens all the time, which is not to say that you should base your opinions on a few isolated examples. As I said, I'd like to look at some real numbers.

As for the series, it's one-one as I write this, and I'm pretty sure it'll go six or seven. I think the Braves will win, but not because of their postseason experience; I think they'll win because they have the better team.

ORIOLES-INDIANS. My wife was watching Game 1 of this series with me, and all she could say was, "Boy, that Erickson guy is *really* good-looking!" And I said, "He sure didn't look this good when he was pitching for the Twins a few years ago." Scott Erickson has really turned his career around, and you have to give a lot of credit to the Orioles' improved infield defense. Erickson is an extreme groundball pitcher—he had the highest groundball-to-flyball ratio in the American League this year (2.88). The addition of Mike Bordick, along with the move of Cal Ripken to third, helped make him a much more effective pitcher.

We at STATS keep a number of sophisticated defensive stats including range factor and zone rating, and yet I still think we wind up underestimating the value of good defense to a major league team. Despite an occasional big hit, Bordick is pretty much of an offensive zero, and most statistical studies would wind up concluding, "Get the guy out of there. He loses more runs with his bat than he saves with his glove." I have my doubts about that, and maybe one problem is that the numbers we produce, good and useful though they are, still don't do a good enough job of interpreting the value of a really good defensive player. But we'll keep working on it.

I wrote an article for a forthcoming issue of *Baseball Weekly* on the National League Cy Young race, and I hope you'll be able to catch it. I don't want to repeat what I wrote there, but here are my choices for the major 1997 awards:

National League

Most Valuable Player: Larry Walker

A tough call, especially since (as I pointed out last week) Mike Piazza probably had the best offensive season by any catcher in major league history. Catcher is a more important defensive position than right field, but I still don't think Piazza is a *good* catcher, and Walker just did so much this year. And as many people have pointed out, he was *not* a Coors Field phenomenon.

Cy Young Award: Pedro Martinez

You'll have to wait for my article to find out why.

Rookie of the Year: Scott Rolen

Not much debate here, is there?

Manager of the Year: Dusty Baker

Any intelligent observer who looks at the Giants' 1997 season will conclude that they were one lucky team, but that doesn't take away from the wonderful job that Baker did. Luck isn't the only reason the Giants beat out the Dodgers.

American League

Most Valuable Player: Ken Griffey Jr.

Again, not a whole lot of room for debate.

Cy Young Award: Roger Clemens

Randy Johnson *almost* won me over at the end, but Clemens was the first American League pitcher since Hal Newhouser in 1946 to win the "Pitcher's Triple Crown" (Wins, ERA, Strikeouts). I have to give it to him.

Rookie of the Year: Nomar Garciaparra

The easiest choice of all.

Manager of the Year: Davey Johnson

Yes, I know they were "supposed" to win (or at least qualify for the playoffs), but Johnson handled every problem he encountered—like a pitching coach not of his choosing (Ray Miller), the shift of Ripken to third, Eric Davis' cancer, the injury to Roberto Alomar—without ever missing a beat. After winning flags with three teams that were each chaotic in their own way (the Mets, Reds and Orioles), Johnson has to be considered one of the best managers in major league history.

October 16, 1997—Postseason Ponderings

Notes on the postseason:

MARLINS-BRAVES. Rob Neyer pointed out in his SportsZone column the other day that according to the Pythagorean Theorem, the Braves' overall record in the LCS and World Series under Bobby Cox should be 38-18. Instead, they're 29-27. How'd that happen? Well for one thing, their record in one-run games in these series is 9-20.

Bad bullpen. . . bad bench. . . bad managing. . . or just bad luck? According to Rob, the bullpen is *not* to blame—in those 29 one-run games, the Braves' pen has had a 2.47 ERA

Poor pinch hitting has been a factor (Braves' PH are 12-for-83 in the LCS and World Series under Cox), and Bobby's made his share of bad moves. But after a long discussion about this on the office e-mail network this morning, we concluded that plain and simple bad luck is a far bigger factor than most people realize. As Steve Moyer put it, "In a short series, the worst of players can be the hero (ask Buddy Biancalana) and the best of players can be the goat (ask Tom Glavine). The 'right' managerial choice all comes down to results and the results are as much luck as anything else in a game or two."

I agree; the best team doesn't always win. But what else is new? Let's give some credit to the Marlins. They might have folded up like a tent when they lost Alex Fernandez and Kevin Brown got sick; instead they took it all in stride and beat what had been the best team in baseball during the regular season. I'm happy for Jim Leyland. . . but I still think the better team lost the series. That's baseball.

INDIANS-ORIOLES. What a wild and wonderful series this was.

My lingering image of the 1997 ALCS will always be Davey Johnson's incredulous face in the Baltimore dugout as one bad thing after another happened to his team. Remind you of 1969, any, Davey? Of course it did; in fact, one of the first things Johnson talked about after yesterday's game was how this series reminded him of his heavily favored Orioles losing the '69 World Series to the Mets in equally improbable fashion (Johnson was the O's second baseman back then, in case you didn't know).

All kinds of crazy things happened to the Birds in this series, but there were two primary reasons why Baltimore lost:

1. The Birds, who outhit (.248 to .193), outhomered (seven to five) and outscored (19 to 18) the Indians in the series, could never seem to come through when the games were on the line. During the series the O's batted .283 with the bases empty, .213 with runners on base, .191 with runners in scoring position and .130 with runners in scoring position and two out. The Tribe hit pretty badly in the clutch also, but the Indians came through with the big hits in Games 2, 4 and 6, and that was the series.

2. The big hits in all three of those games came off Armando Benitez. Johnson, whose faith in Benitez never seemed to waver, went down the drain with him.

After their shocking loss to the Mets in '69, the Orioles blasted their way to 108 wins and a World Championship in 1970. Johnson undoubtedly thinks the 1998 Orioles will do the same, but I really doubt it. This Oriole team is older than the 1970 bunch was, and a lot less talented. I think the Birds will have to hustle just to make the playoffs next year.

As for Benitez, two words come to mind: Calvin Schiraldi.

THE SERIES. The Marlins are favored, and rightfully so. But I have this feeling that Cleveland's magical autumn is going to continue. The Tribe in seven, it says here. Don't bet a lot of money on it.

In last week's column, I offhandedly commented that there was "not much debate" that Scott Rolen would win the National League Rookie of the Year award. Several readers took issue with this and pointed out the virtues of the Cardinals' Matt Morris, who had a very fine rookie season (12-9, 3.19).

My mistake. Morris had an excellent first year and is a very viable ROY candidate. The same goes for the Pirates' rookie closer, Rich Loiselle.

But Rolen's gonna win it.

October 23, 1997—The World Series

Ah, the World Series. The Fall Classic. The sporting event of the year. The two best teams in baseball showing off their skills while an entire nation stops to watch in rapt attention. . .

I'm talking about the 1977 World Series, of course. Or maybe 1957, or 1937. Anything but 1997.

This has gone way beyond painful, what with the frigid weather, the pitchers whose fingers are too numb to throw strikes, the fielders who are too frostbitten to catch or throw the ball (poor Edgar Renteria looks likes he's about to develop rigor mortis any second now), the endless number of at-bats which begin ball one/ball two, and the constant pauses while everyone blows on their hands, rubs their fingers together, visits the space heater, etc., etc. I'm not surprised that the TV ratings for this World Series are so bad. . . I'm surprised they're so *good*. My wife, who always finds a way to get to the heart of things, summed it up best: "God, I hope they're not still playing on Sunday."

NBC has the very same wish.

This is almost karmic. It's like all of baseball's demons are coming home to roost in a single one-week period. This is a combination of:

1. Baseball's insistence on playing night baseball in the Midwest and East at the end of October.

2. Baseball's inability to get the umpires to enforce the strike zone.

3. Baseball's further inability to get the players and umpires to move at a faster pace.

4. Baseball's greed in giving the networks more and more time for between-inning commercials.

5. Baseball's expanded playoff system, which extends the season, invites mediocre teams into the postseason tournament, and increases the chances that the survivors are going to be worn out and beaten up by the time the Series rolls around.

The result is what you see on your screen—if you're hearty enough to sit through the "action." For the most part, I have been, but that ninth inning of Game 3 put me to sleep. And when a World Series game puts the Zee-Man to sleep. . . well, I tremble for baseball.

Is there a solution to this? Well, you could reduce the schedule to 154 games, but I don't see either the players or the owners voting to reduce their revenues. Or you could go back to two divisions in each league, thus eliminating the Division Series. This is one of my favorite fantasies in life, and it could possibly come true if the big networks decide they simply don't want to televise so much postseason baseball. In all likelihood, however, one of the cable networks like ESPN or TNT or Fox SportsNet would jump at the chance to broadcast postseason games, albeit at a lower rate than NBC and Fox are currently paying. So late-October World Series games are probably going to stick around.

Which means we'll be stuck with one of two bad choices: either risk playing the games in frigid weather, as we're doing now, or move the World Series to a neutral warm-weather (or domed) site. Whitey Herzog campaigned for this idea around 15 years ago, insisting that it would make the Series bigger than the Super Bowl. I doubt *that*, and in fact I fear that there might be a lot of empty seats until the idea catches on.

The big disadvantage to this idea, of course, is that you'd be taking the Series away from the home fans. And won't the baseball-hating press jump on *that*, not to mention all those purists from Bismarck, N.D. who write letters to *The Sporting News*. Too bad, but consider the advantages:

1. The games would be played in decent weather.

2. With the players not fighting the elements, the games might not only be better-played— they might move along at a decent pace instead of putting everybody to sleep. (Of course, we'd need more than warm weather to guarantee *this*.)

3. With the site of the games set a year or more in advance, people could plan vacations around the Series.

4. Promoters would schedule conventions and other events around the Series, which would pull in people from all over the globe and turn the Fall Classic into a week-long celebration.

5. Baseball would get a chance to promote the hell out of the World Series and hopefully regain a little of the ground it's lost over the last few years.

I used to think that this was a terrible idea, and the sort of thing that baseball should never resort to. And even if the idea were adopted, you'd still have to deal with the umpiring, the pace of the game, the mediocre teams in the playoffs, etc. But they have to do *something* to heighten interest in the game, and I don't think the solution is continuing to stage the World Series as a Winter Carnival. I'd rather have a neutral-site Series than have to sit through another fiasco like this year's games in Cleveland.

October 30, 1997—My Fans Speak Out

Last week's column suggesting the possibility of a neutral-site World Series seemed to touch a few nerves. Let's start with my biggest fan:

> Don, you are simply an asshole. Neutral Sites would kill baseball. As a long-suffering Indians fan, I would consider never watching baseball again if my home team were to battle into the Series again only to watch a bunch of rich bastards from around the country go sit in a Teflon dome sipping cocktails, with an almost complete indifference to the game being played. Baseball is for the *home* fans!. . I guess your solution to this would be to kick all of the Midwest teams out or move them to warm weather cities. Then your pansy-ass might not be so cold!

Actually, I've lived in the Chicago area my whole life, which means my pansy-ass is *always* cold. Of course, it also means I don't have to worry much about ever getting to watch a World Series game. But if I ever get lucky, I sure hope that

a) it isn't snowing, and b) I'm not sitting next to *that* guy.

Actually, that particular message was downright *thoughtful*, compared with this one:

> what are you an idiot? your there screaming your head off because of too many changes in baseball already and you want to go and move the world series to a neutral site, u call yourself a baseball purists with this idiotic idea. . .

That's me, all right—Don, the pansy-ass baseball "purists." Mr. Grammar (or is it Ms.?) goes on:

> if the players cant handle there jobs in extreme conditions then why in god's name are they making 6 or 7 million a year?. . . and to your claim that these are second rate teams playing in the world series. . . how are they so second rate if the marlins not only beat the braves but swept the orioles in the regular season and took two of three from the yankess. . . how do u explain a second rate team winning all those games???? your no baseball purists, your a loud mouth they gave a sports column to.

Yes, and aren't we all lucky that they did? But I guess you could say the Marlins are lucky too—after all, they didn't have to play those mighty "yankess" in the World Series.

Actually, there were a number of thoughtful, well-expressed e-mails written to me on this subject. . . all of them agreeing with my point of view, of course. Actually, that's not true; the letters were about five-to-one against the idea of playing the Series at a neutral site, which is certainly understandable. But I'll reiterate the main point of my article: badly played games in 30-degree weather aren't good for baseball, and do nothing to foster the growth of the sport. One way or another, we need to find a way to avoid this sort of thing.

We now head into the offseason, and one of the big events of November will be the expansion draft to stock the Diamondbacks and Devil Rays. Both *Baseball Weekly* and *Baseball America* ran mock drafts in their current issues, and the results couldn't have been more different. *Baseball Weekly* had Lyle Mouton of the White Sox going to the Diamondbacks as the top overall pick... *Baseball America* had Mouton going to the Devil Rays as the 49th pick. *Baseball America's* choice as the first player picked was Al Leiter of the Marlins; *Baseball Weekly* had Leiter lasting until the 42nd pick, though both publications thought he'd wind up with the Diamondbacks.

Overall, the folks in the STATS office felt that *Baseball America's* picks were a little more thoughtful, but nobody really knows how this thing will actually play out. But judging from the experience of past expansion drafts, two things are likely to happen:

1. The teams will each wind up with only a few players who prove useful for more than a year or two.

2. When and if these teams start winning championships, the expansion draft will have had little to do with it.

Point number two will probably be more true than ever, now that the Marlins have won a World Series. Florida's success in the free-agent market will likely spur the Diamondbacks, in particular, into making aggressive free-agent signings in an attempt to win quickly. All in all, it should be a very interesting offseason.

November 6, 1997—Minor League Equivalencies

Our "Fall Books"—the *Major League Handbook*, *Minor League Handbook* and *Player Profiles*—are out, and I thought it might be fun to focus on a fascinating chapter in the *Minor League Handbook*: the section on Major League Equivalencies. MLEs, as they're called, were invented by Bill James a number of years ago. Their purpose is to translate a Double- or Triple-A hitter's minor league statistics into equivalent major league numbers—that is, the stat estimates how a player's 1997 minor league numbers would have looked had he been performing for his parent club this year. How do we do this? By making a series of adjustments for the player's minor league ballpark, the strength of the league he was playing in, and the park factors of his major league parent club. The idea may seem far-fetched at first, but it works: over the years, Bill's MLE formulas have proven their worth again and again.

MLEs aren't perfect, of course. One limitation is that they're based on the previous year's stats, and only that year. Young players often improve significantly from one year to the next, and the MLE won't be able to capture that. They don't take injuries into account, either. There are other limitations as well, but as we said, MLEs have proven themselves over the years. For instance, look at Scott Rolen, whose MLE was in the 1997 *Minor League Handbook*:

	AVG	OBP	SLG
Rolen 1996 MLE	.292	.363	.447
Rolen 1997	.283	.377	.469

Or Derek Jeter from the 1996 book:

	AVG	OBP	SLG
Jeter 1995 MLE	.295	.365	.380
Jeter 1996	.314	.370	.430
Jeter 1997	.291	.370	.405

Not bad. So without further ado, let's look at the 1997 MLEs of some of baseball's most heralded prospects:

Paul Konerko	AB	H	HR	RBI	AVG	OBP	SLG
1997 MLE	440	113	21	78	.257	.316	.448

Konerko put up some huge numbers for the Dodgers' Albuquerque farm club last year, but there are two factors which you need to keep in mind about him: first, Albuquerque is a great place to hit, and second, Dodger Stadium is a really *difficult* place to hit. Thus Konerko's MLEs may seem a little disappointing. But project these figures to 550 or 600 at-bats, and you get 25 to 30 homers and around 100 RBI. He figures to be a strong Rookie of the Year candidate.

Ben Grieve	AB	H	HR	RBI	AVG	OBP	SLG
1997 MLE	454	142	22	102	.313	.392	.537

Grieve also put up big minor league numbers last year, but unlike Konerko, he compiled them in parks that were basically neutral for hitting. He'll be playing next year in an Oakland park that is much more favorable for hitting now that it's been reconfigured. Grieve played there for a month at the end of the year, and his numbers for 93 at-bats—.312 average, .402 on-base, .473 slugging—are very close to the MLE. He's the real thing, and he could turn out to be one of the best rookies in recent memory.

Todd Helton	AB	H	HR	RBI	AVG	OBP	SLG
1997 MLE	388	134	14	70	.345	.417	.541

Helton played in a good hitter's park in Triple-A ball last year (Colorado Springs), and he's going to be playing in one of the best hitter's parks ever next year: Coors Field. The result could be some huge 1998 numbers. Like Grieve, he got 93 at-bats at the big-league level in 1997, but unlike Grieve, his major league numbers didn't approach the MLE. I don't think the MLE is far off what he's likely to do next year, however.

Juan Encarnacion	AB	H	HR	RBI	AVG	OBP	SLG
1997 MLE	475	141	23	75	.297	.339	.512

Encarnacion was only 21 last year, which makes these numbers even more impressive. He doesn't have much patience at bat, but that's his only weakness: he figures to be a 30-plus homer guy for the Tigers within a year or two.

Travis Lee	AB	H	HR	RBI	AVG	OBP	SLG
1997 MLE	214	55	9	32	.257	.323	.453

Lee's numbers are harder to analyze, for two reasons: he's only had 227 at-bats above Class-A ball, and no one really knows yet what kind of characteristics the Arizona Diamond-backs' new park will have. We basically projected it as neutral, but there's good reason to think, based on the climate, altitude, Pacific Coast League numbers, etc., that it'll be a fine place to hit. Thus these numbers probably underestimate how Lee will perform in 1998. He should be good, but maybe not quite as good at the start as some people are predicting.

I could go on forever with this, but you get the idea. Check out the numbers in the Minor League Handbook: they'll open your eyes a little, and they're a LOT of fun. One last MLE—the legendary Josh Booty:

Josh Booty	AB	H	HR	RBI	BB	SO	AVG	OBP	SLG
1997 MLE	430	82	13	41	16	177	.177	.206	.307

Sixteen walks with 177 Ks? A .206 OBP? I'd call that positively "Bootyesque."

See ya soon.

January 8, 1998—Hall of Fame

Well, I'm back. I didn't *intend* to take this much time between columns, but November and December are our big baseball book months, and then there were the holidays, and the STATS '98 budget to work on, and blah blah blah. Whatever. I'm back.

Let's talk about everybody's favorite subject, the Hall of Fame. I have more than just a fan's interest in this subject, since I'm a member of the BBWAA, the organization that does most (but definitely not all) of the electing. Unfortunately you need to be an active member of the organization for at least 10 years before they let you vote for the Hall, and I've still got about seven years to go. Pretty stupid, because I'm as well-qualified as most of the people voting now, and a *lot* more qualified than many of them. But then, so are most of my readers. Oh, well; life ain't fair.

But let's say I *did* have a vote in this year's election. Who would I have voted for? Here's my list, which is fairly short.

RON SANTO. I put him first because this was his last year of eligibility for election by the writers, though I guess he'll get another chance with the Veterans Committee in a few years. That's good, because Santo was easily one of the best third basemen in history. It's true that he was greatly helped by his home park, but you could say that about a ton of players, and anyway, he could hit home runs and field and draw walks wherever he was playing. The main reason he didn't get in was that he retired at age 34—he had diabetes and other health problems—and as a result didn't stick around long enough to hit 400 home runs, which surely would have gotten him in. He belongs.

DON SUTTON. I concur with the critics who say that Sutton was helped by his teams, that he was often the third-best pitcher on his staff, that he never had a Cy Young-caliber season, and all that. But long-term excellence should count for something, and Sutton was an excellent pitcher for a *long* time. Some of his assets:

1. He was a consistent winner. Sutton won at least 15 games *twelve* times in his career. How many active pitchers have had even half that many 15-win seasons? There are only six: Maddux 10, Clemens 8, Langston 7, Finley 6, Gooden 6, Hershiser 6. Sutton also had 15 different seasons in which he posted a winning record. Only Alexander (18), Spahn (16), Ryan (16) and Seaver (16) have had more winning seasons since 1900 (minimum 10 decisions in a season).

2. He kept guys off base, which is one of the first things to look for in a pitcher. Sutton's career opponents' on-base average was .287. Among pitchers whose careers began since 1920, only Sandy Koufax (.276), Juan Marichal (.278) and Tom Seaver (.285) have had a lower OOBP.

3. He was a successful power pitcher for a long, long time. Sutton struck out at least 100 batters in 21 different seasons. Only Nolan Ryan, with 23, has had more.

4. He didn't just win 300 games. . . he won 324 friggin' games. That's 111 more wins than the current active win leader, Roger Clemens. Among all pitchers since 1920, only Warren Spahn (363) and Steve Carlton (329) have won more. Shouldn't that be enough?

GARY CARTER. One of the greatest catchers in major league history. I'm surprised he didn't get more votes.

I considered a number of others: Bruce Sutter, Tony Perez, Jim Rice, Dwight Evans, Steve Garvey, Bert Blyleven, Luis Tiant, Jim Kaat, Tommy John, Minnie Minoso. All very good players, and I have no doubt that one or more of them will make the Hall of Fame eventually. I don't have a big problem with that, but basically my attitude is this:

1. The Hall of Fame should have very high standards.

2. If winning 324 games isn't good enough for you, your standards are *too* high.

About STATS, Inc.

STATS, Inc. is the nation's leading independent sports information and statistical analysis company, providing detailed sports services for a wide array of commercial clients.

As one of the fastest-growing sports companies—in 1994, we ranked 144th on the "Inc. 500" list of fastest-growing privately held firms—STATS provides the most up-to-the-minute sports information to professional teams, print and broadcast media, software developers and interactive service providers around the country. Some of our major clients are ESPN, the Associated Press, Fox Sports, Electronic Arts, MSNBC, SONY and Topps. Much of the information we provide is available to the public via STATS On-Line. With a computer and a modem, you can follow action in the four major professional sports, as well as NCAA football and basketball. . . as it happens!

STATS Publishing, a division of STATS, Inc., produces 12 annual books, including the *Major League Handbook*, *The Scouting Notebook*, the *Pro Football Handbook*, the *Pro Basketball Handbook* and the *Hockey Handbook* as well as the *STATS Fantasy Insider* magazine. These publications deliver STATS' expertise to fans, scouts, general managers and media around the country.

In addition, STATS offers the most innovative—and fun—fantasy sports games and support products around, from *Bill James Fantasy Baseball* and *Bill James Classic Baseball* to *STATS Fantasy Football* and *STATS Fantasy Hoops*. Check out the latest STATS and Bill James fantasy game, *Stock Market Baseball* and our immensely popular Fantasy Portfolios.

Information technology has grown by leaps and bounds in the last decade, and STATS will continue to be at the forefront as a supplier of the most up-to-date, in-depth sports information available. For those of you on the information superhighway, you can always catch STATS in our area on America Online or at our Internet site.

For more information on our products, or on joining our reporter network, contact us on:

America On-Line — (Keyword: STATS)

Internet — www.stats.com

Toll Free in the USA at 1-800-63-STATS (1-800-637-8287)

Outside the USA at 1-847-676-3383

Or write to:

STATS, Inc.
8131 Monticello Ave.
Skokie, IL 60076-3300

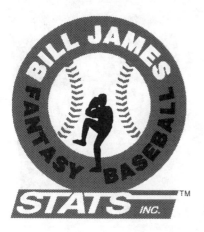

Track YOUR Fantasy Team

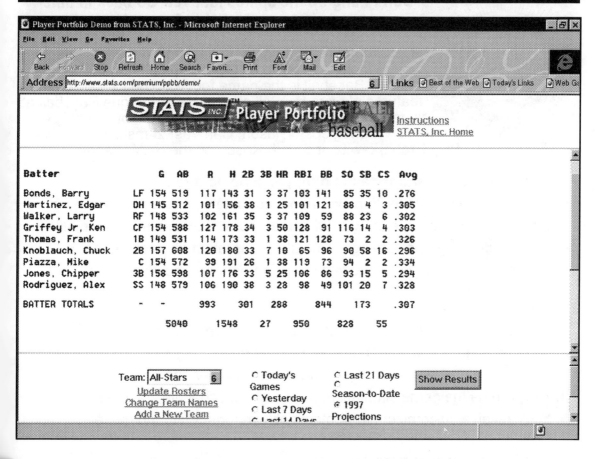

Every Play. Every Game. Every Day.

Manage your fantasy player's statistics with **STATS Player Portfolio for Baseball**

Interactive & fully customizable fantasy roster-tracking software

Player & team stats — search today, yesterday, this week, last week, season-to-date...

Real-time results. Log-in to in-progress games...*see how your ace pitcher is doing after 5 innings*

In-depth info keeps you totally informed! (Upcoming schedules, injury reports, player projections and more)

STATS makes your fantasy life easy. Track all your players with no fuss.

www.stats.com

There is NO Offseason!

Don't hang up the spikes just yet! Go back in time to compete on the field of your dreams!

If you're not ready to give up baseball in the fall, or if you're looking to relive its glorious past, then Bill James Classic Baseball is the game for you! The Classic Game features players from all eras of Major League Baseball at all performance levels—not just the stars. You could see Honus Wagner, Josh Gibson, Carl Yastrzemski, Bob Uecker, Billy Grabarkewitz and Pete Rose...on the SAME team!

As owner, GM and manager all in one, you'll be able to...

- "Buy" your team of up to 25 players from our catalog of over 2,500 players
- Choose the park your team will call home—current or historical, 72 in all!
- Rotate batting lineups. Change your pitching rotation for each series
- Alter in-game strategies, including stealing frequency, holding runners on base, hit-and-run and much more!

How to Play The Classic Game:

1. Sign up to be a team owner TODAY! Leagues form year-round
2. You'll receive $1 million to buy your favorite major leaguers
3. Take part in a player and ballpark draft with 11 other owners
4. STATS runs the game simulation...a 154-game schedule, 14 weeks!
5. You'll receive customized, in-depth weekly reports, featuring game summaries, stats and boxscores

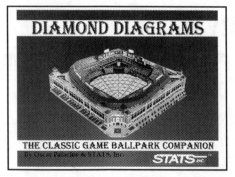

ADMIT IT. You're always looking for that edge against your Classic Game competition. ***STATS Diamond Diagrams 1998*** takes you on a stroll through every major league ballpark, as featured in Bill James Classic Baseball. You'll visit over 75 parks, complete with historical summaries, pictures, park dimensions, scouting reports and more. A great read for every student of the game! **Item #DD98, $19.95, Available NOW!**

Order from STATS INC. Today!

Use Order Form in This Book, or Call 1-800-63-STATS or 847-676-3383 or visit www.stats.com

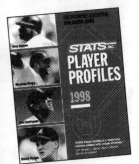

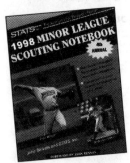

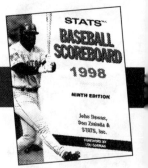

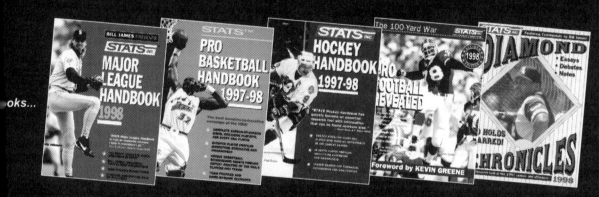

ROUNDING OUT THE STARTING LINEUP. . .

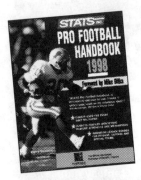

STATS Pro Football Handbook 1998

- A complete season-by-season register for every active NFL player
- Numerous statistical breakdowns for hundreds of NFL players
- Leader boards in a number of innovative and traditional categories
- Exclusive evaluations of offensive linemen
- Foreword by Mike Ditka
- **Item #FH98, $19.95, Available NOW!** *Comb-bound Available.*

STATS Pro Football Revealed 1998
The 100-Yard War

- Profiles each team, complete with essays, charts and play diagrams
- Detailed statistical breakdowns on players, teams and coaches
- Essays about NFL trends and happenings by leading experts
- Same data as seen on ESPN's *Sunday Night Football* broadcasts
- **Item #PF98, $19.95, Available 7/1/98**

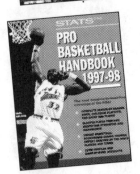

STATS Pro Basketball Handbook 1997-98

- Career stats for every player who logged minutes during 1996-97
- Team game logs with points, rebounds, assists and much more
- Leader boards from points per game to triple doubles
- Essays cover the hottest topics facing the NBA. Foreword by Bill Walton
- **Item #BH98, $19.95, Available Now!** *BH99 Available 9/1/98.*

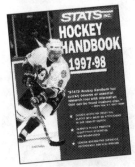

STATS Hockey Handbook 1997-98

- Complete career register for every 1996-97 NHL player and goalie
- Exclusive breakdowns identify player strengths and weaknesses
- Specific coverage for each team, plus league profiles
- Standard and exclusive leader boards
- **Item #HH98, $19.95, Available Now!** *HH99 Available 8/15/98.*

Order from STATS INC. Today!

Use Order Form in This Book, or Call 1-800-63-STATS or 847-676-3383 or visit www.stats.com

Get Into STATS Fantasy Hoops!

Soar into next season with STATS Fantasy Hoops! SFH lets YOU make the calls. Don't just sit back and watch Grant Hill, Shawn Kemp and Michael Jordan—get in the game and coach your team to the top!

How to Play SFH:
1. Sign up to coach a team
2. You'll receive a full set of rules and a draft form with SFH point values for all eligible players—anyone who played in the NBA last year, plus all NBA draft picks
3. Complete the draft form and return it to STATS
4. You will take part in the draft with nine other owners, and we will send you league rosters
5. You make unlimited weekly transactions including trades, free-agent signings, activations and benchings
6. Six of the 10 teams in your league advance to postseason play, with two teams ultimately advancing to the Finals

SFH point values are based on actual NBA results, mirroring the real thing. Weekly reports will tell you everything you need to know to lead your team to the SFH Championship!

PLAY STATS Fantasy Football!

STATS Fantasy Football puts YOU in charge! You draft, trade, cut, bench, activate players and even sign free agents each week. SFF pits you head-to-head against 11 other owners.

STATS' scoring system applies realistic values, tested against actual NFL results. Each week, you'll receive a superb in-depth report telling you all about both team and league performances.

How to Play SFF:
1. Sign up today!
2. STATS sends you a draft form listing all eligible NFL players
3. Fill out the draft form and return it to STATS, and you will take part in the draft along with 11 other team owners
4. Go head-to-head against the other owners in your league. You'll make week-by-week roster moves and transactions through STATS' Fantasy Football experts, via phone, fax or on-line!

STATS Fantasy Football on the Web? Check it out! www.stats.com

Order from STATS INC. Today!

Use Order Form in This Book, or Call 1-800-63-STATS or 847-676-3383 or visit www.stats.com

STATS, Inc. Order Form

Name_____

Address_____

City_____ State_____ Zip_____

Phone_____Fax_____E-mail Address_____

Method of Payment (U.S. Funds Only):
❏ Check   ❏ Money Order   ❏ Visa   ❏ MasterCard

Credit Card Information:

Cardholder Name_____

Credit Card Number_____ Exp. Date_____

Signature_____

PUBLICATIONS (STATS books include FREE first class shipping; magazines — add $2)

Qty.	Product Name	Item #	Price	Total
	STATS All-Time Major League Handbook	ATHA	$54.95	
	STATS All-Time Baseball Sourcebook	ATSA	$54.95	
	STATS All-Time Major League COMBO (BOTH books!)	ATCA	$99.95	
	STATS Major League Handbook 1998	HB98	$19.95	
	STATS Major League Handbook 1998 (Comb-bound)	HC98	$21.95	
	STATS Projections Update 1998 (MAGAZINE)	PJUP	$9.95	
	The Scouting Notebook 1998	SN98	$19.95	
	The Scouting Notebook 1998 (Comb-bound)	SC98	$21.95	
	STATS Minor League Scouting Notebook 1998	MN98	$19.95	
	STATS Minor League Handbook 1998	MH98	$19.95	
	STATS Minor League Handbook 1998 (Comb-bound)	MC98	$21.95	
	STATS Player Profiles 1998	PP98	$19.95	
	STATS Player Profiles 1998 (Comb-bound)	PC98	$21.95	
	STATS 1998 BVSP Match-Ups!	BP98	$19.95	
	STATS Baseball Scoreboard 1998	SB98	$19.95	
	STATS Diamond Chronicles 1998	CH98	$19.95	
	Pro Football Revealed: The 100-Yard War (1998 Edition)	PF98	$19.95	
	STATS Pro Football Handbook 1998	FH98	$19.95	
	STATS Pro Football Handbook 1998 (Comb-bound)	FC98	$21.95	
	STATS Basketball Handbook 1997-98	BH98	$19.95	
	STATS Hockey Handbook 1997-98	HH98	$19.95	
	STATS Diamond Diagrams 1998	DD98	$19.95	
	STATS Fantasy Insider: 1998 Baseball Edition (MAGAZINE)	IB98	$5.95	
	STATS Fantasy Insider: 1998 Pro Football Edition (MAGAZINE)	IF98	$5.95	
	Prior Editions (Please circle appropriate year)			
	STATS Major League Handbook '90 '91 '92 '93 '94 '95 '96 '97		$9.95	
	The Scouting Report/Notebook '94 '95 '96 '97		$9.95	
	STATS Player Profiles '93 '94 '95 '96 '97		$9.95	
	STATS Minor League Handbook '92 '93 '94 '95 '96 '97		$9.95	
	STATS BVSP Match-Ups! '94 '95 '96 '97		$5.95	
	STATS Baseball Scoreboard '92 '93 '94 '95 '96 '97		$9.95	
	STATS Basketball Scoreboard/Handbook '93-'94 '94-'95 '95-'96 '96-'97		$9.95	
	Pro Football Revealed: The 100-Yard War '94 '95 '96 '97		$9.95	
	STATS Pro Football Handbook '95 '96 '97		$9.95	
	STATS Minor League Scouting Notebook '95 '96 '97		$9.95	
	STATS Hockey Handbook '96-'97		$9.95	

FANTASY GAMES

Qty.	Product Name	Item Number	Price	Total
	Bill James Classic Baseball	BJCB	$129.00	
	STATS Fantasy Hoops	SFH	$79.00	
	STATS Fantasy Football	SFF	$69.00	
	Bill James Fantasy Baseball	BJFB	$89.00	

1st Fantasy Team Name (ex. Colt 45's):_____ _____

   What Fantasy Game is this team for?_____

2nd Fantasy Team Name (ex. Colt 45's):_____ _____

   What Fantasy Game is this team for?_____

NOTE: $1.00/player is charged for all roster moves and transactions.

For Bill James Fantasy Baseball:

Would you like to play in a league drafted by Bill James?   ❏ Yes   ❏ No

MULTIMEDIA PRODUCTS (Prices include shipping & handling charges)

Qty.	Product Name	Item Number	Price	Total
	Bill James Encyclopedia CD-Rom	BJCD	$49.95	

TOTALS		Price	Total
Product Total (excl. Fantasy Games)			
Canada—all orders—add:		$2.50/book	
Magazines—shipping—add:		$2.00/each	
Order 2 or more books—subtract:		$1.00/book	
(**NOT** to be combined with other specials)			
Subtotal			
Fantasy Games Total			
IL residents add 8.5% sales tax			
GRAND TOTAL			

For Faster Service, Please Call 800-63-STATS or 847-676-3383
Fax Your Order to 847-676-0821
Visit STATS on the World Wide Web at www.stats.com
or on AOL at Keyword STATS
STATS, Inc • 8131 Monticello Avenue • Skokie, Illinois 60076-3300

NOTE: Orders for shipments outside the USA or Canada are Credit Card only.
Actual shipping charges will be added to your order.